WESTERN CIVILIZATION

VOLUME I: TO 1715

Resources for Instructors available at
www.mesharpe-instructor.com

WESTERN CIVILIZATION

A GLOBAL AND COMPARATIVE APPROACH

VOLUME I: TO 1715

KENNETH L. CAMPBELL

M.E.Sharpe
Armonk, New York
London, England

The EuroSlavic fonts used to create this work are © 1986–2012 Payne Loving Trust.
EuroSlavic is available from Linguist's Software, Inc.,
www.linguistsoftware.com, P.O. Box 580, Edmonds, WA 98020-0580 USA
tel (425) 775-1130.

Cover photos: *(bottom, left to right)* Roman aqueduct in Portugal *(© Ionut David/Fotolia.com)*;
Neptune, god of the sea sand sculpture *(© alma_sacra/Fotolia.com)*; Roman Colosseum at night
(© Ariy/Fotolia.com); colossal statues on Mount Nemrut, Turkey *(© Orhan Çam/Fotolia.com)*.

Library of Congress Cataloging-in-Publication Data

Campbell, Kenneth L., 1955–
   Western civilization : a global and comparative approach / by Kenneth L. Campbell.
      p. cm.
   Includes bibliographical references and index.
   ISBN 978-0-7656-2253-2 (pbk. : alk. paper)
   1. Civilization, Western—History—Textbooks. I. Title.

CB245.C295 2012
909′.09821—dc23   2011039106

Printed in the United States of America

The paper used in this publication meets the minimum requirements of
American National Standard for Information Sciences
Permanence of Paper for Printed Library Materials,
ANSI Z 39.48-1984.

IBT (p)   10   9   8   7   6   5   4   3   2

To my parents,

Lloyd and Barbara Campbell

Man is a history-making creature who can neither repeat his past nor leave it behind.

—W.H. Auden

Contents

List of Tables, Maps, and Charts

List of Illustrations

Preface

Every aspect of our lives has been shaped by the past and is helping to shape the future. We get to make individual choices and decisions, but only in a context that has been shaped not only by our own past, but also by broader historical developments—including some that may go back hundreds or even thousands of years. The Industrial Revolution, the Protestant and Catholic Reformations, the migration of Europeans to the Americas, the beginnings of parliamentary democracy, and the rise of religions such as Judaism, Buddhism, Christianity, and Islam are all examples of developments that have shaped in a direct way the world that we still inhabit today and, frequently, the way that we live our lives and think about our place in the world. Our own decisions and actions, in turn, become part of the history that will help shape the future—both our own and that of others. When we study history, we become more conscious of the influence of the past and obtain knowledge that can help us not only to understand ourselves and our world, but also to decide what range of options employed by people and cultures in the past is most appealing, useful, or inspiring to us. Furthermore, the study of history trains our minds to analyze and interpret a vast amount of information in our attempt to understand or make sense of the past. History as an academic field of study does not—or at least should not—consist merely of memorizing names, dates, and facts. So much of what constitutes and shapes history consists of beliefs and myths that may not be based on hard facts, rational analysis, or concrete evidence. It would be a very foolish historian who would ignore these to concentrate on just the facts, as important as these may be.

Yet history must be based on what we know about the past; as one of my colleagues frequently says, "you can't just make it up." Historians formulate their own views about the past, but those views must be based on critical thinking and analysis as well as on the evidence and testimonies of people who have lived in the past. In order to understand the contemporary relevance of the past or the impact that it has had on our world, it is important to attempt to understand the past on its own terms and not on the basis of what we think it should have been. This volume, which takes a chronological approach to history from prehistory to the present, is divided into chapters that examine different aspects of history—social, cultural, religious, political, economic, and intellectual—from particular, sometimes overlapping, periods. Each chapter is followed by a set of questions intended for the purposes of both review and analysis of some of the main themes treated within it. Each chapter also contains at least one image, an excerpt from some written source from the period covered therein, at least one map, and a comparative feature that accompanies the section dealing with an area of the world outside of the West. It is hoped that this approach will provide enough of a basis for students to begin to form their own ideas about the past based on their own critical thinking and analysis.

This book, then, is intended to provide a stimulating and thoughtful brief text that will engage students in the study of history. It differs from other Western civilization texts primarily in its emphasis on making comparisons between the West and different civilizations in the different periods considered in each chapter. This approach is based in part on the premise that understanding other societies will further an understanding of Western civilization. In addition, other cultures and civilizations are worthy of study for their own sake and provide the student/reader with different perspectives on the past. In an age of increasing globalization, it is important that students broaden not only their knowledge of Western civilization, but also their awareness of different parts of the world and their understanding of some of the underlying similarities of the human experience.

Beyond that, I have attempted to present an interesting, intelligible study of the past from ancient times to the present that will be relevant to contemporary readers. I have not pursued a particular agenda related to the superiority of social history over political history or vice versa. Consequently, different chapters receive different emphases, based on what seemed called for by each individual chapter. In the end, these decisions were based on my perspective on the past alone. I am all too aware of what and how much has been left out of this text, but if I had tried to include or give equal attention to every kind of history or every country or region throughout the text, this would have become an encyclopedia and not a textbook. Instead, I have treated history in this text as a coherent, if sometimes confusing and unpredictable, story made up of many complex threads.

Although the reader will find a number of themes and issues included here, three will receive special emphasis. First, because religion has done so much to shape human experience and since religious issues continue to unite and divide people, it seemed appropriate at the beginning of the twenty-first century to give special attention to the history of religion, particularly to issues related to religious persecution and religious toleration. Second, although there is not as much emphasis on social history as in texts that make it a primary point of emphasis, I have tried to acknowledge some relationship between broad historical developments and the everyday lives of people during the different periods covered by the text, including the experiences of women. Third, I frequently make use of the phrase "the shaping of the past," generally designating at least one section of each chapter to particularly develop this theme. Sometimes the course of history seems beyond our control, and yet people's individual decisions, thoughts, and actions can and have shaped history. Transforming moments that have shaped the past include not only key political events, major wars between rival civilizations, and revolutions, but also those ideas, religious changes, and social transformations that influence the course of subsequent historical development in a major way.

The idea for this book originated many years ago when as a graduate student I made a conscious decision to become something of a generalist in an age of increasing specialization among historians. This is not intended as a criticism of specialization; I have my own, and no decent textbook would be possible without the work of countless numbers of specialized scholars who have labored to make their areas more comprehensible and their findings readily accessible. It is impossible to acknowledge them individually; even a complete bibliography would have expanded the text to an unreasonable length. But one of the goals of history texts such as this one is to bring the learning and insights of specialists to a wider readership. Another is to synthesize the current state of historical knowledge and understanding. I hope that I have accomplished these goals in this book and that the student and reader will profit by it and enjoy the result.

Acknowledgments

I am extremely grateful to M.E. Sharpe for giving me the opportunity to complete this work and for bringing it to publication, particularly Steve Drummond, Pat Kolb, Kimberly Giambattisto, Henrietta Toth, Laurie Lieb, Katie Corasaniti, and Nicole Cirino. Many people have believed in this project over the years I have been working on it, but Steve's vision did much to shape the final product. Laurie is a terrific copy editor. Thanks to Pat for "recalling me to life." Prior to publication by M.E. Sharpe, Betty Slack and Melanie White provided invaluable editorial assistance and advice. Monmouth University awarded me precious time during sabbaticals in fall 2006 and summer 2008 to work toward the completion of the manuscript. My chair, Fred McKitrick, and all my colleagues in the Department of History and Anthropology have been extremely understanding and supportive of the time I devoted to this book. In particular, I need to thank Chris DeRosa for reading and commenting on the chapters on World War II and the Cold War, as well as my treatment of the Vietnam War, and Ken Stunkel for his constant encouragement and for allowing me to use his comparative chart for Chinese and Western civilization. Joan Manzo has been of invaluable assistance, especially with the maps and illustrations. Erica Moreland read and commented on my chapter on the Renaissance, as well as assisting me with numerous permissions needed for material used in the text.

Anyone who has ever worked on such a project knows what a collective and collaborative experience this really is, even though it involves endless hours of solitude. Julius Adekunle, Rich Leiby, Linda Bregstein, Bill Mitchell, Rayeanne Keevish, Ellen Frye, William Norman, Rich Veit, Rekha Datta, and Sharon Arnoult all read parts and contributed to the text's development at various stages along the way. Yvette Lane was a terrific research assistant during the time she worked for me. Rick Pachman also provided assistance for a brief period. In addition, the students that I have taught in my Western Civilization in World Perspective survey courses over the past twenty-plus years, as well as those in my upper-level and graduate history courses, have contributed more than they can imagine by allowing me the privilege of teaching and learning from them. I am sorry that I cannot acknowledge them all, but special acknowledgement must go to the students in my senior seminar in European history in the spring of 2008—Ryan Adams, Tom Andrykovitz, Jenel Bramante, Kevin Cuneo, Tristin

Fleck, Norma Jean Garriton, Robert Gregorka, Colin Grimm, Jennifer Huey, Molly Kline, Megan Leonard, Renee Neale, Karisa Playter, Jennifer Rubin, Andrew Vanderbeck, and Danielle Vitorla—for producing an exceptionally good set of research papers; this text has benefited from their work and insights. The text has also benefited from the feedback of numerous anonymous reviewers—my extreme gratitude to the most critical of them as well as the most encouraging, the blend of which was the perfect combination to make me more determined and inspired to bring this work to fruition.

I would also like to thank Paul Knight for his lifelong friendship and encouragement and all my friends at Virginia Commonwealth University who many years ago accompanied me on Saturday trips to the Virginia Museum of Fine Arts and indulged my passion for history, especially Bill Armstrong and Marilee Candino, who continue to do so after so many years. Bill Gorman has been a constant and faithful friend, colleague, and supporter for over twenty years. Matt O'Brien and Pasqualle Simonelli have provided much intellectual stimulation and loyal friendship as I worked on this project. Thanks as well to Tom Pearson, Stan Green, and Paul Gaffney for their encouragement and support. I would also be remiss not to acknowledge my former mentors, especially William Young, William Blake, Gerald Straka, Tai Liu, John Bernstein, Raymond Callahan, George Basala, and Lawrence Duggan. I apologize to anyone I have neglected to mention; I am sure that I have left out more than a few people who deserve better. Finally, and most importantly, I offer my fondest appreciation to my wife, Millie, who designed the timelines for the book and never begrudged me the time that I devoted to it, and my fourteen-year-old daughter, Stephanie, who accompanied me on many trips to the library without complaining (too much). While I owe thanks to so many people, I take full responsibility for any errors of omission or commission in the text.

WESTERN CIVILIZATION

VOLUME I: TO 1715

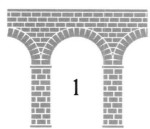

1   The Beginnings of History and the Ancient Near East

The story of Western civilization did not begin during the Italian Renaissance, the Middle Ages, or even with the classical cultures of Greece and Rome. Human history—at least as far back as we can possibly trace—exists on a continuum in which human beings always learned something from their predecessors. Developments, ideas, and inventions from many hundreds or thousands of years earlier influence what human beings are doing at any given moment in their history. Climate and geography play a role, too—and these have been known to change over the course of time as well. There are reasons why the first civilizations emerged where and when they did, just as there are reasons why Western civilization would emerge where and when it did. The larger context of Western civilization demands at least some consideration of the history that preceded it.

What we know about human origins and the prehistoric past is part of the history of humanity that provides that larger context for Western civilization. We can trace the existence of art, religion, magic, and the attempt to understand the natural environment deep into the prehistoric period. The transition to settled agriculture made possible many later historical developments, but was itself a gradual process that was part of the continuum of history. In fact, even after the rise of the first urban civilizations and well into recorded history, the vast majority of the people made their livings from agriculture. The complex and detailed histories of the first ancient civilizations are only briefly discussed here, but with an emphasis upon the main course of their history, their basic characteristics, and their relationship to one another. The Sumerians and Babylonians, the Egyptians and the Hebrews all made their contributions to the legacy of the ancient world that later influenced and shaped Western civilization. But they also deserve attention in their own right for the vital role that they played in the emerging human experience.

Human Origins and Prehistory

A series of startling discoveries in the twentieth century raised as many questions as they provided answers about the distant origins of human beings. Still,

3

4

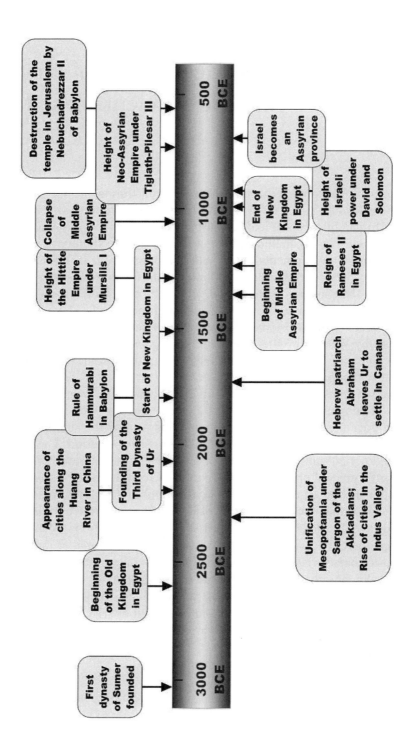

we know much more than we did 100 years ago, and new evidence continues to increase our knowledge and understanding. The pioneers in this field were the British husband-and-wife team of Louis (1903–1972) and Mary (1913–1996) Leakey. Their discoveries of early human-like remains in Kenya and Tanzania, including fossils and footprints that dated to approximately 3.7 million years ago—combined with the discovery of a 1.6-million-year-old skeleton of the species *Homo erectus* by their son Richard—helped to establish Africa as the site of the origins of humanity. These discoveries were reinforced by two finds in Ethiopia, the first a 3.25-million-year-old female skeleton given the name of Lucy, found by a University of Chicago-trained paleoanthropologist named Donald Johanson (b. 1943). The second was the discovery in 2006 of a more complete skeleton and skull of a three-year-old child of the same species as Lucy (*Australopithecus afarensis*). At some point representatives of the species *Homo erectus*, which walked upright and more closely resembled modern humans than the earlier *Australopithecus*, migrated from Africa, as evidenced by the earliest discovery of the species in 1890 on the island of Java in Indonesia by a Dutch paleontologist, Eugène Dubois (1858–1940). The discovery of additional remains of *Homo erectus* in China and more recently in 1991 in Georgia in central Asia indicate a great expansion of hominids about 1.3 million years ago, perhaps as a result of a dietary change toward increased meat-eating that led them to expand their habitat. The first appearance of humans in Europe has now been dated to about 780,000 years ago, which is much earlier than paleontologists had previously thought.

Given the long periods during which these human ancestors inhabited the earth, the appearance of the more recognizably human *Homo sapiens* and Neanderthals occurred relatively recently, within the past 150,000 to 200,000 years. The Neanderthals, named after the Neanderthal valley in North-Rhine Westphalia, Germany, where their remains were first discovered in 1856, were long thought to be the ancestors of modern humans, but are now considered a separate and distinct line of humanity, sharing only a distant ancestor with their *Homo sapiens* cousins. Neanderthals, known for their large bones, sloping foreheads, and short limbs, were capable of a wide range of human skills, activities, thoughts, emotions, and communication, although not through verbal language as we know it. They had brains equal in size to those of contemporary humans and, if they worked differently, they worked successfully enough for them to survive and flourish for 170,000 years, much longer than our current species, *Homo sapiens sapiens*, has been in existence. What most distinguished the line of human beings from which we descend was the use of language, a greater ability to innovate and adapt new technologies that were more effective at manipulating the environment, and a capacity for abstract thought, although Neanderthals did believe in an afterlife and buried their dead. The novelist Jean Auel (b. 1936) has provided a fascinating and speculative look at the possible relationship between Neanderthals—who died out around 30,000 years ago—and *Homo sapiens sapiens* in her Earth's Children series.

During the Paleolithic period, otherwise known as the Stone Age, prehistoric humans developed certain types of tools that defined their culture, including mainly knives, scrapers, and related instruments for shaping, cutting, polishing, grinding, and making notches. These same basic tools, usually made of flint, served humans for millions of years until a noticeable shift late in the Paleolithic period—the so-called Upper Paleolithic, around 40,000 years ago—to new tools made of animal materials such as bones, antlers, or ivory. It is difficult to say whether humans changed because of these innovations or if they made these innovations because they had changed. Steven Mithen (1996) has suggested that the human brain actually underwent significant changes during this period that allowed it to better integrate knowledge of the natural world with technological skills. In addition to the creation of new tools, which included hunting weapons such as spear-throwers made from antlers, bevel-pointed flint tools known as burins, and small geometrically shaped tools known as microliths, the people of this period also demonstrated great creativity in the splendid artworks that have survived from it. Paleoanthropologists have placed the origins of human art between 75,000 and 91,000 years ago, with the 2007 discovery in Morocco of painted shells used as beads for a bracelet or necklace now considered to be the oldest known example. By the time of the Upper Paleolithic, jewelry made of animal teeth or stones and other examples of bodily ornamentation were fairly common, but it was the beginnings of cave painting around 30,000 years ago that marked the most spectacular artistic development of this transitional period. Using flint knives and paint made from clay, artists produced images of bison, deer, lions, bears, horses, and woolly rhinoceroses in caves in southeastern France discovered in 1994 by Jean-Marie Chauvet, which supplemented earlier finds at Lascaux Cave near Montignac in the southwest of France and at Altamira in northern Spain.

One thing that all prehistoric people had in common was that they lived in a society of hunter-gatherers. They traveled wherever necessary to find food. These migrations were made more necessary, at least on the European continent, by the last Ice Age, which did not begin to thaw until around 10,000 BCE. The art of the period between 20,000 and 10,000 BCE, which includes the caves at Lascaux and Altamira, reflects a strong preoccupation with the sacred dimensions of the hunt but also—in the form of smaller bone-carvings and the like—with signs of spring that were so eagerly awaited every year. These foragers lived off the land and depended heavily on available resources; their societies could only be as large as the land would sustain. This meant that for

the most part their groups remained small, leading to a particular type of social organization that was clan-based. Coastal regions might sustain a slightly
larger population because of the ability to supplement their food supply from
the sea, although the groups who lived in these regions practiced hunting and
gathering as well. But populations seem to have been getting larger, beginning
as early as 30,000 BCE, which made necessary greater levels of cooperation
and adaptation within and even among these groups. At some point they began
to supplement their diet by deliberately planting and cultivating a portion of
their food supply, leading to a gradual shift in human social and economic
organization that produced perhaps the greatest single change in human history: the agricultural revolution.

The Shaping of the Past: The Agricultural Revolution

The transition from a hunger-gatherer society to a society based on settled
agriculture was a gradual process; it did not occur as a result of a single
breakthrough in one place, or even several. If this transition occurred in a
number of places in the period from roughly 10,000 to 5000 BCE, this was
largely because of a change in environmental conditions that made settled
agriculture advantageous, especially for feeding the expanded populations of
particular regions. But archaeological evidence suggests that other factors were
involved that made the process less deterministic than a simple environmental
explanation would indicate. Furthermore, the gradual and extremely slow pace
of the transition indicates that a dichotomy of hunter-gatherers versus settled
agriculturalists is far too simplistic. Many hunter-gatherer societies made some
use of the deliberate cultivation of food-producing plants long before 9000
BCE, the date by which grain-based agriculture had taken root in southeast
and southwest Asia. In addition, long after settled agriculture had become
established in places such as the valley where the Huang River makes a huge
bend in northern China, agricultural societies continued to supplement their
food supply by practicing traditional hunting and gathering techniques.

It makes sense that hunters and gatherers near advantageous sites for grain
agriculture—which also included the Tigris and Euphrates River valleys in
southwest Asia and the Indus River valley in the northern part of the Indian
subcontinent—would first experiment with settled agriculture in close proximity to the woodlands that provided traditional food sources from foraging. But
this does not preclude the use of agricultural techniques for food production
by numerous other hunters and gatherers, even in places that did not yield the
later spectacular successes of river valleys such as that of the Nile in Egypt.
In other words, the agricultural revolution did not occur simply because the

climate improved at the end of the last Ice Age, leading to larger, more settled populations that were more likely to create a stable food supply by turning to the cultivation of grains—though this could easily have been one factor. Rather, it occurred as the result of a large number of individual decisions that occurred at different times in different places and for a variety of reasons, some of them perhaps unique to particular societies—such as the creation of a sanctuary at Göbecki Tepe in Turkey by hunter-gatherers who needed to provide for all the people that would have been drawn to it.

Whatever its origins, agriculture brought many other changes to human society. First, the cultivation of more food and the existence of a more predictable supply would have encouraged further population growth. In addition, the greater availability of food encouraged the construction of more permanent buildings near agricultural sites, the making of pottery and utensils for storing and consuming the food, and systems of mathematics and writing for recording and tracking transactions involving large amounts of grain. Social organization seems to have been affected as well. Societies became less collectivized wholes with a common food supply and more divided into individual family units with separate residences, as archaeologists have confirmed from buildings dating to 8000 BCE found at the town of Jericho on the lower Jordan River.

As populations increased in the regions where agriculture was most successful, these societies began to expand into other regions still populated by hunter-gatherers. This does not mean that the main agricultural centers were solely responsible for the spread of agriculture, which, as previously stated, hunter-gatherers proved perfectly capable of discovering on their own, as they did in many places. Nor does it mean that agriculturalists either displaced or converted hunter-gatherers to their way of life. Populations in places such as the Greek mainland or along the Danube River in Europe were so sparse throughout the first several millennia after the agricultural revolution had begun that farmers and hunter-gatherers could have lived independently within the same region, much as Neanderthals and *Homo sapiens* once had. Still, expansion of peoples had its effects, especially after about 4000 BCE when such influences can be more easily traced. Knowledge of crops, domestication of animals such as sheep and goats, and technological innovations such as the ox-drawn wooden plow (invented around 5000 BCE) would have provided great advantages and do seem to have spread from southwest Asia to Europe during this period. Languages spread along with the people who spoke them, affecting the evolution of language throughout Europe, Asia, and northern Africa. The one main agricultural center that remained relatively isolated—northern China—only very gradually received influences from the Indus valley and central Asia and continued to develop independently, but with many of the same characteristics of agricultural societies elsewhere.

The arrival and consolidation of agriculture gave rise to the earliest civilizations in those exact areas where it most flourished. (This happened in the great river valleys in the interiors of continents, not along the coasts, where availability of food from the sea actually discouraged the adoption of agricultural techniques.) With the coming of agriculture, then, we arrive at the beginnings of history. Many scholars believe that when humans through agriculture gained greater control over their own environment, they changed their attitudes and behavior in other quite significant ways. Private ownership of land became crucial to economic success, making land the basis of political power and authority as well. The possibility of food surpluses created opportunities to trade for different kinds of food or nonfood items, such as weapons, tools, pottery, and even works of art. Some scholars have traced the origins of warfare to the competition for economic resources as agriculture made particular lands more valuable, though others argue that violence is intrinsic to humanity and commonly found among hunter-gatherers as well. Beyond dispute, however, is the impact that the agricultural revolution had on mythology and how humans defined themselves in relation to the natural and supernatural worlds.

The First Civilizations and the Earliest Evidence for Religion

The earliest evidence for religion predates the agricultural revolution and goes back far into the prehistoric period. Early humans, including Neanderthals, buried their dead, often with an assortment of artifacts, arguably indicating some belief in the supernatural and possibly a conception of the afterlife. In 2006 archaeological researchers led by Sheila Colson of the University of Oslo discovered a rock shaped like a snake and marked with hundreds of tiny notches in an isolated cave in Botswana in southern Africa. The spearheads dug up in the immediate vicinity of the snake were dated to 70,000 years ago, allowing researchers to argue that the snake, which appeared to flex in a certain light, currently represents the earliest evidence for religion. (Significantly, snakes play an important role in the mythology of the local San people.) Previous estimates had placed the origins of religion about 40,000 years ago, and even so some scholars have argued that this is too early and remain unconvinced that human burials alone constitute evidence for religion. But the stone-shaped snake confirms the existence of ritualistic behavior far back in the Paleolithic period. Furthermore, the discovery of bone flutes dating to 36,000 years ago in a cave in southern Germany known as Geissenklösterle provides further evidence of early religious behavior. The cave—one of the earliest discovered in Europe that had been inhabited by modern humans—contained flutes believed to have been made of swan bones with three distinct finger-holes that were not spaced evenly, indicating that this was probably not the prototype. Steven Mithen believes strongly that the origins of music derive from an intention to communicate with the supernatural since music was not the most effective way for early humans to communicate with each other.

Opinions vary on the religious significance of rock art and cave paintings later in the Paleolithic period as well, but musical instruments, human burials, and cave art all indicate some belief in the existence of a reality that transcends that which humans experienced in their everyday world. For example, the belief in the afterlife among hunter-gatherers is confirmed by the Deer Island cemetery in northwest Russia dating to between 6700 and 6000 BCE. The most plausible explanation for the 170 burial sites discovered at Oleneostrovski Mogilnik in Lake Onega (containing a total of some 500 burials) is that these people felt the need to isolate the spirits of the dead in order to protect their settlements and hunting grounds. In addition, the portrayal of men wearing bird-masks in the cave paintings of Lascaux and Altamira indicates some type of shamanic (or priestly) activity, which would have been associated with flight or out-of-body experience. Hunters had to rely on favorable circumstances beyond their physical control and were likely to believe that shamans could help to ensure a successful hunt. Evidence from a 50,000-year-old Neanderthal site provided evidence of a leopard skin worn as a human costume, an indication that shamanic activity predated that associated with the cave art by tens of thousands of years.

But already by the time of the cave art at Lascaux and Altamira, there is evidence of another type of religious sensibility that went beyond attempts to connect with the supernatural and a belief in the afterlife. The discovery of sculptures and pendants representing a goddess figure—such as the 21,000-year-old "Venus of Laussel" found carved in a cave near the Dordogne River in southwest France—seems to indicate the origins of a fertility cult centered on the Great Earth Mother that probably predated but gained in strength during the transition to settled agriculture. Portrayed as nude and pregnant (an obvious symbol of fertility), the mother goddess appeared under different names in the emerging civilizations of Sumer, Babylon, Canaan, and Egypt. There is thus plenty of evidence that in prehistory and the early history of civilization people did not conceive of divinity in exclusively masculine terms. This is further confirmed by the discovery of female clay figurines, with their hands beneath each breast, excavated at Jericho dating to 7000 BCE.

Beyond the few generalizations made in this section, archaeology does not tell us a great deal more for certain about prehistoric and early religion, but there was clearly some continuity between the religions of the late prehistoric period and those practiced in the earliest civilizations. This continuity is confirmed not only by the Goddess religions, but also by the discovery of temples built on the same site of Eridu in southern Iraq from around 5500 BCE to about 2000

BCE. The names of gods among the Assyrians and Babylonians bear traces of those embraced by their predecessors, the Sumerians and Akkadians. The Egyptians used a cloth-wrapped pole as a symbol for the divine God before incorporating it into their hieroglyphic system of writing. Perhaps additional discoveries will shed further light on the origins and nature of humanity's earliest religions, but once we enter the historic period in which the invention of writing accompanied the rise of cities, religious developments and other aspects of the earliest civilizations become far more accessible and clear.

The Urban Revolution in Mesopotamia, the Indus Valley, and China

In the fourteenth century CE the Muslim historian Ibn Khaldun (1332–1406) explained to his readers why cities are founded and why they are usually located on or near great rivers. In the *Muqaddimah: An Introduction to History* (1370), he theorized that towns first develop only after royal authority has come into existence. He states that the cities are built out of a ruler's desire to provide tranquility and the blessings of civilization to his people. Cities also provide a source of manpower for royal armies and serve as a defensive fortification (which is why early cities were all surrounded by walls). He provocatively suggests that luxuries give birth to cities, rather than the other way around. As for the location of cities on rivers, he cites several logical explanations. If a city is on a river, it can only be approached from one side, making it easily defensible, especially if other aspects of the location are taken into consideration. Rivers provide a source of fresh water, an essential for urban life. But, he notes, other criteria need to be taken into consideration when determining the location of an urban settlement as well. It needs to be located near good pastureland for domestic animals and livestock, as well as near fields that can sustain an adequate grain supply for its residents. Finally, Khaldun lists accessibility of firewood and building materials as another main criterion.

About 4000 BCE, according to the Australian-born archaeologist V. Gordon Childe (1892–1957), the first cities started to arise in Egypt and Mesopotamia; the result was what he termed an "urban revolution" that represented the next great stage in human history. This revolution, he argued, was accompanied by a complex of additional changes that included the first monumental buildings in history and the construction of large defensive fortifications largely absent from the earlier Neolithic period. Increased trade accompanied the rise of cities, which needed to import many of their goods from the countryside or other cities, giving rise to a monetary economy that permitted rulers to tax their inhabitants. Technology became advanced, primarily through the smelting of tin and copper to form bronze, which was useful for weapons, pots, and

Ziggurat of Ur, Mesopotamia. This reconstruction captures how the famous ziggurat would have looked in Sumerian times. It is believed that the Biblical story of the Tower of Babel may have been based on the construction of such a ziggurat, which was a temple tower designed to reach toward the gods.

everyday utensils, while the advent of writing gave rise to greater intellectual activity, codified laws, and helped define changing ideas about religion.

A similar complex of developments occurred in later centuries in the Indus Valley and China, but the earliest cities are associated with the area known as the Fertile Crescent, formed by the Tigris and Euphrates Rivers in ancient Mesopotamia (modern Iraq). By comparing and contrasting the rise of cities in these three regions (Egyptian civilization will be dealt with later in this chapter), we can begin to formulate some ideas about the usefulness of Ibn Khaldun's theories, as well as the validity of Childe's concept of an urban revolution. In Mesopotamia, the rise of cities seems to have been preceded by a general population shift toward the banks of the Tigris and Euphrates as a result of advances in irrigation techniques and a climate change in the direction of cooler and drier weather. The first large cities appeared around 3000 BCE, characterized mainly by monumental temple constructions known as ziggurats. Key to the success of these cities was the successful irrigation of a land that suffered from a lack of rainfall. A new religious sensibility emerged that better resonated with an urban population, specifically one in which the gods became somewhat distanced from

Check this website—www.metmuseum.org/toah/hd/zigg/hd_zigg. htm—sponsored by the Metropolitan Museum of Art for additional images and more detailed descriptions of Mesopotamian ziggurats, as well as access to maps, timelines, essays, and art from the ancient Near East.

humanity, which had proved capable of great accomplishments on its own. Still, the people built their ziggurats in cities such as Ur, Erech, and Kish to honor the gods, who were now credited with the origins of urban civilization.

The major cities of the Indus Valley, such as Harappa and Mohenjo Daro in modern Pakistan, flourished between 2600 and 1900 BCE and were also located on a great river, the lower part of the Indus. These cities were remarkably well planned and made effective use of water, even beyond using it for irrigation (as suggested by Khaldun and used in Mesopotamia). They had a sophisticated system of sewage disposal and baths heated by underground furnaces; their temples even contained tanks of water that may have been for ritualistic purification similar to that practiced by modern Hindus. These cities contained impressive walls and examples of monumental architecture. However, because the language of this civilization has not yet been deciphered, much less is known about its origins than those of the earlier Sumerian civilization of Mesopotamia.

Most Chinese scholars consider the lower valley of the Huang (or Yellow) River, which flows east from north central China, the cradle of Chinese civilization. The excavations carried out at the ancient Chinese city of Anyang between 1928 and 1937 began to confirm the existence of impressive palaces and noble residences in a recognizable Chinese architectural style, indicating a highly developed imperial state behind this urban center, which flourished from 1380 to 1040 BCE as the last capital of the Shang dynasty (ca. 1750–1040 BCE). But discoveries at Anyang also seemed to reveal the existence of the previous Xia dynasty (ca. 2200–1750 BCE), long thought to be legendary. What archaeologists have confirmed for certain is the existence of a number of cities along the lower course of the Huang River by 2250 BCE, around the time that China began its Bronze Age (2200–500 BCE). Here technological change and the rise of urban civilization did seem to coincide with the establishment of centralized authority and the beginnings of China's religious traditions. The fact that the Chinese practiced a different method of bronze casting from that of the other urban civilizations seems to indicate that these changes in Chinese history occurred independently of those in Mesopotamia and the Indus Valley and without outside influence. Unfortunately, we cannot know for certain whether the urban revolution in China occurred as a result of the rise of royal authority or vice versa.

In comparing these three river valley civilizations, however, some commonalities and tentative conclusions begin to emerge, beyond the obvious geographic similarities explained by Khaldun. First, they most likely all arose independently—the writing of the Indus civilization is quite unique and dissimilar from any produced in Mesopotamia or China, for example. This makes the similarities among them all the more significant since they were not merely copying from each other, despite the fact that they appeared at different times. Although the religions, technologies, and art of each civilization had significant differences, changes and new developments in all three areas seem to invariably accompany the rise of urban civilizations. They all built monumental architecture and constructed walled cities, two developments entirely compatible with Khaldun's theory about royal influence and motivations behind the construction of cities. The size of the Mesopotamian cities has been estimated at between 30,000 and 40,000 and it is not inconceivable that the cities of the Indus Valley and China could have held as many; it would have taken a strong central authority to organize and control so many people in a constricted area. The urban revolution seems indeed to have been an undeniably important phase in the history of humanity, giving rise in each of these regions to writing and advanced ideas and artistic styles.

However, the differences among these three civilizations perhaps have something to teach us as well. First, whereas the origins of cities in Mesopotamia initiated a civilization that endured in one form or another for over 2,000 years and China's emerging cities became part of a long continuity to Chinese history as it shifted from dynasty to dynasty, the Indus Valley civilization collapsed after less than 1,000 years, and many mysteries about it remain despite the growing intensity of archaeological excavations there. Does this say something about the variability and contingency related to general historical processes? One of the ways in which the Indus civilization differed from the other two, based on the archaeological evidence, is that there was not a strong military presence there. Nor is there evidence from the Indus Valley of royal palaces or even of a wealthy, hereditary elite with palatial homes compared to those of the rest of the population. By contrast, there was a significant gap between rich and poor in Mesopotamia; in early Chinese cities peasants lived in squalid hovels compared to the splendid residences of the aristocracy. Finally, although the religions of these urban civilizations all shared some similarities, they were distinct enough to take each civilization in entirely different directions. This might suggest the importance of religion in defining the history of a people and shaping other aspects of their histories and societies. Of the three, it was the religious sensibilities of the peoples of Mesopotamia and southwest Asia that had the greatest impact on the later civilization that would become defined as Western.

Mesopotamia: Sumer, Akkad, Assyria, and Babylon

Based on Sumerian king lists recorded on surviving clay tablets, the outlines of Mesopotamian history began around 3100 BCE with the establishment of the first dynasty of Sumer. The Sumerians, who based their power in southern Mesopotamia, dominated the region until Sargon of the Akkadians conquered and unified the region around 2350 BCE. The early Sumerian period is known as the Heroic Age, in which details on individual rulers and dynasties are scanty and much of what was later remembered was steeped in legend. But this early period prepared the way for the Akkadian dynasty and the Third Dynasty of Ur (2113–2004 BCE), both of which ruled over well-developed states based on bureaucratic administration and territorial conquest. The Akkadians preserved the Sumerian language and did not cause a sharp break in the basic culture of the region. Evidence for continuity, for example, includes the remarkable similarities between monuments constructed for Sargon and earlier Sumerian steles. The Akkadians were also artistically and culturally advanced—Sargon's daughter, Enheduanna, the first identifiable author in history, composed hymns to the Mesopotamian fertility goddess, Inanna. At its height the Akkad dynasty ruled all of Mesopotamia, Syria, and part of Asia Minor; however, such an extensive empire may have been historically premature for it could not withstand an invasion from eastern tribes around 2150 BCE.

After a period of relative decline caused partly by the overirrigation of the soil, which raised the salt levels of the soil too high for the crops to grow, a new ruling dynasty from a people known as the Amorites emerged around 1830 BCE. The Amorites established their capital at Babylon and did much to shape the history of the region. (Dates in Mesopotamian history have been established by use of Babylonian king lists, which began using regnal-year dating during this period; previously years were named for the most significant event in the preceding year.) Babylon proved a particularly wise choice for a capital as it was surrounded by the most fertile soil in the region and a plethora of vegetation, including plenty of xerophytes that could survive on limited amounts of water and helped to sustain domestic animals such as sheep and camels. The most significant ruler of this early period of Babylonian history was Hammurabi (1792–1750 BCE), who conquered all of Mesopotamia except for Assyria. Babylon sits on the Euphrates in southern Mesopotamia, while the Assyrians later settled on Ashur near the Tigris in the northern part of the region and established their own empire beginning in 1365 BCE. This Middle Assyrian Empire lasted until 1078 BCE, but a new empire—sometimes called the Neo-Assyrian Empire—was founded by a strong ruler named Ashur-dan II (934–912 BCE), whose inscriptions celebrate his savage but successful attacks on the invading tribes that had occupied parts of Assyria. In the eighth century BCE, the Assyrians subjugated the Babylonians to their rule as well. During the reign of Tiglath-Pileser III (744–727 BCE), the Assyrian empire stretched from the Persian Gulf to the borders of Egypt. Within a century, however, this empire had exhausted itself by numerous wars and conquests—of which the people themselves must have tired—and the new or Neo-Babylonian Empire that followed only lasted another eighty-six years; in 539 BCE Mesopotamia fell prey to the rising power of the Persians from the east.

Throughout this period and amid the changing political fortunes of dynasties, some of which actually ruled for a very long time, the Mesopotamian rulers and their people never ceased to pay heed to their gods or to give a significant amount of power and authority to their priests. For the Sumerians, the dominant gods were the sky god, Anu, and the fertility goddess, Inanna, both of whom were seen as paramount in ensuring the harvest on which the entire civilization depended. Mesopotamia was subject to extremes of nature that could produce droughts or floods, so it was important to keep these temperamental gods appeased. The first king of the Third Dynasty of Ur, Ur-Nammu (2112–2095 BCE) dedicated an entire sanctuary to the moon god, Nanna, which his son Shulgi (2095–2047 BCE) saw through to completion. The Sumerians also cared a great deal about life and death; in their defining literary accomplishment, the *Epic of Gilgamesh*, the hero embarks on a fountain-of-youth quest for a source of eternal life. After being told of a plant that could provide this, Gilgamesh dives underwater to retrieve it (despite its thorns), only to have it snatched away by a serpent. The Babylonians believed that their society mirrored that of their gods, the earthly city a reflection of the heavenly city, their temples modeled on the homes of the gods. In order to account for the imperfections and sins of the human world, they celebrated elaborate New Year festivals that ritualistically restored the beginning of time and washed their sins away. They conceived every act that they took as in some way reflecting an action once performed by a god, a principle that contributed to their sense of a social and moral order. Still, the rulers of ancient Mesopotamia frequently made use of divination in order to determine or understand the will of the gods. The Mesopotamians also believed in a realm of the dead beneath the earth, which they envisioned as a flat disc floating on an ocean bed surrounded by mountains. But since time was always being recreated in Mesopotamian cosmology, there was a basis for believing that their life would be repeated in an endless cycle. In the tale of Gilgamesh, however, the hero found no such consolation.

Frequent warfare marked Mesopotamian society as one prone to violence and destruction as much as one marked by civilization and creativity. The surviving clay tablets, preserved by baking in the Mesopotamian sun, reveal much about the daily lives of the people, in addition to records of wars, conquests, and the achievements of kings. Such information comes from tablets recording financial or administrative transactions or contracts, others that contain personal correspondence, and, finally, omen texts, such as the one that attributed the death of a ruler to "the bite of a shoe" (probably a foot infection). In fact, the vast majority of these tablets deal with business, illustrating the importance that trade occupied in the urban culture of ancient Mesopotamia, although the vast majority of the people made their living from agricultural occupations. In addition to the soldiers, farmers, and merchants that dominated Mesopotamian society, numerous craftsmen, scribes, artists, metalworkers, cloth weavers, and jewelers were much in demand by this sophisticated civilization that produced and has left us many fine examples of their work, including the vast treasure of exquisite jewelry and delicately embroidered linen garments discovered in the tombs of Assyrian queens.

Scientifically, the Babylonians stand at the beginning of a tradition that featured significant achievements in mathematics and astronomy. They evolved their system of mathematics mainly to accommodate the needs of business and first discovered the concept of position numbering, based on the number 60. If a merchant wanted to charge someone 20 percent interest, for example, this could be represented by a decimal of .12. They divided their calendar year into 360 days and their days into twelve hours, which probably provided the basis for their mathematics. They divided the sky into twelve constellations—giving us the signs of the Zodiac—through which they observed the path of the planets since around 2000 BCE. Among the cuneiform tablets discovered in Mesopotamia there also appear examples of more practical scientific knowledge, including instructions for extracting perfumes, manufacturing mercury from the mineral cinnabar, which contains mercuric sulfide, and deriving ammonium chloride from dung.

Mesopotamia, then, not only represented one of the earliest civilizations, but also played a critical role in the politics and history of the region that later became known as the ancient Near East. The region produced a vast amount of wealth, contained desirable and valuable farm land, and featured some of the greatest cities in the ancient world. Throughout the 2,500-year period briefly covered here, its greatest rival and competitor lay to the southwest in northeast Africa—Egypt, whose civilization was based almost exclusively on its own great river, the Nile.

Egypt: Politics, Religion, and Everyday Life

The Nile River cuts its way through the Sahara Desert, one of the only rivers in the world that flows from south to north, its waters flooding every year and depositing the rich silt that fertilized the soil and made Egypt one of the most successful agricultural societies of the ancient world. The Nile, like the Tigris and Euphrates in Mesopotamia, also provided a major avenue for transportation and commerce, leading to the growth of towns and cities along its banks. Egyptian civilization predated the rise of the first recorded ruling dynasty at the beginning of the Old Kingdom around 2650 BCE: archaeologists have discovered hieroglyphic writing there dating to about 3300 BCE and ceramic clay pottery estimated from the period around 4000 BCE. Although it is still not completely clear how they did it, the rulers of the Old Kingdom, which lasted until 2150 BCE, created a unified and effective state that became a dominant power in its region. It was these rulers who built the Great Pyramids, not—as was once thought—through the use of slave labor, but through the employment of highly skilled architects, engineers, and paid workers who were dedicated subjects of the Egyptian kings. During the Old Kingdom, Egyptians also mastered the art of mummification and developed, particularly among the upper classes, a new religious sensibility that moved from a pantheon of animalistic gods to worship of their own sky god, the sun god Ra. The collapse of the Old Kingdom, probably resulting mainly from the personal weakness and short reigns of its last rulers, was followed by a less centralized Middle Kingdom that lasted until 1680, after which Egypt fell prey to an invasion from outsiders known as the Hyksos.

By 1558 BCE, Egypt had recovered its independence and produced under the New Kingdom (1558–1085 BCE) an even stronger state, in which the kings—now called *per-aa*, later translated as *pharaoh*, meaning "great house"—claimed divine status as the sons of Ra. The New Kingdom, however, faced a crisis during the reign of an eighteenth-dynasty king named Amenhotep IV who took the name of Akhenaton (ca. 1353–1336 BCE). Akhenaton viewed himself as a reformer and even relocated his capital to Tell El-Amarna; thus this period in Egyptian history is known as the Amarna Age (even though Akhenaton changed the name of the city to Akhetaton, meaning "horizon of the sun"). During the Amarna Age about 30,000 people resided in the city, a population that seems to be fairly standard for cities of the ancient world. Akhenaton's major initiative involved challenging the position of the priests of Ra (also called Amon-Ra after the merger of Ra with a local Theban god) in favor of emphasizing the worship of the sun god Aton, a shift that at least bordered on monotheism. Akhenaton shared power with his wife, Nefertiti, who supported his reforms, but their son, Tutankhamen, reversed their reforms and restored the old gods (and priests) to power. However, the people who shape history are also shaped by it, and Akhenaton had responded to forces at work during his age that did not disappear with his death. Influential army leaders reviled Akhenaton's military weakness, but his nonimperialistic agenda may have represented his attempt to refocus Egypt's priorities as a result of a perception that Egyptian power was already waning. Specifically, Suppululiumas (ca. 1375–1345 BCE), the king of the Hittites, had begun expanding his empire from Asia Minor to Syria up to the borders of Egypt.

The Hittite Empire reached its height under his successor, Mursilis I (1344–ca. 1310 BCE). The brief reign of the boy-king now known as King Tut (ca. 1347–1338 BCE)—whose spectacular tomb was famously discovered by

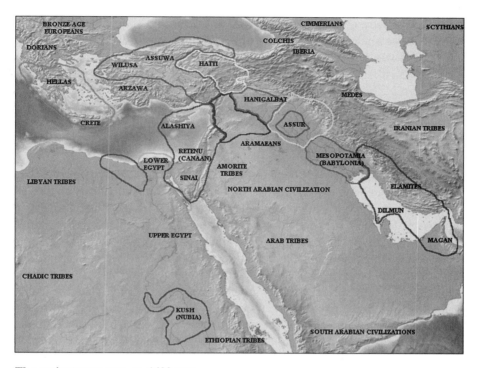

The ancient near east, ca. 1400 BCE

the English archaeologist Howard Carter (1874–1939) in 1922—did nothing to strengthen Egypt. Egypt never fell to the Hittites, however, who were content to share their dominance with the power on the Nile until both empires suffered at the hands of new invaders—which the sources simply identified as the "sea peoples"—in the twelfth century BCE. Unlike the Hittite Empire and other powers in the region such as the Mittani and the Kassites, however, Egypt managed to keep the invaders at bay, maintaining its independence if not its former power.

When Akhenaton attempted to reform Egyptian religious practice, he risked offending a number of Egyptian gods and goddesses, as well as the priests and people who were devoted to them. But Egyptians did not fear the unpredictable whims of their gods in the same way that the Mesopotamians did, probably because the Nile was so regular and predictable. Still, the Egyptians valued their gods, and according to the Greek historian Herodotus (ca. 485–425 BCE), practiced animal sacrifice, presenting offerings of bulls and bull-calves (but not cows) to their mother goddess, Isis. Perhaps they sacrificed only bulls because of the sacred nature of cows in Egypt, as indicated by the presence of cow horns on their ancient goddess of love and childbirth, Hathor. Isis was said to be married to Osiris, who was murdered by his brother Seth, after which he became god of the underworld. Although versions of the myth of Isis and Osiris varied over time, the underlying theme is always rebirth, for Isis brings Osiris back to life and conceives a child who becomes the god Horus. At this point the myth becomes confusing because in some accounts Horus merges with Osiris as the husband of Isis, though Osiris continues to rule the underworld—to which the Egyptians were admitted only after undergoing judgment in which their heart was weighed against truth on a scale watched by a jackal-headed god named Anubis.

Egyptian religion and belief in the afterlife were integrated fully into the lives of the Egyptian people and never separate from the main concerns of society. For example, while it is a commonplace that the pyramids stood above vast tombs for the rulers who had them built, in ancient Egypt they were integrated into a lively complex of buildings and walkways that would have been teeming with people there to honor the dead, much as tourists today in Washington, DC, might pay homage to past leaders such as Lincoln and Washington or the fallen soldiers of the Korean and Vietnam Wars. In addition to the spectacular tombs of Tutankhamen and other members of the royal family discovered in the Valley of the Kings, archaeologists have also uncovered the tombs of some of the workmen who built the pyramids and excavated the villages in which they lived. These finds have provided a valuable glimpse into the lives and values of ordinary workers who drank beer and wine, ate twelve different types of bread, were mostly monogamous (but not always), and had a life expectancy of about thirty-seven years. Some workers had offering tables and small statues buried with them, indicating that they shared with their rulers a concern for what they could take from this world to the next.

This did not mean, however, that they did not value this life, as is indicated by the Egyptians' concern with science and medicine, and the lengths to which they would go to save a life—even for a member of the working class. The Egyptians knew how to heal broken bones, prevent wounds from becoming infected, and even perform brain surgery; evidence reveals that one worker survived fourteen years after having a brain tumor surgically removed. They very much believed that the gods had a role in healing and were not averse to the use of magical incantations, but over the course of time they began to favor known remedies and therapies as their first choice in healing people from accidents or disease. They applied the same approach to chemistry, technology, mathematics, and astronomy. The construction of the pyramids becomes less of a mystery given the Egyptian emphasis on experimentation and learning from experience that is reflected in all aspects of their thought and life. But experimentation took them only so far, as they lacked theoretical knowledge. They had a practical knowledge of geometry that they used in their buildings, but did not understand the mathematical principles behind it; they practiced medicine and mummification without ever really understanding the internal workings of the human body.

Despite Akhenaton's attempt to introduce a brand of monotheism, ancient Egypt remained a polytheistic society for the length of its history. Its gods were adapted to Egyptian society rather than the other way around. Egypt's great cities—particularly Memphis in the north and Thebes in the south—still depended on the success of the farmers who cultivated the lands fertilized by the Nile with extreme regularity. The people in turn depended on the favor of their gods, as well as on the effective administration of the pharaohs, which regulated the balance between city and countryside. The pharaohs' reputations, however, were also built on war and conquest, which helped to sustain the people's confidence, as well as to confirm their semidivine status. It was, according to tradition, during the reign of one such conqueror, Rameses II (1290–1224 BCE), that a small Semitic people called the Hebrews left Egypt to take their own religious beliefs to the land bridge between Africa and Asia known as Palestine.

Israel and the Religion of the Hebrews

The Hebrews did not originate in Egypt, nor did they enter Palestine for the first time when they left Egypt some time close to 1250 BCE. About 500 years earlier, perhaps around 1750 BCE, the Hebrew patriarch Abraham had left the city of Ur in Mesopotamia, following the command of his god to settle in the land of Canaan, later known as Palestine. He brought with him many aspects of Mesopotamian culture, including stories about the creation of the world, a garden paradise, and a great flood, all of which made their way into the Hebrew Bible.

The Hebrews, also known as the Israelites, may have migrated to Egypt sometime in the seventeenth century BCE—because of a famine in Canaan, according to the book of Genesis. Whether they escaped from slavery (as the Hebrew book of Exodus suggests) or were driven out of Egypt by Rameses II, they returned to Canaan just as the sea peoples were in the process of disrupting the stability of the region. In their own conflict with the Philistines—whom many scholars have identified with the sea peoples themselves—the Hebrews claimed one great advantage: the support of their god, Yahweh, whom they believed had promised them possession of the land. After some initial success with a system of decentralized tribal administration under the leadership of men called judges, Israel turned toward kingship and centralized monarchy under the pressure from the Philistine threat in about 1030 BCE. About twenty years earlier, the Philistines had captured the sacred Ark of the Covenant, which symbolized the divine presence of Yahweh to the Hebrews, thus increasing their sense of desperation. According to one Old Testament tradition, the prophet, judge, and political leader Samuel warned the Hebrews against selecting a king instead of relying on Yahweh. Israel's first king, Saul, does seem to have struggled to retain popular support. The basis for the monarchy had been established, however, and was fully capitalized on by Saul's successors, David (r. ca. 1000–965 BCE) and his son, Solomon (r. ca. 965–931 BCE), who transformed Israel into a strong, wealthy kingdom and leading power in the region.

Despite their political and military success—and archaeology has confirmed the creation of a new royal palace by David in Jerusalem, as well as the magnificent building program and wealth amassed under Solomon—the main historical significance of these Hebrew kings is the role that each occupies in the narrative accounts that became the Hebrew scriptures and, later, the Christian Old Testament. Historians, archaeologists, and religious scholars who have attempted to use the Bible as a historical source have long been baffled by its silence on many points of history, mainly because the writings it contains were never intended to serve as a historical source for later researchers. They were intended as works of religious and spiritual inspiration, but they are useful to historians because they incorporate so much history. They do so because the religion of the Hebrews was, first and foremost, a historical religion. The Hebrew scriptures were meant to reveal the relationship between Yahweh and his chosen people, the Hebrews—a relationship that was forged in history and unfolded over the course of time. Archaeology has confirmed many of the historical events, circumstances, and names provided in the Bible, but for others, such as the exodus from Egypt, the Bible remains our only account.

Whereas there are some blanks in the historical account of the Hebrews, however, these sacred writings provide much insight into their religion. Its major characteristics, as it unfolded over time, were the belief in a single, universal God who had chosen the Hebrews to fulfill his divine will on earth; the idea of a covenant between Yahweh and his people in which Yahweh promised to defend and prosper the Hebrews as long as they obeyed his commandments and worshipped only him; and, eventually, the idea of a Messiah, or savior, who would redeem Israel for its sins and transgressions. David played a particularly important role in the unfolding of the relationship between Yahweh and his people because he strove to follow Yahweh to such an extent that Yahweh promised that the Messiah would come from among his descendants. David, however, was not perfect and Yahweh did not allow his transgressions to go unpunished, even among his children and future descendants. Solomon, too, a wise and great king according to the Biblical account, incurred Yahweh's displeasure—and that of his people—when he imposed heavy taxes and forced labor on his people to fulfill his own ambitions. The Hebrew people were supposed to learn from these examples and to imitate the good qualities of their leaders while forsaking the bad.

The next stage in Israel's historical development prepared the way for the next stage in its religious development. Solomon had built a magnificent temple in Jerusalem to serve as a permanent home for Yahweh and a central, unifying place of worship for the Hebrew people. However, following Solomon's death, the nation became divided into two separate kingdoms, Israel in the north and Judah (from which the Hebrews also became known as Jews) in the south. This obviously weakened Israel and later made it prey to the rising power of the neo-Assyrian Empire. Religiously, the Hebrews interpreted the decline of Israel's power as the result of its people's failure to do the will of Yahweh. A series of prophets arose to call people back to the covenant and to do God's will; they frequently criticized the ruling powers in both kingdoms. The religion of the Hebrews remained a worldly religion in the sense that the prophets called for repentance in search of God's favor and blessings on earth. Most of the rulers of the kingdoms, beginning with Solomon's son Rehoboam, stubbornly refused to acknowledge the authority of the prophets and regarded their calls for reform as direct challenges to the kings' rule. The only solution that could restore the unity of Israel's people proved to be the actual destruction of their earthly kingdom and their exile from the Promised Land. In 734 BCE the Assyrian ruler Tiglath-Pileser III invaded Palestine and within two years had rampaged through both kingdoms. The last king of Israel, Zechariah, having been assassinated in 734, the northern kingdom became a province of the Assyrian Empire (renamed Samaria). In 586 BCE, the Babylonian king, Nebuchadnezzar II (ca. 604–562 BCE) destroyed Jerusalem and its temple, made Judah a Babylonian province, and forced a number of Jewish captives into exile.

Human and Divine Law: Governing Human Behavior

The establishment of law as a means of reinforcing authority and promoting justice was another major development that helped to shape the ancient world and its legacy for Western civilization. First arising in Mesopotamia toward the end of the third millennium BCE, law as distinct from the commands of the ruler was not the inevitable destiny of advanced civilizations. But in Mesopotamia people began to regard their rulers as their liaisons with the gods and the representatives of the divine will on earth. In the earliest known law code—that of Ur-Nammu from the third Ur dynasty—the Sumerian ruler committed himself to principles of social justice and demonstrated a desire to correct the abuse of power within the royal administration.

These concerns continued to receive emphasis in the most famous Meso-potamian law code, that promulgated by the Babylonian ruler Hammurabi (1792–1750 BCE). Other law codes besides that of Ur-Nammu predated Ham-murabi's, but his is the most complete and detailed that has been preserved and reveals much about both the nature of Babylonian society and the principles upon which the code was based. Hammurabi's code incorporates important distinctions among members of Babylon's three main social classes: free citi-zens, a middle or secondary class, and slaves. His law code shows the concern of the ruler with commercial activity and interpersonal relationships. The code took a harsh stand against adultery, particularly if committed by the wife, who, along with her lover, was subject to death or mutilation on her husband's au-thority if she were caught. A woman who wished to divorce her husband was permitted to do so, but only if a city council determined that she was not to blame for the problems in her marriage. Hammurabi's code prescribed very specific penalties for violations of the law. But its overall purpose was "to cause justice to prevail in the country, to destroy the wicked and the evil, that the strong may not oppress the weak" (Roux 1992, 202). There is evidence of similar concerns in other law codes from the ancient Near East, including the code of Urukagina of Lagash from about 2400 BCE, which prescribed measures to restrict the power of priests and royal administrators. This general concern for social justice was seen as consistent with the will of the gods, but it is clear that these are human laws, not divine commandments. The laws of Hammurabi and other Mesopotamian rulers took justice as their province and stipulated conditions governing human behavior so that their people would know the consequences of particular transgressions.

The Hebrews believed that their law had been handed down by God himself to their leader Moses, who had led them out of Egypt and, according to the book of Exodus, established a direct personal relationship with Yahweh. The most important laws that appear in the Pentateuch (the first five books of the Bible) were the Ten Commandments, also known as the Decalogue. Unlike the conditional laws of Hammurabi and the Babylonians, the Ten Command-ments were absolute laws that people were simply supposed to obey. The seventh commandment does not say that if you commit adultery, such and such would happen—it simply states that you shall not commit adultery. The Commandments—which in addition to prohibiting killing, stealing, lying against your neighbor, and worshipping false images, commanded absolute devotion to Yahweh and obedience to your parents and made it a sin to desire anything that did not belong to you—became the foundation of the covenant between Yahweh and Israel because they represented what the Hebrews needed to do in order to fulfill their part of the treaty.

The ancient civilizations discussed in this chapter all took different ap-

---

Prologue to the Laws of Hammurabi

When the lofty Anu, king of the Anunnaki gods, and Enlil, lord of heaven and earth, he who determines the destiny of the land, committed the rule of all mankind to Marduk, the chief son of Ea; when they made him great among the Igigi gods; when they pronounced the lofty name of Babylon; when they made it famous among the quarters of the world and in its midst established an everlasting kingdom whose foundations were firm as heaven and earth—at that time, Anu and Enlil named me, Hammurabi, the exalted prince, the worshiper of the gods, to cause justice to prevail in the land, to destroy the wicked and the evil, to prevent the strong from oppressing the weak, to go forth like the sun over the black-headed people, to enlighten the land and to further the welfare of the people, Hammurabi, the shepherd named by Enlil, am I, who brought about plenty and abundance; . . . the powerful king, the sun of Babylon, who caused light to go forth over the lands of Sumer and Akkad; the king who caused the four quarters of the world to render obedience; the favorite of Ishtar, am I.

When Marduk sent me to rule the people and to bring help to the country, I established law and justice in the language of the land and promoted the welfare of the people . . .

Source: Nels M. Bailkey, ed., *Readings in Ancient History: Thought and Experience from Gilgamesh to St. Augustine,* 4th ed. (Lexington, MA: D.C. Heath, 1992), pp. 31–32. Based on the translation by Robert F. Harper, *The Code of Hammurabi* (Chicago: University of Chicago Press, 1904).

What does Hammurabi identify here as the purposes of his law codes? Why does he include so many references to the gods? How does he define his relationship to the gods? How is the relationship between the gods and his law code defined?

---

proaches to law, yet some underlying similarities provide an indication of a common set of cultural values that help define what it means to live in human society. Egypt had no written law codes because the ancient Egyptians accepted the divine status of the pharaoh, whose word was law. The Mesopotamian rulers claimed to represent the will of the gods, but they inscribed their laws in stone and thus limited the authority of individual rulers to depart from codes partly intended to prevent the oppression of the weak by the powerful. In ancient Israel, laws—even the more specific codes that appear in the books of Leviticus and Deuteronomy—were treated as divine laws that helped people to do God's will in all areas of their lives, including diet. But the similarities include sets of common concerns with particular problems of human behavior as well as a general concern with social justice. Whereas the laws of Moses have an absolute quality about them, the concerns of later laws—which some scholars refer to as the Covenant Code—display a clear concern for protecting the weaker members of society, including widows, children, and the poor. The Code of Hammurabi and the Mesopotamian codes share this concern, but also have in common with the Hebrews an emphasis on the preservation of property rights and retributive justice—the "eye for an eye" mentality. Even the Egyptians relied heavily on precedent in their court cases and legal transactions in a way that was designed to preserve the social order and protect property rights. Whether they were regarded as human or divine, these civilizations all used the concept of law to regulate behavior, preserve social order, and provide mechanisms for restitution when crimes were committed.

Conclusion

When considered as a whole, the ancient Near East established certain fundamental patterns that defined future expectations and did much to shape the future history of the West. First, these early civilizations all tended toward strong, centralized monarchical rule bordering on despotism. Although some variation existed among these early states, their leaders all seemed to recognize that absolute authority was necessary in order to hold large populations together and keep them working to sustain the conditions of civilization. Once these civilizations accumulated enough wealth to make them targets of potential invaders, they needed a strong military to defend themselves. This need reinforced the trend toward strong monarchies, which would use their military strength to expand their own empire whenever possible.

Second, mythological and religious beliefs underwent changes in ways that made them more applicable to these advanced urban civilizations. Exactly how this happened is unknown, but a definite shift occurred away from a close relationship between the nature gods that predominated in hunter-gatherer and early agricultural societies toward a greater emphasis on remote sky gods who operated outside of the earthly plane. Most ancient societies remained polytheistic; even the early Hebrews recognized the existence of other gods and at first viewed Yahweh only as their special god. But monotheism had become a religious option, as indicated by the religion of Akhenaton, one that the Hebrews came to believe in and left as a major legacy to the world.

Other texts and documents related to the religious history of the ancient near east are available at www.fordham.edu/halsall/ancient/asbook1.html.

Monotheism in Ancient Egypt and Israel

The following passages are from the *Hymn to Aton*, associated with the Egyptian pharaoh Akhenaton, who is credited with introducing monotheism into Egypt, and *Psalm 104*, from the book of Psalms from the Hebrew Old Testament.

Hymn to Aton

Thy dawning is beautiful in the horizon of heaven,
O living Aton, Beginning of life!
When Thou risest in the eastern horizon of heaven;
Thou fillest every land with Thy beauty;
For thou art beautiful, great glittering, high over the earth;
Thy rays, they encompass the lands, even all Thou hast made
Thou art Ra, and Thou hast carried them all away captive;
Thou blindest them by Thy love
Thought Thou art from afar, Thy rays are on earth;
Though Thou art on high, Thy footprints are the day.

When thou settest in the western horizon of heaven,
The world is in darkness like the dead.
Men sleep in their chambers
Their heads are wrapped up,
Their nostrils stopped, and none seeth the other.
Stolen are all their things that are under their heads,
While they know it not.
Every lion comes forth from his den;
All serpents, they sting.
Darkness reigns,
The world is in silence:
He that made them has gone to rest in His horizon.

Bright is the earth, when Thou risest in the horizon,
When thou shinest as Aton by day,
The darkness is banished
When Thou sendest forth Thy rays.
The two lands [of Egypt] are in daily festivity,
Awake and standing upon their feet,
For thou hast raised them up.
Their limbs are bathed, they take their clothing,
Their arms uplifted in adoration to Thy dawning.
Then in all the world they do their work. . . .

How manifold are thy works!
They are hidden before us.
O Thou sole god, whose powers no other possesseth.
Thou dids't create the earth according to Thy desire,
Whilst thou wast alone:
Men, all cattle large and small,
All that are upon the earth,
That go about upon their feet,
All that are on high,
That fly with their wings. . . .

O Sun of day, the fear of every distant land,
Thou makest [also] their life.
Thou hast set a Nile in heaven,
That it may fall for them
Making floods upon the mountains, like the great sea,
And watering their fields among their towns.

How excellent are thy designs, O lord of eternity!
The Nile in heaven is for the strangers,
And for the cattle of every land that go upon their feet;
But the Nile, it cometh from the nether world for Egypt. . . .

Thou art in my heart,
There is no other that knoweth thee
Save Thy son Akhnaton,
Thou hast made him wise in Thy designs
And in Thy strength.
The world is in Thy hand,
Even as Thou hast made them.
When thou hast risen they live,
When thou settest they die.
For Thou art duration, beyond mere limbs,
By thee man liveth.
And their eyes look upon Thy beauty
Until thou settest.
All labour is laid aside
When thou settest in the west.
When thou risest they are made to grow . . .
Since Thou didst establish the earth
Thou hast raised them up for Thy son,
Who came forth from thy limbs,
The King, living in truth . . .
Akhnaton, whose life is long;

[And for] the great royal wife, his beloved
Mistress of the two Lands, . . . Nerfertiti,
Living and flourishing forever and ever.

—Translated by James Henry Breasted

Source: www.brainfly.net/html/books/aton.htm.

Psalm 104

Bless the Lord, O my soul. O LORD my God, thou art very great; thou art choked
with honour and majesty.

Who coverest [thyself] with light as [with] a garment: who stretchest out the
heavens like a curtain:

Who layeth the beams of his chambers in the waters: who maketh the clouds
his chariot: who walketh on the wings of the wind:

Who maketh his angels spirits; his ministers a flaming fire:

[Who] laid the foundations of the earth, [that] it should not be removed
forever.

Thou coveredst it with the deep as [with] a garment: the waters stood above
the mountains.

At thy rebuke they fled; at the voice of thy thunder they hasted away.

They go up by the mountains; they go down by the valleys unto the place which
thou hast founded for them.

Thou hast set a bound that they may not pass over; that they turn not again to
cover the earth.

He sendeth the springs into the valleys, [which] run among the hills.

They give drink to every beast of the field: the wild asses quench their thirst.

By them shall the fowls of heaven have their habitation, [which] sing among
the branches.

He watereth the hills from his chambers: the earth is satisfied with the fruit of
thy works.

He causeth the grass to grow for the cattle, and herb for the service of man:
that he may bring forth food out of the earth;

And wine [that] maketh glad the heart of man, [and] oil to make [his] face shine,
and bread [which] strengtheneth the man's heart.

The trees of the Lord are full [of sap]; the cedars of Lebanon, which he hath
planted;

Where the birds make their nests: [as for] the stork, the fir trees [are] her
house.

The high hills [are] a refuge for the wild goats; [and] the rocks for the
conies.

He appointed the moon for seasons: the sun knoweth his going down.

Thou makest darkness, and it is night: wherein all the beasts of the forest do
creep [forth].

The young lions roar after their prey, and seek their meat from God.

The sun ariseth, they gather themselves together, and lay them down in their dens.

Man goeth forth unto his work and to his labour until the evening.

O LORD, how manifold are thy works! in wisdom thou hast made them all: the earth is full of thy riches.

[So is] this great and wide sea, wherein [are] things creeping innumerable, both small and great beasts.

There go the ships: [there is] that leviathan, [whom] thou has made to play therein.

These wait all upon thee; that thou mayest give [them] their meat in due season.

[That] thou givest them they gather: thou openest thine hand, they are filled with good.

Thou hidest thy face, they are troubled: thou takest away their breath, they die, and return to their dust.

Thou sendest forth thy spirit, they are created: and thou renewest the face of the earth.

The glory of the Lord shall endure for ever: the Lord shall rejoice in his works.

He looketh on the earth, and it trembleth: he toucheth the hills, and they smoke.

I will sing unto the Lord as long as I live: I will sing praise to my God while I have my being.

My meditation of him shall be sweet: I will be glad in the Lord.

Let the sinners be consumed out of the earth, and let the wicked be no more. Bless thou the Lord, O my soul. Praise ye the Lord.

Source: King James Version (London and New York: Collins' Clear Type Press, 1956).

What do these two passages reveal about the religious viewpoints of both authors? What is the significance of their similarities and differences?

Third, the civilizations of the ancient Near East—in addition to those of China and the Indus Valley—developed techniques of irrigation and other changes in technology associated with the coming of the Bronze Age that made large-scale urban civilization possible. Although these technologies seemed to develop independently in different parts of the world, collectively they stimulated a complex of changes that increased the possibilities of wealth and trade, bringing more cross-cultural contact. Increasing contact between different peoples furthered more rapid historical change because of the interchange of ideas, knowledge, and technologies. This is one of the reasons for some of the similarities among different Near Eastern cultures. It also helps to explain the influence of ancient Near Eastern civilizations on Western civilization, beginning with the emergence of the civilization of ancient Greece.

1. What major historical changes accompanied the development of settled agriculture? Was this a sudden or a gradual process? Was it an isolated phenomenon in particular regions?
2. Is there historical validity to Childe's concept of an "urban revolution"? What is the basis for such a concept?
3. What are some of the main characteristics of the ancient civilizations of Mesopotamia and Egypt? What were some of the main factors that contributed to their success?
4. What were the main religious beliefs of the ancient Hebrews? In what ways were these similar to and different from beliefs found elsewhere in the Near East?
5. What were the main characteristics and purposes of law in these early civilizations? Did these early peoples make a distinction between human and divine law?

Suggestions for Further Reading

Bauer, Susan Wise. 2007. *The History of the Ancient World*. New York: W.W. Norton.

Brewer, Douglas J., and Emily Teeter. 2007. *Egypt and the Egyptians*. 2nd ed. Cambridge: Cambridge University Press.

Cahill, Thomas. 1998. *The Gifts of the Jews: How a Tribe of Desert Nomads Changed the Way Everyone Thinks and Feels*. New York: Nan A. Talese.

Mithen, Steven. 1996. *The Prehistory of the Mind*. London: Thames and Hudson.

———. 2003. *After the Ice: A Global Human History, 20,000–5000 BC*. London: Weidenfeld and Nicolson.

Roux, Georges. 1992. *Ancient Iraq*. 3rd ed. London: Penguin.

Suggested Websites

www.anthropology.si.edu/humanorigins

The Smithsonian Institution in Washington, DC, provides this regularly updated website related to the anthropological study of human origins.

www.metmuseum.org/Works_of_Art/deartment.asp?dep=3

This website of the Metropolitan Museum of Art allows for the viewing of ancient Near Eastern artworks from its fascinating collection.

http://oi.chicago.edu/OI/DEPT/RA/ABZU/YOUTH_RESOURCES.HTML

This is a valuable website designed by the University of Chicago to provide resources related to the ancient Near East for students and teachers.

www.sacred-texts.com/ane/index.htm

This website provides access to both primary and secondary sources on ancient religious texts, including the *Epic of Gilgamesh* and other texts from the ancient Near East. It is an excellent site for comparing the religions of the various civilizations discussed in this chapter.

www.witcombe.sbc.edu/ARTHneareast.html

This website, provided by Dr. Christopher Witcombe of Sweet Briar College, contains links to numerous resources related to the history of art in the ancient Near East.

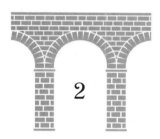

2

Greece and the Mediterranean World, ca. 2000–350 BCE

In 1900 the British archaeologist Sir Arthur Evans began to excavate a palace at a place called Knossos on the relatively poor Mediterranean island of Crete. Crete seemed an unlikely place for a thriving Bronze Age civilization, but Evans had taken an interest in the site on a previous visit in 1894 when he noticed the presence of some carved stone seats. What he found confirmed the existence of a powerful civilization that must have been a major center of political and economic power in the ancient Mediterranean. Evans found a series of palaces with expansive courtyards at their center and large rooms where massive amounts of commodities such as grain, wine, and oil had been stored. The earliest of these palaces date to about 2000 BCE. These large palaces suggest a strong, centralized rule, supported by a bureaucracy capable of managing the huge imperial storerooms. An even more fascinating find was the discovery of clay tablets, some containing a form of writing similar to Egyptian hieroglyphics and others from a later period with a new written language based on syllabic symbols that scholars now refer to as Linear A. The evidence suggests that Crete was a fertile and flourishing land during the Bronze Age, perhaps benefiting from the rich soil characteristic of areas that had experienced volcanic activity in the past.

Beginning with the rise of the Bronze Age civilization on Crete, the Greeks evolved a unique civilization in the ancient world. Greek civilization culminated in the classical culture of the Greek city-states during the period from about 700 to 350 BCE. This chapter covers the history of Greece from the early Minoan and Mycenaean civilizations of the Bronze Age to the thought of the philosopher Aristotle in the fourth century BCE. Aristotle lived to see the Greek city-states conquered by Philip of Macedon and his son, Alexander the Great, Aristotle's own pupil. But during the preceding centuries, the Greek city-states fostered new lines of thought and practice in politics, art, literature, philosophy, and science. The Greeks explored fundamental questions concerning the relationship of human beings to the

34

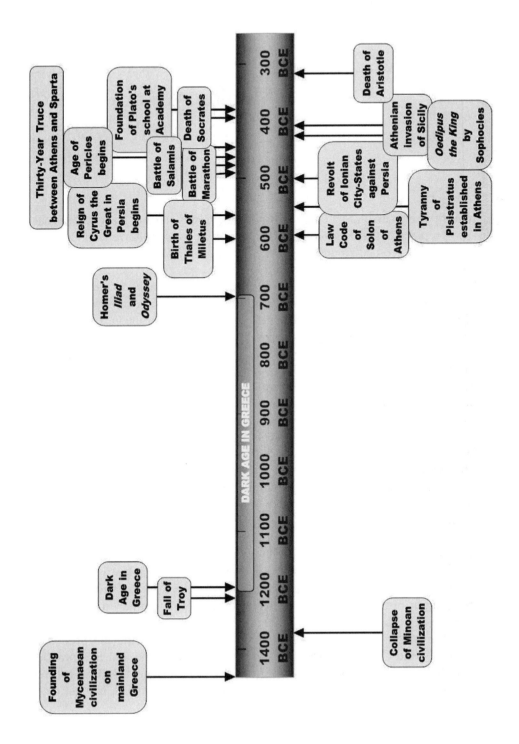

state and the role of the gods and of fate in human affairs. They attempted to understand the underlying physical reality of the universe. They reflected on such important issues as the role of women in society, the causes of warfare, and the justifications for power, to name just a few. Athens became the first state to experiment with democracy, which deteriorated under the pressure of a major war with its archrival, Sparta. Before the fifth-century conflict that the Athenians referred to as the Peloponnesian War, the Greek city-states had combined to fight a war against Persia, which was a dominant power at the time and represented a different culture against which the Greeks could measure and define themselves.

The geography and economy of Greece worked against unification and facilitated the tendency of the Greeks to organize themselves into smaller, self-contained political units. The Greek mainland and islands had been physically shaped by numerous earthquakes and volcanic activity that produced a rugged, mountainous peninsula; the terrain made trade routes across land difficult and increased a sense of political and social isolation in different regions. Sparta, for example, was located on a plain on the mountainous southern peninsula of the Greek mainland known as the Peloponnese. The fundamental Greek political organization was called the *polis*, usually translated as "city-state." The Greek city-state system extended across the Aegean to the region called Ionia, which comprised the island city-states of Chios and Samos and ten more on the mainland of Asia Minor. As in the rest of Greece, these city-states made a transition from monarchy to oligarchy from the eighth to the sixth centuries BCE. They collectively formed a loose organization known as the Pan-Ionian League, though each retained its independence. Of the twelve Ionian city-states, Samos was the most prosperous, mainly a result of its location on the safest trading route across the Aegean. The culture of Ionia was largely Greek, but showed strong traces of Near Eastern influences because of its location. But it took some time for a distinctively Greek culture to develop. The history of early Greece may be divided into three main periods: the Minoan period, lasting from about 2000–1350 BCE; the Mycenaean period, which overlapped with the Minoan and flourished from around 1450–1200 BCE; and the period known as the Dark Age, which lasted from about 1200–700 BCE. Each of these periods made contributions to the future development and shape of Greek civilization.

Read more about and see images of the archaeological finds from the Minoan period at Knossos at www.interkriti.org/visits/knosos.htm.

Minoan fresco on wall of Palace of Knosses, Crete *(Photograph by George M. Groutas)*

Early Greece

Minoan Crete shared some characteristics with the Egyptian and Near Eastern monarchies, but it still stands at the beginning of Greek civilization. The legends that came to surround Crete attributed its origins to the legendary King Minos, whose father was believed to be Zeus, the powerful sky god of Greek mythology. According to legend, Zeus, in the form of a bull, had made love to Minos's mother, Europa. Then Zeus sent a white bull out of the sea to Minos as a sign that he was the legitimate ruler. Pasiphae, the wife of Minos, made love to the white bull, after which she gave birth to the Minotaur, a creature who was half bull and half human. Ashamed and embarrassed, Minos had the inventor Daedalus construct a labyrinth to confine the Minotaur, which was fed with human sacrifices. Cretan art suggests a cult of bull-worship that could be related to the legends surrounding King Minos. Cretan religion did not solely revolve around a bull cult, however; some of the familiar Greek gods were already worshipped at Crete, including Zeus, Poseidon (who controlled earthquakes as well as the sea), and Dionysus, the god of wine. In addition, the Minoans worshipped a birth goddess named Eleitheia, and their religious objects included images of birds (perhaps an Egyptian influence) and lilies, a later Christian symbol associated with the resurrection of Christ.

Most of the objects found at Knossos, especially from the Early Palace

Period (ca. 2000–1700 BCE), indicate a peaceful society. However, after 1700 BCE more objects suggestive of warfare begin to appear, though they could have been introduced by outside influences instead of resulting from a more aggressive policy of the Minoan rulers. The decline of Minoan civilization was most likely accelerated by earthquake activity. A cataclysmic earthquake decimated the settlements at Thera during the Bronze Age, evidence of which only began to come to light with archaeological digs starting in the 1960s. The archaeological finds at Thera suggest greater North African influence there than at Crete, evident in the portrayal of both animals and people in the paintings. Archaeologists have found evidence of a number of Minoan settlements that were never reoccupied after being completely destroyed by volcano, earthquake, fire, tidal wave, or other unknown causes that could have been either natural or human in origin. The volcanic eruption on Thera may have contributed to destruction of a number of sites on Crete around 1500 BCE, though the main palace at Knossos seems, based on the dating of pottery, to have survived to approximately 1380. The palaces of Minoan Crete survived until the twelfth century BCE, though sometime around 1450, Crete seems to have lost its independence to a powerful civilization that had emerged on the Greek mainland among people known as the Mycenaeans after their capital city, Mycenae.

The Mycenaeans had risen to power on the Greek mainland through the use of horses and chariots. They entered Greece sometime before 1900 BCE and exploited the native population as serfs and laborers. They had a warrior culture that has been revealed in the artifacts and oral traditions that they left behind. While the Mycenaeans borrowed extensively from the culture and civilization of Minoan Crete, they also had their own practices and culture that distinguished their civilization from that of the Minoans. Mycenaean palaces that date from the fourteenth century BCE contain impressive throne rooms that do not resemble anything found on Crete. In Mycenaean art, human figures appear heavier and more solid than in Cretan art. The area of Mycenae lacks the mountain shrines and cave idols found on Crete, indicating the practice of a more centralized official religion on mainland Greece. The Mycenaeans were also seafarers who had stronger connections with other Mediterranean civilizations than with those on the European continent. These connections were probably based on trade, indicating that the Mycenaeans had developed a successful agricultural economy centered on the production of olive oil, wine, and wool, which they would have exchanged for precious metals, jewels, and dyes, as well as tin and copper for use in the manufacture of bronze weapons. Their graves contained goods from throughout the Mediterranean, indicating the extensive contacts that the Mycenaeans had over a wide region, including contact with the Egyptians, the Syrians, and the Hittites.

The central event for which the Mycenaeans are remembered was the fall of the city-state of Troy on the northwest coast of Asia Minor at their hands in 1260 BCE, when they were ostensibly at the height of their power. Yet by 1200 BCE the Mycenaeans themselves entered a period of decline that preceded the virtual disappearance of their civilization by 1100 BCE. The exact cause of the fall of Mycenae has been a subject of debate among scholars of ancient history. Since the main fortress at Mycenae is set inland from the Argos Bay, it was not vulnerable to a surprise attack, though it had no defenses against a large invading force. The mysterious sea peoples may have attacked Mycenae solely to loot it and then destroyed the fortress with fire. The abrupt demise of the Hittite kingdom around 1200 adds support to the theory that sea robbers from the eastern Mediterranean posed a significant threat in the twelfth century BCE. Such piratical raids could account for a general decline in civilization and the economy of the Mediterranean at the end of the Bronze Age. The fall of the Mycenaeans set the stage for the onset of the Dark Age of Greek history, about which even less is known than these earlier periods. With the fortress of Mycenae in ruins, the Mycenaeans must have scattered throughout the Greek mainland, blending with other peoples and disappearing from history. Mycenaean culture, however, bequeathed an oral tradition of songs and poetry to the generations of Greeks that followed the destruction of Mycenae.

By the time that the poet Homer gave the stories and legends from the Mycenaean period their final form some time toward the end of the eighth century BCE, other Greek poets had preserved tales of the great victory in the Trojan War and the wealth and glories of the reign of the Mycenaean king, Agamemnon. Two long epic poems attributed to Homer—*The Iliad* and *The Odyssey*—have become enduring masterpieces of world literature. *The Iliad* deals with the war between Troy (Ilium) and the Greeks (Homer's Achaeans). The plot revolves around the character of Achilles, the greatest Greek warrior and son of a sea-nymph who had warned her son that his fate was to die if he went to Troy. After nine years of warfare, the Trojans appear to gain the upper hand because of a division in the Achaean ranks between Agamemnon and Achilles; Achilles holds back from the fray, but joins the fighting upon the death of his good friend, Patroclus, at the hands of Troy's great warrior, Hector. Achilles kills Hector and drags the body behind his chariot—an affront to the gods. (Throughout the poem, the gods play an active role in the struggle and wage their own war as a counterpart of the earthly conflict.) The Trojans recover Hector's body and hold their own funeral for him, ending the *Iliad*. In this poem, Homer treats war as part of the human condition and combines descriptions of glory and valor with accounts of undeniable tragedy and horror. When the Achaeans do not accept offers of ransom from the wealthy Trojans and do not allow them to redeem their captured countrymen, Homer indicates that the normal rules of civilization have broken down, as they frequently do in times of war. *The Odyssey* recounts the travels of the Greek hero, Odysseus, after the fall of Troy at the hands of the Achaeans. The gods decide to punish the Achaeans on their way home because the victors failed to give the deities proper recognition after their victory. Odysseus thus endures ten years of trials, hardships, and adventures fraught with danger and distractions before he manages to return home to his beloved wife, Penelope. He then has to endure a final test to prove his identity; Penelope, long assuming that her husband has died, is expected, despite her resistance, to marry one of the many wealthy men contesting to take the place of Odysseus. Odysseus has to compete with them and prove his identity in order to win back his own wife. The story became symbolic for the Greeks of the many trials and tests to which the gods may put humans, and the rewards that await those who learn humility and reject the Greek sin of hubris, by which men aspired to superiority over the gods or in their pride thought that they could gain success solely on their own merits without divine assistance.

The Dark Age in Greek history (ca. 1100–700 BCE) is so named because the period left fewer sources and traces than earlier or later periods. But the poems of Homer and his contemporary Hesiod suggest a vibrant cultural tradition that moved from oral to written during this period. Hesiod's *Works and Days* celebrates work and contains advice on a number of topics ranging from sailing to farming, while also carrying strong religious and moral overtones. Furthermore, recent archaeological work on Crete suggests that the period may not have been so dark to the people who lived during that time. Evidence of imported works of art and craftsmanship argues for the continuation of some trade and suggests that cultural and creative stimuli existed for the natives of the island during these centuries; scholars no longer assume that the downfall of Minoan civilization meant that high-quality work on Crete must have been imported.

The Shaping of the Greek Polis

Each polis or city-state had its own special associations with the Greek gods that were recognized throughout the peninsula. Both Sparta and Athens chose the goddess Athena as their patron deity, but their historical development took them in entirely different directions. Sparta was one of the most venerable of the Greek city-states with its own unique political and social conditions. The Spartans' emphasis on discipline and military development made their city-state the dominant power in their region of Laconia, if not in all of Greece.

Politically, Sparta was an oligarchy, with political power and the right to vote confined to relatively few individuals. As an oligarchy, Sparta was not a dictatorship; members of the main political assembly, the *gerousia*, enjoyed lifetime membership and complete freedom of speech. The Spartans were quite conservative; they maintained political stability by resisting change, sublimating any differences that might result in divisions among the ruling class, and repressing any potential sources of rebellion or turmoil. Spartan veneration of the legendary founder of their state, laws, and constitution, Lycurgus, made the Spartans extremely reluctant to adopt any political changes. In 706 BCE the Spartans shipped some of the illegitimate sons of citizens to their only successful colony of Taras (Tarentum) in southern Italy, afraid that they might cause trouble because of their exclusion from the body politic.

Socially, the important division that characterized Sparta involved the distinction between citizens and noncitizens. A Spartan citizen was, first and foremost, a soldier; to encourage military discipline and a feeling of equality, Sparta required its citizens to live in barracks and eat together in communal mess halls. Since all male citizens of Sparta served as soldiers, they did not become merchants or adopt a profession. The Spartan economy was not based on trade; they tried to produce whatever they needed or they relied on the subjugated residents (known as *perioikoi*) of country villages in their region. The Spartans used the helots, socially inferior serfs who were tied to the land, to sustain the state economically, enabling the Spartan citizens to remain in a constant state of military preparedness.

The Athenians developed their city-state in an entirely different manner from Sparta. Sparta may have dominated the Greek mainland militarily, but Athens ruled the seas. Whereas Sparta's political constitution remained stable and entrenched oligarchy as the dominant political force, Athens made its way from oligarchy to democracy by way of tyranny. Whereas the Spartans looked back to the legendary Lycurgus as the founder of their constitution, the Athenians revered their famous lawgiver, Solon, who formulated his own code in about 594 BCE in direct response to an extremely harsh and inflexible code instituted in 620 by Draco (*draconian* has become an adjective describing severe and punitive legislation). The Greek historian Plutarch (ca. 46–120 CE) said of Solon that his main concern was the application of morals to politics. Solon tried to protect the poor without alienating the wealthy; he canceled all debts and had Athens purchase the freedom of the slaves, enabling them to become citizens. However, while Solon ended some of the exploitation and abuses of the old system, he had not mediated successfully between the rival aristocratic and merchant classes, both of whom sought power.

Pisistratus (ca. 600–527 BCE), an outsider to both groups, succeeded in transforming Athens into a tyranny about 546 BCE. The word *tyranny* did not then have all the negative connotations that it does in the modern world, and Pisistratus proved a relatively tolerant ruler who did not provoke intense opposition. He ruled successfully until his death in 527, maintaining peace between the town and the countryside in Attica. Pisistratus's son, Hippias, however, reversed the lenient policies of his father and had a number of Athenian citizens killed in retaliation for an assassination attempt against him and the successful assassination of his brother, Hipparchus in 514. Hippias's revenge led to rebellion and his overthrow around 510, led in part by a powerful aristocratic family known as the Alkmeonids (with whom Pisistratus had forged a marriage alliance) and supported by the Spartans, who viewed the rebellion as an opportunity to gain political control over Athens. The Athenians, however, naturally resisted Spartan dominance, led by Cleisthenes, a member of the Alkmeonid family, who sensed that he could benefit from the support of a popular faction in Athens. In the years that followed, he became a prominent supporter of democracy whose reforms stood until the end of the Peloponnesian War a century later.

Aside from these historical developments, certain conditions contributed to the rise of democracy in Athens. The growth of the Athenian population raised the possibility of democracy as one means of redressing the imbalance caused by the rule of a few aristocrats. Whereas the Spartans severely restricted their citizenship and oppressed everyone else, the Athenians opened the doors for wider citizenship and reduced the number of potential leaders of a rebellion against the state. Furthermore, Athens had a democratic tradition, dating from the seventh century BCE, that included the right of Athenian male citizens to attend meetings of the assembly, called the *ecclesia* (although the assembly seems to have met infrequently and had as its main purpose the election of the archons, the chief magistrates of the city-state). Moreover, democracy guided village and community life on an informal basis. Athenian politics included voluntary political associations that mainly consisted of Athenian citizens and might be associated with a particular craft or trade, a military unit, interest in a particular religious cult, or simply based on social class. In the end, the Athenians claimed no divine sanction for their form of government, nor did they create a constitution against which all future decisions could be measured. Athenian democracy mainly relied on precedent, looking back to past laws, statutes, and judicial decisions. But Athenians reserved the right to change their minds according to what seemed called for by the situation. Athenian democracy began to flourish, however, before Athens had acquired its vast wealth at a time when people could still perceive a wider degree of basic equality.

When Corinth overthrew and abandoned tyranny, it—unlike Athens—did not proceed to democracy, but instead evolved into a stable merchant oligarchy. Corinth rivaled Sparta in its political stability, but the Corinthian regime seems to have been less prescriptive than that of Sparta and to have done more to cultivate the support of its citizens. Corinthian colonies lined the Aegean and the Adriatic Seas and were integrated into a single political and economic unit, each using the same coins and ruled by a governor appointed by Corinth. Welcoming travelers from all over Greece to its central location on the slender isthmus between the south and the north, Corinth became a prominent trading port and derived a great deal of revenue from the ships that paid taxes and bought supplies while docked in its harbor.

Although each was independent, the Ionian city-states shared a sense of unity and common destiny, symbolized by a temple devoted to Poseidon on Mount Mycale on the coast of Asia Minor in southern Ionia. Settlers from mainland Greece intermingled with the native population of the region to forge a unique Ionian identity. The unity of the Ionian city-states was fostered by their precarious position between mainland Greece and the powerful Persian Empire. Herodotus, the fifth-century BCE Greek historian, tells us that the Ionians were the weakest of the Hellenic peoples at the time of the rise of Persia in the sixth century BCE. Tradition ascribed the origins of the Ionian city-states to Athens and its surrounding region, Attica; it was to Athens that the Ionians turned when they decided to revolt against the mighty Persians in the early fifth century BCE.

Persia and Greece

When the Greeks came into conflict with the Persian Empire in the early fifth century BCE, they encountered a culture significantly different from their own. Unlike the politically disunited Greeks, the Persians had created a huge empire under the dominance of a single, autocratic ruler. While the Greeks had certainly been influenced by Egyptian and Near Eastern cultures, the Persians were much more imitative of their Babylonian and Assyrian predecessors, as well as the culture of Egypt, which they also conquered. Of their religion, Herodotus said that the Persians did not build temples, altars, or religious statues because they did not view their gods as having human qualities, as the Greeks did. While this is not entirely true—since the Persians embraced the gods of many cultures and had a large pantheon—some Persians had abandoned polytheism in the sixth century BCE under the influence of the prophet Zoroaster, who taught a dualistic religion that included equally powerful gods of light and darkness, each served by a set of demons. In addition, the Persian emperor Darius I (548–486 BCE) gave special recognition to the Lord God Ahura-Mazda, who took precedence over all other gods. The Persian religion lacked the subtlety and multidimensional character of the Greek beliefs about their Olympian gods. But the Persians tolerated the religions and customs of their conquered subjects as long as they provided deference and tribute to the emperor, in whom all power ultimately resided. Under Darius, the empire was effectively structured into twenty administrative districts known as satrapies, ruled over by governors and a growing bureaucracy that allowed this vast empire to function. The Greek political tradition was entirely different, making it difficult even for Herodotus (who came from Asia Minor and probably had direct experience with the Persians) to fathom the workings of such a vast empire.

Nor could the Greeks identify with the extent of the luxury and the massively impressive palaces in the major centers of the Persian Empire: Persepolis, Pasargadae, and Susa. Although Athens and Corinth, in particular, had flourishing mercantile economies, the economy of the Persians was entirely geared toward channeling wealth and resources to support the emperors and their large army and administrative structure. Even Greek art and craftsmanship were geared more toward public and popular consumption compared to the Persian cultivation of opulent jewelry, tableware, and beautiful, luxurious palaces built on a grand scale for the benefit of the emperor and his intimate family members and associates. The complete subjugation of people to the power of the emperor would have had little appeal for the fiercely independent Greek city-states. Even some Greeks, however, expressed admiration for Persian political stability, which offered a stark contrast with Greek political life.

The Persians first appeared as a threat to Greece around the mid-sixth century during the reign of Cyrus the Great (r. ca. 560–529 BCE), when their conquest of Asia Minor brought them in contact with the Ionian city-states. Under Darius (r. 522–486 BCE), the Persians continued to expand their empire in all directions, from Afghanistan in the east to Egypt in the west. They had expanded to the regions of Thrace and Macedon north of Greece by 514. By about 500 BCE the Spartans had become head of an alliance of a number of Greek states formed in the face of the Persian threat; however, when the Ionian city-states revolted against Persia in 499 BCE, the Athenians, not the Spartans, lent their support and thus became open enemies of the Persian Empire.

Herodotus said that the ousted tyrant Hippias moved "heaven and earth" to get Persia to invade Athens, hoping to rule as a vassal of the Persian king if such an invasion were to succeed. The Persians waited until they had crushed the Ionian revolt in 494 before making their move on Athens. During the Persian Wars, the Greeks benefited from a military revolution that had occurred in the sixth century involving the emergence of infantry troops known as hoplites as a deadly efficient fighting force. Hoplite soldiers advanced in close formation holding their shields in a position to protect their neighbor and leaving their strong arm free to engage the enemy. They fought in unison and as a unit became much stronger than the number of individual soldiers involved. It was difficult to break their ranks because the soldiers had strength together, but

Sculptural Representations in Greece and Persia

These two images are somewhat representative of the differences between Persian and Greek art and culture. In the first, located at the great palace at Persepolis begun by Darius the Great in approximately 500 BCE and later completed by Xerxes, priests are on their way to offer tribute to the Persian emperor. The second image is representative of a revolutionary new type of artistic sculpture that occurred in Greece about the same time. Human figures were carved to adorn temples that commemorated the lives of deceased men and, as depicted here, women.

Priests' procession, Apadana Palace staircase, Persepolis
(Photograph by Patrick Charlot)

Kore statue at the Acropolis Museum, Athens

What does the subject matter of each work reveal about the cultures that produced them? What is the significance in the difference between the two in artistic style?

were doomed if they split apart. In 490 the Persians launched a naval invasion of Attica, landing at the town of Marathon, twenty miles from Athens. They hoped to disperse the hoplite soldiers with their archers and cavalry, a strategy that represented the key to a Persian military victory against the Greeks. At Marathon, however, the Greek hoplites advanced quickly enough to surround the Persian infantry before the archers could do their work; the result was a great Athenian victory in which approximately 6,400 Persians died compared to 192 Greeks.

The victory at Marathon did not eliminate the Persian threat, but it proved that the Persians could be defeated, an important psychological realization for both the Athenians and the Persians. In 486 Darius died, having failed to avenge the defeat suffered at the Battle of Marathon, but the Persian threat had not ended. The new emperor, Xerxes (r. 485–465 BCE), formed a large army of about 180,000 men and launched what became known in Greece as the Second Persian War. The Persians marched through a largely sympathetic Macedonia into the northern Greek region of Thessaly, where they met little opposition. After a force led by the Spartan king Leonidas failed—despite a valiant and heroic effort—to stop the Persians at Thermopylae, just south of Thessaly, the Athenians abandoned their city, which Xerxes set ablaze in retaliation for the burning of the city of Sardis in Asia Minor during the Ionian revolt of 499. But the Athenians had devoted themselves to strengthening their navy and looked to the sea for their salvation. At Salamis in 480 BCE the Athenian navy forced the Persian ships into an engagement that resulted in a resounding naval victory in which the Athenians destroyed almost all that remained of a Persian fleet already decimated by violent storms.

A final decisive battle at Plataea in 479 ended the Persian threat once and for all and signaled the rise of Athens as the leading power of the Greek world. Running woefully short of food and water (thanks in part to the Persians poisoning a spring), the Greeks needed a successful retreat to avoid having their troops crushed by an onslaught of the Persian cavalry. The Greek commander, Pausanias, managed this retreat under cover of night, enabling his troops to fight the Persians in conditions that neutralized the strength of the Persian cavalry.

See additional images of the Apadana Palace, along with a description and a diagram of its layout, at http://oi.uchicago.edu/museum/collections/pa/persepolis/apadana.html.

Explore the collection at the Acropolis Museum at www.theacropolis-museum.gr/?pname=Home&la=2.

Herodotus praised the valor of the Persians, but, with their cavalry neutralized, the Greeks won a crushing victory in hand-to-hand combat. Frustrated by the heavy losses, Xerxes had no choice but to declare a retreat and began to lose interest in Greece; the Greeks followed up their victories at Salamis and Plataea by liberating their Ionian allies and pushing on to the Black Sea.

Greece in the Classical Age

The Persian Wars and the subsequent Greek victory, in which Athens had played a leading role, facilitated the rise of Athens as the dominant city-state in Greece. Even prior to the Persian Wars, Athens had aligned itself with the Ionian city-states and begun to establish colonies such as those on the islands of Salamis and Euboea. The farmland in Attica did not provide enough grain to feed the growing population of Athens, making the city-state dependent on food imported from the Black Sea region. But Athenian motivations for expansion were complex and their support for the Ionian city-states, for example, could have been partially motivated by the Athenian commitment to democracy and hostility to Persian autocracy.

The dominant political figure of fifth-century Athens was Pericles (ca. 495–429 BCE), a strong advocate of democracy who became so powerful that he dominated Athenian politics for more than thirty years (461–429). A relative of Cleisthenes on his mother's side, Pericles showed his commitment to democracy in his proposal that public officials chosen by lot, including members of juries, be paid for their political service, allowing even the poorer citizens to serve. Pericles realized, however, that Athens could not have all positions filled by lot, because some positions required skill, knowledge, or leadership ability. Since the most important military and political leaders—including Pericles—did not receive any money for their service, they all came from the wealthier classes. In addition, Pericles was the man most responsible for the impressive public projects undertaken during his rule. The Athenians used their treasury to fund construction of some of the most important buildings of the classical period, including the Parthenon, a temple dedicated to the goddess Athena and built in 447 on the hill known as the acropolis. Such projects as the Parthenon provided employment for skilled craftsmen and unskilled laborers alike. In addition, the Athenian government under Pericles financed the expansion of the navy and the construction of defensive walls around Athens and its ports. Although a political opponent accused Pericles of misuse of public funds in 443 and attempted unsuccessfully to drive him out of office, throughout this period Pericles remained popular with most people, including members of the lower classes who viewed him as an advocate for democracy. Furthermore, colonies provided an outlet for

Classical Greece

the surplus population of Attica, providing greater resources for those who remained. Athens prospered under Pericles and used its wealth and strength to solidify its dominant position within the Greek world. Citizens took great pride in their association with such a prosperous and powerful city-state, their ability to serve in politics and get paid for it, and their own contributions in the navy or the construction of public works.

Public life in the Greek city-states centered on the agora, a public market-place where people met for a variety of purposes, from political assemblies to personal rendezvous. Theatrical performances, religious festivities, and athletic competitions were held there as well. Archaeological evidence from the Athenian agora has revealed religious shrines, meeting places for the great council and law courts, and shaded colonnades, which would have made for pleasant private meetings. The agora helped to shape a city's identity and would have witnessed a great deal of bustle and activity every day, contributing to the public nature of Greek life.

It should be noted, however, that—at least in Athens—women were largely excluded from these public areas. Women in some Athenian households lived segregated existences, designed to keep them in their place and to encourage them to perform their assigned duties. It was not acceptable practice for Athenian women to dine with their husbands if guests were present in the household.

Upper-class Athenian women were generally not permitted to leave the house without male permission or accompaniment and frequently even sent their maids to do the marketing. There were some exceptions to these restrictions, such as the religious festival of Thesmaphoria, which was dedicated to women's fertility. Women could attend this festival freely without their families or the permission of their husbands. The Peloponnesian War (see below) changed the women's situation in Athens to a large degree, giving them greater access to public areas and more freedom in the absence of the many men who were called away to fight.

Women outside of Athens had a good deal more freedom than did Athenian women. Greek women outside Athens generally had the right to own their own property. Spartan women had more freedom than women in any other city-state, but only after they reached adulthood. Young Spartan girls shared with Spartan boys a strict, disciplined upbringing, but Spartan women had the freedom to socialize with men and even participated in military drills alongside them. The Greek historian Xenophon (ca. 435–354 BCE) reported that elderly Spartan men could allow their wives to have children by other men. He added that men might also allow their wives to have children for unmarried men who desired a family without marriage.

Most of the Greeks placed a great emphasis on family relationships and attempted to regulate them through their various law codes, thus blurring the distinction between public and private life. For example, Solon pre-scribed that fathers teach their sons a trade; sons were expected to care for their parents in old age, but Solon's law exempted those who had not been adequately trained by their fathers. Inheritance laws ensured that sons who cared for their parents would be rewarded at their parents' death. Greeks could not marry anyone in their immediate family, but it was not uncommon for first cousins to marry in the Greek world as a way of strengthening family relationships. The Spartans, however, did not emphasize family life. They practiced infanticide on babies that did not seem robust enough to grow into strong soldiers. They separated wives from husbands for long periods of time and boys from their mothers at the age of seven (Spartan girls, however, stayed with their mothers until they got married). Husbands were not even allowed to live with their wives until the age of thirty; fathers were expected to devote themselves to the state rather than to their family. In addition to the Spartan exception, the common practice of homosexuality and bisexuality among Greek men (and sometimes among women) in the classical period might seem to contradict their emphasis on traditional family relationships. However, although homosexuality was a frequent theme of Greek art and poetry, it remained proscribed for members of the lower classes, and only certain types of homosexual relationships were tolerated. For example, the most accepted homosexual relationship occurred between an unmarried aristocratic young man in his twenties and a teenage boy who would benefit from his elder partner's tutelage; it was considered a disgrace for older men to engage in homosexual relations.

The Shaping of the Past: The Peloponnesian Wars

The Athenian rise to power did not go unnoticed by its rivals, such as Sparta, who began to question the desirability of one state becoming so singularly dominant. To counter Athenian power, Sparta formed the Peloponnesian League and allowed its member states to complain about any mistreatment that they felt they had received from Athens. A first Peloponnesian War ended in 446 BCE when Sparta agreed to a Thirty-Year Peace with Athens, but by 435 the Spartans were already contemplating whether or not another war was justified. In that year, Corinth complained to Sparta regarding Athenian protection of Corcyra, with whom it was quarrelling over the colony of Epidamnus. Athens sent ships to support Corcyra, but hoped to remain in a defensive position to avoid abrogating the Thirty-Year Peace. The Athenian navy, however, found it impossible to support Corcyra without confronting the Corinthians and entered the fray when it appeared that the Corinthian navy had won the battle and would seize Corcyra's ships. The Spartans, who now had their justification, accused Athens of violating the peace agreement. They called representatives of their allies together and asked for their support in declaring war on Athens. The Greek historian Thucydides (ca. 460–ca. 400 BCE) viewed the Spartans' decision as a foregone conclusion because of their fear of the growing power of Athens. The problem with his interpretation is that Athens had not significantly expanded its power in the years leading up to the conflict, nor was it acting in a manner that posed a direct threat to Sparta itself. Sparta, however, needed the Athenian threat in order to maintain its alliances and therefore condemned Athens and went to war in order to preserve its own power and influence within Greece.

At the beginning of the Second Peloponnesian War, it seemed that Athens had an advantage based on its wealth and resources. Pericles, however, advocated a defensive war and refused to pander to the people who demanded a more aggressive approach. After Pericles died in a plague that decimated the Athenian population in 429 BCE, political leadership in Athens passed to Cleon, a radical democrat who guided Athens through the first phase of the war, which lasted until 421.

Pericles's democratic ideals could not survive in the context of a destructive war in which leaders increasingly appealed to the basest emotions of the masses to increase their own support. Cleon was a long-time political opponent of Pericles who relied on demagoguery to increase his power over war strategy. Athens began to pursue an expansionist policy that had little justification beyond a blatant grab for additional power. In 422 Cleon died at the Athenian defeat at Amphipolis, leading to a frequently violated truce that lasted from 421 to 416, after which Alcibiades (ca. 450–404 BCE), a student of the famous philosopher Socrates, became the leader of the Athenian war effort and pursued a far more aggressive military policy. He launched an invasion of Syracuse on the island of Sicily in 415. The Athenians, recalling the burning of their city by the Persians, preferred to fight farther from their home base rather than see their own city threatened (by contrast, the Spartans, wary of the potential discontent of their subject population, preferred to fight closer to home). Alcibiades, however, did not see the invasion through to a successful conclusion because he was accused of sacrilege. Rather than returning to Athens, he defected to Sparta and provided information that contributed to the defeat of the Sicilian expedition in 413. The defeat suffered by the Athenians there presaged their ultimate defeat at the hands of the Spartans.

The Peloponnesian War was a vicious affair that undermined many of the foundations of Greek civilization. It lasted for three decades and constantly fueled the hatred of each side against the other. The war dragged on without any decisive battles, escalating the fighting and the number of atrocities. In Thucydides's history *The Peloponnesian War*, the Mytilenean debate and the Melian dialogue illustrate the shift in values that occurred in Athens during the war. In 427 the Athenians sent a squadron to kill the entire male population of Mytilene and enslave all its women and children, before changing their minds. While it was significant that the Athenians considered such drastic measures, they quickly pulled back from such a cold-blooded and ruthless decision, recognizing that the innocent would have been punished along with the guilty. In 416 the Athenians demanded that the Melians—who wished to maintain their neutrality—support Athens in its war effort or else Melos would be considered a hostile state. Thucydides stressed the argument made by the Athenians that nature supported the principle that the strong should rule the weak. In the context of war, this argument presented a new and dangerous interpretation of Athenian imperialism. When the Melians refused to support Athens, the Athenians had the entire male population of Melos killed and all the women and children sold into slavery. Although Athenian democracy under Pericles had sanctioned slavery and imperialism as economically necessary to support the state, the Peloponnesian War had destroyed whatever redeeming values the empire possessed, which had included toleration of differing viewpoints and new ideas.

Classical Greek Culture (480–338 BCE)

The Greeks contributed many ideas and insights to the cultural development of Western civilization. For example, although belief in the physical existence of the Greek gods ceased long ago, people have continued to find profound psychological and human insight in Greek religion. In addition, Greek art and architecture provided models and inspiration for many periods from Roman times to the present. Greek literature established certain models from which much of Western literature derived and contained insights into the human condition that make these works still interesting, challenging, and relevant. Finally, Greek philosophy and science charted courses that influenced all aspects of Western thought. Through a critical examination of what the Greeks did, wrote, and thought, we can come to a better understanding of Greek civilization and, perhaps, ourselves.

Greek religion was polytheistic and derived from the Homeric epics and other works of mythology from both the archaic and classical periods. The Greek gods were associated with Mount Olympus in northern Greece, the point at which the Greeks believed heaven and earth connected. Among the gods and goddesses of particular importance to the Greeks were the sky god Zeus and his brothers, Poseidon, the god of the sea, and Hades, the god of the underworld. Ares, the god of war; Athena, the goddess of wisdom; Apollo, the god of the sun who also symbolized rationality and health; Aphrodite, the goddess of love; Hermes, the messenger god; Artemis, the goddess of the hunt and the moon; and Hephaestus, the god of the forge, constitute the other main deities in the Greek pantheon. The anthropomorphic Greek gods and goddesses shared all the qualities of human beings, both strengths and weaknesses.

The Greeks of the classical period inherited their gods from an earlier period and had to make sense out of myths that often characterized the gods as petulant and flawed beings. The continuing appeal of Greek mythology in an age of growing rationality can be understood if one focuses on the practical purposes that mythology served for the Greeks instead of viewing it as a set of irrational superstitions. The flaws of the gods might have helped the Greeks to accept their own humanity a little more easily. The myths about the gods presented a set of characteristics that individuals could decide to emulate or reject. The variety of personalities among the gods may have made the Greeks more tolerant of the different types of personalities among humans, on which their ideas about the gods were clearly based. This does not mean, however, that the Greeks did not believe in the gods and goddesses, who could be viewed as manifestations of diverse aspects of the divine that were reflected in the world around them. In many ways, the oracle at Delphi epitomized the Greek approach to religion, which was characterized by a devotion to ritual and valued for its worldly usefulness. A temple believed to contain the oracle of Apollo sat in the town of Delphi on the southern slope of Mount Parnassus. A high priestess called the Pythia—Apollo had allegedly killed a python at Delphi—

presided over the oracle. She wore a veil and sat on an altar, unseen by those who came seeking her insight or advice. Under the influence of smoke and ingested laurel leaves, the Pythia would utter her oracle, which could usually be interpreted in whatever way the petitioner desired. The Greeks might respect the gods, petition the gods for assistance, or blame the gods when things went wrong, but they did not develop a strong emotional attachment to them. The Greeks quarreled over many things, but they did not go to war over religion or persecute people for their religious beliefs, or lack thereof.

Much art in ancient Greece served a religious purpose. The statue of Athena in the Parthenon provides a good example of the religious purposes of much Greek statuary and its association with architectural structures such as temples. Pericles appointed the master sculptor Phidias to supervise the sculptures at the Parthenon, which was adorned with a number of representations of Greek gods and heroes. The architects of the Parthenon, whose names were Ictinus and Callicrates demonstrated the ability to combine form and function into a harmonious design that could be appreciated for its own sake—even as people gathered in devotion to the goddess Athena. The Greeks took art seriously and were devoted to the cultivation of beauty, harmony, and proportion. They valued art, collected it, and made it an integral part of their lives and culture.

Art helped the Greeks to define who they were and what they believed and valued. Greek art—or Greek civilization, for that matter—never existed in complete isolation from the other cultures of the Mediterranean world. For example, the seventh century BCE has been noted by specialists on ancient history as a period of significant Egyptian influence upon Greek culture and art, particularly sculpture. Greek artists, however, enjoyed the freedom to express themselves, whether they were adding beauty to everyday objects such as pottery or creating statues or paintings in the search for beauty itself. Classical art was characterized by an idealization of the human form, attention to a balance between vertical and horizontal lines, and the subordination of each part to the beauty of the whole. The Greeks also made the nude human form a staple of Western art and the means through which they idealized humanity. The emphasis in Greek art was not so much on depicting individual human beings as it was on making general observations about human physicality. The emphasis on the ideal in Greek art found expression in Greek philosophy (see below) in the ideas of Plato (428–347 BCE). Plato stressed the existence of perfect forms in the divine realm in which physical examples participate by their resemblance to them.

The Greeks also expressed themselves in poetry, for which the Homeric epics provided a model. The poems of Homer and Hesiod taught the Greeks their values and provided them with many of their basic ideas about religion.

Other writers built upon their work, but branched out to explore a variety of themes and topics. The seventh-century poet Stesichorus, who came from a Greek settlement in southern Italy, wrote verses that built on the Greek myths established by Homer and contributed significantly to the evolution of Greek mythology and the development of Greek lyrical poetry. The seventh-century Spartan poet Tyrtaeus wrote songs glorifying military courage and the civic spirit of the Spartan troops, in keeping with the martial spirit of his city-state. Another seventh-century poet, Archilocus, was a hoplite soldier who wrote about his military experiences, often in a satirical and self-mocking way. He also wrote poems on everything from the colonization efforts of his native land of Paros to the poor quality of food there. In the late seventh century, Mimnermus, from the Ionian city-state of Colophon, wrote pleasant poems about the sun and Aphrodite, but also kept alive historical traditions about how the Greeks came to settle in Asia Minor. The poet Sappho (ca. 610–ca. 590 BCE), who came from the island of Lesbos, explored personal emotions and sexual longings in verse, inaugurating a new direction in Greek literature. She allegedly killed herself by jumping from a cliff after a man rejected her love, but she also wrote lesbian poems, including her one complete surviving poem, which was an appeal to Aphrodite to help her deal with the love she felt for another woman. The poet Pindar (ca. 522–440 BCE) attempted to preserve some of the vanishing values of ancient Greece at a time of great political and cultural change. At a time when democracy was flourishing in Athens, Pindar lent his support to tyrants in Sicily and Cirene because of their continued support for the Olympic Games. This was in keeping with Pindar's devotion to his own aristocratic class and his disdain for democracy with its emphasis on equality and catering to the masses.

Greek tragedy was based on the premise that human beings might find themselves in situations where they take actions for the right reasons and yet end up with disastrous results. The three great playwrights of the classical age were Aeschylus (ca. 525–ca. 456 BCE), Euripides (ca. 480–ca. 406 BCE), and Sophocles (ca. 496–406 BCE). In the seven surviving tragedies by Aeschylus, his characters suffer from fatal flaws that they prove incapable of remedying. Aeschylus thus seems to have regarded human character as static, as his characters do not evolve during his plays. Aeschylus finds it difficult to rationalize the suffering inflicted by gods upon humans, but his plays imply that people do become ennobled through suffering. In one of his earliest and most important plays, *The Persians*—first performed in 472 BCE, shortly after the end of the Persian Wars—Aeschylus celebrates the Greek victory and heightens the effect on his audience by revealing the failure and suffering of the Persians. In contrast to Aeschylus, Euripides introduced character development into his plays. In one of his best-known plays, *Hippolytus*, the lead character is accused by his stepmother, Phaedra, of harboring incestuous love for her after rejecting her amorous advances. Phaedra commits suicide immediately after making the accusation. Hippolytus then has a curse placed upon him by his father, Theseus; unable to prove his innocence, Hippolytus dies soon afterward.

In the plays of Sophocles, characters act on the basis of what they believe to be right, but meet tragic ends because their knowledge is limited. His plays deal with the powerlessness of human beings to alter their destiny. In *Oedipus the King*, written around 425 BCE in the aftermath of the plague that struck Athens early in the Peloponnesian War, the central characters of Oedipus and his wife Jocasta seem to believe that they can change their fates. They are mistaken, but Oedipus at least gains wisdom through the many trials he endures; the prophet Teiresias tells him that even his wisdom has been part of his destiny.

In *Antigone*, the daughter of Oedipus comes into conflict with her uncle, King Creon, who has issued a decree that forbids rebels who had opposed him on the battlefield from being given a proper burial. Unable to stomach the thought of her brother Polyneices (one of the dead rebels) becoming food for the vultures, Antigone decides to ignore Creon's decree, arguing that there is a divine law that supersedes the earthly law. Creon regards Antigone as a traitor and does not believe that he can tolerate open disobedience to his decrees without undermining order in the state. Creon argues that he is doing that which he thinks best for the state and that private concerns must give way to the public welfare. For Creon, there is no middle ground—one is either with the state or against it. Both Antigone and Creon make persuasive cases for their positions, making the situation tragic because a legitimate disagreement must lead to Antigone's death. Creon's ideals force him to put his own niece to death, making the denouement of the play even more poignant to the Greeks, who would have recognized the importance attached to family ties.

The Athenian comic playwright Aristophanes (ca. 488–ca. 388 BCE) provides our main source of Greek comedy. A significant difference between the comedies of Aristophanes and Greek tragedy lies in the freedom that comedy allows Aristophanes to employ fantastic sets and elaborate costumes, and to abolish the unities of space and time that bound the tragic playwrights. In addition, Aristophanes is concerned less with destiny, fate, and humanity's relationship with the gods than with contemporary political and social issues, such as Athenian foreign policy or disturbing trends in the education of Athenian youth. In his earliest surviving play, *The Acharnians* (425), written in the midst of the Peloponnesian War, an elderly Athenian named Dikaiopolis laments that his suffering has far outweighed happiness in his life and says that in his old age he looks at his fields and lusts for peace.

Meanwhile, the two historians of classical Greece, Herodotus and Thucy-

The Chorus Speaks, from *Oedipus the King*

Fate
Be here let what I say be pure
Let all my acts be pure
Laws forged in the huge clear fields of heaven
Rove the sky
Shaping my words limiting what I do
Olympos made those laws not men who live and die
Nothing lulls those laws to sleep
They cannot die
And the infinite god in them never ages

Arrogance insatiable pride
Breed the tyrant
Feed him on thing after thing blindly
At the wrong time uselessly
And he grows reaches so high
Nothing can stop his fall
His feet thrashing the air standing on nothing
And nowhere to stand he plunges down
O god shatter the tyrant
But let men compete let self-perfection grow
Let men sharpen their skills
Soldiers building the good city
Apollo
Protect me always
Always the god I will honor
If a man walks through his life arrogant
Strutting proud
Says anything does anything
Does not fear justice
Fear the gods bow to their shining presences
Let fate make him stumble in his tracks
For all his lecheries and headlong greed
If he takes whatever he wants right or wrong
If he touches forbidden things
What man who acts like this would boast
He can escape the anger of the gods
Why should I join these sacred public dances
If such acts are honored

—Sophocles, *Oedipus the King*

Source: Oedipus the King, translated by Berg and Clay (1978), pp. 62–63
© Stephen Berg and Diskin Clay. Reprinted by permission of Oxford University Press, Inc.

What does this passage reveal about Greek attitudes toward religion and the gods? How is fate intertwined into this petition? Is Sophocles also expressing a political view here in this speech by the chorus?

dides, initiated the Western tradition of viewing events in a larger historical context and recording both events and context for posterity. Herodotus believed that history followed certain repetitive patterns that taught human beings valuable moral lessons. He set out to write the history of the Persian wars and tell the story of how the relatively weak and disunited Greek city-states overcame the mighty Persian Empire. His emphasis on history as a series of morality tales limits the extent of his historical analysis, but contributes to his book's enduring interest and appeal. What gives his *Histories* a level of sophistication, however, is his refusal to portray the Greeks and the Persians in black and white terms. Herodotus also had an interest in other cultures, displayed in lengthy geographical and ethnographical digressions within the text, yet he retained a belief in a fundamental underlying human nature that crossed cultural and geographical boundaries. His book provides the main source of information about the Persian wars and a wealth of information about the ancient world, even if some of his specific facts, stories, and interpretations require skepticism and cannot be relied upon. The work of Thucydides differs significantly from that of Herodotus. Thucydides was a general on the Athenian side in the Peloponnesian War, which he chronicled and analyzed in great depth. Thucydides believed that the historian could most reliably write about his own age, but also he believed that his period was more significant than any that had come before it. He thought that this war was the most important that had been fought in history and he wanted his work to preserve the story of it for posterity. But he wrote not to record a series of events, but rather to analyze the causes of the war and record the lessons of how a society can deteriorate under the pressures of such a violent conflict. Thucydides never completed his work, which does not extend to the end of the war. In addition to providing the main source of information on the Peloponnesian War, Thucydides interweaves a heavy dose of political philosophy into his work, some of which is embedded in speeches that he reconstructed from his own perspective.

Philosophy, also present in the works of these historians, was another major part of Greek intellectual and cultural life. The Ionian city-states played a large role in the development of Greek literature and philosophy because of their location at the crossroads of a variety of cultures from Greece, Egypt, and the Near East. The Ionian city-state of Miletus produced the first three significant Greek natural philosophers: Thales (ca. 620–ca. 555 BCE), Anaximander (ca. 611–547 BCE), and Anaximenes (ca. 585–528 BCE). At a time when the Greeks were mostly interested in politics, Thales, a contemporary of the Athenian lawgiver Solon, started Greek philosophy in a new direction by speculating on the ultimate nature and composition of the universe. In doing so, Thales, who believed that the fundamental substance in the universe was water, gave Greek philosophy a more practical bent than in those societies that sought to discover why God had created the universe.

Anaximander, who thought that one form of matter could not be the under-lying reality behind every other form, rejected the theory of Thales. Instead, he thought there must be a single fundamental substance that could exist in a variety of forms. He gave that substance the name of the Boundless, because of his belief that the universe supplied an infinite amount of matter. What gave that basic substance different forms were the different combinations of four basic qualities—hot, cold, wet, and dry—that gave matter its physical reality. Whereas Thales had chosen water as the fundamental substance of the universe, Anaximenes believed that the universe was composed of air, which produced other substances through the processes of condensation and rarefac-tion. Thales, Anaximander, and Anaximenes all believed in the existence of a simple, unifying truth that could be discovered behind all the apparent diver-sity and multiplicity in the universe. Even if their answers were wrong, they had started an intellectual inquiry that shaped the future direction of Greek philosophy. The ideas of the Milesian philosophers, Thales, Anaximander, and Anaximenes, influenced the Greek philosopher Empedocles (ca. 490–ca. 430 BCE), but he rejected the idea that one single substance existed in all matter. Instead, he theorized in his work *On Nature* that there were four basic elements in nature—earth, water, air, and fire. His ideas influenced Aristotle, through whom this conception became orthodoxy in medieval Europe.

Inspired by the ideas of these and other thinkers who sought explanations for the universe that went beyond mythological explanations, a group of think-ers known as the Sophists began to question traditional notions of ethics and morality as well. The term *Sophist* meant "wise teacher" and thus originally had a positive connotation. One of the leading Sophists, Anaxagoras (ca. 500–428 BCE), denied the existence of the Greek gods, viewing the sun as a burning disc without any association with Apollo and the moon as a dark object that appeared light because of reflections from the sun. Another Sophist, Gorgias (ca. 485–ca. 380 BCE), took the skeptical position that nothing was true, or, at the very least, that truth, if it did exist, could not be known by human beings. The Sophists acquired a negative reputation in ancient Greece because of their skepticism and their ability to confuse people through argument and rhetoric, but they had a great influence on the seminal thinker Socrates (469–399 BCE).

Socrates's student, Plato recorded many of Socrates's teachings in his *Dia-logues*, though it is impossible to tell how much Plato himself may have added to or altered them. Unlike the Sophists, Socrates did believe in the attainability of knowledge, through lengthy questioning and examination. He stressed self-understanding as the beginning of knowledge and advised others to "know thyself." The Greek educational ideal, promulgated by Socrates, was to give equal attention to cultivating the health of the body and the mind. Cultivation of the mind included attention to music and the arts in addition to other forms of learning. Socrates's main contribution to Greek thought, however, was his constant questioning of tradition and established wisdom. Such questioning may have been acceptable during the age of Pericles, but the Peloponnesian War demanded absolute loyalty to the state and allowed Socrates's opponents to charge him with disloyalty. In 399 one of his enemies had Socrates charged with corrupting the morals of Athenian youth and irreverence toward the gods. At his trial, as recorded by Plato, Socrates defended his teaching methods and his life without responding to the charges against him. A jury found him guilty and sentenced him to death. Instead of fleeing for his life, Socrates poisoned himself with hemlock, believing that he had remained true to his own values. In 386 BCE Plato, seeking to continue the legacy of his great teacher, went to a place called Academy outside of Athens and founded his own philosophical school in an olive grove there.

As a philosopher, Plato addressed virtually every subject with which philosophy deals, from morals to aesthetics. In his *Republic*, Plato put forth some of his most important ideas about politics and social organization, such as the idea that a society worked because it allowed different individuals to pursue activities that they were good at and that they most enjoyed. In addition, he opposed democracy and believed that a philosopher-king would provide the best government for society; this view is understandable because Plato had witnessed the deterioration of democratic ideals in Athens during the Peloponnesian War that culminated in the death of Socrates.

Plato is best known for his theory of universals, the belief in an ideal world that provided abstract concepts through which people could understand themselves and the world around them. Plato believed in the real existence of ideals such as goodness, beauty, truth, and justice; he also believed that the world of ideals provided prototypes on which people could model their behavior. By contrast, his student, Aristotle (384–322 BCE), did not completely reject Plato's world of ideals, but he placed less emphasis on it and contented himself with studying what could be learned from observation of the world around him. Aristotle was more of an inductive thinker, basing his conclusions on sense experience, whereas Plato distrusted sense experience and relied on deductive reasoning to lead him to the truth. Whereas Plato had written *The Republic* to describe an ideal city-state that could provide a model against which all real city-states could be measured, Aristotle wrote his *Politics* to consider what practical elements were required of a successful city-state. Aristotle stressed the need for food, arts, armed forces, revenue, devotion to the gods, and a judicial system for civil and criminal cases, with particular emphasis on the last two. He advocated the exclusion of workers and farmers from politics on the grounds that their professions did not allow them enough time for the cultivation of virtue; thus, like Plato, Aristotle opposed democracy.

Although Aristotle wrote on a diverse variety of subjects, including ethics, drama, poetry, rhetoric, and metaphysics, perhaps his greatest contributions were in science, which also rested on a strong foundation laid by earlier Greek thinkers. Here again, the cultural crossroads along the Ionian coast proved a fertile breeding ground for new ideas in the seventh and sixth centuries BCE. Here Greeks became exposed to astronomical knowledge, scientific ideas, and technology from Egypt, Babylonia, and Phoenicia. In addition to his speculation about water as the fundamental substance of the universe, Thales of Miletus had an interest in astronomy and accurately predicted a solar eclipse. The sixth-century philosopher and mathematician Pythagoras, from the island of Samos off the Ionian coast, and his followers emphasized the importance of numbers; by applying them to nature they had a significant impact on the future direction of Western science. The four elements of Empedocles provided a framework for the Greeks' basic understanding of the natural world.

The earliest application of scientific thinking to a practical field in ancient Greece occurred in the area of medicine. Hippocrates (ca. 460–ca. 377 BCE), from the island of Cos, became the most famous and in-demand physician in the Greek world. Seventy ancient medical works that belonged to his school of thought have survived. Although Greek physicians sought to understand illness, the Greek approach to medicine concerned more than simple pathology. Greek physicians began with the premise that the body is naturally healthy. They viewed the main role of medicine as preserving or restoring the health of the body as opposed to fighting or curing illness.

Greek physicians had ample opportunity to observe the physical symptoms of diseases and to draw conclusions from them. Two early works, *On Ancient Medicine* and *On the Nature of Man*, emphasized the importance of empirical observation and evidence at the expense of abstract speculation. Another, *On Regimen in Acute Diseases*, rejected divination as a means of understanding and treating disease. *On the Sacred Disease* denies the intervention of the gods in matters of disease and health. However, the physicians' approach to medicine remained limited by several factors. Surgery in the Greek world was extremely rare. Especially in the temples dedicated to healing, some physicians used dreams to help them determine treatment, and some works encouraged them to do so. Greek physicians were all male and they did not seem to understand well the differences in physiology between the sexes or have a good understanding of medical concerns particular to women; they were not good gynecologists. Aristotle recognized that animals and humans reproduced through copulation, but believed that sperm acted on undifferentiated matter within the female womb.

Aristotle greatly influenced the scientific thought of the Greeks and, later, the Europeans through a number of his ideas. He believed in teleology, the idea that everything in the universe had a purpose and had been designed to serve a particular end; he therefore believed that causes in nature had to be explained by understanding the ultimate purposes that they served. He believed that every species (both animate and inanimate) had a specific purpose within the natural order of the universe, which he conceived as a hierarchical scale that formed the basis of the medieval conception of the Great Chain of Being. In his book on *Physics*, Aristotle distinguished among three kinds of changes in the physical world: first, transmutation, whereby a substance became transformed into a different substance; second, growth and decay, which he witnessed mainly in the biological realm; and third, translational change, which involved a change in location or physical movement such as spinning. He believed in a first cause (or God) that set the universe in motion. Another influential idea of Aristotle's was his theory that the four elements of earth, air, fire, and water represented different combinations of four qualities—hot, wet, cold, and dry. But Aristotle was also interested in collecting information and became obsessed with ordering and classifying it; thus, he combined an inductive approach to knowledge with certain deductive principles.

Conclusion

Plato and Aristotle both flourished after the Spartan victory in the Peloponnesian War. That victory had put an end to the position of Athens as the dominant power in ancient Greece. It ended the Athenian experiment with democracy as well. Although the Spartans emerged in the dominant position, they did nothing to unite the Greek world. In fact, the rivalry between Sparta and Athens continued, leaving Persia, which regained control over the Ionian city-states, as the main beneficiary. In the 360s the city-state of Thebes emerged as a rising power in Greece, but Greek disunity still made the mainland vulnerable to foreign conquest. The Greeks continued to resist the powerful Persians, but the glories of their former victory were now a distant memory, enshrined in the works of Herodotus and Aeschylus. Soon the Greek city-states would fall under the control of the rising power of Macedon and its kings, Philip, and his son, Alexander. The Athenian empire had collapsed as the Greeks made the painful transition from conquerors to conquered. But their cultural and intellectual traditions still mattered, as even Philip realized when he asked Aristotle to tutor his son.

The Greeks had placed a strong emphasis upon the cultivation of the mind. Even though most of the Greeks continued to believe in their gods and goddesses and to accept the Homeric myths, they had no dominant priesthood to censor or restrict intellectual inquiry. Literature had flourished in fifth-century Athens during a period with little censorship. The ideas of thinkers from Thales to the Sophists created a tradition that produced in Plato and Aristotle two of the greatest thinkers in the history of Western thought. The Greeks debated ethical issues and questioned established truths, seeking knowledge about the world at the same time that they sought guidelines for how to live. None of this was lost, but these traditions were altered as Greek civilization spread throughout the Mediterranean during the Hellenistic period.

1. What were some of the primary features and characteristics of the Minoan and Mycenaean periods of Greek history? What are some possible explanations for the downfall of these early civilizations?
2. Why did city-states emerge as the main form of political organization among the Greeks? What distinguished the leading city-states from one another?
3. What were some of the ways in which Greek and Persian civilization differed from one another? What role did these differences play in wars between the two?
4. What was the significance of the Peloponnesian War in Greek history? Why did Thucydides think that it was worth writing a history of this war?
5. What are some of the most striking cultural and intellectual achievements of Greek civilization? What conditions produced such a flourishing and vibrant culture?

Suggestions for Further Reading

Herodotus. 1972. *The Histories*. Edited by John M. Marincola. Translated by Aubrey de Sélincourt. Harmondsworth: Penguin.

Holland, Tom. 2005. *Persian Fire: The First World Empire and the Battle for the West*. New York: Doubleday.

Homer. 1990. *The Iliad*. Translated by Robert Fagles; introduction and notes by Bernard Knox. New York: Penguin Books.

Hornblower, Simon. 2002. *The Greek World, 479–323 BC*. 3rd ed. London: Routledge.

Pomeroy, Sarah. 1997. *Families in Classical and Hellenistic Greece: Representations and Realities*. Oxford: Clarendon Press.

Thucydides. 1972. *The Peloponnesian War*. Translated by Rex Warner with an introduction and notes by M.I. Finley. Harmondsworth: Penguin Books.

Suggested Websites

www.ancientgreece.co.uk

This website, sponsored by the British Museum, provides glimpses into war, daily life, gods and goddesses, and other dimensions of Greek life and history.

www.ancient-greece.org/index.html

This website contains descriptive sections devoted to the archaeology, history, art, and culture of ancient Greece, as well as maps, images, information about Greek museums, and resources for teachers and students.

www.fordham.edu/halsall/ancient/asbook07.html

Fordham University's online sourcebook includes excerpts from numerous primary sources related to ancient Greece, including the writings of Homer, Herodotus, and Thucydides, as well as selections related to religion, philosophy, literature, and many other topics.

www.metmuseum.org/works_of_art/greek_and_roman-art

This website allows access to highlights of the permanent collection of ancient Greek and Roman art from the Metropolitan Museum of Art.

www.pbs.org/empires/thegreeks/htmlver

This companion website to a PBS documentary on the Greeks includes interactive maps, a guide to pronunciations in the Greek languages, and a feature on the building of the Parthenon.

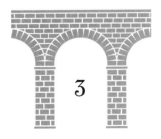

3　The Hellenistic Age and the Rise of Rome, ca. 350–30 BCE

The Hellenistic period, like the later medieval period in European history, suffers from frequent comparison to the ages immediately preceding and following it. The medieval period fell between the two supposed golden ages of ancient Rome and the Italian Renaissance; the Hellenistic period between the classical age of Greece and the height of Roman civilization. However, there are very good reasons why both comparisons are misleading. As we will see in Chapter 7, medieval Europe produced the first universities, great works of literature, and magnificent architecture, while featuring developments in politics, religion, and science that would serve as the foundations for the Renaissance and Reformation periods that followed. The Hellenistic period produced the rise of two great empires that changed the course of world history and that spread the ideas and achievements of Greek civilization far and wide. In addition, new philosophical responses to the changing political situation in the Mediterranean changed the ways that many people thought and even their basic approach to life. New discoveries and ideas in science, technology, and medicine contributed to a remarkable and thriving civilization.

This chapter begins with the rise to power of Macedonia under its dynamic and intelligent king Philip II (382–336 BCE) and his even more ambitious son, Alexander (356–323 BCE). The Macedonians first conquered Greece and then embarked on a mission of world conquest that enhanced the cultural unity of the Mediterranean region and even brought Greece into contact with India, which was developing its own important traditions and philosophies. But Alexander's empire did not remain intact beyond his death, preparing the way for the rise of other great powers in the Mediterranean, such as Carthage and Rome. The Romans, having first solidified their position in Italy, reacted defensively to Carthaginian naval power and encroachment on islands off the coast of Italy. After defeating the Carthaginians, they found themselves in a position to rival any of the successor kingdoms set up after the death of Alexander. Rome became the dominant power in the world. But the rise of empire brought wealth and with it came changes in Roman society and politics.

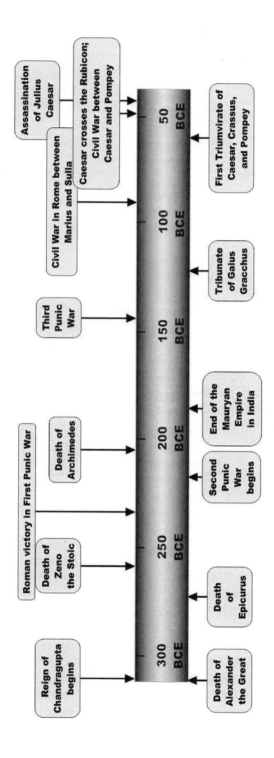

Internal struggles for power created violence that at times bordered on anarchy. An obscure Roman nobleman named Julius Caesar emerged from a series of civil wars with the ambition to provide Rome with the stability that it had lost. Some Romans, fearing that whatever stability he had provided came at the expense of the ideals on which the Roman state had been built, decided on a course of action to rid Rome of Caesar. Most Romans, however, had come to fear instability even more. Another civil war following upon Caesar's death proved the fears of the majority well founded. It ended with the rise of Caesar's own grandnephew, Octavian. This dramatic story lay behind the utterly compelling rise of the Roman Empire.

Philip of Macedon, Alexander the Great, and the Hellenistic World

The decline of Athens created a power vacuum in the Greek world into which stepped a mighty ruler from the rugged, isolated region north of Greece called Macedonia. If Macedonia seemed an unlikely candidate to emerge as a great power among the Greeks, it would only have been because of Greek ignorance of some natural advantages possessed by the region, as well as of some recent historical developments there. First, Macedon contained an abundance of gold. This gave an enterprising leader who knew how to use it a tremendous opportunity to assert his power over the rest of the independent Macedonian aristocracy. Philip II of Macedon came from a line of kings who claimed royal authority in the region based on their alleged descent from the Greek god Zeus. Archaeological evidence from Philip's capital of Pela reveals a certain amount of grandeur and organization associated with the rising power of a centralized monarchy. Although wealth supported Philip's ambitions, the key to his transformation of Macedonia into a major power was his makeover of the army into one of the great military organizations in history. Philip's Macedonian army would prove capable of defeating Greek hoplite armies thanks to an impenetrable, closely packed infantry that fought with lengthy pikes (known as *sarissas*) measuring between fifteen and eighteen feet. Philip used his army to assert his authority over the Greek city-states, formally bringing an end to the classical period of Greek history.

In 338 BCE Philip soundly defeated the Athenians at the Battle of Chaeronea, southeast of Mount Parnassus in east-central Greece. Philip, who viewed himself as Greek, did not rule oppressively over the Greek city-states, which began to experience a renewed prosperity under his stable influence. The conquest of Greece provided Philip with the opportunity to contemplate his next great ambition: the conquest of the Persian Empire. In proposing to go to war with that mighty empire, he posed as a defender of Greece and an avenger of the

Persian invasions of the fifth century. The Greeks, however, did not regard Philip as one of them; they believed that power had gone to his head, and they probably regarded his hubris as the main cause of his murder by an obscure assassin named Pausanias.

The main beneficiary of Philip's death was his twenty-year-old son, Alexander, whose inheritance had been potentially threatened by Philip's marriage to a new wife and the birth of a son to them shortly before Philip's assassination. There is no proof that Alexander was involved in the plot to kill Philip or knew anything about it, though his dispossessed mother Olympia could certainly have orchestrated it. But Alexander wasted no time in claiming his right to rule and building on his father's legacy. For example, in partial imitation of his father, Alexander further developed the cult of kingship by sitting for numerous portraits and perpetuating his image on coins, statues, and engravings. He retained his father's military and administrative organization. He even picked up his father's plans for an invasion of Persia and prepared to implement them. Alexander's claim to fame, then, is not originality, but rather the scale of his ambition and the success he achieved as a military leader within a single decade—success that brought much of the world within the realm of Greek influence.

With the impetuosity and extreme confidence of youth, combined with a growing conviction of his own divinity and immortality, Alexander embarked on a dizzying whirlwind of aggressive military invasions. He began his invasion of Persia and his mission of world conquest when he crossed the Dardanelles from Greece to Asia Minor in 334 BCE. Persian power was not what it once was and—however much Alexander regarded himself as the champion of Greek civilization—this new Persian War was not a conflict between Persian despotism and Greek democracy. The inhabitants of the territories that he conquered did not regard Alexander as in any sense a liberator; once conquered, Alexander himself faced frequent revolts from his subject territories. Those conquests included not only Asia Minor and Persia, but also Syria, Mesopotamia, Egypt, and regions as far away as India and modern Afghanistan.

One of the most famous rulers in world history, Alexander's legacy has been much in dispute ever since his lifetime and much given to superficial generalizations and stereotypes. His education at the hands of Aristotle, his commitment to the Greek gods, and his devotion to Homer, whose poems accompanied him on his military campaigns, have contributed to Alexander's reputation as a civilizing influence spreading Greek culture far and wide. Such a reputation belies the savage, violent nature of many of Alexander's conquests, which included the destruction of cities and the massacre of civilian populations who continued to oppose him. At other times, however, Alexander could display leniency and tolerance toward the peoples he defeated. Displaying the

contradictions to which men in their twenties (and sometimes older) are particularly prone, he could display personal loyalty and religious devotion—he
is reputed to have offered sacrifices to the gods at the reputed burial sites of
Achilles and Patroclus in Asia Minor—or descend into exhibitions of drunken
debauchery and jealous rage.

Although Alexander's brief reign left a legacy of destruction that has given
him an evil reputation in places like Iran and Iraq (ancient Persia and Mesopotamia), its effects were slightly more complicated than that. He built cities—the
most famous of which was Alexandria in Egypt—and imported Macedonians,
who brought Greek culture with them, as colonists. The process of the spread
of Greek culture during the reign of Alexander is known as Hellenization (from
the word "hellene," meaning "Greek"), so the Hellenistic Age that followed is
defined as a period characterized primarily by the heavy influence of Greek art,
history, and culture. But the conquerors from this point forward were also shaped
by the lands and cultures that they conquered. For example, Alexander and his
generals encountered wealth in Persia that was beyond their wildest imagination
and contributed to an atmosphere of Eastern luxury within their courts. Rather
than build new structures of government and administration based on Greek
models, Alexander and his successors found it easier to adopt the autocratic
ruling styles that had predominated in ancient Near Eastern history.

In 331 BCE at a sanctuary of Zeus in Palestine, Alexander dedicated twenty-
five bronze statues of his leading cavalrymen who had died at the hands of
the Persians at the Battle of Granicus three years earlier. This act commemo-
rating the war dead displayed some of the ambivalence toward war and its
consequences that appeared in Alexander's favorite book, *The Iliad*. There
was a ceremonial aspect to Alexander's rule that it is easy to forget amid the
legends and the constant battles. Alexander's early death in 323 at the age of
thirty-two could have symbolized to the Greeks, again, the dangers of hubris,
as well as the frailty of the life of a conqueror. Taking advantage of an army
created by his father, Alexander had achieved enormous success, power, and
fame. Alexander sought to enshrine that success by leaving monuments and
memorials to himself and his empire, even as he destroyed cities and built
new ones. He lost many of his closest Macedonian generals, commanders, and
ordinary troops to dismissal, desertion, or death by illness and warfare, leaving him increasingly isolated and at the head of an army that could no longer
be considered Macedonian. The unrest that his rule provoked throughout his
empire makes it questionable whether he could have continued to maintain it
had he lived longer. He had created the largest empire that the world had ever
seen, but not the institutions needed to effectively rule or administer it. His
premature death ensured that his empire would not last intact for long; indeed,
it barely survived his death at all.

The Division of Alexander's Empire

Alexander may have intended to focus more on administrative matters for his empire and might even have gotten around to the issue of the succession if he had lived longer, but his death of a stomach ailment (some believe that he was poisoned) precluded him from doing either. His death consequently set off a struggle for power among rival generals and claimants to the throne. The strongest and leading candidate to succeed Alexander—and the one with the best chance of keeping the empire intact—was Antigonus (382–301 BCE), Alexander's one-eyed general who immediately sought to establish his control over the Asian portion of the empire. But Antigonus's ambitions provoked the opposition of several of Alexander's other leading generals. His opponents included Cassander (ca. 358–ca. 297 BCE), who murdered Alexander's mother, Olympia, his Persian wife, Roxanne, and her infant son, born after Alexander's death, in the process of assuming control of Macedonia. A second opponent was Ptolemy Lagi (ca. 366–ca. 283 BCE), who assumed control of Egypt on his way to founding a dynasty that would also rule over Palestine, Cyprus, and some territory in Asia Minor. A third member of the alliance against Antigonus was Alexander's former bodyguard, Lysimachus (ca. 355–281 BCE), who became king of Thrace. The most formidable opponent of Antigonus, however, turned out to be another of Alexander's former generals, his infantry commander Seleucus (ca. 358–281 BCE). As satrap—Alexander had employed this Persian designation for his local commanders—of Babylon, Seleucus gained the support of the Babylonian priesthood and people by ruling peacefully. Antigonus, by contrast, sought to conquer by violence and angered the Babylonian people by his destructive tendencies. Seleucus proved to be too firmly entrenched and too skilled a commander for Antigonus to oust from the region, even after Antigonus had made peace with his other three rivals. Fighting raged among Alexander's military successors for decades after his death, but eventually the main lines of division within his empire started to emerge with some clarity.

The successors of Alexander could not keep the empire intact because they simply did not trust each other enough to cooperate in its governance. The rivals were all ambitious men who claimed Macedonian descent and had a roughly equal status while Alexander had ruled. Although Alexander had divided his empire into approximately twenty satrapies, three main kingdoms emerged out of the chaos and warfare that followed his death. Ptolemy established a kingdom in Egypt in which he took on the royal trappings of the ancient pharaohs, while Seleucus gained control over most of the Asian portions of Alexander's empire. The grandson of Antigonus the One-Eyed, Antigonus Gonatus (ca. 319–239 BCE) finally emerged in 276 BCE as the ruler of Macedon, the third of the major successor states. Even then, he continued to face threats to his power. Macedon, as the homeland of Alexander, remained a prize territory for ambitious men.

Although Alexander's empire was carved up after his death, it was significant that it was divided up among fellow Macedonians who considered themselves Greek. This ensured that Greek influence would continue to spread throughout the Mediterranean and western Asia, particularly in the form of cultural traditions. Most cities in the Hellenistic world had amphitheaters for the performance of plays, public arenas for games and sporting events, and public squares for celebratory festivals. Rather than spreading Greek political traditions, however, the Ptolemaic and Seleucid rulers adopted those of their native lands. An emphasis on military life survived the establishment of these kingdoms as well; their rulers, seldom content just to retain what they had, were always looking for the chance to annex additional territories. The rulers of these kingdoms thus continued to fight among themselves and identified themselves with the militaristic traditions and ambitions of their predecessors. The Greek city-states sought to recover some semblance of their former political autonomy throughout the various wars and struggles of the period and did continue to operate as independent states, at least in relation to each other.

The division of Alexander's empire, therefore, represents as much a turning point in history as was the foundation of that empire in the first place. Once the three main successor states had been established, wars were fought at the peripheries of these states rather than for control of the states themselves. This allowed the Ptolemaic and Seleucid rulers to concentrate some attention on constructive activities such as administration and governance, building and facilitating commerce. Although these states and the Hellenistic period with which they are associated are often viewed as part of a transition from classical Greece to the rise of Rome, this period provided the context for significant changes in the way that people thought that would define their world and help to shape that of ancient Rome and beyond.

The Shaping of the Past: Hellenistic Philosophy

Philosophers and historians sometimes disagree about the extent to which new ideas in philosophy arise in response to changes in historical circumstances or in direct response to the ideas of previous philosophers. The three major new philosophies of the Hellenistic period—Cynicism, Epicureanism, and Stoicism—could be used to support either side of the argument. They all shared enough in common, particularly a general indifference to politics and an emphasis on individual happiness in a troubled world, that they collectively represent a response to the violence, chaos, and uncertainty that accompanied the decline of Athens and the dismantling of Alexander's empire. But none of these schools of thought can be well understood without reference to previous developments in Greek philosophy. It was, in fact, the combination of their relevance to their own times—and the Roman period that followed—and the solutions that they offered to thorny problems in Greek philosophy that made these philosophies so significant in the shaping of the Hellenistic period and beyond.

Cynicism was the earliest of the three philosophies, originating in the fourth century BCE in the thought of Socrates's student Antisthenes (ca. 445–370 BCE) and his follower, Diogenes of Sinope (412–323 BCE). The Cynics had the least uniform system of thought of the three major schools, its proponents adopting the ideas that appealed to them and rejecting the others. They all tended, however, to reject traditional social conventions, preferring a simple life in which they did not get caught up in the trivial anxieties of society or politics. Led by Diogenes and his loyal follower Crates of Thebes, the Cynics sought a life of individual freedom marked by possession of a minimum of material goods and a desire to keep their needs basic and simple. They adopted simple dress and took little care of their personal appearance. Diogenes was said to have walked through Athens dressed in a barrel in order to illustrate his point about the unimportance of social conventions. Diogenes also challenged traditional ideas about marriage and social class, while content to live a homeless and beggarly existence that was imitated by many of his followers. But this extreme behavior was rooted in a philosophical conviction that the individual could be happy once freed from societal constraints and the throes of ambition and greed.

Epicurus (341–270 BCE) also saw philosophy as the key to personal happiness. In one of his few surviving writings, he advised that people are never too young or too old to seek wisdom or attend to the state of their mental and spiritual health. But, unlike the Cynics, Epicurus believed that happiness could be found through the cultivation of personal pleasure, which he defined mainly in intellectual and social terms. Intellectually, Epicurus believed the world too complex for individual understanding and therefore thought that people should use reason mainly to govern their own personal lives and behavior. He taught that people should avoid anything that might become a source of anxiety or distress, intellectual or otherwise. Socially, he regarded association with friends as among the greatest pleasures. He gathered around himself in Athens a large group of disciples who shared with him his famous "garden." For Epicurus, the search for pleasure consisted of a shared, comfortable life free from pain rather than a constant hedonistic search for pure physical sensation. But, like the Cynics, Epicurus advocated a withdrawal from public life and a rejection of traditional norms. For example, he did not believe in gods that were at all interested in human affairs; he taught a rejection of traditional Greek religion as not conducive to human happiness.

The Philosophical Teachings of Epicurus

Those things which without ceasing I have declared to you, those do, and exercise yourself in those, holding them to be the elements of right life. First believe that God is a living being immortal and happy, according to the notion of a god indicated by the common sense of humankind; and so of him anything that is agrees with whatever may uphold both his happiness and his immortality. For truly there are gods, and knowledge of them is evident; but they are not such as the multitude believe, seeing that people do not steadfastly maintain the notions they form respecting them. Not the person who denies the gods worshipped by the multitude, but he who affirms of the gods what the multitude believes about them is truly impious. For the utterances of the multitude about the gods are not true preconceptions but false assumptions; hence it is that the greatest evils happen to the wicked and the greatest blessings happen to the good from the hand of the gods, seeing that they are always favorable to their own good qualities and take pleasure in people like to themselves, but reject as alien whatever is not of their kind.

Accustom yourself to believe that death is nothing to us, for good and evil imply awareness, and death is the privation of all awareness; therefore a right understanding that death is nothing to us makes the mortality of life enjoyable, not by adding to life an unlimited time, but by taking away the yearning after immortality. For life has no terror for those who thoroughly apprehend that there are no terrors for them in ceasing to live. Foolish, therefore, is the person who says that he fears death, not because it will pain when it comes, but because it pains in the prospect. Whatever causes no annoyance when it is present, causes only a groundless pain in the expectation.

—Epicurus, Letter to Menoeceus
Translated by Robert Drew Hicks

Source: http://classics.mit.edu/Epicurus/menoec.html.

What are the social and religious implications of these ideas? On what does Epicurus seem to base them? What does Epicurus believe to be the goal of philosophy?

The founder of Stoicism was Zeno of Citium (336–264 BCE), which was located in Cyprus. Like Epicurus, who came originally from Samos, Zeno moved to Athens, the philosophical capital of the Hellenistic world. Zeno shared with the Greek thinker Heraclitus the view that the universe is governed by *logos* or reason, that there is a fundamental order to reality beyond the apparent changes that we perceive and experience. If the universe is logically ordered and basically good, as the Stoics believed, then the goal of life can be to live in harmony with the natural order of the universe. This gave the Stoics a large popular appeal because they combined an advocacy of ethical behavior with an acceptance of the nature of the world that was beyond the control of the individual. Reacting against Plato's vision of the ideal state, Zeno put forth his own ideas, which were heavily influenced by the Cynics in their rejection of property, money, and social conventions such as marriage. But he then shifted to a stronger emphasis on the importance of living a virtuous life, which in Stoicism is regarded as the key to human happiness. Stoicism became the most popular of the three philosophies during the Hellenistic and Roman periods and a guiding force and incentive for ethical behavior among people with no strong commitment to religion.

These three philosophies thus seemed particularly suited to a world that was subject to the constant vicissitudes of war and political changes that characterized much of the Hellenistic period. But they also appealed to the rulers themselves because of their emphasis on an acceptance of the political order; Antigonus II was said to have attended Zeno's lectures whenever he visited Athens. These philosophies combined to attach a positive value to the actions of individuals for their own sake rather than in service to the state or some external entity. Epicurus found politics too volatile for an individual who sought happiness to attach much importance at all to it. Diogenes attacked the phoniness of politicians, but blamed the problem on a thoroughly corrupt system. It was irrational for anyone to enter politics in order to make a difference when the system was to blame, he argued. It was equally irrational, according to Epicurus, to fear death, another reality that was beyond human control. Epicurus was influenced by the ideas of the philosopher Democritus (ca. 460–370 BCE), who believed that the entire universe was composed of atoms that moved constantly and randomly interacted with each other, creating a constant state of change. Epicurus did not believe in an afterlife, since the atoms that exist in our bodies would simply be reabsorbed into the natural world. But Zeno, under the influence of Heraclitus, denied the existence of atoms and rejected the randomness of events in the material world. The Stoics believed in a universe that had purpose and order behind it, one that was evolving toward a state of perfection. To the extent that individuals aligned themselves with this evolution, they could join in harmony with it. They could not, however, affect the general direction of the cosmos. Virtue was still its own reward. Thus, in responding to previous issues in Greek philosophy as well as to the circumstances of their times, the Stoics successfully founded a philosophy with a strong moral appeal that did not reject faith in a larger purpose to the universe. Indeed, all three philosophies provided answers to the problems of their age and contained insights that many would continue to find valuable, especially under authoritarian political systems.

Hellenistic Science, Technology, and Medicine

The scientific achievements of the Hellenistic period alone should call into question any generalizations about the decline of Greek civilization after Alexander. The center of scientific learning switched to Alexandria in Egypt, but almost all of the scientific accomplishments of the period were made by people who would have considered themselves Greek. The establishment of a museum and a magnificent library in Alexandria meant the end of Athens's intellectual predominance, although, as we have seen, philosophy still flourished there, as did the schools established by Plato and Aristotle. There were also close connections between the two cities; the careers of some teachers led them to both places. Alexandria, however, attracted the best minds from all over the Greek world, such as Herophilus of Chalcedon (ca. 335–280 BCE), Erasistratus of Ceos (ca. 250 BCE), Aristarchos of Samos (third century BCE), and Eratosthenes of Cyrene (275–194 BCE). Herophilus and Erasistratus were responsible for Alexandria's preeminence in the study of anatomy and medicine, while Aristarchos and Eratosthenes made their contributions in astronomy and geography, respectively. Euclid, the man regarded as the founder of geometry, taught in Alexandria around the beginning of the third century BCE, while another great Greek geometer, Apollonius (fl. 250–220 BCE) came from the city of Perga in Asia Minor. And the greatest scientific thinker of the age came from Sicily: Archimedes (287–212 BCE), who was killed in the Roman invasion of his native Syracuse, allegedly because he was so entranced by a mathematical problem that he ignored the Roman soldier who confronted him.

The scientific tradition established in classical Greece provided important background for the achievements of the Hellenistic age. For example, one of Aristotle's students, Theophrastus (ca. 372–287 BCE) wrote two works on botany—*The Natural History of Plants* and *Causes for Vegetable Growth*—that would not be surpassed for another 1,500 years. He absorbed Aristotle's passion for observation and classification, accurately describing the pollination of date palms, as well as other aspects of plant anatomy, pathology, and sexuality. The head of Aristotle's school, the Lyceum, from 286 to 268 BCE, Strato of Lampascus (in Asia Minor) directly responded to and challenged some of Aristotle's ideas on the motion of rising and falling bodies. His realizations that all elements have weight—Aristotle had suggested that air and fire were completely light—and that heavy bodies accelerate as they descend demonstrate the stimulus that Aristotle provided to scientific thinking at the same time that they reveal that the Greeks kept an open mind when it came to their own scientific authorities.

The openness to new ideas among the Hellenistic Greeks was not restricted to philosophy and scientific theory. The appearance of the first dependable water clocks introduced a new attitude toward time that most scholars associate exclusively with the mechanical clocks that appeared in early modern Europe. Herophilus and Erasistratus studied human anatomy through the novel practice of human dissection; according to some sources, they even practiced vivisection on condemned criminals who were still alive. Erisistratus studied the anatomy of the heart and discovered its connection to the body's veins and arteries. Eratosthenes used his scientific calculations of the earth's circumference—which he calculated to within fifty miles—to produce better maps that accounted for the earth's circular shape. (The idea that everyone before Columbus believed that the world was flat is a complete myth.) Archimedes, in addition to formulating fundamental laws of physics and mathematics, designed catapults and other war engines for Hiero II, the ruler of Syracuse from 275 to 215 BCE. The early twentieth-century discovery of the Antikythera mechanism—a mechanical calculator used to predict astronomical positions—in a Greek shipwreck dated to the second century BCE completely altered previous views concerning the technological proficiency of Hellenistic Greeks. An intricate device about the size of a modern laptop computer, the mechanism contained as many as thirty-seven gears. Although research on the device is ongoing, it seems to have had the capability of predicting the positions of the sun, moon, and up to five planets, as well as eclipses and lunar months. These diverse achievements all testify to a vigorous intellectual world that belies its reputation among some scholars as technologically stagnant.

The study of scientific medicine at Alexandria combined with the botanical work of Theophrastus to provide Hellenistic physicians with an unprecedented amount of medical knowledge. Theophrastus was interested in the medicinal uses of plants and wrote about them in his treatises. Erisistratus and Herophilus belonged to a school of medical thought known as the Dogmatists, who based their practice exclusively on empirical evidence, supported by some medical experimentation. Herophilus recognized the importance of drugs in treating illnesses and of taking the patient's pulse in order to diagnose them. Surgery, already practiced by the ancient Egyptians, became a more practical option in Hellenistic times both because of increased knowledge and improvements in medical instruments. The dissections performed at Alexandria allowed Herophilus to understand even minor organs, such as the spleen and duodenum, to which he gave its name. He also provided descriptions of the brain, liver, sexual organs, and even the nervous system. Herophilus understood the difference between sensory and motor nerves. Unfortunately, from a scientific standpoint, the practice of dissection was halted by religiously conservative rulers after the death of the more open-minded Ptolemy II in 246 BCE. The practice would not be revived in any significant way until the sixteenth century. This limited the extent and the accuracy of Greek medical knowledge that was passed on through the work of the second-century Greek physician, Galen (ca. 130–201 CE).

As the conquests of Alexander brought the Greeks in closer contact with the Babylonian and Egyptian scientific traditions, Greek astronomers were able to draw from their observation-based knowledge to reach a better understanding of the heavens. The Greeks even adopted the Babylonian system of the zodiac and the division of the heavens into 360 degrees for the purposes of astrological prediction. But the Hellenistic Greeks came to their own remarkable conclusions regarding astronomy. Heracleides of Pontos (ca. 388–310 BCE), a disciple of Plato, suggested that the earth rotated on its axis on a daily basis. While he still believed in an earth-centered universe, he argued that the movements of Venus and Mercury could best be explained if they revolved around the sun. Aristarchos of Samos went even further and developed the first heliocentric theory of the universe in which the earth and planets all revolved around the sun.

The Greeks' fascination with astrology played to their interest in numerology, which resulted from their misunderstanding of the relationship between mathematics and the physical world, one of the key deficiencies in Greek science from a modern perspective. The heliocentric system of Aristarchos, for example, was based on a qualitative evaluation of the movement of heavenly bodies rather than rooted in mathematics, as was the case with the sixteenth-century system of the Polish astronomer Nicolas Copernicus. The lack of a mathematical foundation for Aristarchos's theory helps to explain the fifteen-hundred-year predominance of the geocentric system of the later Greek astronomer and mathematician, Ptolemy (fl. 127–145 CE). (Ptolemy, however, had to use epicyles, in which planets at times went backward in their revolutions, in order for his mathematical calculations to match observable phenomena.) Ptolemy was also an important geographer whose more accurate maps built on the earlier achievement of Eratosthenes. Yet the achievements of Euclid and Archimedes were rooted in a sophisticated understanding of mathematics that made their texts relevant into the modern era. Archimedes, for example, demonstrated that a right triangle with sides equal to the circumference and radius of a circle would be equal in area to that circle. Archimedes also had an outstanding understanding of physics and its relationship to mathematics.

It is, thus, not easy to characterize Hellenistic science, and any attempt to do so in a general way is bound to falter on numerous exceptions. The Hellenistic Greeks engaged in observational astronomy and even Aristarchos attempted to use mathematical data to conduct astronomical measurements, but also they engaged in theoretical speculation. Archimedes was a brilliant theoretical physicist who famously discovered the principle of the displacement of volume of water when he got into his bath (at which point he ran naked through the streets screaming *Eureka*—"I have found it") as well as the principles upon which levers and pulleys work to move large and heavy objects (he said he could move the earth if he could stand on another planet). But he also built war machines and fortifications based on innovative technology. Religious considerations may have had something to do with the rejection of Aristarchos's ideas, as with the halt to the practice of human dissection. Yet most of the scientific and technological developments of the period occurred without reference to any religious considerations whatsoever. The Hellenistic Greeks discovered how to use steam for energy, but they applied this discovery to toys and curiosities. In short, this was, like most periods, a complex one, and one with too many notable ideas and characteristics to regard simply as an interlude between the achievements of classical Greece and the rise of Rome.

India in the Hellenistic Age

After the death of Alexander the Great, India did not fall under the control of one of his successor dynasties, but was left to discover its own rulers and to follow its unique historical path based on its own traditions. The most ancient Indian traditions had been gathered under the broad umbrella of religious beliefs collectively known as Hinduism. Although the varieties of Hinduism are too complex and varied for this text, it is important to understand something of this religious philosophy that saw the presence of the divine in every aspect of creation and believed in the fundamental unity of the universe.

The concept that one universal law governs all aspects of existence the Hindus referred to as *dharma*. Dharma also had a second meaning in Hinduism—the duty of all individuals to act according to the expectations and traditions of their caste. For Hindus, the caste system was part of the divine order of the cosmos. There were thousands of castes in Hinduism, subdivisions of the four great classes in Indian society. These were the Brahmins, or priestly class; the warrior class, known as the Kshatriyas; the Vaishyas, which comprised craftsmen, merchants, and peasants; and the Shudras, or working class. This system gave Indian society a level of stability that did not depend upon strong monarchical rule to enforce order. Hindus also taught that the universe was governed by the principle of *karma*, according to which every action caused an effect that was a direct result of and proportionate to that action. The principle of karma encouraged Hindus to practice acts of kindness and generosity and to avoid acts of cruelty and selfishness because the universe operated according to an unvarying law of rewards and punishments. This did not make Hindus perfect any more than the adherents of any religion with high ideals, but it did provide a standard for behavior and the only possibility of escaping the wheel of life and death that was the cause of so much human suffering.

By the Hellenistic period, Hinduism had been supplemented by Buddhism, which originated in northeastern India in the life and ideas of Prince Siddhartha (ca. 563–483 BCE). Though not a member of the priestly class of Brahmins, Siddhartha, like many others of his age, had set off on a spiritual quest because of a lack of fulfillment in an increasingly materialistic age. After he achieved enlightenment, Siddhartha, now the Buddha, preached and taught others what he had discovered without challenging traditional Hindu beliefs. Buddha believed in the illusory nature of what we perceive as reality, even of the human personality. He taught that we could attain happiness by restraining our desires and our ego in order to attain a state of perfect detachment, peace, and harmony, which he called *nibbana* or nirvana. Buddha did not stress the existence of an external god, but the divinity within each person that only had to be accessed through a spiritual approach. Buddha was not interested in setting up an established religious orthodoxy, much less becoming a religious authority for others to obey and imitate. He believed that people had to find their own path to enlightenment and that he was merely a guide to help them along their way. He compared himself to a raft that could help someone get to shore, but would become a hindrance and need to be abandoned once land was reached.

At the beginning of the Hellenistic age, the traditions of Hinduism continued to dominate Indian life. Buddhism still represented something of a reform movement, although Hinduism and Buddhism provided enough latitude that people could embrace them both. The conquests of Alexander in the fourth century BCE, however, had introduced Greek ideas into India, as well as an element of power politics as he demonstrated the possibility of uniting India through war. This became the ambition of Chandragupta Maurya (r. ca. 322–297 BCE), who fought to unify India and founded the powerful Mauryan dynasty, the first one to rule over most of India. Chandragupta thus had more in common with the rulers who succeeded to other parts of Alexander's empire than he did with any of his Indian predecessors.

His grandson Ashoka came to the throne in 269 BCE. At first, Ashoka adopted the expansionist policies of his father and grandfather, going to war to conquer the northeastern Indian kingdom of Kalinga. But Ashoka, who had allegedly murdered his older brothers to gain the throne and had witnessed firsthand the bloody, gruesome effects of a conquest that killed tens of thousands, underwent a religious conversion to Buddhism shortly after the conquest of Kalinga. For the rest of his reign he did his best to avoid violence and warfare. He had thousands of pillars carved throughout his kingdom as a testimony to his faith and conversion. In doing so, he challenged both the realistic approach to politics adopted by Chandragupta and the social traditions associated with Hinduism. He substituted Buddha's emphasis on *ahimsa* or nonviolence and the simpler teachings of the Buddha on love and righteousness that cut across India's class and caste boundaries.

Ashoka's pillars provide much more evidence for his reign than we have for any other Mauryan or ancient Indian ruler. They stand in direct contrast to much of ancient Indian religious art, which focused on various gods or manifestations of deity as paths to spiritual awareness. They reveal Indian influences, but also the assimilation of other cultural influences from western Asia. They reveal Ashoka's dedication to his people and his attempt to guide them safely through this world and beyond to the next life. But the pillars also reflected other aspects of royal policy and thus served as an instrument of governance. Though a Buddhist, Ashoka saw no need to give up his throne. He continued to take action to defend it and to enforce his policies, including the prohibition of animal sacrifice, restrictions on religious festivals, and a kind of prescription drug program that called for medicinal herbs and roots to be imported into areas where they did not grow.

In 185 BCE the Mauryan Empire came to an end and India once again politically disintegrated into numerous decentralized states. Political chaos ensued. While the Greek world was being conquered—and its culture and philosophies were being preserved—by the Romans, India, beyond the reach of even the Romans, experienced a period of darkness and decline. Buddhism, like Stoicism—and Epicureanism to a degree—taught detachment from suffering in this world and remained more of an individually meaningful faith than an organized church or religion. A new form known as Theravada Buddhism, with a greater emphasis on the spiritual enlightenment of the individual, became popular after 200 BCE—an individual, spiritual solution to the problems of the world. Through Ashoka's influence, Buddhism had started to spread throughout India and beyond to the rest of southeast Asia; it would continue to do so, just as other faiths, such as Christianity, would later spread throughout the Roman world in its times of trouble.

Early Rome and the Shaping of the Roman Republic

The peninsula that historically came to be called Italy contains a diverse geography that combines rugged, irregular mountainous terrain with extremely fertile valleys and plains. As in Greece, the geography of Italy lent itself to political division rather than unification. As different peoples settled there, including the Greeks, they carved out their own niches based on their choice of location. The most successful of the early settlers were the Etruscans, a

▲▼ ▲▼ ▲▼ ▲▼ ▲▼ ▲▼ ▲▼ ▲▼ ▲▼ ▲▼ ▲▼ ▲▼ ▲▼ ▲▼

Indian and Greek Religious Architecture

What similarities and differences are there between these two temples? How might each represent the different spiritual visions of the two cultures?

Buddhist stupa and torana (gateway) of Stupa, India. Known as the Great Stupa, it was built by the Emperor Ashoka in the third century BCE, at Sanchi, Madhya Pradesh.

Greek Temple of Hercules, Agrigento, Sicily, ca. 520 BCE

▲▼ ▲▼ ▲▼ ▲▼ ▲▼ ▲▼ ▲▼ ▲▼ ▲▼ ▲▼ ▲▼ ▲▼ ▲▼ ▲▼

people still shrouded in mystery, who produced an advanced culture in what is now Tuscany in central Italy by the seventh century BCE. The city of Rome was founded a bit farther south in the midst of seven hills that sat close to the Tiber River, according to legend in 753 BCE by Romulus and Remus, twin sons of the god Mars. Like the Trojan War and the early history of Greece, the founding and early history of Rome are steeped in mythology, including a story about Romulus and Remus being cast adrift in a river as infants to be found by a she-wolf who nursed and protected them.

In the case of the Etruscans, it is their tombs that tell us the most about this

Find additional images, as well as discussions of the history and symbolism of the stupas, at the website of the Shambala Mountain Center at www.shambhalamountain.org/stupa.html.

See more images of the famous Valley of the Temples at Agrigento, Sicily, at www.agrigento-sicily.it/home.htm.

obscure but apparently extremely successful civilization. They had twelve primary cities, the most important of which seems to have been Tarquinia, which became the head of an Etruscan confederation against Rome. Tombs there of Etruscan aristocrats contain realistic animal figures such as birds and leopards, as well as human figures depicted in paintings and statuary in native garb and elegant poses. These figures are shown in motion and in relationship to one another. Because scholars have still not had much success in deciphering the Etruscan language, we can only surmise that the figures in these tombs were believed to enjoy similar relationships in the afterlife. The figures in the tombs are clearly based on individuals, given the variety of physical characteristics portrayed, such as the differences in length (or absence) of beards among the men. The tombs are exotic and yet strangely familiar in their vague resemblance to classical Greek and Roman art; artifacts found in the tombs reveal strong commercial connections with Greece, which no doubt exerted some cultural influence over the Etruscans.

Trade was initially important to the early Romans as well and certainly had a good deal to do with the real reason why the city was founded at the exact point on the Tiber that was as far inland as seagoing vessels could sail (the same factor that determined the location of London along the Thames River). Trade was, of course, supported by agriculture, which still employed the majority of people in both societies. But if trade was the basis for Etruscan wealth, the Romans learned early that military conquest could be an equally effective means to that end. By the third century BCE, the Romans had expanded their economic base by territorial expansion in Italy at the expense of peoples such as the Sabines, the Samnites, and the Etruscans.

The early history of Rome is traditionally divided into two main periods: that of the Roman monarchy, which lasted until 509 BCE, and the Roman Republic, which officially lasted from 509 until 27 BCE. Many later political traditions originated in Rome, including the word *republic*, which comes from the Latin *res publica*, meaning "the public thing." Through both of these periods, however, Rome remained a patriarchal society in which a relatively few noble families known as patricians dominated public life. In the fifth century BCE, the lower classes, collectively known as plebeians, had to put pressure on the patricians just to make Roman laws public so they could not be interpreted according to the whims of the ruling class. Romans also continued to place a strong emphasis on military service and martial values under the Republic.

Around 509 Rome began to make the transition from a monarchy to a state with republican institutions after the overthrow of the last king, the Etruscan Tarquin the Proud. The Romans then formalized the senate, which had probably acted in an advisory capacity under the monarchy, into an elected representative body and began to give the plebeians some say over political decisions. The leading political officials in Rome after the downfall of the monarchy were two officials known as consuls who served for only one year at a time. Different officials presided over the military and other aspects of the government; the quaestors, for example, oversaw state finances.

The Roman moralistic historian Livy (59 BCE–17 CE) later glorified the early Republic as a time of noble deeds and active citizenship in order to condemn the vices and apathy of his own age. But even the early Republic involved fierce competition for political office and a system that heavily favored the wealthy and powerful at the expense of the common people. The imposition of term limits for Roman political offices only went so far since one could not normally get elected consul without the support of powerful citizens and a wide network of clients who received special treatment in exchange for their political support.

In ancient Rome, social mobility was strictly limited by the closed nature of the patrician class; one became a patrician by birth only. Birth status meant everything; individuals were associated not only with their own immediate family, but also with a *gens*, an extended family grouping. The male head of the gens exercised absolute authority within it according to a principle known as *patria potestas*, or patriarchal power. According to later accounts of the Twelve Tables, the fifth-century Roman law code, a husband could divorce his wife simply by ordering her to take her property and leave. The male head of the household, or *paterfamilias*, even had the power to sell his sons and daughters into slavery. In fact, descent into slavery, generally for failure to pay debts, represented the main form of social mobility, although slavery was not as widespread in the early republican period as it later became with the establishment of large commercial farms and olive groves.

Still, compared to other ancient societies, the Romans did maintain some balance between the power of the patricians and the rights of the people—in principle if not always in practice—a factor certainly in the allegiance that most Romans felt toward their state. This theoretical balance was based on the existence of a plebeian assembly and of officials called tribunes—established in 494 BCE after a plebeian revolt—who were supposed to represent the interests of the common people. The Republic also created a common bond between patricians and plebeians by requiring all property-owning male citizens to serve in the army as necessary. In fact, the Republic established a *Comitia Centuriata*, or assembly based on army units, as a complement to the *Comitia Curiata*, which was organized according to family association. The consuls, however, retained complete power or *imperium*, which allowed them to declare war, impose death sentences, and take any necessary measures to preserve order in the city. The only exceptions to this power were the tribunes, who were immune from physical assault and who actually possessed veto power over any consular decisions. Government in the Roman Republic, then, consisted of some contradictory tendencies that were generally overcome by appeal to whatever the Romans came to regard as accepted tradition. In the third and second centuries BCE, those traditions would be challenged by new realities of increased Roman power and a growing population within the city.

Among the other responsibilities of the consuls, each had the right to control any legion in the Roman army. This prevented one from dominating at the expense of the other. In its early centuries, the Republic made no distinction between armies based on individual commanders, however; the Roman citizens who served did so out of allegiance to the state, not their commanders. As property owners, they were expected to serve the state out of a sense of civic virtue before retiring to private life. This ideal was relatively easy to maintain as long as Rome did not acquire additional territories outside of Italy. Rome did not set out to become an empire and did not merely rely on military might to establish its position in Italy; at times the Romans furthered their interests through peaceful alliances. When they did fight, they usually campaigned only from spring to autumn, affording even the infantrymen the opportunity to return home for part of the year.

Rome began its period of military expansion not out of blatant aggression but as a result of the desire to defend the position it had achieved in Italy. Rome, like Athens, was a Mediterranean power, which depended upon access to sea trade for its economy. The Roman military tradition and the commitment of the people to what had emerged as the Roman ideal prepared the Romans for the next stage in their history. Their rivalry with one state in particular—Carthage—shaped and defined Rome during that next stage.

The Punic Wars and Overseas Expansion

The Phoenician state of Carthage on the coast of North Africa had begun to achieve a dominant position in the western Mediterranean by the third century BCE. Carthage had established a military presence on the islands of Sicily and Sardinia, placing its navy in close proximity to Rome. In response, Rome, for the first time, committed to becoming a naval power itself. Inevitably a clash of the two powers ensued. The Romans defeated Carthage in 241 BCE in the First Punic War—the term *Punic* deriving from the Latin name for the Phoenicians. The Romans ousted the Carthaginians from Sicily and seized control over the islands of Corsica and Sardinia. Surviving to fight another day, Carthage awaited the opportunity to exact revenge upon the Romans. A proverb stated that a lion would not fight with a whale, but Rome had transformed itself from a lion into a whale. Now Carthage would transform itself from a whale into a lion; no longer possessing clear naval supremacy, the Carthaginians launched a new strategy to become a land power from a new base in Spain.

In the Second Punic War (218–201 BCE), the Carthaginians came extremely close to defeating and conquering Rome. Once again, conflict over Sicily was the root cause of the fighting since the Carthaginians had not resolved to accept its loss. But the background to the war occurred in Spain, where the Carthaginian general Hamilcar Barca (ca. 270–228 BCE) had established a strong military presence. Like Alexander the Great, his son Hannibal (247–182 BCE) benefited from his father's military preparations. But, also like Alexander, Hannibal turned out to be an immensely skilled and successful military leader in his own right. First solidifying his position in southern Spain, Hannibal launched a surprise invasion of Italy from the north, bringing a huge army complete with African elephants across the Alps. He defeated the Roman army in Italy in a series of major battles from 218 to 216 BCE. These defeats challenged the Romans' confidence in themselves and their self-image, which was largely based on their military abilities. With the enemy practically at the gates of Rome, the Romans determined to raise yet another army and continue fighting. They resorted to defensive warfare and took advantage of the Carthaginians' vulnerability so far from their supply lines in the midst of a hostile land. Meanwhile, the ruler of Syracuse had panicked in the face of all the Carthaginian victories in Italy and made an alliance with Carthage. By 214 the Romans were able to send a military force to place Syracuse under siege. The city fell in 212 and the Romans reestablished their influence in Sicily. The innovative general Scipio Africanus (236–c. 183 BCE) pursued the Carthaginians first to Spain and then to North Africa itself. Scipio received the adulation of the Romans for his defeat of Hannibal, which he had first achieved in Spain through tactics that included placing his strongest troops on the flanks to crush the weakest troops of the enemy, while his center troops delayed action long enough to allow the two wings of the army to encircle the best troops in the Carthaginian army. But his victory was possible only because Rome had survived its darkest days based on sheer determination to keep fighting and the loyalty of other peoples in Italy who in the end preferred Roman rule to that of the Carthaginians.

Legend has it that Hannibal at the age of nine pledged to destroy Rome; in the end it was Carthage that suffered destruction. Rome continued to expand its empire after the Second Punic War, but some Romans never got over the enmity they felt toward their old enemy. Fearful of a revival of Carthaginian power, Rome supported Carthage's neighbor state of Numidia. When a border dispute arose between Carthage and Numidia, Rome used the provocation toward its ally as an excuse to launch the Third Punic War

(149–146 BCE). This time the Romans left no chance for a fourth Punic war. They totally decimated the city of Carthage and dispersed the Carthaginian people throughout the empire, leaving no historical traces of this once-proud people. With the Carthaginian threat over, Rome began to enjoy unrivaled power in the Mediterranean.

The general who led the Romans to victory in the Third Punic War, Scipio Aemilianus, also known as Scipio Africanus Minor (ca. 185–129 BCE) moved on from the conquest of North Africa to establish Roman hegemony over Spain as well. Perhaps such expansion had been Rome's intention or destiny all along—the historian Polybius (ca. 200–120 BCE) thought so. The Romans had become the strongest military power in the Mediterranean world and had a state that could draw on the support of not only its own people, but also the other tribes in Italy to whom it had granted Roman citizenship. In between the Second and Third Punic wars, Rome had defeated the Seleucid kingdom in Syria and placed itself in a position to exercise influence in the Near East as well. As outsiders, the Romans were in a good position to arbitrate the conflicts among the various Hellenistic rulers there. The Romans had become a force of power and intimidation that their enemies might annoy but not seriously threaten. However, the rise of Roman power provided some cause for concern within Rome itself. As wealth, goods, and food supplies from other territories flowed into Rome, a rise in inflation and accompanying social changes led some citizens to demand political reform.

The Revolution of the Gracchi Brothers

The Roman Republic experienced its first major internal crisis from 133 to 121 BCE, a period that was defined by the proposed reforms of two brothers, Tiberius and Gaius Gracchus. When Tiberius became a tribune of the plebeians in 133, he turned his attention to the issue of land reform because of his concern over the amount of land in Italy that was falling into the hands of the wealthiest Roman citizens. Recent surveys of land in the region that was Etruria have revealed a number of small farms still in existence at the time of Tiberius's proposed reforms. But according to his biographer Plutarch, Tiberius had been disturbed at witnessing gangs of slave laborers at work on farmland in the region. Even if Tiberius did underestimate the number of small farms still in existence, he had identified a trend that he believed would be detrimental to Rome in the long run. Plutarch observed that Tiberius did not draft his law on a whim, but rather with the advice and support of some of Rome's best legal minds and most distinguished citizens. Furthermore, Tiberius did not advocate the abolition of private property nor propose confiscation of privately owned land, but rather restricted his reform proposals to land owned by the state that he wished to see distributed to ordinary Roman citizens who had fought in the army. The Roman senate—whose members felt more threatened by Tiberius's political tactics, which ignored senatorial prerogatives, than by his actual proposal—passed a land reform bill, but only after Tiberius and a number of his supporters had been murdered.

Gaius, having witnessed his brother's political defeat and subsequent murder, determined to learn from them. Whereas his brother had a calm, rational disposition, Gaius displayed a strong temper and a passionate nature. As tribune (123–122 BCE), he began to solicit the support of the equestrian class of knights (*equites*) and sought through legislation to detach their interests from those of the senate. For example, in his law on extortion he called for decisions in cases of provincial corruption to fall to juries of knights, a privilege that had previously belonged to senators (who were likely to acquit other senators). This law caused great offense among the senatorial class. Compared to Tiberius, Gaius was also much more aggressive in pushing his reform program, which was more ambitious than his brother's, seeking not only to end injustice but also to make the Roman political system more participatory and inclusive. The desire to include the people in the political decision-making process was what made the program of the Gracchi brothers so revolutionary. Aristocrats themselves, they became proponents of democracy. They provided a model for later Roman politicians of the patrician class who would appeal to the people for political support.

The Roman political system worked against the Gracchi brothers. Their power came from their position as tribune of the plebeians, but that position only lasted for one year; Gaius shockingly overcame the Roman commitment to tradition when he successfully stood for reelection for a second term. He needed more than one year for his ambitious reform program, which also included granting citizenship to all residents of Italy and state subsidies for grain distribution to the poor. He actually needed more than two, but when he attempted to secure election to a third term he met the same fate as his brother. But his ideals lived on. To the Romans, the Gracchi were either heroes or devils, depending on one's political viewpoint.

The Gracchi brothers had also made Roman politics much more personal. Gaius, in particular, was a charismatic figure described by Plutarch as pacing frenetically, raising his voice, and at times even tearing at his toga when making speeches. Gaius was murdered, along with 3,000 supporters, during riots that followed the passage of a notorious law—the *senatus consultum ultimum*—allowing the consuls to execute without trial any Roman citizen that they believed represented a threat to the Republic. Scandal, the threat of anarchy, and the rise of dictatorial tendencies would continue to shape Roman history for the next century.

The Career of Caesar and the Collapse of the Roman Republic

Toward the end of the second century BCE, the Roman Republic was having difficulty harmonizing the growth of its empire and its political traditions.

In 107 BCE, Gaius Marius (ca. 157–86 BCE), an increasingly powerful Roman general, called for volunteers to enter the Roman army in direct contradiction of the tradition restricting military service to those from the property-owning classes. This move greatly upset the patrician class, not only because it violated tradition but also because it gave Marius a base of political support among the lower classes. Marius's political clout provoked a challenge from Lucius Cornelius Sulla (ca. 138–78 BCE), who posed as a defender of senatorial privilege, but turned out to be a cruel and pitiless dictator. In Rome, *dictator* was a legal title for a ruler with emergency powers to guide the state at a time of crisis. Sulla used the office to strengthen his own power and to destroy his numerous political enemies. He held the position for two years after defeating Marius in a blood-soaked civil war (88–82 BCE), before retiring—surprisingly—in 79 BCE.

The struggle between Marius and Sulla set a precedent for military leaders riding their own armies on their path to power. Generals without ambition suddenly found the road to power open to them if they achieved great military success. Politicians who had ambition found it essential to secure a military command and to seek military glory to advance their career. Of the three rulers who divided power among them in the First Triumvirate in 60 BCE, Marcus Licinius Crassus (ca. 115–53 BCE) and Gnaeus Pompeius Magnus (known as Pompey the Great) fell into the first category. The third, Julius Caesar (ca. 101–44 BCE), fell into the second. Crassus was an extremely wealthy citizen who achieved fame when he ruthlessly crushed a large-scale slave rebellion led by a gladiator-slave named Spartacus, while Pompey returned victorious from a series of wars in Spain and Asia Minor with more money than he knew what to do with. Caesar secured command over the Roman armies across the Alps in Gaul (modern France), which he used as a platform for achieving even greater power.

Caesar's successes in Gaul and his obvious political ambitions led to distrust among his co-rulers. They began to maneuver to exclude him from

Explore a digital model of the Roman Forum—created by the UCLA Cultural Virtual Reality Laboratory—at http://dlib.etc.ucla.edu/projects/Forum.

Roman Forum. Although it attracts mostly tourists today, in Caesar's time the forum was a vibrant public meeting place for politicians, lawyers, and businessmen.

power while he was away, while Caesar bided his time annihilating the Celtic people of Gaul and writing cool, detached third-person annual accounts of his brilliant military leadership, the bravery of his men, and the technological superiority of the Romans. His accounts, collectively known as *The Gallic War*, like the war itself, clearly served the political purpose of enhancing his reputation at Rome at the same time that he built up his support among his own army.

Crassus died in 53 BCE, leaving Pompey and Caesar to contend for mastery over Rome. In 49 BCE, Caesar ignored a law passed by Sulla that forbade a Roman general from returning to Rome without the government's consent. Already facing senatorial prosecution for corruption during an earlier term as consul, Caesar believed he had nothing to lose when he crossed the Rubicon River in northern Italy with his army, intent on invading Rome itself, if necessary. Unnerved by his fierce military reputation, the Italians did nothing to resist him, while Pompey chose to flee and prepare for a civil war. The following year, after losing a battle at Pharsala in Greece, Pompey went to Egypt, which he would use as a base in his war against Caesar. At the time

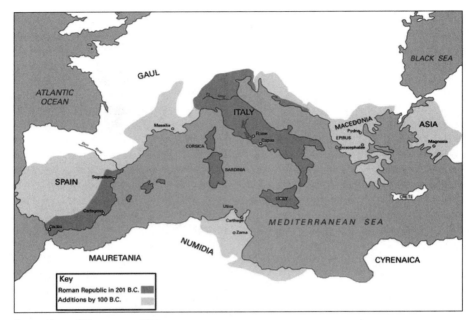

Expansion of Rome, ca. 100 BCE

Egypt was ruled by the daughter of Ptolemy Auletes, a young, ambitious, and determined woman named Cleopatra VII (69–30 BCE), who was embroiled in a power struggle with the advisers of her younger brother. Following the murder of Pompey in Egypt, Caesar followed him there to settle the succession dispute and ensure no disruption in the flow of Egyptian grain to Rome. Not only did he settle the issue in favor of Cleopatra, he also fell in love and conceived a child with her.

Caesar had steadily accumulated power and now, with his two rivals deceased, prepared to return to Rome in triumph. The changing political realities in Rome that had first produced a Marius and then a Sulla had culminated in a figure with truly grandiose visions of unlimited power. Sulla's defense of senatorial privilege had not lasted, leaving Caesar's political opponents to watch helplessly as each of his victories seemed to signal a further step in the decline of the republic. Upon returning to Rome, Caesar secured from a compliant senate the title of dictator for life and began a period of autocratic rule. Republicans had long feared that Rome might descend into a monarchy, which had been political anathema in Rome for centuries. Therefore, although he attempted to rule justly and in the interests of the people, Caesar faced mounting opposition from his adversaries.

Caesar never actually overthrew the republic. He was popular because, as dictator, he restored order and brought an end to civil war and political strife. His rule was more a product of changes in Roman society that had threatened the republican ideal than a cause of its decline. In fact, Caesar had risen up through the ranks of power and had himself come from an ancient aristocratic Roman family. The anarchy in Rome was not of Caesar's making and seemed to call for extreme measures; the senate had passed another *senatus consultum ultimum* in 52 BCE in an attempt to restore order. Caesar, in order to reduce population pressures in Rome, dispersed citizens throughout the empire, primarily to Spain. He preserved private property, but set up a system of arbitration to resolve disputes over debts, the amounts of which were to be determined with reference to prewar property values. Caesar could rationalize everything that he did—including the destruction of the Gauls—as ultimately being in Rome's best interests. But he underestimated the continuing appeal of the old senatorial traditions. A faction led by two former friends—Gaius Cassius Longinus (d. 42 BCE) and Marcus Junius Brutus (85–42 BCE)—plotted and carried out his assassination on March 15 (the Ides of March), 44 BCE. They stabbed Caesar twenty-three times about the face, eyes, and groin while a stunned and speechless senate sat and watched. The senators did not stay, however, to listen to Brutus's intended explanation; they could not leave the frightful scene fast enough. Caesar's murder left a political void in Rome. A distraught Cleopatra, fearing that she and her son would be next, returned to Egypt. Caesar had not named his son by Cleopatra heir, but instead designated a great-nephew and adopted son by the name of Octavian (63 BCE–14 CE). One thing soon became clear: the assassination of Caesar did nothing to preserve the republic nor did it put an end to the ambitions of powerful military leaders.

The career of Caesar, then, did not directly bring about the collapse of the Roman republic. But his death helped to ensure its further demise. His successors would rule as absolute monarchs—emperors—the very thing that Caesar's opponents had most feared. But Rome was more prepared to accept a virtual monarchy after yet another civil war following Caesar's murder. Furthermore, Rome, having long outgrown the traditions suitable to a city-state, needed an emperor to rule an empire. The great republican orator Marcus Tullius Cicero (106–43 BCE) blamed the ambitions of men like Pompey and Caesar for the downfall of republican traditions and for a long time tried to support whoever he thought was most committed to preserving them; he died a year after Caesar—murdered by Mark Antony (ca. 83–30 BCE), an ally of Caesar who contended for power after his death—without ever realizing that the system he defended was simply no longer viable.

Conclusion

Cato the Elder (234–149 BCE) grew up in the shadow of the First Punic War, participated in the second, and died on the eve of the third. Although he did not come from Rome, during his lifetime he came to embody—or at least so he thought—all that it meant to be Roman. He was a wealthy landowner and influential politician who shared the lifestyle of the laborers who worked on his farm. As an administrator, he was said to be incorruptible and completely devoted to Roman law. He viewed himself as the guardian of Roman morals, opposing new fashions and supporting a law that forbade women to wear colorful clothing or to own more than a pound of gold. He was so committed to what he considered Roman values that he completely opposed any Greek or foreign influences, especially Greek philosophy. Cato earned the nickname of "the censor" for the intolerance he displayed when holding the position of that name in 184 BCE.

Cato's stance in support of the older Roman tradition and his hostility to the ideas of Greek thinkers and an increase in luxury among the Romans testifies to the extent of their growth during his lifetime. Cato was an earnest and learned man who believed that knowledge should serve practical ends; he wrote a book on agriculture that is the oldest prose work extant written in Latin. But Cato's personal and political conservatism included hostility to Carthage—Rome's great enemy. "Carthage must be destroyed," became his slogan, repeated in Latin grammar books down to the present. Cato, however, failed to realize the extent to which war would bring about the very changes he sought to prevent—for Rome's success in the Punic Wars consolidated Roman power and wealth and brought change in its wake.

Meanwhile, another chain of events was set in motion during Cato's lifetime that would have an even greater impact on Roman—and world—history. A resistance movement had arisen in Palestine among the Jews in opposition to religious and political oppression imposed by the Seleucid king of Syria, Antiochus Epiphanes (ca. 215–163 BCE) Although this movement was not successful, resistance to foreign rule did not end, provoking a variety of religious responses among the Jews to their situation in the second and first centuries BCE. When Pompey the Great intervened in a succession dispute, he involved Rome in the affairs of Syria, which soon came under Roman authority. Within a century, the Jews, now seeking deliverance from Roman authority, would produce a leader who would revolutionize the meaning of power and do more to change the course of world history than Caesar or any Roman ever would.

1. Why is this period referred to as the Hellenistic age? What would you identify as its defining characteristics?
2. What were the main factors in the rise and decline of the Macedonian empire? What were its legacies to the ancient world?
3. In what ways did Hellenistic philosophers respond to the problems of their own age? In what ways did they respond to earlier Greek philosophy?
4. What were the main features of the Indian religious tradition? What was the significance of the Mauryan Empire in Indian history?
5. What led to the emergence of Rome as a major power in the Mediterranean? What consequences did the rise to power have for internal Roman politics?

Suggestions for Further Reading

Boatwright, Mary T., Daniel J. Gargola, and Richard J.A. Talbert. 2004. *The Romans: From Village to Empire*. New York: Oxford University Press.

Errington, R. Malcolm. 2008. *A History of the Hellenistic World, 323–30 BC*. Malden, MA: Blackwell.

Freeman, Philip. 2008. *Julius Caesar*. New York: Simon & Schuster.

Green, Peter. 2007. *The Hellenistic Age: A History*. New York: Modern Library.

Polybius. 1979. *The Rise of the Roman Empire*. Translated by Ian Scott-Kilvert. Selected with an introduction by F.W. Walbank. London: Penguin Books.

Russo, Lucio. 2000. *The Forgotten Revolution: How Science Was Born in 300 BC and Why It Had to Be Reborn*. Translated by Silvio Levy. New York: Springer.

Suggested Websites

http://classics.mit.edu
This site allows for the exploration of works written during this period, including writings by and about individuals, such as Epicurus, treated in this chapter.

www.fordham.edu/halsall/ancient/diogeneslaertius-book7-stoics.html#Zeno
This address will direct readers to the life of Zeno the Stoic and the lives and works of other Hellenistic philosophers.

www.fordham.edu/halsall/India/kautilya1.html#Book%20III,%20
Chapter%202

Here readers will find a work written for the Mauryan emperors on the duties of a king that greatly influenced Chandragupta and Ashoka in the early years of his reign.

www.roman-empire.net

This popular site contains many details and images related to Roman history, divided into well organized sections for easy navigation through the site.

www.unrv.com

This well-maintained site features book reviews, bibliography, and expanded content on the aspects of Roman history dealt with in this text.

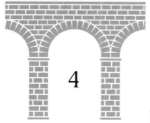

4

The Roman Empire and the Enduring Legacy of the Ancient World, ca. 30 BCE–500 CE

When Julius Caesar was assassinated in 44 BCE, a symptom of Rome's problems had been removed but not the cause. The institutions of the Republic were no longer capable of responding to the growth of military power. They were inadequate for administering the vast empire that Rome had accumulated. Caesar was dead, but what plan did the conspirators have to prevent another Sulla or Caesar from seizing power? Brutus and Cassius had to resort to military strength to defend themselves, thus contributing to the continuation of Rome's civil wars. Even if Caesar's supporters had not risen against them, Rome still needed a huge military to defend its widespread frontiers. The Roman state had changed and it needed leadership and institutions that reflected that change. It also needed a leader that could bring an end to civil war and political chaos and restore peace to the Roman world.

The changes that had occurred with the rise of the Roman Empire called forth other kinds of responses besides political disorder. Rome had expanded into other areas of the world that possessed cultures and traditions that were hundreds or even thousands of years old. The Romans began to interfere in the affairs of the Hellenistic kingdoms and eventually to take control of them. In Palestine they would find themselves in the middle of a lengthy dispute between patriotic, devout Jews determined to worship their god alone and Hellenistic kings who had begun to insist on outward religious conformity to pagan gods. The Romans, who were generally tolerant of the cultures and religions of the peoples they ruled, merely wanted peace and stability. By the first century BCE, Hellenistic Judaism had produced a variety of responses to the situation in Palestine. The region was turning into a fertile ground for new ideas and new religious approaches. Out of this atmosphere came a prophet named Jesus, whose life and teachings would soon reverberate throughout the Roman Empire. Roman authorities executed him, even though they were not entirely convinced that he represented the political threat that his Jewish

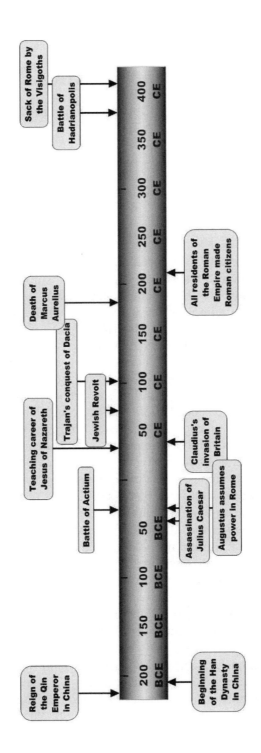

enemies had claimed. Jesus's Jewish followers believed that he had risen from the dead and started a new faith that at first appeared to be just another variant of Judaism. It soon became more. Missionaries such as Paul of Tarsus began preaching to the non-Jewish people of the Greek and Roman world, thus initiating one of the world's great religious traditions.

Rome, meanwhile, adopted an imperial system of government, even as it attempted to dress this up in republican clothing. For almost three centuries, its rulers took little notice of the Christians, except for the occasional ruler who for political or personal reasons decided that they deserved to be persecuted. For the most part, Roman emperors either had enough power that they did not perceive Christians as much of a threat or were contending with more serious problems. Second-century emperors generally fell into the first category, third-century emperors into the second. By the third century CE, foreign threats from beyond the borders and internal threats from their own military rivals increasingly weighed on the crowned heads of Rome. Claims of the Roman emperors to a status of divinity did not make them bleed any less when struck by an assassin's sword or dagger. And though Rome possessed the most powerful military machine on earth, constant warfare with Germanic tribes on its northern borders was still a legitimate cause for concern. Parallels between the Han Empire in China and the Roman Empire illustrate some of the common problems faced even by great empires that might eventually lead to their demise. But such a scenario was a long way off in the first century BCE when Rome finally resolved its constitutional crisis and found its first emperor.

Augustus and Augustan Rome

The man who emerged triumphant from the civil wars in the first century BCE was Octavian, who would later become known as Augustus, "the consecrated one." Octavian, like Caesar before him, had to overcome the opposition of conservatives who sought to preserve the Republic, as well as the ambitions of a formidable rival. Mark Antony—who was to Octavian what Pompey had been to Caesar—assumed power in Rome upon Caesar's death and claimed the support of Caesar's army. Antony even followed Caesar into the bed of Cleopatra, whom he met in Cilicia in the autumn of 41 BCE and then accompanied to Egypt. Octavian and Antony at first attempted to share power—along with Marcus Aemilius Lepidus (d. 13 BCE), a former supporter of Caesar who was given control of Rome's Africa Province. They combined their forces to crush those of Cassius and Brutus. Lepidus retired when his soldiers refused to take up arms against Octavian, leaving the field to Antony and Octavian. The ambitions of both men led to another civil war that culminated in Octavian's decisive victory in the naval battle of Actium off the coast of western Greece

Augustus of Prima Porta. This marble statue dates to 20 BCE.

in September of 31 BCE. Cleopatra chose to commit suicide rather than humble herself before Octavian, who took control of Egypt and its wealth for his own private treasury.

In the years following the Battle of Actium, Octavian transformed himself into Augustus, a dignified and aloof ruler who posed as Rome's savior. The poet Virgil (70–19 BCE) had predicted a return of Rome's golden age in his Fourth *Eclogue* (37 BCE) and celebrated Rome's traditional rural values in his *Georgics*, completed two years after the Battle of Actium. Augustus assumed full power over Rome in 27 BCE, after which he patronized poets and artists who celebrated his heroic and divine qualities in works such as the Prima Porta statue.

He took the title of *Imperator*, which meant "Supreme Commander," but at the same time preserved the various offices that had existed under the Republic. The nature of Augustus's rule is summed up in a speech composed two centuries later by the Greek historian Dio Cassius (ca. 155–235 CE) that purported to reflect the advice that Augustus, upon assuming power, received from his chief adviser Maecenas (d. 8 BCE). Maecenas's reputed advice—which at any rate matched the strategy actually employed by Augustus—called on him to rule Rome in a moderate way, but to rule it as a monarch would, accepting responsibility for the safety and well-being of the state and people.

Like many rulers who must fight to gain power, Augustus became an ardent advocate of peace once he had achieved power. To eliminate the possibility of future civil war, he reorganized the government and the military, making sure that he held all the key positions of power within both. Augustus personally took control of the senate in the newly created position of *princeps senatus*.

Read more about Augustus and other historical figures at the history website of the BBC at www.bbc.co.uk/history/historic_figures/augustus.shtml.

Augustus Defends His Rule

I ask and implore you one and all both to approve my course and to cooperate heartily with me, reflecting upon all that I have done for you alike in war and in public life, and rendering me complete recompense for it all by this one favour,—by allowing me at last to be at peace as I live out my life. Thus you will come to know that I understand not only how to rule but also how to submit to rule, and that all the commands which I have laid upon others I can endure to have laid upon me. I ask this because I expect to live in security, if that be possible, and to suffer no harm from anybody by either deed or word,—such is the confidence, based upon my own conscience, which I have in your good-will; but if some disaster should befall me, such as falls to the lot of many (for it is not possible for a man to please everybody, especially when he has been involved in wars of such magnitude, both foreign and civil, and has had affairs of such importance entrusted to him), with entire willingness I make my choice to die even before my appointed time as a private citizen, in preference to living forever as the occupant of a throne. Indeed, this very choice will bring me renown,—that I not only did not deprive another of life in order to win that office, but went so far as even to give up my life in order to avoid being king; and the man who dares to slay me will certainly be punished, I am sure, both by Heaven and by you, as happened, methinks, in the case of my father. For he was declared to be the equal of the gods and obtained eternal honours, whereas those who slew him perished, miserable men, by a miserable death. As for immortality, we could not possibly achieve it; but by living nobly and by dying nobly we do in a sense gain even this boon. Therefore, I, who already possess the first requisite and hope to possess the second, return to you the armies and the provinces, the revenues and the laws, adding only a few words of suggestion, to the end that you may not be afraid of the magnitude of the business of administration, or of the difficulty of handling it and so become discouraged, and that you may not, on the other hand, regard it with contempt, with the idea that it can easily be managed, and thus neglect it.

Source: Dio Cassius, *Roman History,* translated by Earnest Cary. Loeb Classical Library, vol. 6 (Cambridge, MA: Harvard University Press, 1917).

In this speech, as recorded by Dio Cassius, Augustus seems to decline monarchical status. Not everyone thought that he was being completely honest. Why does Augustus say that he is acting in this way? What else might he have hoped to achieve from such a speech besides his stated intention here?

He created a number of new administrative positions staffed by members of the equestrian class. Augustus directly controlled appointments to these positions. One such position was the *praefectus annonae*, which oversaw grain provisions for the city, which Augustus increased in an attempt to satisfy the poor. He also controlled new appointments to the senate, but he appeased the old senatorial class with its share of provincial appointments and outwardly retaining traditional Roman institutions. In order to alleviate fears of military dictatorship, Augustus dismissed 100,000 members of his army after the Battle of Actium and settled them on their own lands. But he retained a standing army and created the Praetorian Guard, part of whose responsibility was to protect Augustus. The army of about 165,000 legionnaires was stationed across the empire, while auxiliary troops could be called upon when needed. The army sustained peace and thus did not cause great resentment. Order had been restored; Augustus reformed the Roman system of coinage; trade flourished; Augustus was hailed as a hero and a god.

Augustus was such a skilled politician and successful ruler that he even reconciled his former opponents to his authoritarian regime. The poet Horace (65–8 BCE), for example, became one of his leading supporters and a member of the literary circle of Virgil associated with Augustus, despite his earlier support of Cassius and Brutus. It is easy to accuse Horace of political inconsistency and self-aggrandizement, but the explanation for his change of heart lies as much with Augustus as it does with Horace. Augustus made dictatorship easy to swallow, even for former republicans, by restoring Roman glory, rebuilding the city, and ruling with a moderation seldom seen in history among rulers who achieve absolute power. It was only later in his reign that the Battle of Actium became a clear-cut symbol of Augustan triumph; people first needed reassurance that the civil wars were indeed over. By 14 BCE, Horace was celebrating Augustus in verse for preserving the safety of Rome, improving Roman laws, and laying down new guidelines for civilized behavior. Critics such as the historian Tacitus (ca. 55–120 CE) came along only after Augustus's successors had demonstrated flagrant abuses of the power that he had accumulated.

Augustus's absolute rule even extended into Roman society, which he sought to make worthy of a great empire. The golden age could not be just about power and money. For example, in 18 BCE he oversaw the promulgation of laws intended to preserve the sanctity of marriage among Roman citizens. He made adultery a criminal offense in the *lex Iulia de adulteris*. Augustus also sought to promote social stability and the survival of Rome's elite classes with another law that placed restrictions on marriages between people of different classes. Inheritance laws from his reign disadvantaged those who refused to marry and married couples who had no children. Although there were practical reasons for these laws, Augustus had a deep conservative strain that included a strong moral sensibility. In addition to his attempt to improve Rome's morals, he also improved the safety of the city, not only with regard to crime, but also in areas of public health. He had more fresh water channeled into the city via aqueducts and sought to improve the quality as well as the quantity of the food supply.

The appearance of Rome changed dramatically under Augustus, who sought to make the capital city worthy of the empire as well. In addition to a new forum, he financed many buildings of marble throughout the city that gave Rome the classical look that many today associate with the ancient city. It seemed to many of his contemporaries that Augustus had created a golden age, but behind the marble facade was unbridled power that had been seized by military conquest. The Republic had evolved means of conveying legitimate authority and passing it down from one year to the next. Augustus attempted to establish his own divinity in an attempt to achieve recognition for his legitimate claim to authority over the empire. This was not much of an issue during the forty years that he exercised power, tempered by restraint. But as Augustus approached death, the problem of the succession loomed. (Augustus had only one legitimate child, a daughter by his first marriage whom he had exiled for adultery.) The legitimacy of Roman imperial authority became an issue, not only in Rome, but also in the one place that refused to accept Roman legitimacy during the reign of Augustus—the tiny but troublesome territory called Palestine.

Hellenistic Judaism and the Dead Sea Scrolls

The Jews had not lost faith in the covenant that they believed they shared with God, even though as a people they had endured the trials of the Babylonian Captivity and the subsequent scattering of their people to many nations in what was known as the Diaspora. They had also lost political control over the land of Palestine, and, in the aftermath of the conquests of Alexander, their way of life itself was threatened by the spread of Hellenism. While many Jews accommodated themselves to Hellenistic culture and philosophy, others reacted strongly to Greek infringement upon Jewish traditions. The Hellenistic Jews gained power through an alliance with the Seleucid king, Antiochus IV (215–163 BCE). Antiochus enticed Jewish priests to follow Greek practices (at the expense of their devotion to religious services) in the gymnasium that he had built in Jerusalem. However, when Antiochus had a statue of the Greek god Zeus—referred to in the Book of Maccabees as the "Abomination of Desolation"—placed in the Jewish temple in 167 BCE, a party of religious zealots led by Judas Maccabeus started a revolt that ultimately cost the Seleucids control over Palestine. Although many Jews had been attracted to Greek ways, Antiochus had made the mistake of attempting to force the Jews to accept the Greek gods and to abandon their own cultural traditions, such as circumcision. The Romans might have learned from this error as they were much more tolerant of Jewish beliefs and practices once they gained control of the region in the first century BCE. However, by then Jewish belief and practice were anything but monolithic. Some scholars have gone so far as to refer to Judaisms during this period rather than Judaism. Judaism could not avoid being influenced by the multitude of religious and cultural traditions with which Jews came into contact during the Hellenistic period.

The most radical and important change that occurred in Judaism at this time was the rise of the Pharisees, Jews who believed that God's law did not appear in its entirety in the Torah. They fully believed in the validity of the written law that God had revealed to Moses, but they also believed that another law had been revealed to Moses that had been transmitted orally from generation to generation. Their belief in this twofold law led to a bitter rivalry with the Levites, the more traditional and hereditary priestly class who presided over the religious rituals and guarded the legal heritage of ancient Judaism. The Pharisees believed that the oral law had contained teachings that included a belief in human resurrection and God's promise of eternal life, which did not appear in the Pentateuch (the first five books of the Bible). The Pharisees also believed that religion was not a set of scripted practices that were performed ritualistically at certain times, but rather a constant attention to the laws of God in one's daily life—laws that essentially consisted of treating others with love and kindness.

There is a great diversity among the Jewish writings from the Hellenistic period down to the first century BCE. They include a collection of writings later known as the Apocrypha, as well as those collectively known as the Dead Sea Scrolls, which were preserved for 2,000 years in caves near the northwestern shore of the Dead Sea until their discovery by shepherds in 1947. The Apocrypha includes, among other books, an account of the Jewish revolt against Seleucid rule in the two books of the Maccabees, several stories that revolve around the heroic figure of Daniel, who lived during the time of the Babylonian captivity, and the very popular (judging from the number of manuscripts found) book of Tobit, which involves a moralistic tale set in the eighth century BCE. The Dead Sea Scrolls include the oldest known copies of some of the books of the Hebrew Bible, which alone would have made this an exciting discovery for archaeologists and Biblical scholars. The scrolls also include a collection of previously unknown writings that testify to the beliefs and practices of another Jewish sect known as the Essenes that emerged during the Hellenistic period. The Essenes were a semimonastic community that sought to isolate themselves in the Judean wilderness in order to live a more purified life that would hasten their deliverance by God. The location of their community at Qumran, in the vicinity of the discovery of the Dead Sea Scrolls, makes it likely that the scrolls constituted their library. One particular book, *Rule of the Community* (also known as *Manual of Discipline*), appears to contain the rules, regulations, and disciplinary code to which the sect adhered. Even the ruthless Herod the Great (c. 73–4 BCE), appointed king of Galilee by Julius Caesar in 47 BCE, greatly respected the Essenes and exempted them from oaths required of other Jews. The Essenes particularly objected to a third major group within Judaism known as the Sadducees.

To the Essenes—and many other Jews, including the Pharisees—the Sadducees were too corrupt, powerful, and conservative in their approach to Judaism. The Sadducees drew their support from the high priesthood and the Jerusalem aristocracy, who lauded their commitment to the Pentateuch as the exclusive repository of divine truth and to Yahweh as the God of the nation of Israel. During Herod's reign, the influence of the Sadducees was waning, while that of the Pharisees was on the rise. Even more importantly, however, the Jewish people were becoming increasingly divided into separate camps, based upon their political views about accommodation with Rome, their social and economic class, and their religious perspectives. The rise of the Pharisees and the Essenes testifies to the historical bankruptcy of the spiritual approach of the Sadducees, who continued to believe that God would favor the Jews if they just upheld his written law. To the Pharisees, God's salvation was to be expected in the next life, not in this one, while the Essenes' *Rule of the Community* speaks of leaving everything in the hands of God.

Out of the area around Qumran came an individual who became the most famous of Jewish prophets to emerge from this religious atmosphere. He was known as John the Baptizer and he emerged from the wilderness preaching a message of baptism and repentance. The beliefs and practices of the Essenes, whose community featured a number of baptismal fonts, were leading Judaism in a new direction and starting to spread outside of their isolated community. Their texts speak of a Teacher of Righteousness, a conflict between the spirit of truth and the spirit of perversity, of angels and demons, of the advantages of celibacy and communal living. It was John the Baptizer who told his followers that he would be followed by someone greater than he, who would baptize not with water but with the holy spirit—someone whose life and teachings continued to reflect—and extend—the new directions within Judaism.

The Shaping of the Past: The Life and Teachings of Jesus

In about 30 CE, during the reign of the emperor Tiberius, Roman authorities executed a Jewish prophet who, it was charged, had claimed to be the king of the Jews. In the two or three years before his death, Jesus of Nazareth had attracted a small group of loyal followers who believed that he was the Messiah, or savior of the Jewish people, foretold in the Old Testament as well as in intertestamental Jewish literature. During those years he traveled throughout Palestine teaching, healing, and—according to the first-century Gospel writers who recorded his biography—performing various miracles. These later writers believed that Jesus was divine—the Son of God—because of eyewitness accounts that Jesus had risen from the dead three days after he had been crucified by the Romans The earliest evidence for this belief comes from the letters of Saul of Tarsus (ca. 10–ca. 66 CE), a Jew who had begun his career persecuting the followers of Jesus. After having a vision in which Jesus appeared to tell Saul to stop persecuting him, Saul, for unknown reasons, changed his name to Paul and then joined Jesus's previous disciples and a growing number of converts—both Jews and non-Jews—in proclaiming Jesus's divinity and offering hope of eternal life through belief in Jesus as the savior of humanity. These Christians—as they soon became known after the Greek name *Christ*, or "anointed one," given to Jesus after his death—believed that they had been granted authority by Jesus to perform God's will on earth. By this they meant the authority to forgive sins, not political authority; Jesus had told his disciples that his kingdom was not of this world and that whatever they should do on earth would be done also in heaven.

Not much is known about the life of Jesus outside of the four Gospel accounts written under the names of Matthew, Mark, Luke, and John, although some late first- and second-century accounts known as the Gnostic Gospels purport to provide additional details. Mark's Gospel was written first, around 70 CE, and thus is regarded by historians as the most reliable, as there are some inconsistencies that appear among the four. Despite these inconsistencies, however, some things seem clear about Jesus—besides the fact of his crucifixion (verified in Roman texts) and the belief in his resurrection—based on the similarities that do exist in these accounts of his life and teachings. Jesus came from the small town of Nazareth, and nothing in his boyhood seems to have marked him as particularly extraordinary among the people who knew him there. When he began his career as a prophet teaching from the Hebrew scriptures, people in Nazareth were incredulous that the son of the carpenter, Joseph, would presume to speak as he did. When he began his career as a teacher, he followed many of the teachings of the Pharisees, saying that he had come not to destroy the law but to fulfill it, sharing their belief in eternal life, and distilling the main intent of the law as devotion to God and the practice of loving-kindness toward others. Jesus also followed John the Baptizer (who some had come to believe was the Messiah) in preaching a strong message of the need for repentance because of the nearness of the kingdom of God (Mark 1:15, 12:34; Luke 10:9). His followers took this to mean that the end of the world was near, but Jesus also stated that "the kingdom of God is within you" (Luke 17:21), a message consistent with a comment attributed to him in the Gnostic Gospel of Thomas that the kingdom of God is already present and not something to be waited for.

The Gospels provide a great deal of information about Jesus, but their weakness for historians is that the writers did not intend to write a traditional biographical or historical account of his life. Many scholars believe that the first three Gospels derive from a single earlier source that is lost to us, accounting for their many similarities. Whether or not this earlier source contained more biographical information cannot be known, but it is clear that the main purpose of the Gospel writers was to attract followers to the teachings of Christ and belief in his divine nature and mission. The Gospel of John, currently regarded as the work of several authors, is the least biographical of the four, dealing mainly with the last week of Jesus's life and with a theological interpretation adhered to by Christians who believed that they were following the teachings of one of Jesus's disciples. Archaeology, however, is now supplementing the biblical accounts with new insights into his world, such as the recent identification of Nazareth as a suburb of a much larger city rather than an isolated rural village, as it is often portrayed, and the discovery of Jesus's main residence during his ministry in Galilee, a house in Capernaum believed to have belonged to Peter, Jesus's chief disciple.

Even in the first century, Christians had apparently already started to differ on the meaning and significance of the life and teachings of the crucified prophet that they followed and revered. For example, early Christians such as Peter and Paul seem to have largely ignored the role that women played in the life and ministry of Jesus, including Mary Magdalene, who was with Jesus at his crucifixion (unlike his male disciples) and who some believe to have been his wife. Jesus's mother, Mary, also appears prominently in the Gospels, as do a number of other women, such as a pair of sisters named Mary and Martha, with whom he stayed in Bethany. The Gnostic Gospels reveal the existence of a variety of Christianities in these early centuries when Christians frequently lived an underground existence because of the hostility of Roman authorities. At the same time, the survival and spread of the Christian faith during this period testifies to the sincerity of the believers, however divided they were in their interpretations of the meaning of Jesus's teachings. After enduring within the Roman Empire for several centuries, Christians would eventually find themselves in positions of power, from which they more clearly defined their beliefs.

The Roman Empire to 284 CE

Before Augustus's death in 14 CE, he designated his stepson Tiberius as his heir. The achievement of Augustus became magnified after his death by the vices, corruption, and incompetence of most of the first-century rulers who succeeded him. Rome retained its power and stability despite the inattentiveness of Tiberius (r. 14–37), the insanity of Caligula (r. 37–41), and the cruelty and pomposity of Nero (r. 54–68). Of Tiberius, the German historian Theodor Mommsen said that "women disliked him, and to rule Rome without the favor of women was impossible" (Mommsen 1996, 129). Hated because of his reputation for vices that scandalized even the generally uninhibited ancient Romans, Tiberius spent much of his time away from Rome in the villa that he constructed on a cliff high above the sea on the island of Capri. Still, he received reports from Rome and for the most part the business of politics proceeded as it had under Augustus. Consuls were elected annually, a process in which Tiberius sometimes took an interest and sometimes did not. He warned candidates against accepting bribes, probably to preserve the facade of legitimacy that the consular elections provided to the regime. The power behind the throne continued to be the Praetorian Guard, established by Augustus. Tiberius proved capable enough as an administrator, but he had no sense of vision and no ideals to motivate him. He contributed to the development of Roman bureaucracy; if government ran smoothly, the less he would have to worry about. He remained indifferent to the growth of slavery within his empire and we do not know if he was even aware of the crucifixion of Jesus. Roman power was at its height and Tiberius did just enough to keep the system of Augustus running smoothly.

In the first century, Rome remained first and foremost a military state. Foreign expansion was still regarded as necessary to provide revenue and to protect what Rome already had. But the strength and the justification for the Roman Empire was the Pax Romana, the "Roman Peace." Thus, peace and war shared an uneasy coexistence in first-century Rome; if the Romans had so much power they were eventually going to use it. Having already gained control of Spain and North Africa, Rome looked to the north and east for further opportunities for expansion. The emperor Claudius (r. 41–54 CE) established Roman rule as far north as Britain. The native inhabitants of Britain, even though they fought to protect their homes and family, were no match for the professional armies of Rome. In 101 CE, the emperor Trajan (r. 98–117) conquered the territory of Dacia (modern Romania), extracting an enormous amount of gold from local mines in the process. The Romans, provided with spectacular games and public festivals following such campaigns and a renewed economy by the money pumped into it from foreign wars, did not mind the violence and warfare that made them possible.

Still, the historian Tacitus, writing in the early second century, discerned in the Roman imperial history of the first century cause for concern about Rome's future. Augustus had claimed divine status for himself as emperor.

Tacitus records that the Temple of Augustus approved for the Spanish settlement of Tarraco became a precedent for every other province. But after the death of Augustus, Roman citizens and subjects would find it increasingly difficult to accept his successors as gods, starting with Tiberius (who did not even believe in his own divinity). In 41 CE, members of the Praetorian Guard killed Caligula, no longer willing to accept the indignities to which he subjected them, members of the court, and the Roman people (who went hungry when Caligula closed the public granaries). The army was responsible for the deaths of three more emperors by the end of the century, further damaging the prestige of the position. Hereditary succession became less important than the respect of the army or the Praetorian Guard. This led to the rise to power of people of humble origins, such as Vespasian (r. 69–79 CE), whose father was a provincial tax collector. The disparity between the divine pretensions of the emperors and the realities of their personalities and power, according to Tacitus, sapped the allegiance that Roman citizens felt toward their state.

Nero, however, is the emperor who has come to stand for all that was wrong and infamous about the Roman state in the first century. His mother, Agrippina, had schemed to bring her son to the throne by marrying the much-older emperor Claudius in 49 CE. To further solidify his claim to the throne, she had Nero marry his stepsister, Octavia, four years later. Educated by a renowned Stoic philosopher, Lucius Annaeus Seneca (5 BCE–65 CE), Nero took more of an interest in music, poetry, and philosophy than in politics. These interests at first allowed Agrippina to exercise power in her son's stead, but when Nero tired of his domineering mother, he scandalized Rome and the court by having her murdered. Meanwhile, Nero's neglect of the military and his indifference to politics demonstrated the weaknesses of the new imperial system and laid bare the demise of the Republic for all to see. The army took particular offense and longed for a stronger ruler who would provide it with the necessary support. One assassination plot failed in 65 CE; within three years support for Nero within the senate and army had so totally collapsed that he asked a servant to kill him to spare him from the wrath of his enemies. Galba (ca. 3 BCE–69 CE) led the rebellion at the head of the Gallic legions. The military had been forced to play a role in Roman politics, one that it would not easily relinquish. Nor did the precedent take long to repeat itself—Galba himself was overthrown and killed by the Praetorian Guard less than a year later.

Meanwhile, additional trouble had been brewing in Palestine. The Jews had never reconciled themselves to the divinity of the Roman emperors, and a political group known as the Zealots remained committed to the overthrow of Roman authority. The contemporary Jewish historian Josephus (b. ca. 37 CE) details the sufferings and insults that the Jews endured from a series of governors from Caligula to Nero. These included an incident during the

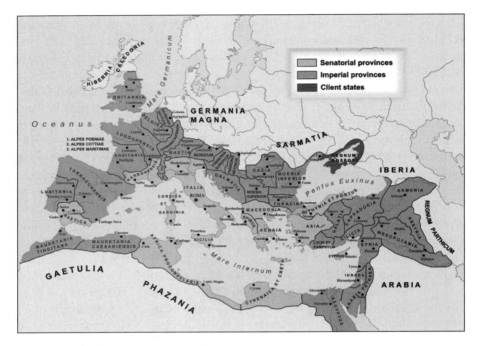

The Roman Empire at the death of Trajan, 117 CE

reign of Claudius in which a Roman solider exposed his derriere and farted in front of a crowd of Jews during the Feast of Unleavened Bread, provoking a disturbance that resulted in the deaths of 30,000 Jews. Finally, in 66 CE, the Zealots organized a full-scale revolt that swept through the Holy Land, leading Vespasian to intervene with 60,000 Roman troops. It took two years for the army to confine the rebels to Jerusalem and another two to crush the revolt, resulting in the establishment of direct Roman rule, the abolition of the Jewish priesthood, and the destruction of the Temple at Jerusalem; the last of the rebels committed suicide three years later at the mountain stronghold of Masada.

Rome demonstrated its power during the Jewish revolt and continued to do so in myriad ways. The establishment of direct Roman rule over Judea was only one example of a general tendency by which Rome appointed its own governors and judges and collected its own taxes throughout the provinces, no longer content to simply make alliances with local rulers. The Romans wanted order and found that direct control of the territories was the best way to ensure it. The letters written by Pliny the Younger (ca. 62–ca. 114 CE) as military tribune of Syria to the emperor Trajan illustrate the growing connection between Rome and the provinces. Trajan's concern for order is revealed by his response to Pliny's query about the growth in the number of Christians in the region. Trajan advised Pliny to persecute the Christians only if they became noticeably troublesome; otherwise he was to leave them alone.

The second century is considered something of a golden age in Roman history in comparison to those that preceded and followed it. Trajan used the income from his Dacian expedition to begin an impressive rebuilding program in Rome that included a new forum, library, and aqueduct, as well as a stone road through the Pontine Marshes of central Italy. His successor Hadrian (r. 117–138) spent most of his time away from Rome, solidifying the boundaries of the empire through the construction of wooden fences and watchtowers in Germany as well as the famous stone wall that bears his name in Britain. Hadrian's Wall, which extends for some seventy miles between the Solway Firth and the Tyne River in northern England, established a boundary designed to keep raiders from the north out of Roman territory. If today it strikes us as a tremendous achievement, at the time the wall represented a point of withdrawal from expansion further northward. The unpopular Hadrian received no great accolades in his lifetime for this achievement. Hadrian's successor, Antoninus Pius (r. 138–161) actually had another wall—the Antonine Wall—built only fifteen years after the completion of Hadrian's, perhaps because he needed to show his support for the army in the frontier regions. He ruled during a time of peace and prosperity for Rome, making him more popular than Hadrian, who devoted most of his time to his army away from Rome. Trajan, Hadrian, Pius Antoninus, Marcus Aurelius—each of these second-century emperors had his admirable qualities and compared favorably to his first-century predecessors. A series of peaceful successions contributed to a sense of political stability and restored respect for the imperial title. Grain continued to flow from Sicily and Egypt. But during the reign of Marcus Aurelius (r. 161–180), a philosopher-emperor who was the most respected of the lot, difficulties that disturbed the golden age began to appear in much of the empire. Marcus Aurelius was forced to fight a series of wars along the Danube River in order to defend the borders of the empire. Furthermore, a devastating plague reached Rome from the east, leading to a serious downswing in the population of the city and the empire.

By the early third century, the inability—or unwillingness—of Rome's emperors to deal with internal problems and external threats was starting to take its toll. Military revolts again became common, leading to an era of political instability and uncertainty. By the middle of the third century, the army began to conduct its own negotiations with invading tribes in order to protect the empire. The economy became depressed as both peace and prosperity waned.

Rome became caught on the horns of a dilemma. Even competent emperors had to make a decision whether to concentrate on strengthening Rome at the expense of the provinces or fortifying the provinces while neglecting the capital. Even strong emperors did not have the luxury of feeling safe on the throne, when any rival aspiring to imperial authority might claim it through murder or assassination. The Roman military was still strong during the time of Marcus Aurelius. Over the course of the next century, threats from Germanic tribes in the north, invaders from the east, and internal rebellion from within gradually ate away at both imperial authority and Roman military strength.

The Han Empire of China

In China, an empire of equally impressive strength and power arose contemporaneously with that of the Romans. The first emperor to establish centralized control over China was the Qin emperor (r. 221–210 BCE), a formidable military conqueror who imposed an oppressive autocracy over the previously feudalized country. The Qin emperor was responsible for the division of China into forty administrative districts or states, the standardization of weights and measures, and the establishment of a centralized legal system. Like the Romans, the Chinese under the Qin emperor undertook enormous building projects, including a new system of roads and canals. Like Hadrian, the emperor sought to erect a wall on his northern boundary (though the Great Wall of China visible today mainly dates from a much later period). The Qin emperor revolutionized Chinese warfare through the innovative use of iron weapons and cavalry (as opposed to chariots). But not all of the Qin emperor's initiatives were devoted to such practical ends. In 1974 farmers discovered the intended (but not actual) burial site of the Qin emperor, which contained an army of more than 7,000 life-size terracotta soldiers and officers, not to mention 4,000 horses, aligned as if to defend the Qin emperor even in death. The site is located roughly twenty miles east of the capital of the Qin emperor, the city of Chang'an (modern Xi'an). It took 700,000 workers and craftsmen thirty-six years to dig the pits that make up this underground compound, to burn in kilns the pieces of clay used for the construction of the soldiers (each of whom has individualized facial features), and to arrange the complex according to the principles of placement known as *feng shui*. The Roman emperors tended to be much more practical and to leave public works and monuments as their legacies; in a way, the planned mausoleum of the Qin emperor testifies to just how absolute his power was, even in comparison to the Romans.

The Qin emperor was extremely powerful, but not very popular. His unexpected death at the age of forty-nine resulted in immediate uprisings against Qin rule and its replacement with a new dynasty within three years. In some ways the founding of the Han Dynasty by Liu Bang (256–195 BCE), a government official from the northern state of Han, resembles the later rise of Augustus, with Caesar in the role of the Qin emperor—a dominant force during his lifetime capable of dealing ruthlessly with any opposing forces but whose very power caused resentment and dissatisfaction, leading to regime change. Liu Bang, who is also known by his posthumous name of Gaodi, established a stronger foundation for dynastic success by sharing his power with other gifted and able men, a tactic in some ways similar to the patronage system supported by Augustus. But in the case of both Gaodi and Augustus, the main legacy of their empire was peace. Both ended the threat of political instability and civil war. Furthermore, the Qin emperor had made imperial power the main principle on which political authority was based. Criticism by one court historian for violating ancient Chinese traditions resulted in the execution of 460 scholars by the Qin emperor, who allegedly had them buried alive, while ordering all books on such impractical subjects as history and philosophy to be burned. By contrast, Gaodi sought to foster traditional Chinese values, based on the thought of Confucius (551–479 BCE), who had advocated the practice of moral virtues by both rulers and subjects. The principles by which Confucius said one should live—such as *jen* or "human-heartedness" and *yi* or righteousness—became the basis for government appointments and the underlying rationale for the Han Dynasty, just as the ideal of civic virtue was used to sustain the Roman Republic and early Roman Empire.

The rule of the Han Dynasty thus represented a radical departure from the strict legalism of the Qin period that featured a rigid code of rewards and punishments. Confucius had seen government instead as part of a harmonious social order in which subjects obeyed the authorities and rulers practiced the principles of *jen* and *yi* out of respect for their subjects. The morality of the ruler is one of the clearest themes in the thought of Confucius, which can, at times, be quite confusing. This does not mean, however, that the Han Dynasty completely abandoned all the policies of the Qin emperor, any more than Augustus forgot what he had learned from Caesar. The military and administrative achievements of the Qin emperor remained intact, as Han rulers continued to defend their frontiers and expand their rule whenever possible. Liu Bang abandoned the harsher measures adopted by the Qin emperor in order to preserve, not to destroy, his empire. He retained those policies and aspects of Qin rule that contributed to the founding of the centralized state. Under the Han, day-to-day governmental administration was turned over to a professional civil service that began to maintain detailed written records. Recent excavations of Han tombs revealed wooden tablets containing population registries and property records of government officials. During the reign of the emperor Wudi (141–87 BCE) the Chinese state took control of the grain supply, just as the Roman authorities would. Wudi also turned his attention to a pressing problem that had plagued the government since the time of the

Qin emperor: the incessant raiding conducted by nomadic tribes on China's western and northern borders.

In addition, the expansionary efforts of Wudi, which led him to send armies into southwest China and northern Vietnam in the south and southern Manchuria and Korea in the north, mirrored the efforts of Roman emperors such as Claudius and Trajan to continue to expand Roman territory. Also like the Roman rulers from the time of Augustus, the successors of Gaodi gradually began to usurp the authority of client-kings in order to establish more direct imperial authority. Sometimes the Han rulers simply subdivided these provinces among the king's heirs, but wherever possible they began to appoint their own governors over them. The death of a king without heirs provided the best opportunity to do so, but, lacking such cooperation, accusing a king of crimes could bring the same result. Such efforts at expansion and political centralization had their theoretical basis in the ideas of Confucian thinkers such as Dong Zhongshu (179–104 BCE), who argued that the emperor was sent by heaven to preside over the people and make them good. By 129 BCE Wudi had consolidated power over the western regions of the empire and established a Chinese military presence in frontier regions that the emperors had never previously ruled.

Whereas Augustus, the founder of the Roman Empire claimed divine status, it took a while for the Han emperors to make such claims. But eventually they did. Wudi elevated imperial authority to cult status, calling for sacrifices to be made on its behalf. During his reign the concept of the Mandate of Heaven—which dated back to the Zhou dynasty (1100–256 BCE) and was consistent with Confucian principles—became firmly established as a justification for imperial rule. The emperor was designated as the Son of Heaven. Wudi attempted to live up to the Confucian ideal, which he believed justified his position and proved that he possessed the Mandate of Heaven. He enjoyed a long and successful rule. But Confucius had said to do what is morally right for its own sake, not because of a belief that it would bring external benefits. Whether Wudi understood this or not, his reign ended in the midst of scandal and factionalism at the court, followed by a period of imperial decline.

The Han dynasty lasted until 220 CE, but the signs of its demise were present long before the final end. The emperors became increasingly isolated from the people and paid little attention to living the Confucian ideal. Bitter internal rivalries within the imperial household among the children of imperial wives

For more on the Han dynasty and a slide show of artifacts from Han China, see www.metmuseum.org/toah/hd/hand/hd_hand.htm.

and concubines combined with the ambitious plotting of eunuchs at court to create an atmosphere of instability at the center of power. In the country a growing landlord class was acquiring more and more land at the expense of the peasantry. Perhaps most importantly, the Han never succeeded in pacifying their northern borders nor did they find a way of dealing with the nomadic raiders ready to capitalize on any sign of imperial weakness. The constant fighting took a toll on the government's treasury, leading to increased taxation. Heavy taxation took its toll on the economy, creating further instability and leading to more internal uprisings against the Han government. These were all problems from which the Romans might have learned if they had been more aware of China. For, at the time that the Han collapsed, the Roman Empire began a steady decline toward its own downfall.

Political and Economic Change and the Decline of the Roman Empire

The authority of the Roman emperors remained absolute through the political turmoil that characterized the third century. At the same time, however, both internal and external forces were at work undermining the stability of the empire. Internally, divisions among members of the senatorial class and the latent possibility that anyone who could obtain a military command might be elevated to the imperial title combined to sap Rome of any sense of either unity or political loyalty. Meanwhile, the population of the empire was declining, as was trade, while rampant inflation ravaged the economy. Emperors spent much of their time away from Rome, often in the field, defending the empire from external threats. The Roman Empire might have collapsed during this period, but two remarkable emperors at the end of the third century and the beginning of the fourth did their best to restore political and economic stability and revive the empire, at least temporarily.

Diocletian (r. 284–305) took on the troubles of the empire with a substantive reform program that included expanding the size of the government. He enlisted the support of first one and then three additional co-rulers so that he did not have to confront Rome's problems alone. He doubled the number of provinces by reducing them into smaller administrative units. In order to ensure that he had enough local officials to run the cities and provinces of the empire, he made their offices hereditary. Of course, this did not always work, but holding government office was becoming less and less attractive and he thought he had to do something. Diocletian personally retained power over the eastern portion of the empire, having ceded control over the west to his friend Maximian when he first decided to split the empire. The government of the empire by four co-rulers during the reign of Diocletian is known as the

Governmental Administration in the Empires
of Han China, and Rome

The charts below illustrate the similarities and differences between the administrative structures of the Han Empire and that of the Roman Empire in the fourth century.

What conclusions might be drawn about the two empires on the basis of this comparison?

Establishment of the Han Empire

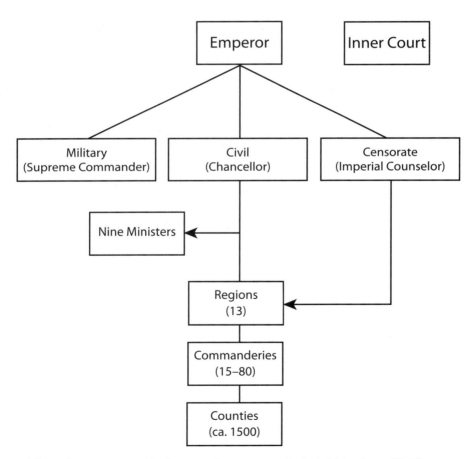

Additional concerns outside the central government included kingdoms 10–30, non-Chinese peoples, and merchants.

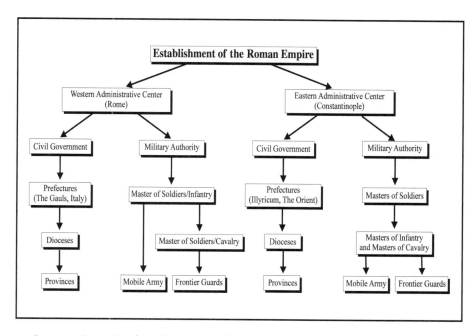

Sources: Grant Hardy and Anne Behnke Kinney, *The Establishment of the Han Dynasty and Imperial China* (Westport, CT: Greenwood Press, 2005), p. 32. Reprinted by permission of Greenwood Press; Chart on Roman government created by Joan Manzo, based on information from www.sjsu.edu/faculty/watkins/barbarians.

Tetrarchy. But Diocletian further organized the empire into at first twelve and then fifteen administrative units known as dioceses, creating another level of administration between the tetrarchs and provincial governments. This expansion of government had economic repercussions at a time when inflation was already making it difficult for tax collectors to meet their quotas. The standard Roman currency, the *denari*, had become substantially devalued against the price of gold by the time of Diocletian. The wealthy landowners horded what gold they had and became richer, while the poor sank even lower into poverty. While Diocletian wished to solve the economic problems of the empire, he did not want to do it at the expense of the money he needed to defend and administer the empire. He had to pay the salaries of his government officials, as well as that of the soldiers, who had gotten used to substantial increases in pay under previous emperors who depended on their support. Diocletian's solution was to assess taxes by region and to charge his provincial administrators with the responsibility of coming up with the required amounts of cash.

This system had the potential to ruin members of the tax-collecting curial class without solving the economic problems of the empire. So, to deal with an ever-worsening inflation, Diocletian issued an edict that essentially froze prices. But this only created a black market that drove prices up even further. The government accumulated a huge debt because the economy simply could not sustain the military and administrative needs of the empire, not to mention the expectation of the poor that it would continue to provide grain.

Why, then, did the great eighteenth-century historian Edward Gibbon believe that Diocletian deserved to be remembered as a new founder of the Roman Empire? For one, Diocletian did reform and strengthen the army, in addition to his administrative reforms. He more clearly differentiated between military and civilian authority, giving the military leaders leeway to control the areas where they were stationed along the frontier. He also revived the power of the emperor by ignoring the senate, which he could easily do since he was never in Rome. He brought an end to the civil wars of the third century. He weakened the power of the Praetorian Guard by reducing its numbers. His administrative reform, if not entirely successful, was a great improvement over the chaos and disintegration of the system he inherited. In order to ensure its effectiveness, Diocletian founded a secret service whose agents acted as internal spies on other government officials. He succeeded for a time in injecting a dose of confidence into the economy, leading to a revival of trade within the empire. Even his decision to instigate renewed persecution of Christians can be seen in the context of his attempt to revive traditional Roman values and the power of the state.

In 305 Diocletian, his health suffering, decided to abdicate his power, as did his co-ruler Maximian, leading to another brief period of instability. Into this breach stepped Constantine (ca. 274–337), the son of Constantius Chlorus (ca. 205–306), who ruled with the title of Caesar over Britain, Gaul, and Spain. In 305 Constantine was in Britain, having just been called there to assist his father. After his father was killed in battle in 306, his army proclaimed Constantine as the new Augustus, a title he sought to extend over the entire empire. He marched toward Rome—winning some significant victories over Germanic tribes along the way—to renew the civil wars and fight for power. The Roman people had acclaimed a rival, Maxentius, as the new Augustus of the West. At the Battle of the Milvian Bridge near Rome, Constantine defeated his rival, who drowned during the battle, and made a triumphal march into Rome itself.

Constantine ended the persecution of the Christians and was said to have converted to Christianity himself because of a vision promising victory in the name of the cross at the Milvian Bridge. He ordered the issue of a new gold coin in order to stop the devaluation of Roman currency and renew confidence in the economy. Seeking religious unity for his empire, he made Sunday a religious holiday and held a council at Nicaea to resolve theological differences among the Christians. He added to the administrative and military reforms of Diocletian. He went one step further than Diocletian by abolishing the Praetorian Guard altogether, an assertion of his independence and power. He founded a new capital in the east, which he named Constantinople. He became known as Constantine the Great; a colossal statue of his head at the Capitoline Museum in Rome provides a reminder of the large shadow that he cast over the empire during his reign. But he no more solved the long-term problems of the Roman Empire than had Diocletian.

At the beginning of the fourth century the Roman army was larger and probably stronger than it had ever been in its history—perhaps as many as 600,000 men. But it was also spread more thinly across the vast frontiers of the empire, which were increasingly attracting the attention of foreign tribes intent on migrating to or invading the empire. More to the point, the term *Roman army* was itself misleading by this time, since it was increasingly composed of foreigners. Furthermore, the balance of power was shifting away from Rome and Italy to Constantinople and the east, giving the empire something of its own identity crisis. Strong emperors could stem the tide of foreign invasions temporarily, but the peace and security of the empire now depended on vigorous military leadership and it was unlikely that every emperor could be a Diocletian or a Constantine. They had restored a sense of peace and order to the empire, but as soon as Constantine died, the old internal strife recurred. This could only encourage a renewed initiative on the part of Germanic armies on the northern border, themselves under increasing pressure from invaders from the east, including a particularly fierce group of Asiatic raiders that became known as the Huns. For the rest of the fourth century, ineffective leadership at the top exposed the military and economic weakness of an empire in decline.

Social and Religious Change and the Decline of the Roman Empire

Caracalla (188–217), the son of Septimius Severus (ca. 146–211), the reforming emperor and founder of a new dynasty, added to the reforms of his father one that turned out to be a turning point in the history of the empire. In 212 Caracalla proclaimed that henceforth all those residing within the boundaries of the empire would be considered Roman citizens. To many in Rome this cheapened the honor. But in that pivotal year this was not the worst of Caracalla's offenses. Appointed co-ruler with his brother, Geta, Caracalla bribed his Praetorian Guard to murder his brother and about 20,000 of his alleged supporters in order to secure the throne for himself. The dead included, in addition to his brother's friends, servants, and common soldiers, a number of senators and high-ranking provincial governors and military commanders. Besides being particularly brutal, Caracalla's attack on Rome's elite signaled another important shift in the vagaries of Roman politics. From this point forward senators knew they could not afford to risk the alienation of the emperor. Many prominent or wealthy citizens retreated to the countryside to live in peace rather than risk their lives in the increasingly powerless senate. In turn, emperors packed the senate with their own supporters. A general trend developed in which the Roman aristocracy withdrew from public life to be replaced by members of the equestrian class, whose families had originally made their money in business. With the withdrawal of the elite, educated class, urban life became less vibrant, leading to a decline in education and literacy.

Depopulation was another major social development contributing to the decline of the Roman Empire. From an estimated height between 70 million and 100 million people during the first half of the first century, the population of the Roman Empire may have sunk as low as 40 million by the early third century. This decline would help to explain Diocletian's measures to fix social classes by forcing sons to practice the same occupations as their fathers. The influx of barbarians from outside the empire contributed to a gradual increase in the population during the fourth century. But—as important as the overall decline in population was—the shifting of the balance of population from west to east in the fourth century was equally significant. Constantine's construction of the new capital of Constantinople in the east played the most important role here. The population of the new capital grew spectacularly—to perhaps as many as a million people by the sixth century—while Rome's population continued to decline. In addition to the impact of disease and plague, citizens in the western half of the empire may have chosen to have fewer children in what were uncertain economic times. Though economic problems were hardly new to Roman citizens, this combination of factors definitely led to a population drop that exacerbated some of Rome's other problems. With fewer citizens to man the Roman defensive armies, emperors turned increasingly to outside mercenaries from the very groups of people against whom they claimed to be defending the empire.

Another major factor often cited in the decline of Rome, most famously by Gibbon, was the impact of Christianity on Roman political values. During the third century a number of Roman emperors did make an effort to reinforce the traditional worship of the Roman gods. Their concern would seem to indicate that devotion to these gods had started to wane. The cult of the emperor had definitely been eroded, particularly during the time of the "barracks emperors" from 235 to 280 in which every emperor came from the military and most suffered violent overthrows at the hands of their successors. Diocletian took steps to remedy the erosion of Roman religious values, just as he attempted to address the other problems that he inherited. His harsh persecution of Christians, however, was only one dimension of his religious initiative to restore traditional Roman worship. For he strove to eliminate other religious beliefs, such as those of the Manicheans, who believed in a dualistic universe involving a struggle between the forces of good and the forces of evil, and persecuted anyone who refused to worship the Roman gods.

If Christians suffered more than anyone else under Diocletian, it was because there were more of them who refused to acknowledge the Roman deities. The new faith had attracted a substantial number of converts during the third century, a trend that did not go unnoticed in Rome. The spread of Christianity—as was also true for other Near Eastern religions such as the Egyptian cult of Isis, the Persian cult of Mithras, and the devotion to the great mother, Cybele, in Asia Minor—had been greatly assisted by the unity of the Roman Empire. Diocletian was not the only or the first emperor to persecute Christians, but during long stretches of time from the first century Christians had been free to worship and proselytize in peace. They began to form a more coherent church organization, based on a hierarchical system that mirrored that of Rome itself. Gibbon believed that this gave Christianity a great advantage over other sects, saying that by the time of Diocletian the Christians had formed "an independent and increasing state in the heart of the Roman empire" (Gibbon 2001, 123). The very prominence of the Christians would have provided Diocletian with even greater incentive to persecute them. Rome was used to tolerating all manner of religious and mysterious beliefs within the boundaries of its empire, but Christianity seemed to represent a new kind of threat that went beyond its adherents' refusal to bow to the altars of Zeus.

It was up to Constantine to demonstrate the compatibility between Christianity and the Roman political order. Although he did not officially convert to the Christian faith until he was on his deathbed, he, along with his co-ruler, Licinius, had issued an Edict of Toleration in 313 and generally favored the church during his reign. He may have waited so long to be baptized simply so that he would not die in a state of sin. He proclaimed the Christian Sabbath a weekly holy day, naming it Sunday—perhaps to appease those who were still pagan or perhaps partly out of his own sun worship, which he may have conflated with his new religion. Constantine sought to unify the faith by summoning more than 300 bishops to meet at a council at the city of Nicaea, where in 325 they agreed on a creed that summarized the orthodox doctrines of Christianity. Constantine's conversion and practice of toleration naturally smoothed the path for millions of new converts. The numbers of Christians in the empire expanded exponentially during the fourth century. Christians went from potential antagonists of the imperial regime to its greatest supporters. But when Rome fell less than 100 years later, there were still those who placed the blame upon the Christians.

The Fall of Rome

Several different dates have been suggested for the fall of the western half of the Roman Empire. Some historians view the Roman defeat at the hands of the Goths at the Battle of Hadrianoplis (modern Edirne) in 378 as a decisive turning point. But others observe that the system of administration set up by Constantine remained intact and that the emperor Theodosius I (r. 379–395) negotiated a peace settlement with the Goths in 382. The sack of Rome itself by the Visigoths in 410 was seen by the Romans as an event of great importance. But the Visigoths moved on from Rome, eventually settling in Spain, with imperial authority continuing in the West for two more generations. For many, 476 marks the traditional date of the fall of Rome, for in that year the sixteen-year-old Romulus Augustulus (r. 475–476), the last Roman emperor in the West, was deposed and imperial authority officially ended. But by then effective imperial authority had already collapsed. The deposition of the last emperor in the West in 476 seems more an act of recognition rather than a decisive, history-altering event. The great Belgian historian Henri Pirenne (1862–1935) even made the case that imperial authority continued in the West after this date, having simply passed on to barbarian rulers who at least formally recognized the legitimate power of the eastern emperors, and only disappeared as a result of the Muslim invasion of the seventh and eighth centuries.

The Battle of Hadrianoplis was part of an ongoing series of battles and agreements through which the Romans attempted to secure the northern borders of their empire. The border along the Danube River was seen as particularly vulnerable, both by the Goths and the Romans. In 363, Julian, the last surviving heir of Constantine, perished, and, after the brief reign of one of Julian's generals, power fell to a career army officer named Valentinian I, who took control of the West, and his younger brother, Valens, who was to rule in the East. Valentinian fought relentlessly against the Germanic tribe known as the Alemanni, concentrating his efforts in the region around the Upper Rhine River. He left Valens to deal with the Goths along the Lower Danube. Valens, overwhelmed by the sheer number of Goths seeking entry into the empire, agreed to their admission on the conditions that they lay down their arms, supply troops for the Roman army, and convert to Christianity. The deal proved to be a failure for both sides. The Goths rebelled against ill-treatment and perceived injustices at the hands of Roman officials, while Valens found the Goths undisciplined and the cause of unrest. Both sides prepared for battle. When the Goths succeeded in repulsing the unsupported Roman cavalry, the cavalry retreated, causing mass confusion among the infantry that ultimately resulted in a Gothic victory. Valens was killed in the Gothic onslaught; the battle, Gibbon said, was equally fatal to the Roman Empire.

Valens's successor, Theodosius, was a formidable military leader, however. (Valentinian had died earlier of a stroke suffered in the midst of heated negotiations with the Germans.) Theodosius attempted to solve the Gothic crisis by allowing the Goths to remain in the empire as Roman allies. As long as Theodosius remained in power, he had the respect of the Goths. After his death, however, the Goths began to migrate westward toward Italy under the leadership of their king, Alaric (ca. 370–410). By 402 both the emperor and the senate had abandoned Rome for the more securely defended location of Ravenna on Italy's east coast. Alaric had converted to Christianity, but the Arian version of it that Roman Christians regarded as heretical. At this point it seemed as if the eastern emperors had completely forsaken Italy and left its fate in the hands of the barbarians. That the Goths were actually highly Romanized, not to mention Christian, was lost on the population at the time. Even though the Goths had been living in the empire for quite some time and had already defeated a Roman army in battle, the sack of Rome in 410 still came as a shock to the Romans.

In the aftermath of the sack of Rome in 410, Augustine of Hippo (354–430), one of the leading thinkers of the early Christian church, wrote a lengthy defense against the charges that Christianity had been responsible for the fall of Rome. In *The City of God*, Augustine offered nothing less than a comprehensive Christian philosophy of history and a historical framework for understanding the disaster that had just befallen the eternal city. For to Augustine, only the city of God, the heavenly city, was truly eternal and not subject to the calamities and vicissitudes experienced by the earthly city, of which Rome was an example. Using numerous historical examples, Augustine argued that Rome had in fact endured many disasters in its long history, thus proving that the Roman gods had not kept it immune from trouble prior to the adoption of the Christian faith; he maintained that the only sure hope for people was to assign their trust not to the things of this world but to look to heaven and, on earth, the church for their salvation.

Even though the sack of Rome in 410 did not physically or officially mark the fall of Rome, it did so psychologically. It was the final blow, the ultimate indignity, capping a long period of gradual decline and an increasing number of disasters. Furthermore, it was at this point that the Romans abandoned Britain and weakened their defenses in Gaul, Spain, and North Africa. They could no longer justify maintaining these outposts of empire when they were incapable of defending their own capital city. Subsequent emperors made some attempt to reestablish their control over the western provinces. But a Germanic tribe called the Vandals, having swept through Gaul and Spain while Rome was preoccupied with the Gothic threat, capitalized on Roman weakness by conquering North Africa from 429 to 439. By midcentury a new threat confronted Rome at its doorstep in the powerful figure of Attila the Hun (ca. 406–453) and his forces. In 451, negotiations with Attila, known as the "Scourge of God," were conducted by the bishop of Rome, not the emperor. That same year, the Roman general Aetius defeated Attila in Gaul at the Battle of the Catalaunian Fields, only to be treacherously murdered by a weak emperor jealous of his success. For the next twenty-five years, the power of the western emperors was restricted to Italy; even there they increasingly shared power with Germanic military leaders.

One such leader, Odoacer (d. 493), became king of Italy in September 476, the year in which Romulus Augustus abdicated power and imperial authority in the west halted. Odoacer did not have the support of the eastern emperor and was later overthrown by the king of the east Goths (Ostrogoths), Theodoric (d. 526), who invaded Italy in 489. At this point the people of Italy had not felt secure for almost a century. After the sack of Rome in 410, they no longer could depend upon imperial protection. Italy became as much a potential battleground as the borders of the empire had been for centuries. Cities became depopulated as people retreated to the more inaccessible villages of the mountains. The eastern empire, meanwhile, survived and even flourished to some degree, even though it was not without threats to its own borders.

The Continuation of the Eastern Empire

At the beginning of the fifth century there was no assurance that the eastern half of the empire would long survive its western counterpart. The eastern empire was subject to the same external pressures from the northern Germanic tribes and had to contend with the powerful Sassanian dynasty in Persia as well. The ill-defined system of succession might have thrown up equally incompetent or ineffective rulers as it would in the west. Eastern emperors had to contend with a variety of peoples within their half of the empire, where social divisions and religious disputes threatened to disrupt the unity and stability of the state. But the eastern empire did possess some advantages that the west did not. Most regions within the eastern empire generally had not suffered a decline in population as the west had. The eastern empire as a whole retained a sizable—and even growing—population capable of supporting the continued maintenance of the administration and military defense of the empire. Trade and urban life remained strong, making the empire more culturally vibrant and further increasing its overall wealth and financial resources. Its capital city, Constantinople, was less susceptible to invasion than

Rome, which was extremely vulnerable once invading armies had crossed the Danube or the Alps. For example, though the Huns threatened the eastern empire and did considerable damage in the Balkans, their leader, Attila, in the end decided to move west toward Rome instead. Meanwhile, other borders remained stable and Constantinople enjoyed uninterrupted trade with Asia Minor, Egypt, and Syria.

Perhaps the most important reason for the continuation of the eastern empire, however, was that by the time the Visigoths attacked Rome the eastern empire had already started to function as a completely separate administrative and political state. Rulers and administrators in the east conducted their business in a different language (Greek) than the west (Latin), and they made their decisions and enacted their laws without the approval or advice of the western emperors. Their destiny was their own, completely insulated from the problems and troubles experienced by Rome.

When Constantine founded Constantinople he had intended it to serve as a capital city with all the layers of administration and bureaucracy associated with that goal. The administrative reforms of Diocletian and Constantine had put in place an effective system of administration and tax collection that served the east, even if it proved incapable of preventing the collapse of the west. This system received further refinement in the *Codex Theodosianus* (Theodosian Code) during the reign of Theodosius II (r. 408–450). Despite its numerous contradictions—the result of an attempt to balance the prerogatives of imperial rule with the need for bureaucratic guidelines and the desire to promote justice—the Theodosian Code represented an attempt to preserve the Roman system of governance while adjusting to the political realities of the fifth century. Theodosius was not an especially strong or competent ruler, but the length of his reign added stability. In addition, he had the positive influence of competent advisers, the chief of which was his older sister, Pulcheria, who was a virtual co-ruler during his reign. Most importantly, the imperial system of government was preserved and even strengthened. Constantinople now possessed a competent, professional bureaucracy that excelled at the day-to-day administration of the empire. Furthermore, in contrast to the situation that would develop in the west, the emperors had begun to be seen by their subjects as the personal embodiment of both church and state.

The eastern emperors thus took on the role of the defenders of the orthodox Christian faith. There was no distinction between western, or Roman, Christianity and eastern Christianity at the beginning of the fifth century. The idea of one empire and one orthodox faith persisted into the fifth century and beyond. But cracks in the concept of religious unity did begin to appear then. The fifth-century emperors did not directly challenge the authority of the pope in Rome, but they began to govern their own church independently, ignoring him much as they ignored the last western emperors. In a way, they had to develop their own position on Christian orthodoxy because so many different forms of Christianity had started to bounce around the east. In 421, when word spread that a new Persian ruler named Bahram V (r. 421–438) had started to persecute Christians, Constantinople came to the rescue. The Persians had apparently become concerned about the rapid spread of Christianity in their empire. This issue led to a brief war between the two powers in 421–422, a violent interlude during a period of relatively peaceful relations. The war was fought to a stalemate, despite the relative weakness of the empire's position in Mesopotamia. Both sides simply agreed not to deal with each other's Arab allies. The war did, however, have the effect of separating the Persian church from that of the empire. This was a rare limitation accepted by the eastern emperors, who became increasingly determined to enforce orthodoxy throughout the vast lands that they controlled.

The concept of the fall of Rome in the fifth century, then, did not apply to the entire Roman Empire. In fact, one historian has suggested that the fall of Rome should be dated to the early fourth century and the decision of Constantine to move the capital of the empire to the Greek city of Byzantium (Ermatinger 2004). Constantine had shifted the focal point of the empire and made it possible to conceive of an eastern empire as a separately administered political entity. After the death of Theodosius I in 395, no emperor ruled over both the east and the west. Yet those in the east still thought of their empire as Roman, even though rulers and subjects communicated in Greek. The scholars who compiled the Theodosian Code had systematized laws since the reign of Constantine from both halves of the empire. Nor had the dream of one day reuniting both halves of the empire entirely disappeared. But in the chaos of the fifth century, the eastern emperors decided to defer such an enterprise to a later date.

Conclusion

The concept of the decline and fall of the Roman Empire needs to be modified in several ways. First, the eastern half of the empire lived on for another 1,000 years after the collapse of the western half. Those emperors still considered themselves the heirs of Rome and for at least several hundred years believed that their authority extended to the west—in theory, if not in practice. Second, barbarian rulers in the west frequently attempted to preserve Roman authority and civilization rather than destroy it. They stepped into a power vacuum that they attempted to fill; the barbarian invasions were as much a symptom as a cause of the decline of Rome. Finally, some historians have questioned the whole concept of the decline and fall of Rome, a theme most famously and eloquently explored by Edward Gibbon in the eighteenth century. They argue that from the perspective of social history, for example, life in the western Mediterranean region had a continuity that transcended the political events that primarily occupied Gibbon's attention. The story of the decline and fall has also tended to be told from a Roman-centered perspective; Gibbon treated it as a great calamity that brought down a superior civilization at the hands of Christians and barbarians. This perspective is now considered by most historians to be out-of-date and inaccurate.

The above qualifications, however, do not necessitate abandoning the whole concept. A case could be made, for example, that the *Roman* Empire did collapse in the fifth century, to be replace in the east by a *Greek* Empire, even if it was not called that at the time (Millar 2006). Judged from the perspective of the transition from the fourth to the fifth century, many contemporaries, especially those from the lower classes, would not perhaps have noticed a sudden break in their history or life experience. But when examined from the perspective of the broad sweep of Western civilization, the decline and fall of the Roman Empire cannot be ignored or simply explained away: a decline did occur, at least in the west—in population, in the economy, in technological craftsmanship and the quality of goods, in the ability of the Roman Empire to defend its borders without resorting to the assistance of those whom they regarded as barbarians, and in the empire's ability to successfully assimilate the newer populations entering Roman-held territory.

This does not mean that Roman culture, language, ideas, institutions, or social practices, to name a few legacies, disappeared. Roman soldiers who retired to the provinces where they had been stationed brought their ways and customs to the far reaches of the empire. The Romans left a system of roads and forts and cities and settlements, many of which survived or were later revived by those who followed. The very idea of the Roman Empire did not disappear in the west; Roman law later became a basis for most European countries. Most significantly, however, the Romans left Christianity as a religious legacy that played a major role in the shaping of medieval Europe.

1. Does Augustus deserve to be considered the founder of the Roman Empire? Why or why not?
2. In what ways is the context of Hellenistic Judaism useful for an understanding of the life and teachings of Jesus?
3. What parallels might be drawn between the history of the Han Empire of China and that of the Roman Empire? What were some key differences?
4. What caused the decline and fall of the Roman Empire? When did Rome fall? Why have some historians challenged this historical concept?
5. What factors account for the continuation of the eastern Roman Empire after the collapse of imperial authority in the west?

Suggestions for Further Reading

Augustine. 2008. *Confessions.* Translated by Garry Wills. New York: Penguin.

Ermatinger, James W. 2004. *The Decline and Fall of the Roman Empire.* Westport, CT: Greenwood Press.

Gibbon, Edward. 2001. *The Decline and Fall of the Roman Empire.* Edited by David Womersley. New York: Penguin.

Lewis, Mark Edward. 2007. *The Early Chinese Empires: Qin and Han.* Cambridge, MA: Belknap Press of Harvard University Press.

Millar, Fergus. 2006. *A Greek Roman Empire: Power and Belief under Theodosius II (408–450).* Berkeley: University of California Press.

Mommsen, Theodor. 1996. *A History of Rome Under the Emperors.* London and New York: Routledge.

White, L. Michael. 2004. *From Jesus to Christianity: How Four Generations of Visionaries and Storytellers Created the New Testament and the Christian Faith.* New York: HarperCollins.

Suggested Websites

www.fordham.edu/halsall/ancient/asbook.html

This website contains a wide range of primary sources dealing with both Roman history and the rise of Christianity.

www.ibiblio.org/expo/deadsea.scrolls.exhibit/intro.html

The Library of Congress put together this informative and interesting website in conjunction with its exhibit on the Dead Sea Scrolls.

www.pbs.org/empires/romans

This companion website to a popular PBS series on empires contains some interesting features, such as a family tree, an emperor game, and a virtual library, as well as interesting information about daily life and other topics related to the Roman Empire.

www.roman-empire.net

This attractive website has many features, including interactive maps, timelines, lists, and narrative chapters on different topics and periods related to the history of the Roman Empire.

www.unrv.com

This website's newsletter contains up-to-date book reviews on recent publications on Roman history, as well as information on various topics and links to related sites of interest.

5 Early Christian Europe, Byzantium, and the Rise of Islam, ca. 410–750

The fall of Rome in the fifth century created a vacuum in political leadership in what had been the western half of the Roman Empire. Strong military leaders of the various tribes that had already infiltrated the empire stepped into that vacuum. The development of kingship among groups known as the Franks, Burgundians, Goths, and Saxons prepared the way for the creation of new political entities in the region soon to be known as Europe. This process began soon after the sack of Rome by Attila the Hun in 451. Germanic kings began to claim that they were the heirs of the authority of the Roman emperors.

Meanwhile, emperors in the eastern half of the Roman Empire—later known as the Byzantine Empire—retained the imperial system of government and ruled over both state and church within their realm. As of the sixth century, Byzantine rulers had not yet even relinquished their claims to the west. The emperor Justinian spent much of his reign and energies attempting to conquer lost territories in Italy, Spain, and North Africa in order to reunify both halves of the Roman Empire. The bishops of Rome, however, refused to subordinate themselves to these emperors in matters of religion. Eastern Christianity gradually diverged from western Christianity from the fifth to the ninth centuries, not only in leadership but also in particular characteristics of the faith. In both east and west, disputes arose about Christian doctrine and practice that led to the further definition and clarification of official Christian beliefs.

In the early seventh century an Arab merchant who experienced mystical visions felt compelled to share his spiritual experiences with the rest of the divided and polytheistic population of Arabia. In 610 this merchant experienced his "night of fire" when he received a vision of the angel Gabriel telling him to spread the word of the one God, Allah. Muhammad had no formal religious training, though he had encountered Jews and Christians in his travels and apparently developed an interest in their beliefs. In 620 he visited Jerusalem's Wailing Wall where, according to tradition, he ascended into heaven and descended into hell. A shaping moment for Muhammad, the Arabs, and world history occurred in 622 when the commercial city of Medina invited Muham-

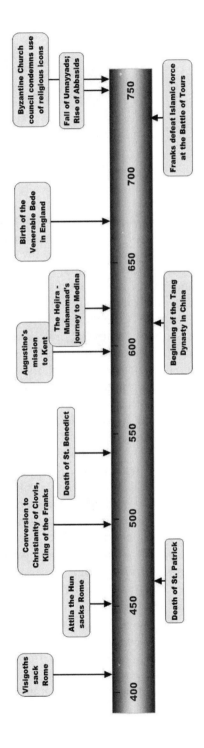

mad to take over the political and religious leadership of the city. Muhammad now occupied a position of power, which he used to eliminate his enemies and potential challengers to his beliefs. The political life of the city became subordinate to the larger goal of establishing Muhammad's religion, now clearly seen as distinct from both Judaism and Christianity. Muhammad forged a new faith out of his ideas and experiences that would provide purpose, meaning, and spiritual guidance for its many followers. Followers were called to submit to the will of Allah; the term *islam* means "submission." Muhammad called for moral reform, but did not impose impossible standards on the faithful. He clearly met a need in the Arab people, who had largely united behind Muhammad by the time of his death in 632. The Arabs expanded throughout the Mediterranean region, conquering most of North Africa and Spain, as well as other parts of the Byzantine Empire within the next 100 years. The Muslim Arabs did not forcefully impose their religion on the people they conquered, but they provided incentives to convert and found many people open to their new spiritual message after years of enforced orthodoxy from Constantinople. In doing so they helped shape the history of the early medieval period and the future course of the history of the West and the world, following on the heels of the spectacular successes of Christianity in the previous few centuries.

The Spread of Christianity

Initially, the most important factor in the spread of Christianity throughout Europe was the conversion of the Roman emperor, Constantine, in 312 and the subsequent legalization of the religion throughout the Roman Empire. Then, after the sack of Rome in 410 and the subsequent collapse of the western empire, many people turned to Christianity for solace in a world that seemed to be falling apart (though some blamed Christianity for Rome's demise). Pope Leo I tried to dissuade Attila the Hun from sacking Rome in 451 in an attempt to provide political leadership in the absence of the emperor, who had retreated to Ravenna for his own personal safety. The exercise of such political authority by the bishops of Rome fostered a tendency for people to look to the Christian church for leadership, comfort, and protection. But the bishops still needed political allies among the rising Germanic kingdoms in order to secure the future of the orthodox Christian church in the west. In 496 Clovis, the king of the Franks, converted to Roman Christianity, largely under the influence of his Christian wife, Clotilda.

At the time of Clovis's conversion, he was the only orthodox ruler in what had been the western half of the Roman Empire. The Vandals who established their kingdom in North Africa and the Visigoths in Spain both had converted to Arian Christianity, which denied the Roman doctrine of the Trinity. But the conversion of Clovis taught future Roman missionaries an important lesson. They recognized that large-scale conversions could best be achieved by converting the kings or political leaders, who were frequently seen by their people as the mediators between them and the gods. When a missionary named Augustine (not to be confused with Augustine of Hippo, the fifth-century author of *The City of God*) arrived in England in 597, he achieved remarkable results through the conversion of Ethelbert, the king of Kent in southern England. It helped, once again, that Ethelbert's Frankish wife, Bertha, was already a Christian. Augustine's mission occurred because the church recognized that much of Europe remained under the influence of paganism and had not yet embraced Christianity. Within a century of Augustine's arrival, most of the native kings and aristocrats of England had come to accept Roman Christianity. The church was instrumental in the development of written law codes there, most of which placed a high priority on protecting church leaders and church property. The church continued to rely on kings for support and protection, while kings began to realize that the church could influence people's behavior and curb the violence that was endemic to society at that time.

The religious situation in the British Isles was complicated by the fact that Irish Christianity had developed independently of Roman Christianity and evolved its own set of traditions. One of the first important missionaries to spread Christianity to Ireland was Patrick (ca. 385–461), a man of Romano-British descent who is credited with almost single-handedly converting the Irish people to the faith. Many of the areas where he preached had never heard of Christianity before. Not content to achieve temporary, surface conversions, Patrick instructed people in the faith and left ordained priests behind to make sure they remained steadfast. He set an example for future Irish Christians who followed his example of missionary zeal and commitment to a monastic calling. For example, St. Columba (ca. 521–597) established monasteries at Derry, Durrow, and, in 565, at Iona. St. Columbanus (ca. 540–615) went even farther afield, establishing a number of monasteries in Burgundy before founding the northern Italian monastery in Bobbio in the heart of Lombard territory.

In order for Christianity to appeal to the Germanic and Celtic masses, its message had to be tailored to their particular sensibilities. The common people accepted Christianity through a process that fundamentally altered the nature of the religion. Christian missionaries had to offer proof of the power of their God over native gods, leading them to emphasize the miracles of Christ and the saints who followed in his footsteps. Rather than explaining complex theological ideas, missionaries stressed the human experience of Christ and the story of the Passion, a dramatic episode that people could understand and to which they could relate as human beings. The church also had to offer people positive benefits in dealing with the uncertainty and problems of this life as opposed to solely offering hope for salvation in the next. The efficacy of prayer, miracles, and Christian signs and symbols were promoted as aids against illness, crop failure, property loss, or other earthly dangers. The flexibility of Christian missionaries was as important a factor as their determination in the successes that they achieved throughout Europe. Throughout these early centuries, Roman Catholic and Irish monks served not only as missionaries but also as living models of their ideal version of the Christian life.

Eastern Versus Western Monasticism

While Christianity rose, evolved, and established itself in the West and Islam emerged in the Near East, religion played a dominant role in the Asian civilizations of India and China as well. The Indian religion of Buddhism contributed immensely to the shaping of Chinese history during this period. In the troubled political and economic times after the collapse of the Han dynasty in the third century, Chinese peasants became attracted to Buddhism and Daoism in their search for a new source of stability and consolation.

Unlike Christianity, Buddhism did not stress the existence of an external God, but rather the divinity within each person that only had to be accessed through a spiritual approach. Prince Siddhartha (ca. 563–483 BCE), subsequently known as Buddha, was not interested in setting up an established religious orthodoxy, much less becoming a religious authority for others to obey and imitate. Buddha believed in the illusory nature of what we perceive as reality, even of the human personality. He believed that we could attain happiness by restraining our desires and our ego in order to attain a state of perfect detachment, peace, and harmony, which he called *nibbana* or nirvana. Buddha believed that people had to find their own path to enlightenment and that he was merely a guide to help them along their way. Nonetheless, Buddha's teachings were written down at a later date and preserved in both the Sanskrit and Pali languages in a collection of sacred works. Once the Buddhist scriptures began to appear, they were regarded as important aids for Buddhists and contributed to the further development of the religion in northeastern India.

Buddhism began to achieve enormous popularity in China during the period between the fall of the Han and the rise of the Sui dynasties (220–581 CE). It is surely no coincidence that the rise of Buddhism in China occurred at a time of political decentralization, partly because no central authority controlled the Silk Road by which Buddhist travelers entered China and partly because Buddhism served a need in those troubled times; the mystical religion of Daoism experienced a revival at the same time. Just as Christianity had seemed to violate all the principles on which the Roman Empire was built, particularly the emphasis on civic virtue and service to the state as the highest ideal, Buddhism seemed to contradict many basic Chinese values, mainly devotion to one's family and obedience to political authority. In both the Roman and Chinese empires, the appeal of Christianity and Buddhism, respectively, was enhanced in unstable political times as people sought for a new sense of meaning in their lives.

Buddhism offered its votaries an opportunity to escape the karmic wheel of birth, death, and rebirth and to avoid future suffering through the achievement of salvation in the form of the imprecisely defined state of nirvana. The practice of meditation or yoga helped to change one's normal pattern of thinking and to achieve a state of mind that approached the true joy offered by nirvana. Buddha himself did not live as a monk and did not advocate total separation from the world, but he did stress the importance of prayer and meditation as the means necessary for cultivating the "right-mindedness" necessary for enlightenment. Many Buddhists did become monks, however, in order to devote more time to liberating themselves from the limited perspective of their own personality and the time and place in which they were born. Different Chinese sects of Buddhism began to emerge by the fourth century; the more traditional sect was known as Theravada Buddhism (from a Sanskrit word meaning "doctrine of the elders"), which held that only the few could achieve enlightenment by becoming monks or nuns who removed themselves from the temptations of society. The rival sect, the Mahayana Buddhists, believed that Buddha had not revealed the complete truth because at the time his followers were not yet ready to receive it, thus justifying their continuing expansion of Buddhist teachings and scriptures. An offshoot of Mahayana Buddhism gained the largest following in China—this was known as Chan Buddhism (called Zen Buddhism by the Japanese). Chan Buddhism in China stressed the importance of communal living, leading to a proliferation of Chan monasteries for men and women. Followers of this sect believed that meditation could be practiced even during routine daily tasks, such as cleaning, preparation of meals, and working in the garden. Chan monasteries were gradually integrated into Chinese society, becoming peculiarly Chinese institutions and influencing the future development of Buddhism in China.

From early in the history of Christianity, some individuals had decided that the best way to live in accordance with their faith and religious beliefs was to withdraw from human society. They believed that a life of isolation away from society would allow them to avoid worldly temptations and concentrate on their spirituality and relationship with God. While some early monks, such as St. Anthony (251–356), fled society in order to live alone, others, such as St. Pachomius (ca. 292–346), formed communities of monks committed to the same ideals. Early monastic leaders claimed to follow Christ's injunctions more closely than other Christians by leaving their families, giving up property, and rejecting the world for the sake of their faith.

For a time in the early church, monasteries operated independently of any official clerical control or supervision. But by the fifth century, when church organization had become more solidified, the church granted bishops jurisdiction over monasteries within their dioceses. From that point forward, all monasteries associated with the Roman church fell under the control of an abbot who answered to the nearest bishop. These monastic communities tended to follow sets of guidelines or rules that governed the life and activities of their members. In time, one set of rules came to predominate in the West—that attributed to Benedict of Nursia (ca. 490–ca. 540), the leader of an Italian monastery at Monte Cassino.

A different type of Christian monasticism evolved in Ireland, where the church was in fact dominated by this movement to a much greater extent than the Roman Church. Celtic monks tended to live in isolated huts that formed part of a village community rather than in a room in a single dormitory; archaeology in Ireland has revealed monasteries with a number of varied buildings designated for specific purposes, such as those serving as kitchens, schools, workshops, and infirmaries, which, along with the residences of the monks, were surrounded by a ditch and earthen rampart.

The history of monasticism in Daoism—an intensely personal faith that advocates living in harmony with nature—bears some strong similarities to Christian monastic development in the West. Both arose first from the impulse of individuals to retreat from society; the word *monasticism* derives from the Greek word *monos*, which meant "single" or "alone." In the medieval period both developed communal forms of living, featuring commitment to a daily ritual, celibacy, and subordination of the individual to the group; in Daoism a transitional stage came in the form of semimonastic households known as "abodes," where one or several monks occupied a household that could be supervised by a founding ruler or aristocrat. The major figure in the history of Daoist monasticism was Kou Qianzhi (365–448), who set the pattern for celibate living according to a set rule within a communal environment. As in Christianity, one rule became predominant in Daoism—the *Fengdao kejie*, which differed from the other prominent Daoist rule (*Yinyuan jing*) in its emphasis on more specific and practical guidelines for living, ceremonies, and rituals. Perhaps a structured practical rule has a greater appeal for most

Compare the websites of a contemporary Buddhist monastery and a modern Benedictine monastery by visiting http://sakya.org and www.benedictine.org.au/index.html.

Buddhist and Christian Religious Imagery

The first image showing Buddha teaching is from a mural at the Sera Buddhist Monastery in Lhasa, Tibet. The second image is of St. Benedict, the founder of the most famous rule in Western monasticism, currently located at the Heiligenkreuz Abbey near Baden bei Wien in Austria. Benedict's rule called for a strictly regimented day that was nonetheless designed to be not too harsh or taxing on the physical well-being of the monks. Specific times of the day were assigned for manual labor, communal worship, private prayer and devotion, eating, and sleeping.

What do these images suggest about the differences or similarities in the monastic vision in East and West? What does the Buddhist image reveal about the religion and the role of monasticism within it? What kind of symbolism is used in this representation of St. Benedict and what is it meant to convey about him?

Buddha teaching *(Photograph by Wonderlane/Flickr)*

Herman Nieg, *St. Benedict,* **1926** *(Photo by Georges Jansoone)*

people inclined toward monastic life; in this regard, the difference between the *Fengdao kejie* and the more philosophical and theoretical *Yinyuan jing* might parallel the triumph of the Benedictine rule over that authored by Augustine of Hippo in early medieval Europe. But both Daoist rules emphasized the importance of Daoist teachings on karma and retribution, just as both Christian rules shared the same theological framework of Christian salvation. The universal claims of the Christian monks for their faith differed, however, from the views of the Daoist monks, who did not reject Buddhist teachings and practices and borrowed much from them. Daoist and Buddhist monasticism both grew during the Tang dynasty (618–907), the same period that saw the spread of Benedictine monasticism in the West.

History thus suggests that monasticism arises from similar impulses and takes similar forms in different religions. Yet monasticism becomes an integral part of societies that share—at least to some degree—its values. Shan-tao (613–681), who entered a Buddhist monastery at a very young age, played an instrumental role in adapting Buddhist ideology to Chinese traditions. In particular, he attempted to reconcile Buddhism with the Chinese emphasis on filial obedience, which could have been problematic given the individualistic focus of Buddhist piety and the fact that the Buddha himself had abandoned his household to seek spiritual enlightenment. Chinese authorities had previously persecuted Buddhists because of their lack of respect for familial authorities, just as Roman authorities had persecuted Christians because of their lack of respect for Roman gods and political authorities. In changing the emphasis in Buddhism, Shan-tao drew on certain traditions within Buddhism itself rather than on a study of Confucianism. In doing so, he contributed to the wider acceptance of Buddhism in China during the seventh century. In order to make Buddhism more acceptable in China, some Buddhists had claimed Chinese origins for the religion, maintaining that Buddha had actually learned from the Chinese philosopher, Laozi, the legendary author of the first Daoist text, the *Tao Te Ching*. Only in the seventh and eighth centuries did Chan Buddhism gain greater acceptance among the Chinese; the Chan leader Huineng (638–713), whose ideas more closely resembled Daoism, emerged as the founder of the important southern school of Chan Buddhism.

Monasteries played an important role in Christian life throughout Europe in the early Middle Ages. Once they became part of the institutionalized church, they served as powerful bastions of Christian orthodoxy, even though most monks were not ordained as priests. Many monks became missionaries who helped to propagate the faith in regions still dominated by paganism. The missionary Augustine brought the Benedictine rule to England at the end of the sixth century under the auspices of Pope Gregory I. In turn, English Benedictine missionaries spread the rule to France in the eighth century. Similarly,

Buddhist and Daoist monasteries contributed to the visibility and spread of their faith and ideas in China. Buddhist monks—as did the early Benedictine missionaries—traveled and established links with different communities in order to spread the teachings of their spiritual leader. Part of the monastic ideal in both religions was that monks should not get too attached to people, places, or things in this world. Celibacy became a prominent requirement of both Buddhist and Christian monks in order to facilitate an attitude of detachment from the world and a single-minded devotion to the faith. The early medieval period represented the height of this ideal in both Western and Chinese culture. In fact, Buddhist monasticism more closely resembles Irish than Benedictine monasticism in the central role that it played in the religion as a whole. The power of the ideals of both Eastern and Western monasticism is in their ability to transcend their historical time and place. But in each instance political circumstances contributed to the appeal of a life of withdrawal and spiritual commitment.

Political Decentralization After the Fall of the Roman Empire

Benedictine monasticism was just one of the responses to the collapse of the western half of the Roman Empire. In addition to the gradual spread and triumph of Roman Christianity in the west, new kingdoms emerged that were associated with the leaders of diverse, multiethnic groups that had invaded and settled in different parts of the Roman Empire. But the immediate aftermath of the fall of the western empire witnessed a period of decentralization that threatened to fragment western society irrevocably. Prior to the collapse of Roman authority in the west, different groups of people had attached themselves to military leaders and entered the empire, in some cases settling peacefully and reinvigorating the regions in which they settled, in other cases raiding and pillaging and hastening the downfall of political authority. At first, Roman landowners formed their own armies to protect their interests and their estates. Then warrior-kings from beyond the Alps began to assume positions of authority over larger areas as the geographical boundaries of the empire in the west receded back toward Rome. Once Roman authorities ceased to provide a sufficient degree of military protection and political order, others inevitably stepped into the vacuum and began to assert control over smaller portions of the empire. This process of political decentralization created a survival-of-the-fittest scenario in which weak authorities looked to those with stronger military forces to provide protection and stability. These military leaders and their followers—under names that they chose but that have continued to give historians a false impression of their ethnic or national unity—shifted locations during the fifth century according to the changing political circumstances in the west. For example, the Burgundians settled in Savoy and the Rhone River valley around the middle of the fifth century as allies of the Romans. The Vandals, who were far more destructive than the Burgundians, migrated to Gaul and then Spain before establishing themselves in Roman lands in North Africa. The Visigoths settled in southern Gaul and Spain, while the Ostrogoths moved into Italy, where they eventually supplanted Roman authority.

In the fifth century, Germanic chieftains did not have much established authority over a set territory or a very sophisticated system of government. This left them free to pick up and move, along with their closest followers, to greener pastures. Groups of people could migrate easily because they were used to producing their own goods without relying on established patterns of trade or contacts with others. But the common people did not necessarily follow their chieftains. They frequently intermarried with members of other groups and shifted their allegiance to other chieftains. This pattern betrays the image of a discrete number of isolated ethnic groups found in the literature of the period. Even in the fifth century, people grouped under a single name, like Goths or Saxons, represented an amalgamation of people of different ethnic backgrounds. As these chieftains became transformed into rulers of emerging kingdoms, they actually sought to preserve Roman authority and to model their administrative and legal systems on the Roman Empire, a token of their continuing admiration. They learned from Rome. They frequently benefited from the assistance of Roman administrators seeking positions in the new regimes. They sought to preserve the image of continuity partly as a way of enhancing the prestige of their own dynasties. But the emergence of new kingdoms could not prevent decentralizing trends in political administration and the economy. Once Roman authority was removed, no language existed among the varied occupants of the west to foster a continued sense of political unity. A general lack of literacy hindered communications across different regions. The western half of the Roman Empire had become a shell of its former self by the middle of the fifth century.

The Emergence of New Kingdoms in the West— Franks, Goths, and Lombards

In the politically chaotic centuries that followed the fall of the Roman Empire in the west, it took a strong leader indeed to establish and maintain power over a new kingdom of any size at all. Theodoric the Ostrogoth, who ruled Italy from 493 to 526, provides a good example of a ruler who attempted to preserve the vestiges of Roman authority and civilization in the aftermath of the decline of the western empire. Taken to Constantinople as a hostage when very young,

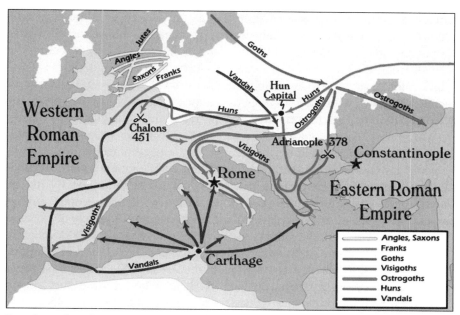

Invasions of the Roman Empire, 100–500 CE

Theodoric experienced the culture of the still thriving eastern Roman Empire. In 484 Emperor Zeno (474–491) made Theodoric a consul and brought him into the political process. In 488 Zeno sent Theodoric as his representative to reassert control over Italy, where imperial authority had disappeared. Zeno expected to take control of Italy himself, but he died in 491 before Theoderic had completed his mission. Theodoric then murdered the Italian king, Odoacer, in 493 and assumed control over Italy himself. Theodoric continued to recognize the authority of the emperor and had coins minted in his name, but he ruled as an independent monarch. The letters of his Roman secretary, Cassiodorus, generally convey the desire of Theodoric to preserve Roman law, Roman customs, and high moral standards.

Under Theodoric's contemporary, Clovis, the Franks rose to prominence in the late fifth century in the northern Roman province of Gaul. Clovis founded the Merovingian dynasty (so named because of an early royal association with a pagan god named Merovech) and greatly expanded the boundaries of his kingdom. Clovis converted to Roman Christianity and—in a dramatic gesture—he ordered his entire army to be baptized in 496. Despite his conversion to Christianity, Clovis was a ruthless ruler who did not hesitate to wage relentless war against his own relatives in order to consolidate his power. Gregory of Tours quotes Clovis as saying, "How sad a thing it is that I live among strangers like some solitary pilgrim, and that I have none of my own relations left to help me when disaster threatens," adding that Clovis said this "not because he grieved for their deaths, but because in his cunning way he hoped to find some relations still in the land of the living whom he could kill" (1974, Book 2.42, p. 158). For Gregory, Clovis's redeeming feature was his conversion to orthodox Christianity and his wars against Arian heretics such as the Visigoths, who did not accept the Roman doctrine of the Trinity. Clovis died in 511 at the age of forty-five, having ruled the Franks for thirty years.

Meanwhile, the Visigoths—who had sacked Rome in 410—established a kingdom in Spain, where they preserved certain aspects of Roman civilization, particularly Roman administration, law, and the taxation system. Nor did the Visigoths alter the earlier social structure, which was dominated by Roman landowners. Visigothic kings ruled the country but their followers quickly became absorbed into the native population. Exact statistics simply do not exist for this period of medieval history, but perhaps 300,000 to 400,000 Visigoths settled in Spain in the fifth century among a diverse population of 9 million native Iberians, Romans, and other recent immigrants. Since Spain had been one of Rome's most prosperous provinces, the chances of the eastern emperors letting Spain go without a fight were bleak. But the Visigoths survived a successful invasion in 554. King Leovigild (568–586) regained control over the lands that the Byzantines had conquered, his success followed by almost 250 years of Visigothic dominance of the Iberian Peninsula.

In Italy, the Ostrogoths were not so fortunate. After the death of Theoderic in 526, the great Byzantine emperor Justinian made a concerted military effort to retake the Italian peninsula from the Ostrogoths. In the mid-sixth century a horrendous war decimated the land and caused widespread misery. King Vitiges of the Ostrogoths desperately clung to power and attempted to hold off the Roman advance; he married the granddaughter of Theoderic to enhance his prestige. However, the Ostrogothic leaders lost the respect of the other peoples who inhabited Italy even before their final surrender in 554. The struggles of the Ostrogoths had encouraged the invasion of other Germanic tribes, such as the Franks and the Alamans. In 539 the Franks sacked Milan. In 554, after twenty years of bloody warfare, Italy was finally restored to imperial rule, as were the islands of Corsica, Sardinia, and Sicily. It was not to last. The local population hardly welcomed a power that had caused devastation to their country and now forced them to pay for it with higher taxes. The Lombards moved into the vacuum created by the collapse of the Ostrogothic kingdom and demonstrated the weakness of imperial authority there.

The Lombards were the last organized group of Germanic people to migrate into the remnants of the Roman Empire in the west, invading northern Italy in 568 and settling there in the late sixth century. King Alboin led the Lombard invasion during its critical stage from 568 to 572, taking over Milan, which had once served as an imperial capital, forcing the surrender of numerous other towns, and sponsoring raids into Frankish Gaul and southern Italy. According to their early historian, Paul the Deacon, the Lombards drew on the assistance of the Saxons, who allegedly contributed 20,000 soldiers to the invasion, providing a further indication of the mingling of Germanic populations in this transitional period. Paul also informs us that Alboin met his death at the hands of his wife, who was incensed that he had commanded her to drink out of a cup made from her father's head. The Lombards eventually became more civilized and peaceful. They established positive relations with the papacy. But they were still capable of causing trouble for their neighbors, including the pope, until their conquest by Charlemagne in the eighth century. They were not the only ones in this violent period causing trouble for their neighbors: the same could also be said of the peoples, collectively known as the Anglo-Saxons, that invaded Britain.

The Anglo-Saxons

According to the *Anglo-Saxon Chronicle*—one of our few primary sources of information about the early centuries in Britain after the fall of Rome—the native British rulers appealed to Rome in 446 for assistance against the Picts, a tribe from the north that had continually made incursions against the south for centuries. At the time, however, the Romans needed all their forces to contend with the prospects of an invasion by Attila the Hun, and no aid from Rome was forthcoming. Instead, the *Chronicle* reports, the British rulers appealed to the Angles who lived across the channel that would eventually bear their name. The Angles arrived in 449 in three ships, the apparent beginning of a migration that would transform every aspect of the history of the British Isles over the succeeding centuries.

Although historical mythology and literature depict the fifth and sixth centuries as a violent, dark age inhabited mainly by heroic warriors, archaeological evidence demonstrates important social changes and the settlement of large numbers of immigrant Germanic farmers during this period. These migrating peoples did not remain isolated from the native population, but soon intermingled and intermarried among them. The native British people did not flee to the hinterlands en masse but instead accepted the leadership of the Germanic rulers as their ancestors had accommodated themselves to Roman rule in earlier centuries. The Angles received lands in the southeast in exchange for military assistance against the Picts. Although details are lacking in the historical record, the Angles must have been successful for they carved out kingdoms for themselves (Northumbria, Mercia, and East Anglia) in the middle and northern regions of what would become known as England ("land of the Angles"). Furthermore, their success led to other migrations. People calling themselves the Saxons established kingdoms in the east, south, and west (Essex, Sussex, and Wessex). Those known as the Jutes founded the southeastern kingdom of Kent. These seven kingdoms composed what was known as the heptarchy, a loosely structured arrangement in which the most powerful king was acknowledged by the term *bretwalda*. Archaeological evidence does suggest important shifts in settlement patterns and material culture from the Roman to the Anglo-Saxon period. Perhaps most significantly, there is strong evidence that Anglo-Saxon England had important trading connections with the European continent, with goods and weapons identified from the Rhine River region, Scandinavia, and areas as far away as the Near East. The amount of wealth and level of skilled craftsmanship with precious metals in Anglo-Saxon England became clearer with the 2009 discovery of an enormous hoard of gold, silver, and beautifully ornamented swords and personal objects in a field in Staffordshire. Archaeologists have estimated that this cachet dates from around the year 700, about fifty years later than the Sutton Hoo Burial ship, which contained only about a third of the amount of gold associated with this later find.

At the end of the sixth century, the most significant kingdom was Kent, whose ruler, Ethelbert, changed the course of English history by converting to Roman Christianity under the influence of his Christian wife, Bertha, and the missionary Augustine, whom Pope Gregory I had sent to England to convert the inhabitants there. The progress of Christianity in Anglo-Saxon England was rapid, but not always steady, as some rulers in the seventh century maintained their pagan ways or directed their people back in the direction of heathenism. Archaeological finds such as the Sutton Hoo burial ship (mid-seventh century) indicate that some rulers practiced both Christianity and paganism at the same time. Anglo-Saxon poetry, of which *Beowulf* is the most famous example, reveals a blending of pagan and Christian elements as well. Politically, the balance of power continued to shift among the different kingdoms. Wars were not infrequent. In the seventh century the Northumbrian kings predominated, although they faced serious competition from certain leaders of Mercia and East Anglia. By the middle of the eighth century Mercia and its king, Offa (r. 757–796), became the dominant power in the east, southeast, and midlands. Intellectually, in seventh- and eighth-century Northumbria the efforts of Irish and British monks created a revival of learning known as the Northumbrian Renaissance, which produced the foremost writer, scholar, and scientific thinker in the West of the seventh and eighth centuries: the Venerable Bede.

Bede (ca. 673–735) produced works on nature, religion, and history that showed the range of his knowledge, learning, and intellectual interests. In his *De Natura Rerum* (On the Nature of Things), Bede considered atmospheric events and natural phenomena such as earthquakes and volcanic eruptions, along with a general consideration of the earth, stars, and planets. In his many religious works, such as his life of St. Cuthbert, Bede displayed his admiration for the traditions of Celtic Christianity and Irish monasticism. But his promotion and celebration of Roman Christianity comes through as well, most clearly in his most important work, his *History of the English Church and People*. Bede details the long history of the struggle between paganism and Christianity on the island and provides some insights on the process by which Christianity triumphed. Given that Bede spent virtually his entire life in the monastery at Jarrow on the North Sea, his history and other works represent an impressive achievement, as does his vision of the diverse ethnic groups that inhabited the island and constituted the "English" people.

Justinian and Theodora

It would take until the second half of the eighth century for the Frankish king, Charlemagne, to revive the idea of the Roman Empire in the west, but to many in the fifth century the Roman Empire had never fallen—it had merely shifted its capital to the east. Constantinople, renamed after the emperor Constantine, had been built on the site of the ancient Greek city of Byzantium. For that reason, historians today refer to the eastern half of the Roman Empire, which continued to exist as a political entity until 1453, as the Byzantine Empire. But the emperors who ruled from Constantinople thought of themselves as the heirs of Rome, and their authority was recognized as such far beyond the borders of the empire, including among the emerging nations of Western Europe. Only when Charlemagne was crowned in Rome in 800 did anyone challenge the claim of the Byzantine emperors to be Roman emperors.

After the deposition of the last emperor in Rome in 476, the emperor in Constantinople, Zeno (r. 474–491), claimed authority over the entire empire, including the west. His successor, Anastasius I (r. 491–518), made similar claims and named the Frankish king Clovis a consul. But the first emperor to attempt to regain those western territories was Justinian (r. 527–565), of whom a claim might be made that he was truly the last "Roman" emperor. In many ways Justinian attempted to demonstrate that he was heir to the entire legacy of the Roman Empire. Justinian spoke Latin and regarded himself as a native speaker, although he came from the territory of Ilyria on the other side of the Adriatic. He had a team of legal scholars codify Roman law into a massive work, the *Corpus Juris Civilis* (Body of Civil Law), which represented the form in which Roman law passed into medieval history. The portion of this work known as the *Institutes* provided some of the basic legal concepts for the Western world, such as its definition of justice as "the constant desire to give to each person his own due right." It taught that the basic precepts of the law are "to live honestly, not to injure another, and to render to each his own." Still, the imperial influence pervades the text, emphasizing that because the people conferred authority on the emperor, his word basically carried the weight of law.

The main way in which Justinian attempted to demonstrate that he was the heir to the entire legacy of the Roman Empire was his attempt to regain the old Roman territories in the west that had been overrun by tribes such as the Visigoths, the Ostrogoths, and the Vandals. War dominated Justinian's reign; although he enjoyed enough success to be motivated to continue fighting, he continued to pour imperial resources into an ultimately fruitless cause. Belisarius, Justinian's leading general, usually receives the credit for the emperor's victories, but his conquests would prove unsustainable over time. In addition to his military ambitions, Justinian had a vision for restoring the empire that was directly linked to his religious views. As the head of the church as well as the state, Justinian regarded the enforcement of religious orthodoxy in the empire as his personal responsibility.

Justinian began his efforts to recover the lost imperial territories in the west by sending Belisarius on a mission against the Vandals in 533. The Vandals, after sacking Rome in 451, had moved on to North Africa, where they controlled a sizeable kingdom that was largely sustained by maritime commerce with Italy. The Vandals made a good first target for Justinian, primarily because their rule was not popular among the native residents of their North African territories. Belisarius was so confident of victory that he brought his wife Antonia along for the ride, as well as the historian Procopius—who would later become Justinian's biographer—to record the story of his triumph. After the destruction of the Vandals and the North African Berbers, Belisarius moved against the Ostrogoths in Sicily and Italy. There both sides waged a war of attrition that brought death and destruction to much of the peninsula. Justinian's armies also temporarily defeated the Visigoths in southern Spain and restored imperial rule there as well, but over a much smaller territory than Rome had previously held. Justinian never tried to retake the entire Iberian Peninsula, where Visigoth rule would last until the Muslims invaded in 711. Justinian may have viewed his gains in Spain mainly in terms of their strategic relationship to his North African conquests.

Despite Justinian's preoccupation with external wars, he faced internal pressures as well. One of the first crises of his reign was a disturbance known as the Nika Revolt, which involved two competing groups in Constantinople that went by the nicknames of the Blues and the Greens. These two parties were associated with sporting rivalries at the Hippodrome, but their rivalry spilled over into the political arena. Before he became emperor, Justinian supported the Blues, but once on the throne he attempted to crack down on both groups in order to preserve order in the capital. In the Nika Revolt of January 532—*Nika* meant "victory" and was taken from a popular cry at the Hippodrome—the Blues and Greens allied to protest the government's refusal to release prisoners from both sides. In the process they set fire to much of the city, including the prison that held those whose release the rioters had demanded, before marching on the palace to demand the dismissal of leading officials. Justinian stalled for time until Belisarius could bring his troops into the city to crush the riot, which he did with savage efficiency, resulting in some 30,000 deaths among the rioters.

In the aftermath of the riots, Justinian was determined to bring all aspects of imperial government under his direct supervision. To assist him with these plans, he relied on his wife Theodora, a former circus performer and prostitute turned empress. Much of the image that we have of Justinian and Theodora has come through the biased lenses of their dual biographer, Procopius, who wrote a *Secret History* revealing all the flaws, weaknesses, crimes, and follies of the imperial couple. Although Theodora assisted Justinian and supported his power in myriad ways, she also had a mind of her own and became a powerful empress in her own right. Theodora has been subject to extremes of interpretation that need to be balanced in any assessment of her character or her achievements as empress. Procopius says that no one ever forced her to do anything against her will. She had her own estates, managed separately from those of her husband, making her at least financially independent. Theodora had a great deal of power, but she did not undermine Justinian's authority. In reality, they ruled together and agreed on more things than they disagreed about. In laws, royal proclamations, and inscriptions they are frequently mentioned as co-rulers.

Procopius followed a convention of the ancient world that did not see character and morality in shades of gray but rather portrayed individuals as good or evil, with fixed characters rather than being capable of moral evolution. Procopius describes Justinian as villainous and guileful, as well as "deceitful, devious, false, hypocritical, two-faced, cruel . . . a faithless friend, . . . a treacherous enemy, insane for murder and plunder, quarrelsome and revolutionary, easily led to anything evil." Of Theodora, he says that she shared with Justinian "rapacity," a "lust for blood," and "utter contempt for the truth." He says that she became a prostitute at a very young age before she was even capable of having sexual intercourse with men and that later she "sold her attractions to anyone who came along, putting her whole body at his disposal." What we have in the *Secret History*, therefore, is a portrait of Justinian and Theodora not so much as real human beings but as the embodiment of evil.

Even if Theodora were a prostitute, it is clearly evident that Procopius wildly exaggerates her sexual exploits and conquests. As empress, she was capable of coming to the aid of women who were poor or abused and of acting as a kind patron to the girls at her court. But she could also be ruthless, especially toward her political enemies. Both these qualities would have fallen well within the typical expectations of a woman in Theodora's position. She restored dignity to the imperial court, but encouraged sycophancy and insisted on deference to her high position. Why did Procopius go to such lengths to condemn Justinian and Theodora? He was mainly concerned with the consequences of their rule, which he must have regarded as deleterious to the empire. Employing a strategy used by many modern political opponents and critics, he chose to tarnish their characters instead of merely arguing against their policies. Since Procopius did not intend the *Secret History* for publication, it may be assumed that he seriously believed the allegations that he made against the imperial couple. If he were just venting, he did so with fervor that surpassed disapproval or disdain, at one point describing Justinian as a demon in human form. Still, the *Secret History* will always remain something of an enigma, given the positive evaluation that Procopius gave to Justinian in his other books about his buildings and wars.

As emperor, Justinian was expected not only to maintain social order and harmony but also to ensure that religious practice reflected the wishes of God. Theodora clashed with Justinian on religious issues, even showing sympathy to the heresy of Monophysitism, which emphasized that Christ possessed a single nature and a single substance, and taking people who would have been prosecuted for heresy under her protection. The Eastern Church placed a great emphasis upon religious orthodoxy and religious unity. The emperor and the church leaders all took the issue of religious orthodoxy extremely seriously, believing correct forms of worship and belief to be of the utmost importance to God. The main religious dispute in the east centered on the nature of Christ, specifically the degree to which he was both human and divine. Monophysitism presented just as much a threat to the religious unity of the east as Arianism did in the west. Whereas the Arians believed that Christ was created by God the Father and was in some sense subordinate to him, the Monophysites stressed that Christ was the Divine Creator incarnated. Both challenged the orthodox doctrine of the Trinity shared by the western and eastern churches. Justinian proved incapable of eradicating Monophysitism from his realm, even after the death of Theodora. But he largely succeeded in encouraging a blending of orthodox and Monophysite clergy within the church that did more to undermine the heresy than persecution would have, at least at the heart of his empire.

As emperor, Justinian ruled over both the state and the church because of a political doctrine that became established in the east known as "Caesaro-papism." First articulated by the church historian Eusebius of Caesarea (ca. 264–340) during the reign of Constantine in the 330s, the doctrine formed a cornerstone of imperial authority in the east. In the west, the bishops of Rome successfully established the papacy and claimed to be the successors of Peter and the representatives of Christ on earth. In the Byzantine Empire, the emperors made the claim to represent God on earth. There the emperor was regarded as head of both church and state. Therefore, the Byzantine emperors took a direct role in the adoption of specific religious policies and even in the formulation of church doctrine. They had the ability to change the religious orientation of the empire and to define and punish heresy, which was regarded as a state offense. But the ideas of Eusebius that had supported the doctrine of Caesaropapism presented a direct challenge to the previous emphasis within Christianity on a separation of church and state. Under Caesaropapism, the emperor was not regarded as divine, but he was regarded as a representative of the divine on earth and believed to have a special relationship with God.

The ideals of Caesaropapism can be found in Byzantine art in its attempt to equate the ways in which earth replicates the order of things to be found in heaven. Portraits of Justinian and Theodora, for example, gave them a semireligious aura that reinforced their roles as the earthly counterparts of the male and female attributes of the divine. Despite their humble backgrounds, once Justinian and Theodora became emperor and empress they were seen as earthly reflections of God chosen by providence. Byzantine art flourished mainly under Justinian, but it set a standard that was hard to build upon. The construction or reconstruction of more than thirty churches, including the church of Sancta Sophia, was Justinian's architectural contribution to the faith over which he presided. According to Procopius, Justinian imported craftsmen from all over the world to work on the construction of Sancta Sophia. Byzantine mosaic art depicted both secular and religious themes, the latter tending to focus on representations of Christ, the Virgin Mary, and the saints. However, Byzantine attitudes toward religious art changed dramatically, leading within two centuries to the greatest religious and political crisis experienced in the early centuries of the Byzantine Empire.

Politics and Religion in the Byzantine Empire After Justinian

In the short term, Justinian had expanded the size of his empire and restored imperial authority in Italy and the west, but many of his gains turned out to be short-lived because he did not leave behind the financial and military means for his successors to preserve them. Justinian's immediate successor was his nephew, Justin II, who had married Theodora's niece Sophia. Justin, who assumed the throne at the age of forty-five, lacked the drive and the administrative abilities of his uncle, while Sophia attempted to emulate her aunt—but she was no Theodora either. Heraclius (r. 610–641) was rather more ambitious. By forging an alliance with the church and drawing on its resources and support, Heraclius succeeded in strengthening his position as emperor. But he proved just as incapable as Justin II at strengthening the imperial defenses. Antioch and Caesarea fell to the Persians in 611, Jerusalem in 614, and Egypt in 616. Heraclius's death in 641 was followed by a period marked by further imperial economic and cultural decline, military weakness, and dynastic instability.

This did not deter Heraclius's grandson, Constans II (r. 641–668), from making yet another attempt to secure imperial rule over Italy and North Africa. His efforts did not bear fruit because he could not afford to send armies to the west and leave Constantinople defenseless against Arab invasions from the east. To his credit, Constans II preserved the empire and managed to hold off the Arab onslaught, largely through a new scheme of provincial administration that involved the establishment of districts known as *themes*, presided over by a new military official called a *strategoi*. But dynastic instability ensued when Constans was murdered in Sicily in 668 and his successor, Justinian II, overthrown in a revolt in 695. After a chaotic period that lasted for two decades, the empire became embroiled in an internal struggle caused by the iconoclast controversy.

The iconoclast controversy arose from a debate within the Eastern Church about whether visual representation of Christ, the Virgin Mary, and the saints constituted a form of idolatry, which the Old Testament specifically condemned. A split on the issue occurred between those known as iconodules (image-worshippers), also known as iconophiles (lovers of icons), and iconoclasts (image-destroyers). Iconoclasts seriously believed that by engaging in a practice specifically condemned by the Bible (according to their interpretation), Christians were inviting God's wrath and jeopardizing the well-being of the empire. Iconophiles continued to believe, however, that icons assisted the believer in the contemplation of the divine. Reports of blood, sweat, and tears emanating from paintings or statues served as confirmation of this belief for many people.

The controversy created a religious culture war within the Byzantine Empire that had serious political ramifications as well. Icons had been associated with the protection of the empire, but iconoclasts pointed to the victories of the Arabs as obvious signs of God's displeasure. In part, their position repre-

The Chora Museum in Istanbul has preserved many fine examples of Byzantine art, including mosaics and frescoes; view them at www. choramuseum.com.

Byzanine mosaic of the Virgin and Child. Located in the Chora Church Museum in Istanbul, this is a good example of the kind of image that iconoclasts wished to destroy during the dispute over icons in the Byzantine Empire.

sented an attack from the secular clergy on the monasteries that had retained a strong sense of independence and isolation from the rest of the church. The high point for the iconoclasts came in 754 when a church council at Hieria condemned the worship of icons, associating the practice with idolatry and devil-worship. During the periods of imperial ban—from 726 to 787 and from 814 to 843—the use or manufacture of icons did not cease altogether, but was done privately and surreptitiously. The iconoclastic controversy took a heavy toll on Byzantine art and culture; in addition to an artistic decline, the Byzantines produced fewer book manuscripts, and fewer schools educated fewer people who could read them.

Everyday Life in the Byzantine Empire

Byzantine society was intended to follow a natural order that reflected that found in heaven. The basic social unit of Byzantine society was the family. Byzantine laws affirmed the sanctity of marriage, as did the church. Women primarily fulfilled their function in society in the context of the family, though monasteries provided another opportunity for them. Men received their identity to a large degree from their families as well, in addition to the profession or trade that they might practice.

Society was hierarchical, with the emperor at the top symbolically representing the divine creator. Everyone else was believed to have their natural place in society, including eunuchs and slaves. Within the rough division of Byzantine society into soldiers, peasants, merchants, clergy, and teachers, there was some degree of variegation. Peasants, for example, might have been traditional farmers or they might have been rural smiths or craftsmen. Most peasants actually owned their own land, rather than serving as tenants on the estates of wealthy landowners. Along the coasts, many people made their living by fishing or other maritime pursuits. Generally, the larger the town or village, the more differentiation there would have been in the professions or activities of the inhabitants. But even small villages in the countryside might contain a local doctor (often of dubious abilities), a fortune-teller, or a sorcerer, among those who practiced nonagricultural professions. Villages played an integral role in a network of trade and food distribution that included market towns and monasteries, in addition to the larger cities. Large cities contained a variety of trades and industries, none more so than Constantinople. Many of these focused on the production of luxury goods, such as silks and jewelry. Within Constantinople, wealthy and poor lived side by side rather than in sections of the city that would have isolated them from one another. Still, a tremendous gap existed between the wealthiest and the poorest members of society.

During the reign of Justinian, the government attempted to provide a number of services that would improve the lives of the people, especially those who resided in the imperial capital of Constantinople. The government had its own equivalent of a national health service, employing physicians to treat people who could not afford medical care and supporting free hospitals. It also attempted to ensure a continual supply of fresh water for the city. Saints and members of the imperial family were the only ones permitted burial within city limits in an attempt to limit the spread of disease by corpses. Not that these measures eliminated disease; in fact, the prohibition against burial inside the city became problematic in times of plague when the corpses piled up faster than they could be carried outside the city walls. The city and the empire were still at danger from epidemics such as the bubonic plague, which struck with particularly deadly force in 541 and lasted till 543. Procopius said that ten thousand people a day were dying at the height of that plague. Six more plague epidemics occurred before the end of the sixth century and another horrible episode from 745 to 747, after which the emperor sought Greeks to repopulate the city. The plague brought with it dramatic inflation, higher taxes on the living, and severe food shortages because of a shortage of laborers to work the fields.

In addition to the threat from plague, Constantinople and its surrounding area faced other threats from natural disasters. The city was particularly vulnerable to earthquakes, two of which occurred within a decade in 732 and 740. Climate still greatly affected the food and water supply. A severe winter in 763–764 actually caused an iceberg to crash against the walls that faced the sea. A particularly bad drought ten years later led the emperor to repair an aqueduct that had been damaged in a siege more than 100 years before. The countryside also had to deal with threats from locusts, beetles, and other pests, in addition to occasional floods and damaging hailstorms. Such natural disasters combined with the plague to take a serious toll on the vitality of the Byzantine capital and the vibrancy of Byzantine civilization in general. An even more serious threat, however, came in the form of Arab conquerors inspired by a new faith.

The Shaping of the Past: The Life of Muhammad

Arabia at the time of Muhammad considered itself the home of numerous gods, one of which was the high God of the Judeo-Christian tradition, whom the Arabs called Allah. All Arabs considered Mecca their religious center, to which many made pilgrimages to pray at the polytheistic temple known as the Kaaba; here resided a sacred black stone that may have been a fragment of a meteorite. Muhammad, having received a prophetic revelation from the angel Gabriel, entered Mecca around 612 believing that he had a mission to preach to the Arabs that Allah was the one true God and should be the object of all their devotion.

Muhammad was an Arab born into the influential Quraysh tribe in Mecca sometime around the year 570 (although this traditional date is based not on any real evidence but on the assumption that he must have been forty—a number of great religious significance in the Middle East—when he received his prophetic calling in 610). As is the case with Moses and Jesus, we know little about Muhammad's youth and early adulthood. We do know that he lost his father before he was born and his mother when he was only six. This could help to explain his later emphasis on the virtue of caring for widows and orphans. Around 595 a woman named Khadija, a wealthy widow with a substantial caravan business, became Muhammad's first wife; she is alleged to have been forty (fifteen years older than Muhammad) at the time of the marriage, but this means that she would have had six children in her forties at a time when most women experienced menopause in their thirties. Muhammad, who seems to have gained some business experience working for his uncle Abbas, assumed control of Khadija's business and became a prosperous merchant. He also had a happy and successful marriage, as indicated by the number of children in the family. Muhammad had become fully integrated into the flourishing, expanding world of Arabian and Middle Eastern commerce. But he also seems to have felt some kind of religious calling because he would on occasion retreat to the desert to pray and meditate. It was during one of these retreats in 610 that he experienced his "night of fire" and received the message to "Recite!" The readiness with which Khadija accepted Muhammad's conversion and converted to his new faith testifies both to the nature of their relationship and the sincerity with which the Prophet must have communicated his vision. That sincerity, however, did not gain him many additional converts in the immediate years following.

Gradually Muhammad gained some followers from among the lesser families of the Quraysh tribe and other tribes that had become dependent on it. In 615 eighty-three of these followers, facing oppression from powerful members of the Quraysh in Mecca, fled the city to take refuge with the Christian ruler of Abyssinia. It is possible that Muhammad, who had not entirely abandoned his business interests, had sent them there with the ulterior motive of opening up further trade connections south of Arabia. Five years later, in 620, travelers from the city of Yahtrib (later known as Medina) encountered Muhammad at a fair. They were impressed. Because Medina had a number of internal problems resulting from factional rivalry and needed peace and unity in order to retain its position as a prosperous trading center, representatives of the city invited Muhammad to take over Medina's political and religious leadership in the hopes that he could become a unifying force. In September 622 Muhammad journeyed to Medina—an event known to Muslims as the Hegira, which marks the beginning of their calendar—and almost immediately transformed it into the first Muslim city.

Yet Muhammad's main target remained Mecca. Mecca had already developed into a thriving commercial and religious center and did not readily accept Muhammad's claims to political and religious authority over all Arabs. Mecca defeated the Muslims at the battle of Uhud in 625. By 627 Mecca, with the support of Bedouin tribesmen and Abyssinian mercenaries, was ready to attack Medina, which Muhammad managed to save by a strategy of digging a huge trench around the city, allegedly on the advice of a Persian believer. Muhammad differed from other religious leaders in history because he also excelled as a political and military leader. He effectively organized a force that eventually took Mecca, destroyed the idols in the temple, and persecuted those who resisted, although these were few by the time that Muhammad actually entered the city.

His closest followers wrote down much of what Muhammad said, recording these sayings as a guide for all adherents of the Muslim faith. Muhammad did not claim to be divine—noting at one point "My sayings do not abrogate the word of God, but the word of God can abrogate my sayings" (Bennett 1998, 22)—but he did consider himself the last of God's prophets. The vast majority of the Arabs agreed and after his death committed themselves to spreading their new faith.

The Rise of Islam

A major question immediately arose, however: if Muhammad were the last prophet, who should assume leadership of the faithful after his death? Muslims did not doubt the validity of his religious message and teachings, but they disagreed about who should succeed him politically. Some advocated for Muhammad's cousin, Ali ibn Abi Talib, who was also the husband of his daughter Fatima, as the preferred choice of the Prophet. More supported Abu Bakr (ca. 573–634), who was unrelated but extremely close to Muhammad.

Islam, which differed from other organized religions in the absence of a real priesthood, viewed political authorities as the guardians of the faith so Muslims took political divisions very seriously. In 656 Ali finally became the fourth caliph (successor). Ali's supporters—later known as Shiites—continued to press the claims of his descendants after Ali's assassination in 661 and after the death of his son Hussein and much of the family at the Battle of Karbala (about fifty-five miles southwest of Baghdad) in 680. But control had fallen to the powerful Umayyad dynasty—named after an ancestor, Umayya—which until 750 became the hereditary rulers of the Islamic world and presided over the continued expansion of the Arabs and the Islamic faith.

The causes of Arab expansion included the rising population of the Arabian Peninsula, available land and wealth in nearby regions, and the decreasing power in the seventh century of the Byzantine and Persian empires, which presented the greatest obstacles to expansion. Disaffected elements within Byzantine lands such as Syria and Egypt, in which many still held Monophysite religious views at variance with the orthodoxy of the emperor, also helped to prepare the way for the acceptance and success of the Islamic conquerors. Contrary to popular belief, the expansionist wars of this period were not considered holy wars nor were they accompanied by forced conversion to Islam. Muslims had respect for Christians and Jews as worshippers of the same God and treated them leniently, though largely in the belief that they would convert once exposed to the higher truth of Islam. Jews and Muslims shared a belief in one God that rejected the Christian doctrine of the Trinity. The vast majority of the people of the conquered territories in the Middle East, North Africa, and Spain did eventually become Muslim but over the course of several generations, not overnight. All of this notwithstanding, these wars did have their origins in the Muslim intention to unify Arabia under the Islamic faith. The wars united the Arabs and spread a unified Muslim culture throughout much of the Mediterranean and Middle East. The Arabs conquered Syria, Palestine, and Egypt in the seventh century; Spain fell in 711, and in 732 the farthest thrust of Arab expansion was checked in the Frankish kingdom at the Battle of Tours.

Even after people in the conquered lands began to convert to Islam, it took time for them to fully know and understand its teachings. Remember that it had taken at least two generations following the death of Jesus before Christians had access to the four Gospels. Following the death of Muhammad, by contrast, his teachings had been collated rather quickly into the sacred text of the Muslims known as the Quran.

The Quran—like most successful religious texts—had a message that was simple enough for common people to understand but complex enough as a text to fascinate and occupy the best minds among its adherents. Muhammad called upon Muslims to submit to the will of the one true God, Allah, and to appreciate his goodness and that of the world he created. He called upon men and women to practice justice and to treat others fairly, especially widows, children, and the poor. He called on merchants to be just in their commercial transactions and to place what is right in the eyes of God above the pursuit of wealth. He encouraged Muslim men to marry women in order to provide protection and increase their well-being—this was the reason that he permitted polygamy. But he restricted men to four wives and said they should only marry once if they could not treat all their wives fairly and equally. Among the numerous other teachings in the Quran, Muhammad said that Muslims should follow Jewish dietary laws because these had been revealed by God to the tribe of Israel.

The Quran is one of the most historically authenticated religious texts of all time. Much of what eventually was included seems to have been written

The Quran: On Allah

In the name of Allah, the Beneficent, the Merciful.

Allah! There is no God save Him, the Alive, the Eternal. He hath revealed unto thee (Muhammad) the Scripture with truth, confirming that which was (revealed) before it, even as He revealed the Torah and the Gospel aforetime, for a guidance to mankind; and hath revealed the Criterion (of right and wrong). Lo! Those who disbelieve the revelations of Allah, theirs will be a heavy doom. Allah is Mighty, Able to requite (the wrong). Lo! Nothing in the earth or in the heavens is hidden from Allah. He it is who fashioneth you in the wombs as pleaseth Him. There is no God save Him, the Almighty, the Wise. He it is Who hath revealed unto thee (Muhammad) the Scripture wherein are clear revelations. They are the substance of the Book—and others (which are) allegorical. But those in whose hearts is doubt pursue, forsooth, that which is allegorical seeking (to cause) dissension by seeking to explain it. No one knoweth its explanation save Allah. And those who are of sound instruction say: We believe therein; the whole is from our Lord; but only men of understanding really heed.

Our Lord! Cause not our hearts to stray after Thou hast guided us, and bestow upon us mercy from Thy Presence. Lo! Thou, only Thou art the Bestower. Our Lord! It is Thou Who gatherest mankind together to a Day of which there is no doubt. Lo! Allah faileth not to keep the tryst. (On that day) neither the riches nor the progeny of those who disbelieve will aught avail them with Allah. They will be fuel for fire . . .

—The Quran, Surah 3

What does this passage reveal about the Muslim conception of God? Does the Muslim conception differ significantly from the Jewish or Christian conception? What does the passage say about the historical relationship between Judaism, Christianity, and Islam?

during Muhammad's lifetime. Of course, these writings were compiled later in a process that Muslims believe was divinely inspired, just as Christians believe that about the canon that made up their New Testament. Zayd ibn Thabit supervised the actual composition of the final version of the Quran accepted by all Muslims around 660—remarkably close to Muhammad's lifetime. Zayd enforced strict standards in determining the authenticity of the writings included in the text. Specifically, at least two people had to have heard the saying and those same people had to be present when the sayings were written down.

Islam, which means "submission," influenced its followers' lives through certain standard practices required of all Muslims—the Five Pillars of Islam.

It taught that all Muslims must declare a confession of faith—the one and only necessary requirement for joining the community of believers and entering into heaven. Muslims were expected to pray five times a day at specified times while facing Mecca. The third pillar required fasting from dawn to sunset during the month of Ramadan. (The sick and the elderly were exempt from this requirement.) Fourth, Muslims were expected to donate a relatively modest proportion (two and a half percent) of their income to charity. Finally, all Muslims, if at all possible, were expected to make a pilgrimage to Mecca at least once in their lifetime. These Five Pillars were supplemented by other guidelines for living, including prohibitions against drinking, gambling, lying under oath, sexual immorality, and charging interest. Islam did not just bring a new faith—in fact, many Muslims would argue that worship of Allah was a very old faith—but it did bring a new way of life to many people.

The last of the Umayyad rulers fell in 750, victim to a revolt originating in Iran. The descendants of Muhammad's uncle, Abbas, assumed power, establishing the Abbasid Caliphate (750–1258). The Abbasids based their claim to power on the concept that the leaders of Islam should be direct descendants of the family of Muhammad. Under the Abbasids, the Shiite branch of Islam gained the ascendancy. Islam began to break down into rival orthodoxies, each claiming that the Quran justified its position. Since the Abbasids combined political and religious authority, any religious differences within the Islamic world carried political overtones as well. The Shiites claimed that authority derived from the family of Muhammad and that religious prophecy would continue through the twelve imams, religious leaders—starting with Ali—who continued to represent the will of Allah to the people. The rival Sunni branch of Islam looked to religious scholars to interpret Islamic law—known as the sharia—based on the Quran and a collection of additional sayings, prescriptions, and prophecies known as the Hadith. Islam had become a dynamic and unifying force for many peoples, but its internal divisions would determine much of its subsequent history and its relations with the West.

Conclusion

By 750, then, Islam had posed a major threat to both the Byzantine Empire and the new kingdoms that had emerged in the West. Islamic rule had replaced Byzantine control of much of North Africa and the Middle East and that of the Visigothic kings of Spain. The Muslims conquered Sicily and Cyprus in the Mediterranean. But the Franks stopped them at Tours and after 750 Islamic military expansion gave way to the development of a rich culture and civilization that achieved spectacular results in science, medicine, art, and literature, as well as preserving much of the rich cultural and intellectual legacy of the ancient Greeks and Romans.

In the sixth century Justinian had sought to continue the legacy of the Roman Empire, but in the two centuries that followed his reign, that legacy fell into a general state of disrepair. The Lombards had control of Italy, with the exception of Sicily and a few isolated areas such as Naples and Venetia. In 751 the Lombards added Ravenna to their territory. The Eastern Church became even more isolated from Rome as a result of the iconoclast controversy. The Byzantine Empire entered a period of population decline, exacerbated by frequent outbreaks of the bubonic plague. Still, the Byzantine Empire survived the Arab invasions, and its emperors had greater wealth and power than any king in Europe. Byzantine society survived as well and remained relatively stable despite the fluctuations of the empire's general fortunes. In 750 the Byzantine Empire was still a powerful force in the east, despite the loss of some of its territory.

However, by 750 a new dynastic power in the West had begun to emerge that would prove capable of dealing and contending with Byzantine and Muslim rulers on equal terms. After Charles Martel drove Muslim forces from France in the Battle of Tours, his son took the next step; he deposed the last Merovingian king and—with the support of the papacy—claimed the throne for the new dynasty that would later become known as the Carolingians. These Frankish rulers would expand the boundaries of their realm at the same time that they fostered the spread of Roman Christianity. These rulers could not completely mask the social and economic legacies of the fall of Rome. Europe remained a largely agricultural society, reduced more and more to division into numerous local economies, even if trade never entirely disappeared. But by 800 Charlemagne had successfully restored the imperial ideal in Western Europe. His reign would be accompanied by a revival of learning in the West and the growth of the church. In 750 the forces of anarchy and decline in the West were about to be challenged and defeated—at least temporarily.

1. What are the main differences and similarities between Eastern and Western monasticism?
2. What were the main reasons for political decentralization in the western half of the Roman Empire in the fifth and sixth centuries around the time of the decline of imperial authority there?
3. How were the histories of the Franks, Goths, and Lombards intertwined in the fifth and sixth centuries? What advantages did the Franks have over the Goths in the preservation of their kingdom?
4. Was Justinian's reign a success or a failure?
5. What factors contributed to the success of Muhammad's religious message and the rise and expansion of Islam in the seventh century?

Suggestions for Further Reading

Bennett, Clinton. 1998. *In Search of Muhammad*. London: Cassell Academic.

Cahill, Thomas. 1996. *How the Irish Saved Civilization: The Untold Story of Ireland's Heroic Role from the Fall of Rome to the Rise of Medieval Europe*. New York: Anchor Books.

Gregory of Tours. 1974. *The History of the Franks*. Translated by Lewis Thorpe. London: Penguin Books.

Herrin, Judith. 2007. *Byzantium: The Surprising Life of a Medieval Empire*. Princeton: Princeton University Press.

Lewis, David Levering. 2009. *God's Crucible: Islam and the Making of Europe, 570–1215*. New York: W.W. Norton.

Wells, Peter S. 2008. *Barbarians to Angels: The Dark Ages Reconsidered*. New York: W.W. Norton.

Wills, Garry. 2005. *Augustine: A Life*. New York: Penguin.

Suggested Websites

www.monasticdialog.net

The North American Benedictine and Cistercian Monasteries of Men and Women sponsor this website, promoting dialogue and comparison between monastic traditions of different faiths.

http://muhammad.net/j/index.php

An educational website devoted to the life and teachings of Muhammad, this site also contains information about Islam in general.

http://orb.rhodes.edu/encyclop/early/pre1000/ASindex.html

This website provides an excellent resource for those wishing access to more information about Anglo-Saxon England. It provides primary source documents, bibliographies, images, links to other sites, and other valuable resources for both teachers and students. It also contains an original essay on Old English.

www.themiddleages.net

This website provides information on a wide variety of topics associated with the medieval period, including much on the early medieval period.

www.wsu.edu/~dee/MA/BYZ.HTM

This is a well-organized, detailed web page about the Byzantine Empire. It is part of a "learning module" on the European Middle Ages. There are additional links to the other pages and topics in a drop-down menu on the bottom of the page.

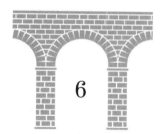

6   The Shaping of Medieval Europe, ca. 750–1100

Although centralized political authority had largely disappeared in the West with the collapse of the Roman Empire, by 750 the Franks had emerged in alliance with the papacy to revive the possibility of its return. By the beginning of the ninth century, Charlemagne (742–814) had achieved success in extending the size and unity of his empire, exercised great political authority, proven himself a formidable military leader, and done much to promote learning and the spread of Christianity. In doing so, he fostered the creation of an emerging European civilization. However, his successes proved ephemeral as Europe was besieged in the ninth century by a number of outside invasions. Charlemagne's successors did not possess his capacity to enforce their authority and hold the empire together. Charlemagne temporarily overcame the obstacles to centralized authority that existed in medieval Europe, but did not eradicate those obstacles, which included—in addition to external invasions—a lack of money, the absence of a well-developed administrative bureaucracy, and the large number of powerful local rulers determined to assert authority over their territories.

The decline of centralized power had an impact on the Christian church in the ninth and tenth centuries. The papacy, in particular, had long depended on an alliance with the Frankish rulers that culminated in the coronation of Charlemagne as Roman emperor by Pope Leo I in 800. Monasteries were a particular target of the marauding Vikings. Those monasteries that did survive were seen to have compromised their original ideals during several centuries of European monastic life. Nonetheless, Christianity continued to spread and both clerics and laymen took an interest in religious reform in the tenth and eleventh centuries.

The absence of strong centralized governments also had an impact on European society. Private bonds between individuals increasingly held the social structure together, assisted by the church's increasing influence over marriage and the family. Subordinate nobles known as vassals swore allegiance to a lord and offered personal and military service in exchange for a fief (*feudum* in medieval Latin, hence the term *feudalism*) that usually consisted of a landed estate. Other personal arrangements existed between landowners and

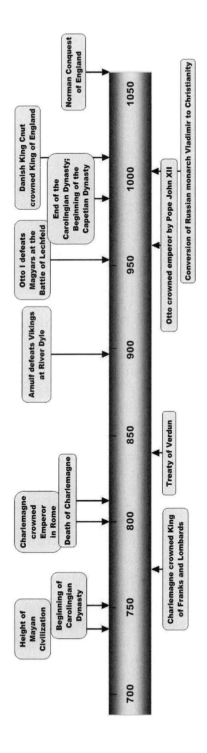

those peasants who worked the land in a system that has become known as manorialism.

Although medieval Europeans did not know it at the time, across the Atlantic Ocean in what is now southern Mexico and Central America an advanced and sophisticated civilization had emerged among the Mayans. Early medieval Europe coincided with the height of Mayan civilization, commonly referred to as the Classic period, lasting from the third to the tenth centuries. Although on the surface medieval Europe and Mayan civilization were very different, an examination of Mayan politics, religion, society, and art provides an interesting basis for comparison between the two. Recent discoveries have shed light on a fascinating culture that Europeans first encountered when the Spaniards arrived in Mexico in the sixteenth century.

Charlemagne

On the European continent in the eighth century an emerging dynasty that later became known as the Carolingians successfully consolidated its power and replaced the ruling dynasty, the Merovingians, whose leadership had been prone to instability and royal weakness. By the end of the century, the king of the Franks, Charlemagne, had unified much of the European continent and revived imperial ideas for the first time since the fall of the Roman Empire. Earlier in the century Pepin of Herestol had used his position as the king's steward (*major domis*) to become the effective ruler of the country; his son Charles Martel ("the Hammer") won a major victory over an Islamic army at the Battle of Tours in 732 to further enhance the family's prestige. In 751, Charles's son, Pepin III ("the Short") officially overthrew the Merovingian dynasty and established a new royal line. The papacy sanctioned this change of dynasty, recognizing the importance of having on the Frankish throne a powerful ruler who could protect and would owe a debt of gratitude to the church. The Carolingians consolidated their position partly by gaining the support of powerful vassals through the distribution of lands and ecclesiastical positions that carried lucrative resources and income with them. Pepin III sought not only to stabilize the Frankish lands, but also to bring order to large areas of the emerging Europe. But Pepin still faced resistance from important areas within and outside Frankish lands. When King Pepin the Short died in 768, the kingdom passed to his two sons, Carloman and Charles, later known as Charlemagne.

Carloman's death in 771 made it easier for Charlemagne to gain control of the whole kingdom, something he surely would have tried to do even if his brother had lived. Well over six feet tall, Charlemagne towered over his contemporaries and impressed his subjects by his sheer physical presence.

Charlemagne was a warrior first and foremost. He fought wars for much of his reign, aiming to expand his territory, further the spread of Christianity, and defend the lands that he already held. In 769 he crushed an uprising by some nobles in the Aquitaine in southwest France. He initiated a war with the pagan Saxons in the German lands to the east in 772 and would fight these implacable foes intermittently until his death in 814. He defeated the Lombards in 774 and had himself officially crowned as king of the Franks and the Lombards. In 778 Charlemagne crossed the Pyrenees Mountains into Spain to campaign against the Muslims, though his most famous battle, the Battle of Roncesvalles, immortalized in a later epic poem titled *The Song of Roland*, was fought against Christian Basques. At one time or another, Charlemagne fought additional campaigns against the Avars, Slavs, Huns, and Danes.

As ruler, Charlemagne refined the emerging feudal system by issuing legislation known as capitularies, which provide great insight into various aspects of Carolingian times. For example, Charlemagne ruled that a vassal could become exempt from the allegiance owed his lord if his lord tried either to kill him, maim him, take away his lands, rape or seduce his wife or daughter, or if the lord failed to hold up his end of the bargain, which called for him to protect his vassals. Charlemagne also divided his lands into administrative units known as counties, appointing counts to govern them in his name and ensure allegiance to royal authority. Counties in border areas where defense was a top priority were known as marches, a new administrative unit introduced by Charlemagne. His biographer, Notker the Stammerer, says that Charlemagne gave single tracts of land to each of his counts, but he made exceptions for those who lived "on the borders . . . of territory held by the barbarians." Charlemagne sought to keep an eye on his noble vassals, the counts, through a group of administrative servants known as the *missi dominici*, or lord's messengers. These consisted of both clerics and laymen, who traveled in pairs consisting of one of each to ensure that Charlemagne's orders were obeyed, his taxes collected, and that law and order prevailed in his realm.

Under Charlemagne, the close alliance between the Frankish monarchy and the Roman papacy continued. Pope Leo III encountered difficulties with local opponents within Rome and found himself in bodily danger. Accounts vary as to whether physical harm was actually inflicted, one reporting that he had his eyes put out, another that the attempt failed. Either way, Leo managed to preserve himself—and apparently recovered his sight if he had been blinded—but still looked to strengthen his alliance with Europe's most powerful ruler. He invited Charlemagne to Rome. Charlemagne, said to have a particular fondness for the Apostle Peter and thus for Rome, welcomed the pope's invitation. Charlemagne made a total of four trips to Rome in his life. He had maintained a good relationship with Pope Hadrian I (r. 772–795), but he had his reservations about Leo. Since the king had a close alliance with the popes, Charlemagne sought to protect the reputation and prestige of the papacy, which Leo seemed to have some difficulty maintaining. On Christmas night in the year 800, Pope Leo crowned Charlemagne emperor during mass, possibly without Charlemagne's prior knowledge or approval. Either way the event proved significant because it provided grounds for both secular rulers and later popes to claim an advantage in the relationship between temporal and spiritual authorities. However, at the time, Charlemagne was so powerful that he hardly had to worry about this, while the pope needed Charlemagne's support so much that he was in no position to claim any type of advantage. Charlemagne died of pleurisy in 814 at the age of seventy-one at his palace at Aachen after an amazingly long and distinguished reign that represented the revival of the imperial idea in the West.

The Carolingian Renaissance and Everyday Life in Carolingian Times

Charlemagne sponsored a revival of learning that is usually referred to as the Carolingian Renaissance. Because Charlemagne relied on the church to provide many important services to his administration, he concerned himself as well with the level of education that clergymen received within his realm. He saw to it that schools were established at monasteries, by bishops at cathedrals and in parishes throughout the kingdom, and at his own palace at Aachen. He then imported prominent teachers, such as Alcuin, a Benedictine monk from York in Britain, to staff them.

The revival of learning meant the revival of writing in a society that had long neglected that art and skill. Literacy increased and more people made written contributions to the culture of the times. Poems, songs, and ballads that had been transmitted orally were copied down for the first time. The script used at the time, known as Carolingian minuscule, became the model for modern writing. Intellectually and philosophically, scholars and teachers in the Carolingian period concerned themselves mainly with preserving and transmitting acquired knowledge and ancient texts rather than with developing new ideas or realms of thought. Even Alcuin, acknowledged as one of the most brilliant scholars of the age, demonstrated his abilities through his understanding of ancient philosophy and the church fathers more than through original contributions. But no ancient text that is known to have existed at the time of Charlemagne is lost to us, due to the intensive labors of monks who made enough multiple copies to ensure the survival of each text. Most of the books that contributed to the revival of learning in Carolingian Europe came from Britain by way of Ireland, where Irish monks had labored for centuries to keep ancient learning alive during a period of intellectual darkness in the former western half of the Roman Empire. The one original thinker who did emerge out of the Carolingian Renaissance was the ninth-century Irishman, John Scotus Erigena (b. 810), who taught in France during the reign of Charles the Bald. Erigena even knew Greek, an accomplishment that was extremely rare in ninth-century Europe, though some scholars associated with the earlier Northumbrian Renaissance were also fluent in it. Erigena demonstrated a deep understanding of the Bible, which he did not interpret literally, stressing how difficult it is for human beings to truly know or understand God.

A study of Carolingian society belies the traditional image of the early medieval period as the Dark Ages. Peasants, in fact, may have been better off than during the height of the Roman Empire. Medieval agriculture benefited from the introduction of a heavy wheeled plow that reduced the amount of labor needed for plowing, required a larger number of oxen than most peasants could afford, making agriculture more of a cooperative than an individual enterprise, and allowed for fields to be cultivated in strips or rows. Their lives were made easier at the same time that they would have had a greater sense of belonging to a community, a notion reinforced by the local church, which was the center of their social as well as their religious life.

Life for many people in Western Europe during the Carolingian period revolved around large estates known as manors, many of which were owned directly by the king himself. Manors and villages tended to be self-sufficient to a very large degree. The residents consumed only food that was grown on the manors or found in nearby forests. They built their homes and other manorial buildings from materials and supplies located in the immediate vicinity. They even made their own clothing to a very large degree, though in Anglo-Saxon England there is already evidence of certain villages specializing in weaving and cloth making. Both women and men participated in cloth making, as well as in other types of work. The use of male and female names for certain occupations (weavers and websters, bakers and baxters) suggests that many activities were not restricted by gender. In peasant society, men would have assisted with household tasks such as cooking, cleaning, and cloth making during the seasons that required less agricultural labor, while women would assist in the fields when extra labor was needed there.

The state and the church took an interest in the lives of the common people during this period. One of Charlemagne's capitularies, titled *De Villis*, dealt with the administration of the manorial estates. Taxes were collected, laws administered, military forces raised through his relationship with his stewards who had the responsibility of running these manors. In *De Villis*, Charlemagne demonstrated concern for the fair administration of the manors by ordering that stewards bring any complaints against them from the manor's inhabitants to his attention. He also ordered that the church receive a tenth of all produce (the traditional tax due to the church, known as the tithe). A church decree under Charlemagne in 789 against unmarried couples living together and forbidding the apparently common practice of dissolving marriages at will represented a move by the church to force people to take the sacrament of marriage more seriously. Otherwise, family life in Carolingian times did not differ significantly from other periods of the Middle Ages. Extended families often lived under the same roof with little privacy. Marriages were generally arranged, even among the peasant class, though peasants would have had more freedom in this area than their social superiors.

The Decline of the Carolingians and the Emergence of Feudal Traditions

The decline of the Carolingians resulted partly from territorial disputes that arose among the sons of Charlemagne's son, Louis the Pious (r. 814–840), partly from the growing powers of the landed nobility, and partly from the Viking invasions that besieged Europe during the ninth century. Following the death of Louis the Pious, his four sons—Louis, Pepin, Lothair, and Charles the Bald—quarreled over the inheritance of the Carolingian Empire. Each son bribed nobles for their support and became heavily dependent on them for military success. Even under Charlemagne, the counts and margraves that he appointed had a great deal of independence because of the sheer size of his empire. Now the nobility took full advantage of the rivalry within the royal family to gain even more authority, particularly over the church and its resources within their territories. Lothair in particular attempted to attract the support of the West Frankish nobility at the expense of his half-brother, Charles—the son of Louis the Pious by Louis's second wife, Judith. (Judith had been instrumental in convincing her husband to leave the West Frankish kingdom to Charles.) The rivalry of the brothers was compounded by a series of Viking invasions that occurred during the 840s, particularly against Aquitaine, Brittany, and Frisia.

The death of Pepin in 838 had strengthened Charles's position in the West, but not enough to ward off the threat of war from his other two half-brothers. The three surviving brothers reached a territorial agreement in the Treaty of Verdun in 843 that left Louis with the German lands in the East Frankish realm, Charles with the West Frankish kingdom, and Lothair with a middle kingdom that included Italy and the borderlands between the kingdoms of Louis and Charles. Lothair, however, did not regard this treaty as a permanent resolution of the conflict. He spent the next five years trying to rescind the treaty. Lothair continued his attempts to strengthen his position at the expense of his brothers,

Division of Charlemagne's Empire at Verdun, 843, and Mersen, 870

largely by trying to attract the support of nobles loyal to either of them. But the main provisions of the treaty held. Lothair died in 855, Louis in 876, and Charles the Bald in 877.

The Carolingian line did not die out with Charles the Bald, but in some respects it may as well have. Louis the Stammerer (r. 877–879) made greater concessions to the nobility without regard for the legitimacy of their claims, antagonizing those whose lands had been given away and creating violent rivalries among his nobles. Charles the Fat (r. 881–887), the nephew of Charles the Bald, temporarily reunited the three kingdoms under his rule. But these kingdoms were not integrated with each other; rather they remained three separate kingdoms with their own nobilities. Descendants of Charlemagne claimed the title of emperor until 924 and ruled in the West Frankish kingdom until 987. However, whatever their intentions, these rulers could not stave off the pressures that caused an almost total collapse of centralized political authority.

The breakdown of central imperial authority in the ninth century led to the emergence of new sets of relationships based on the military needs of the more powerful nobles. Their power became based on the number of men on whose loyalty they could count when they needed political or military support. The lord-vassal relationship that became central to the feudal system originated from these needs in the absence of a strong central government. Men looked for lords as much as lords looked for vassals in these uncertain times.

In fact, such were the military needs of the times that in the Capitulary of Mersen in 847 Lothair, Louis, and Charles commanded that each free man must choose a lord and remain in service to him. This law was an expedient designed to maximize the defense of their realms against the Viking threat. Charles the Bald managed to pay enough tribute to divert the Vikings from his lands, but this tactic only succeeded until 879 when an even greater wave of attacks followed. As military needs continued to increase during the tenth and eleventh centuries, an increasing number of men became drawn into the feudal system, extending the lord-vassal relationship down to the prominent members of the peasantry as well. This made it possible for lords to recruit larger armies, such as that with which William of Normandy invaded England in 1066.

In the tenth and eleventh centuries, kings attempted to turn the use of feudal bonds to their advantage by gaining the allegiance of powerful lords within their kingdoms. In 909 the Frankish king, Charles the Simple, attempted to force the Norman chieftain Rollo to pay homage to him for the grant of lands that became Normandy. Rollo refused to kiss the king's foot as requested. Instead, having some sport with Charles, Rollo commanded one of his warriors to kiss the king's foot. The warrior, instead of bending over, lifted the king's foot to his mouth, dumping Charles on his backside in the process. This comical incident reveals an important political reality of the period—the king's authority was completely dependent on his military power and did not elicit any intrinsic respect from vassals who were often in reality more powerful than the king.

War, Invasion, and the Political Development of Medieval Europe

The main threats to political stability in Europe during the ninth and tenth centuries came from the invasions of the Vikings and the Magyars. Beginning in the eighth century, the Vikings exploded out of Scandinavia intent on raiding and pillaging the wealth of the markets, monasteries, and churches to the south. For the most part, the first Viking attacks on Western Europe, particularly northern France and the British Isles, lasting for about a century from the 780s, exercised a destructive influence on European civilization and political stability. The Magyars, who are now believed to have originated from the Volga River region in Russia, had occupied the area now known as Hungary in the ninth century. They represented the greatest threat to the East Frankish realm. Proficient horsemen with a strong warrior ethos, they overwhelmed their enemies with numbers, speed, and skill.

A number of factors contributed to the expansionist activities of the Vikings in this period. The Danes may have felt pressure from the expansion of the Franks into Saxony and the migration of the Slavs from the southeast, but the Norwegians faced no external pressures and they began their raids at about the same time. Internal rivalries in Norway and Denmark surely contributed to the decision of some to seek their fortunes overseas. The initial violent raids and attacks later gave way to a more peaceful migration of settlers looking for agricultural lands, which were too scarce in Scandinavia to support its rising population. By the end of the ninth century Vikings had started to settle in England, Ireland, and France establishing their own political units or, as in the case of Rollo, accepting grants of territory as fiefs from rulers who were intent on making peace with them. After a period of migration between about 870 and 930, the Danish kings—who were not involved in the early raids carried out by members of the Viking aristocracy but had accumulated wealth through increased trade—embarked on their own program of military expansion. By 1016 the Danish king Cnut had established an empire that included Denmark, Norway, and England.

Meanwhile, the German rulers of the East Frankish realm had enhanced their prestige with a series of military victories, beginning with Arnulf's triumph over the Vikings in 891 at the River Dyle. The decline in the number of Viking attacks following this victory played an important role in the reestablishment of some semblance of centralized authority there. Nobility throughout the East Frankish lands accepted Arnulf's authority, even though Arnulf was mainly active in the regions of Bavaria and Franconia. But Arnulf was succeeded by the weak Louis the Child, whose death in 911 brought an end to the Carolingian line in the East Frankish kingdom. In 911 the dukes of the five most powerful duchies—Bavaria, Franconia, Saxony, Swabia, and Thuringia—elected Conrad I, duke of Franconia, as the new king of East Francia. Significantly, the dukes did not attempt to rule without a king; the election of Conrad showed that they still considered royal authority legitimate even after the Carolingians died out. When Conrad died in 919, the dukes reconvened and elected the duke of Saxony, Henry the Fowler (919–936), nicknamed for his proclivity for hunting, as Conrad's successor. Henry elevated the status of his dynasty with his military victories over the Magyars and Slavs. Henry's successor, Otto the Great (936–973), was more ambitious than any of his predecessors. He signaled this ambition in his coronation ceremony, which was conducted by the archbishop of Mainz at Aachen, the site of Charlemagne's capital.

Otto's biggest triumph came over the Magyars at the Battle of Lechfield in 955. The Magyars had a militaristic society in which young men began training for the army at an early age, perhaps as young as ten, primarily on hunting expeditions. Magyar cavalry could move more than twice as fast as the German armies, covering twenty-five miles a day. Stirrups gave the riders the advantage of being able to pivot in the saddle and shoot their bows and arrows from either the front or the rear. But Otto inspired his outnumbered troops with an impassioned speech portraying his fight against the Magyars as a holy war. Lechfield was the first major setback for the Magyars in their rampage across Eastern Europe.

At a time when France was helpless against the attacks of the Vikings and Italy suffered from the ravages of the Magyars and the Saracens, such a victory elevated Otto to a new level of prestige. Otto took the title of Holy Roman Emperor—an indication that he was interested in the peninsula beyond the Alps as well. In 962 Pope John XII (r. 955–964) crowned Otto as Holy Roman Emperor in gratitude for Otto's support against his enemies among the Roman nobility. Otto used the imperial crown to strengthen his claim to rule, but his Italian policy actually interfered with his designs to increase his power in Germany because his absences gave the dukes an opportunity to assert their independence at the expense of the monarchy. Furthermore, Otto never claimed authority over France or Byzantium; in spite of his title, he remained, primarily, a German emperor.

Just as the Viking and Magyar invasions proved critical to the continuation of royal power in the German lands, the Vikings provided the impetus for the unification of England—at least those parts of it outside of Viking control—under the king of Wessex, Alfred the Great (r. 871–899). Alfred and his successors relied on the native aristocracy and the church to legitimize their rule and in return showed preference for both in their law codes. Gradually, a strong monarchy became the central political institution, supplanting any rival claims to authority such as had occurred under the seven-kingdom heptarchy. The kings took responsibility for issuing coinage, enforcing justice, defending the church, issuing writs (or royal commands) that filtered down to the local level, and dispensing land to their loyal supporters among the nobility. However, the English kings were still mainly martial figures whose power and reputation largely depended upon their military success. This can readily be seen in the fate and reputation of the kings who ruled England during the tenth and eleventh century. For example, Athelstan (r. 924–939) won a major victory over a coalition that included the kings of Ireland, Scotland, and Strathclyde at a place called Brunanburgh. This victory was celebrated in a poem, included in the *Anglo-Saxon Chronicle*, whose author described Athelstan as "Lord among Earls, bracelet bestower and Baron of Barons" who gained "a lifelong glory in battle."

The Battle of Brunanburgh

Athelstan King,
Lord among Earls,
Bracelet bestower and
Baron of Barons,
He with his brother,
Edmund Atheling,
Gaining a lifelong
Glory in battle,
Slew with the sword-edge
There by Brunanburgh,
Brake the shield-wall,
Hewed the linden-wood,
Hacked the battle-shield,
Sons of Edward with hammered brands.

Theirs was a greatness
Got from their grandsires—
Theirs that so often in
Strife with their enemies
Struck for their hoards and their hearths and their homes.

Bowed the spoiler,
Bent the Scotsman,
Fell the ship-crews
Doomed to the death.
All the field with blood of the fighters
Flowed, from when first the great
Sun-star of morning-tide,
Lamp of the Lord God,
Lord everlasting,
Glode over earth till the glorious creature
Sank to his setting.

There lay a man
Marred by the javelin,
Men of the Northland
Shot over shield.
There was the Scotsman
Weary of war.

We the West-Saxons,
Long as the daylight
Lasted, in companies

Troubled the track of the host that we hated.
Grimly the swords that were sharp from the grindstone,
Fiercely we hacked at the flyers before us.

Mighty the Mercian,
Hard was his hand-play,
Sparing not any of
Those that with Anlaf,
Warriors over the
Weltering waters
Borne in the bark's-bosom,
Drew to this island—
Doomed to the death.

Five young kings put asleep by the sword-stroke,
Seven strong Earls of the army of Anlaf
Fell on the war-field, numberless numbers,
Shipmen and Scotsmen.

Then the Norse leader,
Dire was his need of it,
Few were his following,
Fled to his war-ship;
Fleeted his vessel to sea with the king in it,
Saving his life on the fallow flood.

Also the crafty one,
Constantinus
Crept to his North again,
Hoar-headed hero!

Slender warrant had
He to be proud of
The welcome of war-knives—
He that was reft of his
Folk and his friends that had
Fallen in conflict,
Leaving his son too
Lost in the carnage,
Mangled to morsels,
A youngster in war!

Slender reason had
He to be proud of
The clash of the war-glaive—

Traitor and trickster
And spurner of treaties—
He nor had Anlaf
With armies so broken
A reason for bragging
That they had the better

In perils of battle
On places of slaughter—
The struggle of standards,
The rush of the javelins,
The crash of the charges,
The wielding of weapons—
The play that they played with
The children of Edward.

Then with their nailed prows
Parted with Norsemen, a
Blood-reddened relic of
Javelins over
The jarring breaker, the deep-sea billow,
Shaping their way toward Dyflen again,
Shamed in their souls.

Also the brethren,
King and Atheling,
Each in his glory,
Went to his own in his own West-Saxonland,
Glad of the war.

Many a carcase they left to be carrion,
Many a livid one, many a sallow-skin—
Left for the white-tailed eagle to tear it, and
Left for the horny-nibbed raven to rend it, and
Gave to the garbaging war-hawk to gorge it, and
That gray beast, the wolf of the weald.

Never had huger
Slaughter of heroes
Slain by the sword-edge—
Such as old writers
Have writ of in histories—
Hapt in this isle, since

Up from the East hither
Saxon and Angle from
Over the broad billow
Broke into Britain with
Haughty war-workers who
Harried the Welshman, when
Earls that were lured by the
Hunger of glory gat
Hold of the land.

Source: Albert S. Cook and Chauncey B. Tinker, eds., *Select Translations from Old English Poetry* (Boston: Ginn, 1926).

1. What evidence from the poem suggests that this battle contributed to the unification of England? What specific information does the poem provide that would permit a reconstruction of the events leading to war and of the war itself?
2. From what perspective is the poem written? How does the writer convey the historical significance of the battle described?
3. What is the poet's attitude toward war in general? What else does the poem tell us about the author? What else does it reveal about the time period in general? What is the poem's overall value as a historical source?

By contrast, the reputation of Ethelred the Unready (r. 978–1016) (his name was really a pun meaning "noble counsel, no counsel") suffered by his inability to defend his kingdom against the Danes. Ethelred fled to Normandy in 1013, temporarily leaving England under the control of the Danish king, Sweyn Forkbeard (d. 1014).

Ethelred's son, Edmund Ironside, won a major victory over Sweyn's son and successor Cnut in 1016. But when Edmund died in the autumn of that year, the Witan (an assembly of the most prominent men in the realm) awarded the throne to the Danish invader. Cnut solidified his position in England partly by marrying Emma of Normandy, the widow of Ethelred, who died in London in 1016, having returned to England upon Sweyn's death. Cnut (r. 1016–1035) actually strengthened the general position of the English monarchy because as an outsider he could claim jurisdiction over the entire kingdom instead of being associated primarily with a particular smaller kingdom, such as the West Saxon kings were with Wessex. However, it remained incumbent upon the king to demonstrate a strong military presence in the kingdom in order to offset powerful earls. Even Edward the Confessor (r. 1042–1066), the oldest son of Ethelred and Emma who gained the throne after the death of his half-brother, Hardicanute, belied his nickname by taking an active interest in military affairs and showing a willingness to go to war if necessary. But Edward, with no strong military of his own, had to buy the support of the most powerful earl in the kingdom, Godwin of Wessex, by marrying Godwin's daughter, Edith, in 1045. Edward came to depend heavily on his brothers-in-law for their military support, giving them a status that potentially rivaled that of the king. In 1066, Godwin's son, Harold of Wessex, staked his claim to the English throne.

In that famous year, Edward the Confessor died without heirs and all hell broke loose. Harold, earl of Wessex, the most powerful man in the kingdom, brother-in-law to the king, chosen by the Witan, was allegedly designated by Edward on his deathbed as his successor. Harold Hardrada of Norway claimed the throne as the heir to the Scandinavian legacy in England, following in the footsteps of Cnut, who had successfully ruled England for more than two decades. William of Normandy, related by blood to Edward, whose mother was William's great-aunt, claimed to have been designated by Edward sometime before 1051 and to have received from Harold of Wessex a solemn oath to support his claim to the English throne just two years before Edward's death. Actually, by sheer hereditary right, the throne should have gone to Edward the Atheling, grandson of Edmund Ironside and a direct descendant of Ethelred and his first wife. But such matters in the eleventh century were still resolved by a show of force, which emphasizes the martial nature of medieval kingship. In this case, the issue was decided in favor of William at the Battle of Hastings, after Harold of Wessex had first exhausted his army in a march northward to defeat his own brother, Tostig, and Harold Hardrada in the Battle of Stamford Bridge.

Meanwhile, in France, the West Frankish nobility had selected in 987 as the king a French duke named Hugh Capet (r. 987–996), finally bringing a formal end to the Carolingian dynasty. As had occurred in the East Frankish realm, the West Frankish nobles accepted the continued existence of the monarchy even though they had no wish to see their own power and independence curtailed in any way. The main achievement of the early Capetians was the successful establishment of their new dynasty, aided by a history of smooth hereditary successions.

The Capetians held a prosperous agricultural territory known as the Île-de-France, which surrounded Paris in the center of the kingdom. The main strategy of the Capetian kings was to add gradually to their domains as they could without stretching their resources too thin. But the king still lacked the power to force his powerful nobles to obey or enforce his decrees. To partially offset the power of the nobility, the kings turned to the church for assistance. The church responded by attempting to curtail the unruly lawlessness of many of the landed nobility. Originating in the late tenth century in peace councils called by church leaders in Aquitaine and Burgundy, the Peace of God prohibited violence against designated places and individuals, especially churches and members of the clergy. The church also became more integrated with the political system; bishops and archbishops served as royal ministers, advisers, and counselors. In addition, royal service often led to appointment to positions in the church hierarchy, thus blurring the lines further between secular and ecclesiastical offices.

Changing Religious Values

By the tenth century, the Christian church in the West had largely fallen under the influence of powerful members of the landed nobility who had founded churches or gained control of wealthy monasteries that were located on their lands. This was not necessarily a bad thing; laymen patronized and protected their churches in uncertain times. But in doing so, they gained control over clerical appointments and played a role in church affairs that some thought properly belonged to the clergy. A reform movement started to emerge in 909 when William, the duke of Aquitaine, founded a new monastery at Cluny that he placed under the direct control of the papacy. Liberated from lay influence, Cluny became a model of a reformed monastery whose monks adhered to their spiritual calling and a strict religious life. Cluny produced a series of abbots in the tenth century who continually renewed the commitment to monastic reform. Soon other monasteries sprang up on the Cluniac model. They placed themselves directly under the jurisdiction of the abbot of Cluny, who appointed a prior for each of them to manage their daily affairs. In the German lands, the abbey of Gorze became the inspiration for a similar movement of monastic reform. Gorze inspired reformed monasteries in Lorraine, Hesse, Swabia, and Bavaria. In England, the kings of Wessex took the lead in support of monastic reform.

The simultaneous emergence of monastic reform movements in Cluny, Germany, and England is indicative of the changing religious values of the tenth century. The reformed monasteries set a clear example to those monastic establishments that had become more secular. These uncertain times called forth a spiritual response from both monks and laymen who looked to God for inspiration and meaning. In the eleventh century, however, Cluny would form an alliance with the papacy that would push the issue of reform even further than in the tenth century.

In the ninth century the popes had continued to rely on the Carolingian rulers to support their position. As the Carolingians declined, however, the papacy also fell into a weakened state. By the tenth century, the papacy had become an established institution with its own administration and resources that allowed it to claim a measure of preeminence in western Christendom. But few tenth-century popes exhibited much influence over the affairs of local churches throughout Europe. Furthermore, the papacy itself had fallen largely into the hands of lay forces, with powerful Roman families using the institution for their own aggrandizement. In the century between 882 and 984 four popes met violent deaths. The papacy lost much of the power and prestige that it had gained from its association with the Carolingians. The fact that many local churches—and now the papacy—had fallen under the control of powerful laymen made for an intolerable situation to those who sought reform.

In an attempt to rectify this situation, the Holy Roman Emperor Otto III (r. 983–1002) stepped in and supported his own former tutor, the intellectually accomplished Gerbert, who reigned as Pope Sylvester II from 999 to 1003. Gerbert knew Arabic and was one of the first Western scholars to introduce Arab knowledge of science and mathematics to the Christian West. As pope, he brought a certain prestige to the papacy that it had previously lacked, but did not do much to enhance actual papal power during his brief tenure. For example, he did little to extend papal influence beyond the Alps. Still, his appointment indicated a growing desire to restore papal authority that did not just come from the emperor. The restoration of papal authority and the desire to end lay control over the church became the focal points for the eleventh-century reform movement known as the Gregorian Revolution, during which the papacy would assert its authority over the church as never before (see Chapter 7 in this volume).

The position of the papacy had also been affected by a major rift between Pope Nicholas I and the Patriarch of Constantinople, Photius, during the 860s when both churches sent missionaries into Bulgaria, while accusing the other of heretical beliefs. Under Photius—a scholar who sought to purge his church of any heretical influences and initiate a new period in its history—a council in 880 affirmed that the true Christian faith was unchanging and unchangeable. Photius insisted that the early church fathers had received and transmitted the essentials of the Christian faith completely and accurately, including the early teaching on the Trinity. He wanted to defend orthodoxy and to keep it pure from outside influences, particularly a new heresy that had emerged among a group known as the Bogomils. According to Cosmas, an eastern priest who wrote his *Sermon against the Heretics* in 969, the Bogomils fostered a dualistic heresy that saw the world as evil and only heaven as good. They viewed the devil as the creator of humanity and the other creatures of the natural world. They denied the presence of Christ in the Eucharist and rejected the validity of the sacraments. The fact that a Christian sect could depart so radically from religious orthodoxy made it essential for both the Greek and Roman churches to emphasize the divine inspiration that they believed had guided their early Fathers.

Other differences exacerbated the growing division between the western and eastern churches. The main difference between western and eastern Christianity lay in the logical, systematic approach to theology and church doctrine that characterized western thought compared to the more intuitive, mystical approach to religion favored in the east. For example, bishops in the western church, still concerned with the Arian heresy, revised the Nicene Creed in 796 to reflect their belief in the equality of the Father and the Son. Eastern churchmen did not regard the three persons of the Trinity as separate and distinct but rather as a mysterious reflection of an ultimate divine unity that human beings could never fully comprehend. In addition, while the western church emphasized the importance of the clergy as direct mediators between God and the laity, eastern theology left more room for a direct relationship between the individual and God. For example, one tenth-century eastern theologian named Symeon thought that any Christian could experience the Holy Spirit directly and that all Christians needed was the Holy Spirit in order to achieve salvation. By contrast, the western church tended to emphasize the importance of its sacraments and its role as the only means toward salvation. Iconoclasm also represented a sore point between the eastern and western churches. Whereas the western church continued to rely heavily on icons for its religious practices, a new wave of iconoclasm was introduced in the Byzantine Empire at the beginning of the ninth century, though this time it was not accompanied by widespread persecution of those who continued to worship icons. Finally, eastern Christianity was characterized by a much less rigid distinction between the clergy and the laity than occurred in the west. Only monks and bishops practiced celibacy in the east, for example. The division between the two churches widened gradually from the mid-eighth century until a major schism in 1054 after a badly botched attempt at reunion.

Eastern Orthodoxy received a great boon in 988 when Vladimir, the ruler of the powerful new state of Kievan Rus, converted to Christianity and brought his people within the orbit of the Byzantine Empire. Russian Christianity followed a Byzantine model that placed a great deal of emphasis on monasticism and denied women a significant role in the church. A new written language, Church Slavonic, contributed to the development of a new literary tradition based on the translation of liturgical texts from Greek. The conversion to Christianity brought Kievan Rus a new status and respect within the rest of the Christian world. Christianity also strengthened the claims of the Russian rulers by adding a religious sanction for their power that contributed to the social stability of the kingdom. But the strength and prosperity of Kievan Rus only lasted until about the middle of the eleventh century, after which frequent succession crises led to internal weakness and prepared the way for the success of a Mongol invasion in 1240.

From the ninth to the eleventh centuries, changing religious values were also evident among the Jews, especially those in the Islamic world who benefited from the favorable attitudes of Muslim authorities under the Abbasid dynasty (750–1268) in Baghdad. Jewish academies devoted to the study of the Talmud and Jewish law arose in the Islamic world by the ninth century. The heads of these academies were known as "Gaons," and in the ninth century they collectively became known as the "Gaonate." The purpose of the Gaonate was to oversee Jewish law for those Jews living in Islamic territories. The Gaonate reinforced the notion of the twofold law, based on the idea of the Pharisees that Moses had received an oral law—that had continued to evolve in response to the problems of the Jews—in addition to the written law contained in the Pentateuch. Although the Gaonate continued to recognize the validity of the Bible, Talmud, and the Mishnah, the Gaons, interpreted the twofold law in accordance with contemporary circumstances. Meanwhile, other Jews in the Islamic world began to take a greater interest in philosophy during this period. Isaac ben Solomon Israeli (ca. 855–955), a physician from Egypt who turned to philosophy as a means of greater self-knowledge, stressed the moral dimension of philosophy and its role in assisting in the promotion of good and the avoidance of evil. Saadia ibn Joseph (882–942), the Gaon at the Babylonian academy at Sura, believed that God's revelation was intended to make his truth accessible to everyone, but that philosophers could access God more directly. Another Jewish philosopher, Solomon ibn Gabirol (ca. 1022–1070), rejected the idea that God had created the world out of nothing and emphasized the importance of God's complete free will. Medieval Jewish philosophers, like their Christian counterparts, were in search of a synthesis that would combine faith and reason in a single harmonious system of thought.

The Shaping of the Past: Medieval Art and Romanesque Architecture

Throughout the history of Christianity, art and architecture have reflected the times in which they were produced, along with the visions of the faith that predominated during each particular era. During the medieval period, when a relatively small percentage of the population was literate, religious art helped to convey some of the most basic teachings and doctrines of the church. Art and architecture proved perfectly capable of fulfilling this purpose since powerful visual images appeal to the emotions as well as the senses. Art was meant to reflect not actual truth about the physical world, but rather the teachings of faith that represented higher truths about God and salvation. No other subject demonstrated this principle more clearly than the triumph of Christ over his death on the cross. For example, on the cover of the *Lindau Gospels*, which were probably commissioned by Charles the Bald for the abbey of Saint-Denis around 870, Christ does not appear to be suffering at all as he hangs upon the cross, symbolizing his victory even at the moment of his death. As the power of God and Christ dwarfed the significance of individual human beings, medieval art before 1100 did not tend to emphasize the visual representation of specific individuals. Instead, even historical or Biblical figures were portrayed in a rather generic way that downplayed the significance of individual differences among people. Artistic renderings of people became symbolic representations of a fallen humanity, while Christ appeared otherworldly, his divinity emphasized more than his humanity.

Illuminated manuscripts illustrate the importance of symbolism in medieval art in other ways as well. In the *Book of Kells*, which was produced near the end of the eighth century at the Celtic monasteries of Iona and Kells, even the letters that make up Christ's name are so elaborately designed as to seem to possess spiritual significance by themselves. The artists who designed these letters took great care to make them works of art that could stand by themselves as symbols of religious truth. They did not need to convey specific religious truths, only the symbolic nature of religious truth itself.

Architecture also began to reflect the symbolic nature of religious truth. The Romanesque style of architecture and sculpture had emerged by the eleventh century. Rome was still the center of the Christian church in the west and the location of many of the sacred relics associated with the early church. Once the number of invasions decreased significantly around the turn of the eleventh century, more and more Europeans once again started undertaking pilgrimages to Rome. The construction of new churches throughout Europe were inspired by the ancient buildings in Rome, the need to house newly acquired sacred relics in appropriate shrines, and the Roman catacombs that provided a model for the underground crypts in the choirs of Romanesque churches. The monastic revival that centered on Cluny also helped to inspire the Romanesque movement. The tenth-century abbey church there has not survived, but surviving drawings of it demonstrate the influence that it had on medieval architecture. Churches even began to feature new areas called Cluniac choirs, where priests could say masses in order to further the goal of constant prayer

See a slide show of more examples of Romanesque architecture and sculpture and read more about the subject at www.metmuseum.org/toah/hd/rmsq/hd_rmsq.htm.

Jesus Christ at the Last Judgment. This sculpture is above the portal of the Romanesque abbey church at Vezelay.

at the monasteries. Two smaller choirs extended to the side of the main choir, while separate chapels were located on the side of the transepts, the two extensions of the nave that gave the church its shape of a cross. The abbey church at Cluny itself had one of the largest naves because of all the smaller chapels that were located around the church.

The main purpose of Romanesque architecture was to reflect spirituality in stone. It did so in quite a different way from the later Gothic style, which would emphasize opening up the walls with more stained glass windows to allow the cathedral to be suffused with light. Romanesque walls were heavy and solid and bore most of the weight of the structure, containing few windows and admitting little light. Still, the new churches impressed their patrons enough with their size and symmetry, their style and suggestive art work. One of the earliest examples of Romanesque sculpture was the figure of Christ in Majesty in the Romanesque church at Roussillon in southern France. Romanesque sculptures generally depicted Christ, the saints, and religious leaders as authority figures who commanded absolute obedience and subservience, as can be seen in the early tenth-century statue of Saint Faith at Conques and the portrayal of Christ at the Last Judgment at Vezelay.

Medieval architecture acquired other conventions as well, such as the common depiction of the patron of the church being presented before Christ.

The ivory panel done around 968 for the altar frontal at Magdeburg Cathedral depicts Otto I in just such a position. In these ways, Romanesque architecture contributed to the ideas of the religious and intellectual revival of eleventh-century Europe at the same time that they contributed to the heightened spirituality and enthusiasm for pilgrimages that helped shape the religious culture of medieval Europe.

Life and Society in the Ninth and Tenth Centuries

Medieval society was divided into three orders often referred to as "those who fought, those who prayed, and those who worked the land." The nobility, which represented a small portion of the population, justified their land, power, and prestige by their ability to defend the rest of the people from invasion, violence, and anarchy. The clergy were regarded as fulfilling a practical function by catering to the spiritual needs of the people and also by petitioning God's favor for the good of the whole society. The vast majority of the population from the ninth to the eleventh centuries consisted of peasants who worked the fields.

Many peasants worked on estates called manors that had their prototypes in the Roman villas and the German villages, but emerged as well-developed social communities, primarily in England and the West and East Frankish kingdoms. Unlike feudalism, which involved a political relationship between free men who engaged in an exchange of personal and military allegiance in return for land, manorialism represented an economic and social relationship between those who owned the land and those who generally gave up their freedom and labor services in exchange for the use of land and protection. Peasants from 800 to 1100 would generally have considered it a decent bargain to receive land to work and support their family in exchange for their labor services, given the paucity of other economic opportunities and the threats of violence from which their lord shielded them. These unfree serfs regarded the land as belonging to them, even if the lord retained ownership, because by contract they had acquired the full legal use of it. Not all peasants who lived on manors were serfs; some were simply free tenants who contracted to provide rent or services in exchange for the use and benefits of the manorial system.

It must not be thought, however, that all peasants in medieval Europe lived within the framework of the manorial system. Many peasants, even in France and England where manorialism was most prevalent, continued to live on their own lands. The unit of the peasant farm appears in a number of charters and surveys from this period. The manorial system was most characteristic of the area of northern France in the general region surrounding Paris, where royal power remained the strongest. In England, manorialism did not take firm root until after the Norman Conquest of 1066, when William I established a strong royal presence there. As much as nobles valued their autonomy, it seems that they needed the sanction of a king in order to solidify their authority over their estates.

In medieval Europe, manorial and village residents pooled their resources and labor to collectively work the fields and perform other tasks necessary for the survival of the community. Communal agriculture contributed to a strong sense of village identity, even though the produce was not shared communally. The most common agricultural system in Western Europe in the medieval period was the two-field system, in which villagers rotated the fields that they cultivated every year, cultivating half of the land and leaving the other half fallow to allow for the restoration of its nutrients. Agricultural techniques and knowledge were still fairly rudimentary. Crop rotation was the farmers' only means of preventing the land from becoming depleted.

Archaeological evidence from the Rhine River Valley suggests that the number of agricultural sites there declined from the eighth to the twelfth century, a loss sandwiched between two periods of agricultural expansion in the region. This decline occurred in spite of the efforts of the Carolingians, beginning with Charlemagne, to expand settlement into that region. However, this agricultural decline was not consistent throughout the rest of Europe. In lower Saxony, for example, a number of new settlements seem to have emerged around the beginning of the tenth century that survived to form the basis of a significant agricultural expansion that occurred in the twelfth century. Several factors contributed to increases in agricultural productivity in the eleventh century, preparing the way for the growth of the population that occurred at that time, including the use of iron, which allowed for the creation of more efficient plows with heavier wheels that came into wider use; the use of iron horseshoes, which, along with the horse collar, made it more feasible to use horses as draught animals; the adoption of a three-field system that allowed for the cultivation of more land each year; the invention of the harrow, an implement used to cultivate the soil by smoothing it over to make sure that more seeds were covered; and, finally, the growing tendency of the aristocracy in the eleventh century to reserve hunting areas for themselves, making peasants even more dependent upon grains.

Peasants shared with members of the nobility some of the social realities of the period that affected everyday life, especially an increasing emphasis placed upon marriage and the family by the church. The church had a vested interest in promoting a moral order in society centered on the family. The church also had a vested interest in ensuring monogamy and forbidding marriages outside established bounds of consanguinity, or blood relationships. Even powerful kings and nobles generally adhered to the church guidelines on these matters, though the church had less success at enforcing its prohibitions against fornication and adultery. Divorce as a church decree did not exist until the twelfth century, but it was common practice in this earlier period to recognize the right of the husband to set aside his wife for adultery or some other justifiable cause. This choice concerned the families of the couple as much as the individuals since marriages usually involved some sort of property agreement between the families. By the eleventh century, church law had superseded the laws of individual kingdoms in the areas of marriage and sexual morality.

In medieval Europe, marriage represented not only the union between a man and a woman, but an alliance between families in which the wife became a part of her husband's family. Marriage occurred in three separate stages: the petition, which was essentially a proposal often offered by one family to another while the principals involved were still children; the betrothal, which legally obligated the couple to wed; and the wedding nuptials, which finalized the arrangement. At that point, the bride and bridegroom exchanged their wedding gifts, which constituted the dowries that were promised to each other before the wedding. The gift to the bride, which ensured that she would have security if she became a widow, generally consisted of property complete with residence, other buildings, animals, and, among the nobility, serfs, in addition to personal items such as jewelry and clothing. In addition, it was customary in Europe for the wife to maintain control over her dowry property to sell as she wished, with or without her husband's consent. Laws of the English kings Ethelred and Cnut in the early eleventh century designed to protect wealthy widows from being forced into unwanted marriages or religious convents demonstrate the limits of the stereotype of male disregard for women's happiness in the patriarchal society of the Middle Ages.

The Mayan Civilization of Mesoamerica

The Classic period, or golden age, of Mayan civilization overlapped with this period of medieval history, lasting from approximately 250 to 909 CE. The Mayans had a sophisticated, prosperous society that revolved around urban centers and reached its height around 730 CE. Like medieval Europe, Mayan civilization did not consist of a single unified political state or empire. To some extent, the Mayan political order resembled that of France in the feudal period, with over sixty lords controlling independent territories that they were constantly attempting to expand or defend. Sometimes they made alliances or willingly subjugated themselves to an overlord who would help them to defend their interests, making Mayan politics similar to the system of European feudalism that evolved in the ninth and tenth centuries. Nonetheless, the Mayans seem to have evolved during the Classic period a political ideology of sacred hereditary kingship akin to the European conception of theocratic monarchy associated with the Carolingians. Mayan kings may have even claimed that they possessed divine status. Kingship always devolved through the male line and female rulers came to power only in the absence of any male descendants of the royal family, another similarity to European practice.

Each city had a single governor known as a *halach vinic* who exercised virtually complete authority over justice and administration within the city, as well as the right to negotiate agreements with other cities. These ruling lords held an abundance of power over a centralized government unchecked by either religious authorities or representative institutions. There is no evidence of an administration or bureaucracy that operated independently of the political leadership of Mayan states. In the Rosario Valley, for example, no administration buildings have been found that are separate from the centers of political authority. Rulers had a great deal more wealth than their subjects, and family members of the ruler shared with other noble elites something of a monopoly on education. More than one privileged family participated in the government of at least some Mayan polities, but each state had its own supreme ruler who claimed divine favor or status.

Mayan political culture was a largely military one, as was the case in medieval Europe. Warfare was a constant occurrence across the various regions of Mayan rule, particularly among the sixteen states that occupied the Yucatan peninsula. Mayan art often celebrated the warrior ethos through its representations of animal figures such as pumas, coyotes, and jaguars. Other works depict achievements on the battlefield and the practice of taking captives who were often used as human sacrifices. Military conflicts among city-states increased significantly in the second half of the eighth century, leading to the decline of a number of cities and prefiguring the downfall of Mayan civilization, particularly in the southern lowlands.

As in medieval Europe, members of the Mayan nobility served as the military leaders of the society. They also owned large tracts of land, frequently held slaves, and, were the only ones besides family members of the rulers to have access to an education. But Mayan nobles were more likely than their European counterparts to engage in commerce or to become artists or architects. The nobles monopolized trade and food distribution. There was a significant degree of social stratification among the Mayan elites, based mainly on their lineage, which was extremely important in Mayan society, and their relationship to the ruler. For most of the Classic period, Mayan society worked because the nobility and the peasantry performed different roles but shared in the benefits of a functioning and prosperous society. As time went on, however, the Mayan aristocratic elites seem to have become wealthier, creating an even larger divide between them and the rest of the population.

Religion and a powerful sense of the sacred dominated Mayan society no less than in medieval Europe. As Christianity did for Europeans, Mayan religion and cosmology gave meaning to the entire cycle of life and was reinforced by standard rituals. Because of the importance of religion in Mayan society, some scholars believe that the Mayans must have had a powerful priesthood, but no evidence exists for a separate category of priests distinct from the political authorities—a clear difference between Mayan and medieval European civilization. The Mayans also differed from Christian Europe in their cyclical view of time as opposed to the linear concept introduced by Christianity. The Mayans developed a sophisticated interlocking calendar system that reflected their preoccupation with time, the understanding of which they believed held the key to their destiny. In addition to a 365-day solar calendar, another calendar based on the movements of Venus followed a 260-day cycle, which determined the timing of most of their religious rituals. Each ritual had a symbolic significance that related to when it was performed.

Unlike Christian Europe, the Mayans had a large pantheon of gods—166 according to one manuscript. The Mayans recognized as supreme the powerful god Itzamná, who created human beings and exercised control over all areas of life. The Mayans believed in an underworld, and unlike the Christians they sought to make contact with and appease the deities that they believed resided therein. People from all walks of life—from hunters and fishers to comedians and tattoo artists—had their own gods from whom they could seek assistance or inspiration. Mayan war gods resembled the Roman god of Mars or the Persian cult god Mithras, whose worship spread throughout Europe during the later Roman Empire. The Mayans had a large number of nature deities as well, whose appeasement gave the Mayans some sense of control over their environment. Perhaps when the cult of the saints in medieval Europe is taken into consideration, Mayan beliefs did not differ so dramatically from their Western counterparts.

Mayan religious rituals, however, differed most notably in their inclusion of human sacrifice. The Mayans used criminals and slaves for their sacrifices, but more perplexing was their frequent sacrifice of children, particularly illegitimate ones and orphans. They perhaps believed that the blood of children did more to appease the gods to whom the sacrifices were dedicated. The blood of prisoners of war from the elite classes of neighboring territories was also highly valued. Mayan elites valued their own blood and had bloodletting ceremonies for both men and women; men drew blood from their penises, women from their tongues. The Mayan preoccupation with blood was based on the belief that the blood contained the sacred essence that connected humans with the gods and the rest of creation. By contrast, Christians believed that God had sacrificed the life and blood of his son, Jesus, and no longer required sacrificial offerings, though they continued to affirm the importance of this sacrifice in the Eucharist when they symbolically drank the blood of Christ.

▲▼ ▲▼ ▲▼ ▲▼ ▲▼ ▲▼ ▲▼ ▲▼ ▲▼ ▲▼ ▲▼ ▲▼ ▲▼ ▲▼

Illuminated Books from the Mayan and Christian Worlds

This first image is a detail from a Mayan codex, one of only several that survived the destruction of Mayan books in the sixteenth century by the Spaniards, who viewed them as the work of the devil. The second image is from an illuminated manuscript, *The Book of Kells*, produced by Irish monks in about 800 CE.

How would you compare these two images? Are there any similarities in the artistic styles? What were the respective artists trying to convey? What do the differences in artistic styles reveal about the two civilizations?

Detail from a Mayan codex

Image from *The Book of Kells*

Both medieval and Mayan art were largely intended to serve religious purposes. Mayan temples generally contained numerous small shrines in separate rooms or chambers, not dissimilar to the small side chapels of the medieval cathedrals. Although the Mayans gave considerably more attention to architecture than to interior design, some Mayan temples did contain elaborate decorations, such as the colorful paintings that appear on the walls of the temples of Tikal. Mayan art was often quite realistic, compared to Romanesque art, which was almost entirely symbolic. Mayan artists did more to depict movement in their paintings and sculptures, while also appreciating the importance of perspective, characteristics that were largely absent from the art of medieval Europe. European artists were not interested in the natural world of creation, whereas the Mayans valued the natural world as containing sacred qualities. They believed that one sacred essence existed in all parts of creation, from the sun, stars, rocks, and trees to human life itself. Romanesque art was intended to celebrate a higher abstract vision of the faith that separated the natural world from the supernatural. Mayan artists, not bound by the same restrictions, experimented more freely, making their art both more fanciful and more realistic at the same time.

Within the larger framework of religious art, Mayan artists also portrayed war and the daily activities of the common people. As in medieval Europe, Mayan society was primarily based on agriculture; the majority of the lower classes were peasant farmers who, like their European counterparts, worked the land together in a collaborative effort to maximize food production. During the late Classic period, Mayan society generated an increase in wealth, probably the result of a population expansion that is revealed by the appearance of more and larger cities. Increasingly elaborate tombs, palatial homes, and a greater variety of luxury items appeared during this period. But this wealth contributed to a growing social divide that, combined with a lack of sufficient resources to sustain the larger population, may have hastened the decline of Mayan civilization in the tenth century.

Obtain more information and see more images from the Mayan codices at www.library.arizona.edu/exhibits/mexcodex/maya.htm.

The Book of Kells is on exhibit at Trinity College Library in Dublin. For more information, go to www.tcd.ie/Library/bookofkells/book-of-kells.

Conclusion

During the ninth and tenth centuries, it seemed as though all major components of medieval Europe needed to cooperate in order to preserve some semblance of order and stability. Kings gave up local power to their nobles, who in return not only governed and protected their regions but swore an oath of allegiance that at least preserved the idea of royal authority. Nobles formed relationships with each other in the feudal system in an attempt to gain strength through numbers. Peasants gave up their freedom and willingly worked on their lords' estates in exchange for protection and their strips of land. The church did not object to lay interference in its affairs, while laymen bequeathed land to the church and supported its mission and even its reform. Conflicts between rulers and church authorities sometimes arose, but they were not endemic or frequent in this period.

By the eleventh century, Europe had started to escape from under the shadow of invasions from Muslims, Vikings, and Magyars. Improvements in agriculture, a period of relative peace, and a warming trend in the climate, leading to a longer growing season, all contributed to an increase in population. A rising population and a surplus of food contributed to a revival of trade and an increase in the number of towns throughout Europe, along with a growing merchant class and new opportunities for education and employment. Monarchs gradually began to assert their authority over their nobles and kingdoms and to revive theoretical justifications for their power. The church had ambitions of its own, and the idea of religious reform was carried to new extremes, orchestrated by an increasingly radical group of churchmen in Rome who gained control of the papacy in the second half of the eleventh century. The eleventh century and those that immediately followed saw the development of a serious rift between church and state, as both vied for the leadership of Christian Europe. This period also saw the emergence of a much more sophisticated medieval civilization marked by important achievements in art, architecture, education, philosophy, law, and economic and political development.

1. What do the developments in this chapter reveal about the nature of medieval kingship and political authority?
2. What was the basic nature of the relationship between the church and the state from the ninth to the eleventh centuries?
3. What factors shaped the changes in religion and politics that occurred during this period?
4. To what extent do these centuries deserve to be known as the "Dark Ages"?
5. What conclusions might be reached about Mayan and European civilization in this period on the basis of a comparison between the two?

Suggestions for Further Reading

Brown, Peter. 2003. *The Rise of Western Christendom: Triumph and Diversity, A.D. 200–1000*. 2nd ed. Malden, MA: Blackwell.

Coe, Michael. 2005. *The Maya*. 7th ed. London: Thames and Hudson.

Freedman, Paul. 1999. *Images of the Medieval Peasant*. Stanford, CA: Stanford University Press.

Olson, Lynette. 2007. *The Early Middle Ages: The Birth of Europe*. London: Palgrave Macmillan.

Reston, James, Jr. 1998. *The Last Apocalypse: Europe at the Year 1000*. New York: Doubleday.

Thompson, John A. 1998. *The Western Church in the Middle Ages*. London: Arnold.

Suggested Websites

www.chronique.com/Library/MedHistory/charlemagne.htm

This is a good website for those interested in learning more about Charlemagne.

www.fordham.edu/halsall/sbook1i.html

Numerous primary sources can be found in this Internet Medieval Sourcebook, along with a good discussion of the term *feudalism.*

www.historyguide.org/ancient/lecture20b.html

This website relates the changes occurring in Europe during Charlemagne's time to developments elsewhere in the world.

www.pbs.org/wgbh/nova/maya

This companion website for the PBS documentary *The Lost King of the Maya* is an excellent introduction to some detailed research, as well as general information about Mayan history and civilization.

www.themiddleages.net

This website provides detailed coverage of various topics related to medieval history.

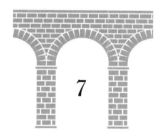

7

The High Middle Ages, ca. 1000–1300

Christianity and the Roman church provided the unifying force that distinguished Europe from the rest of the world from the eleventh to the fourteenth century in the period known as the High Middle Ages. Christianity continued to evolve and expand during this period, while the Catholic Church made even greater claims to authority, power, and influence. Christian ideas about God and his relationship with humanity shaped the cultural vision of this period, while the church played a dominant role in society and asserted itself in the political realm. During this same period, cultural, economic, and political achievements created a new sense of confidence among Europeans, especially among the ruling classes. Population growth and economic expansion went hand in hand and allowed more time for people to devote to education and cultural pursuits. This period saw the rise of cathedral schools in the towns and cities and the creation of the first universities. New forms of literature, innovations in art and architecture, and brilliant achievements in philosophy were among the results of an educational and intellectual renaissance. The application of new ideas to politics created both stronger rationales for royal government as well as the creation of new representative institutions.

A growing sense of confidence contributed to the first efforts at European expansion, which included the attempt of Europeans to conquer the Holy Land and restore it to the Christian faith. The Crusades, which began with a call from Pope Urban II in 1095, brought Europeans face to face with Muslim civilization and initiated a clash of Christian and Islamic cultures that has continued into the twenty-first century. But Christians and Muslims also learned from each other, and their cross-cultural contact during this period did much to shape the future histories of both civilizations. The history of the Crusades demonstrates that religious tolerance is possible even in the midst of frequent and intense conflict.

But Islamic expansion was hardly exhausted as Muslim armies launched new attacks on Spain and spread their faith to new areas in sub-Saharan Africa. As these regions of Africa became more involved in a network of international commerce, they developed new political states and kingdoms to regulate the growing inequality in society that an influx of wealth always produces. Europe

192

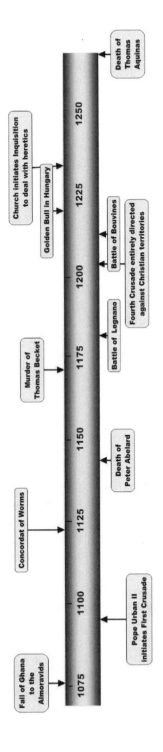

experienced profound political changes and the rise of new kingdoms as well, also deriving largely from the economic expansion that was the prerequisite for so much of the frenzied and profoundly transformative activities that characterized this era.

The Shaping of the Past: Agricultural Expansion and the Development of Urban Centers

Agricultural expansion and urban growth fed each other. Agriculture sustained urban expansion and urban growth placed more demands upon agriculture and supported an increase in agricultural productivity. Throughout Europe, from England to Sicily, forests were cleared, swamps drained, and land reclaimed from the sea. The demand for land in England became so great that people began encroaching on the royal lands and having their claims recognized by the king, who apparently regarded agricultural expansion as a more pressing need than defending his own territories.

Political stability and the end of invasions, which contributed to the growth in the European population, encouraged the rise of towns and the development of urban life in the eleventh century. The Romans had established a number of urban centers throughout their empire as administrative and trading centers, many of which provided the foundation for towns during the revival that occurred during the High Middle Ages. The church had established cathedrals at many of these locations, attracting more people to them as the population expanded and trade revived. The cities that had survived in Europe, such as Venice, were those that had maintained their trading relations with the East even when trade had declined significantly throughout most of Europe. In the early medieval period, urban life had remained most developed in southern Europe because of its proximity to the Mediterranean and trade routes to the East. Córdoba in Spain, which had the additional advantage of its connection to the rest of the Islamic world, became one of the most populous cities in Europe, with a population over 300,000 by the tenth century. In the eleventh century increasing numbers of European merchants began to engage in long-distance trade. Subsequently, the populations of Paris, Milan, Florence, Venice, and Palermo grew to over 100,000 by the end of the thirteenth century. Most towns in Europe during the High Middle Ages, however, did not exceed 6,000 in population. And even in heavily populated areas such as Flanders and northern Italy, more than 80 percent of the population still lived in the countryside and made their living by agriculture.

Population growth brought changes to society and provided new opportunities and advantages in both towns and the countryside. Since population growth promoted the rise of towns, this meant that peasants had options that had been previously unavailable. In order to attract workers, it became common practice throughout Europe for towns to offer incentives for serfs to leave the countryside. Some lords willingly granted their serfs freedom to allow for more flexibility in the use of their land based on market forces. For example, by reclaiming land used by serfs in a traditional manner, lords could have different crops planted or even convert arable land to pasture to take advantage of the demand for wool. Some serfs managed to buy their freedom during this period from profits made by selling their goods at markets. It also became tradition that serfs who managed to reside in a city for a year and a day were considered free.

In many respects, the rise of towns provided the foundation for many of the other major developments of the High Middle Ages. It is difficult to envision the rise of universities and the cultural achievements of the period without the existence of centers that would draw people to exchange learning, knowledge, and ideas in addition to goods. Rulers relied on the income from towns to strengthen their governments. The alliance between monarchs and a growing class of townsmen or burghers (bourgeoisie in French) constituted one of the main political developments of the period. Towns could not have developed or survived without an increase in trade, while trade could not have flourished without a network of towns located along specific routes. Medieval towns rose in conjunction with a trade revival and became centers to and from which merchants could deliver their goods to enough people to make their business profitable. Towns provided for the growth of a class of burghers who simply did not fit into the traditional social categories of clergy, nobles, and peasants.

Society and Everyday Life in the High Middle Ages

Merchants and craftsmen in the rising towns seeking to find their place in medieval society created organizations that provided them with a sense of belonging. Their organizations became known as guilds, which became a dominant force in urban life throughout Christendom. Guilds developed first and became the strongest in places that had the strongest urban traditions, particularly Flanders and northern Italy. Merchant and craft guilds provided their members with the kind of security that land gave to the nobility and peasantry and the church gave to its clergy. Merchant guilds had originally developed out of a need for members to band together for mutual protection. Guild members did not view themselves in competition with one another; instead, they provide an example of the tendency of medieval people to think in terms of collective identities. Guilds were in essence monopolies that prohibited anyone not belonging to a guild from setting up a shop or business within city limits.

Guilds had their own system of apprenticeship that provided training for individuals who would become workers employed by the guilds and, eventually, new members of the guild. Apprentices were usually adolescents who left their families in their early teens to work and learn under a master guildsman in a particular craft or trade. After a period that might have averaged five years, they would become paid workers known as journeymen, who worked for a daily wage. Journeymen could become masters of their craft and join the guild once they had accumulated enough money to open their own shop and proved their skill at their craft through the production of an item worthy of a master (a masterpiece). This system created order and stability within the guild system and contributed to the general stability of medieval society as a whole. Guild regulations covered such matters as the quality of products, the price paid for materials, the wages paid to journeymen, working hours, and the prices charged for products. Selling prices were governed by a concept known as a "just" price, generally the amount necessary to cover the costs of producing an item along with enough profit to allow the guild member to maintain an adequate standard of living. Guilds were also political organizations; prominence in the merchant guild often translated into positions in local government. Guilds provided a number of other services to towns, since they were responsible for such municipal projects as maintaining or improving roads, docks, and harbors, in addition to making sure that their town had an adequate supply of food.

Once merchants began to settle in the towns, they began to build walls for protection that then marked the town's boundaries. The protection offered by towns then attracted additional settlers. The disadvantage of enclosing the towns in such set boundaries as walls is that it inhibited growth beyond a certain point. Eventually, the towns became too crowded, leading to the building of multistoried buildings, with the wealthier occupants living on the ground floor. But those on the ground floor had the disadvantage of living closer to streets that contained sewage and food scraps dumped out of the windows from above. Proximity created the conditions for conflict and necessitated the creation of town watchmen to retain order. In university towns, raucous students came into frequent conflict with other residents of the town who did not hesitate to take advantage of the students by charging high rents and prices.

At first the guild system was antithetical to the rise of capitalism, since the guilds were cooperative organizations that inhibited open competition. Whereas the guilds regulated everything and formed monopolies, capitalism is a system that involves open competition among individuals within a free market economy. But a tension already existed in medieval society between collective identities and individualism. Individuals who sought larger profits and struck out on their own contributed to the rise of capitalism, which by its nature represented a challenge to the guild system. The guild system originated to regulate the economy in a particular town or region and was not particularly well-suited to international trade. The European economy came to rely increasingly on long-distance trade from the eleventh century forward, partly as a response to an increased demand for goods, especially among the nobility and the wealthy members of the towns, who became interested in the greater variety of goods available from the East as a result of the expansion that accompanied the Crusades. But the rise of capitalism could not have occurred without the initiative of individual merchants who sought to increase their own standard of living through more aggressive trading practices. During the High Middle Ages, European merchants began to import spices from the Near East and silks from China. Merchants from the region of the east Baltic and Russia sold lumber, furs, amber, and grain. Scandinavian merchants transported tons of fish, as well as timber and iron. Capitalism did not replace the guild system overnight, but it did begin to develop alongside of it by the thirteenth century, creating an international economy that affected the political fortunes of kingdoms within—and outside—of Europe.

Political Leadership and Kingship in Sub-Saharan Africa and Europe

The growth of large political states and kingdoms in sub-Saharan Africa resulted in part from economic change and more extensive trading connections, particularly with the Islamic territories to the north and east. A variety of states developed from the tenth to the fourteenth century in a region that had previously been dominated by tribal chieftains presiding over societies with a strictly local economic focus. The first such state was the empire of Ghana, whose fall at the hands of the Islamic Almoravids in 1076 helped to prepare the way for the emergence of new political entities such as the Takrur state in the Senegal River Valley, the state established by the Sosso east of the Takrur, Kanem, the seven city-states of Hausaland in what is now northern Nigeria, and the first Yoruban kingdom. The ruling classes of most of these states converted to Islam, as did those of Mali and Songhai, which later became successive dominant powers in the region.

African monarchs, no less than European ones, needed a reputation for strength and charisma in order to maintain allegiances and hold their states together. This was particularly true since most of the lesser chieftains and village leaders did not convert to Islam, instead retaining their traditional religious beliefs. African monarchies were dominated by connections between rulers and the local heads of lineage groups and individual villages. Like feudal princes swearing their allegiance to a liege lord, the local leaders accepted the domination of, say, the Mali kings from the early thirteenth century because

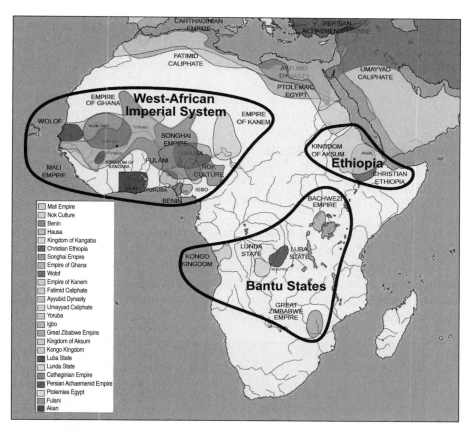

Emergence of states in Africa, 500–1500

outside interest in African gold and the expansion of trade made such alliances desirable both from a defensive and an economic perspective.

The ultimate goal of these kingdoms was peace, a prerequisite for benefiting from trade and economic expansion. The rulers of Mali—centered on the upper Niger River—created a large empire that far exceeded that of Ghana two centuries earlier. Conquest played an important role in the creation of the Mali Empire, beginning with the victories of Mali's Charlemagne, Sundiata (r. 1235–1255). A victory over the Sosso king Sumanguru in 1235 cemented his reputation among his warriors and prepared the way for future conquests. Like his European contemporaries, Sundiata, although celebrated in legend as a powerful warrior, tried to centralize his administration while supporting both trade and agricultural development. For the rest of the thirteenth and most of the fourteenth century, Mali dominated the lucrative gold and salt trade throughout the region. European monarchs were only just beginning to

▲▼ ▲▼ ▲▼ ▲▼ ▲▼ ▲▼ ▲▼ ▲▼ ▲▼ ▲▼ ▲▼ ▲▼ ▲▼

Royal Women in Twelfth- and Thirteenth-Century Africa and Europe

The first image is a terracotta figure of a Yoruba queen from Nigeria. The second is the famous Eleanor of Aquitaine, wife of Henry II of England and a powerful woman in her own right by virtue of her possession of the wealthy province of Aquitaine in southern France. Prior to her marriage to Henry, Eleanor had been married to Louis VII of France, whom she divorced. After Henry's death, she continued to play an active role in politics under her sons Richard and John, both kings of England.

Do the artists of these two works portray royal women in a fundamentally different way? If so, what are the differences? Are these artists attempting to convey something about these individual women or about the nature of royal women in general? Is there a connection between the comparison of these two images and the comparison of African and European kingship in this chapter?

Yoruba queen *(Courtesy of Getty Images)*

Eleanor of Aquitaine, ca. 1122–1204

▲▼ ▲▼ ▲▼ ▲▼ ▲▼ ▲▼ ▲▼ ▲▼ ▲▼ ▲▼ ▲▼ ▲▼ ▲▼ ▲▼

Learn more about Yoruban art and culture at http://hearstmuseum.
berkeley.edu/outreach/pdfs/yoruba_teaching_kit.pdf.

View other works of art from medieval Europe at www.metmuseum.
org/Works_of_Art/medieval_art.

appreciate the potential for income from trade when Mali kings were taxing all imports and exports in their kingdom.

Another prominent empire in medieval Africa that profited from increased trade with the Islamic world was that of Kanem, northeast of Lake Chad. The first ruler, Hummay, to bring Islam to Kanem did so around 1075, concomitant with the establishment of the new Sefuwa dynasty, which ruled until the mid-nineteenth century. The existence in this period of seven independent Hausa city-states confirms the importance of trade; like the Hanseatic League, a loose organization of commercial towns in northern Europe that formed around this time, the Hausa states worked together to achieve their mutual goals of defense and promotion of their commercial interests. With a solid agricultural base, these states continued to prosper into the fifteenth century and grew more culturally sophisticated with the introduction of Islam by foreign merchants around 1300.

Medieval African monarchies possessed highly developed and polished governments, frequently relying on educated Muslims to staff their administrations. The trend toward keeping more and more written records was shared by the European monarchs of the High Middle Ages. Taxes, effective administration, and strong armies were the main ingredients for successful monarchies on both continents. African monarchs, though, acquired additional sanction for their rule through marriage alliances with a number of different lineage groups within their kingdoms—for this reason they sometimes had several hundred (or thousand) wives. In Mali, Sundiata strengthened his prestige and authority by cultivating ceremony surrounding his kingship and isolating himself from his people, while oral traditions emerged about a miraculous childhood in which he overcame paralysis in his legs and suddenly began to walk at the age of seven. These traditions were finally recorded in written form by the historian D.T. Niane in 1960 as *Sundiata: An Epic of Old Mali*. Myths surrounding European kings such as Arthur, Alfred, and Charlemagne were used to support the legitimacy of later rulers; such may have been the case with Sundiata in Mali. But in neither place did such stories substitute for the practical abilities, especially in warfare, that ultimately validated the power of a medieval ruler. The history of Mali substantiates this, for within thirty years of Sundiata's death a man named Sakura, a military leader from a different family, seized control of Mali's government and initiated a new period of conquest. Still, the belief in the legitimacy of the dynasty must have counted for something because in the end Sakura abdicated in favor of Sundiata's descendants. African monarchies tried to preserve the best of both worlds: a system of hereditary monarchy that asserted the legitimacy of the dynasty without following primogeniture so that the most capable child of the monarch could be selected to rule. European monarchies followed much the same principles, though this system could sometimes produce intense competition and military feuds between rival claimants to the throne. Thus, the concept of throne-worthiness was a legacy from the original foundation of a dynasty. In Sundiata's case, he allegedly had to overcome the jealousy of other wives of his father who would have preferred their own children to inherit the throne.

During the eleventh century the monarchs of England and France started to use feudal traditions to strengthen their claims over their kingdoms. After the Norman Conquest in 1066, William I laid the groundwork for a strong English monarchy by combining elements of Norman rule based on feudal traditions with Anglo-Saxon traditions such as the local hundred and shire courts and the use of royal administrative decrees known as writs. The English king who did the most to enhance royal authority in the High Middle Ages was Henry II (r. 1154–1189). A powerful military ruler, Henry created a huge empire comprising vast territories in France, including Normandy, Anjou, and the Aquitaine, in addition to his English kingdom. Henry's own skill as a fighter and military leader commanded the respect of even his greatest nobles, who could not match the king's leadership, resources, or determination. Henry was a powerful and charismatic figure who reveled in the role of king and, knowing that land equaled power, acquired as much territory as he could. He sought to boost the sources of royal revenue through collection of feudal aids (payments owed by vassals for special occasions such as the knighting of the king's eldest son and the marriage of his eldest daughter), the imposition of additional taxes, and the substitution of monetary payments called scutage for the military service owed by his vassals. He granted charters to towns and used the income and political support that the townsmen offered to strengthen his government at the expense of the nobility.

Henry's attempt to expand his power was not without obstacles: his desire to have royal courts override ecclesiastical courts brought him into a serious conflict with his archbishop of Canterbury and former chancellor, Thomas Becket (1118–1170). When Henry decided to appoint Becket to the position of archbishop of Canterbury, he completely underestimated the extent of both Becket's dedication to the privileges of the church and his stubbornness in insisting upon his own prerogatives. Ironically, the pope supported Henry in his quarrel with Becket, mainly because Alexander III was more concerned with his rivalry with the Holy Roman Emperor (Frederick Barbarossa) and had no wish to alienate a potential ally in Henry. Becket fled England on multiple occasions for France, but each time that he reconciled with Henry enough to return, he refused to temper his opposition to Henry's policies toward the church. John of Salisbury—an intellectual cleric who served Thomas Becket as his personal secretary before becoming chancellor to Henry II—argued in his influential political treatise *Policraticus* (written in the 1160s at the height of the Becket controversy) that kings could claim a moral justification for their power as long as they did not abuse that power or ignore the best interests of their subjects. John's argument supported the growing power of the monarchy because he left no recourse for the church if a monarch did rule as a tyrant. On Christmas night in 1170, four of Henry's knights, acting in the belief that they were enforcing the will of their monarch, murdered Becket as he celebrated mass in Canterbury cathedral. The murder provoked an intense public reaction against Henry, who underwent a period of penance that included beatings by monks and temporarily backed off his challenge to the ecclesiastical courts. He may have felt a profound regret over the death of his former friend and chancellor, but his repentance served a political purpose as well. The death of Becket did nothing to deter Henry in his efforts to build a strong secular monarchy and to extend royal power at the expense of the church.

The relative weakness of Henry's immediate successors created serious problems that limited the power of the English monarchy while the French kings slowly but surely continued to expand their lands and extend their authority. The rise of the power of the English monarchy was more rapid and spectacular than that of the French kings during the eleventh and twelfth centuries, but the Capetian dynasty had a stability founded largely on a long line of smooth transitions from one reign to the next, based on the principle of hereditary succession. Between 987 and 1316 every Capetian king left a male heir, of whom only one had not yet reached his majority. The Capetian kings carefully avoided alienating their nobility, remaining content to secure their authority over their own realm in the prosperous and strategically advantageous region known as the Île-de-France, gradually expanding their patrimony as circumstances and resources permitted.

Philip II (r. 1180–1223), who was so sick in 1179 that a planned coronation as co-king had to be cancelled, turned out to be a shrewd, manipulative, and savvy ruler. He made great strides in the expansion of royal power in France, especially at the expense of the English kings, who were technically his vassals for the lands they held in France. In 1189 Philip embarked on the so-called King's Crusade, along with Richard I of England and Frederick Barbarossa, the Holy Roman Emperor. But Philip, wishing to devote his attention to expanding his royal patronage at home, returned home because of a suspect illness. His plans came to fruition when he declared that Richard's successor, John, had forfeited his lands in France by marrying the daughter of another vassal of Philip without permission; Philip made good his declaration through military victory at the Battle of Bouvines in 1214. Philip also concentrated on building up the royal treasury, largely through cultivating an alliance with the French towns, and on extending royal justice through the use of officials known as seneschals—educated lawyers who owed their positions directly to the king.

Meanwhile, in the German lands of the Holy Roman Empire, semi-independent dukes and princes looked for opportunities to curb the power of the emperor whenever possible. The long reign (1152–1190) of Frederick I, duke of Swabia, as the Holy Roman Emperor provided a measure of political stability and should have given him time to consolidate his power over the other duchies. Frederick, however, had serious aspirations south of the Alps and did not focus exclusively on Germany (Frederick's Italian nickname, "Barbarossa" or "red-beard," testified to his preoccupation with Italy). Frederick knew that if he could derive income from taxing the wealthy towns in northern Italy, he would be less dependent on feudal dues from the German nobility. However, Frederick suffered an important military defeat at Legnano in 1180—partly as a result of a betrayal by one of his most powerful vassals, Henry the Lion—and was forced into a compromise with the northern Italian towns.

Frederick's successors, Henry VI (r. 1190–1197) and Frederick II (r. 1215–1250) retained Barbarossa's obsession with the south. By 1197 Henry had successfully asserted his authority over the northern Italian towns and was threatening Rome. But his sudden death from a fever in that year left the throne to the three-year-old Frederick II, leaving an opening for more powerful men to lay claim to the imperial title. Frederick gained the throne after the 1214 Battle of Bouvines, where Pope Innocent III had cast his lot with Philip II of France and the winning side against John of England and Frederick's rival, Otto of Brunswick. Frederick II was a strong ruler who believed strongly in the monarchical principle and had a sense of his own power; he simply chose to exercise that power more in Sicily than he did in the German lands, making concessions to the German princes to the detriment of royal power there.

The preoccupation of the German emperors with the south and the subsequent weakness of the German monarchy contributed to the emergence of new monarchies in Eastern Europe. The Roman church supported this development as it looked to spread and strengthen Christianity in that region. Administratively, the church established bishoprics that served as a model for the political organization of the new kingdoms of Bohemia, Poland, and Hungary. Like the new sub-Saharan African kingdoms, these Eastern European kingdoms benefited from the cultural influence of a new religion, the growth of trade and a monetary economy, and the hiring of court officials to keep written records. But these lands had also been settled and claimed by powerful barons who did not completely subordinate themselves to the new monarchies. In order to win their allegiance and access to some of their wealth, Andrew II (r. 1205–1235) in Hungary granted some political concessions in the famous Golden Bull in 1222, seven years after John of England had made similar concessions to his barons in the Magna Carta (Great Charter). In Poland, Boleslav III (r. 1102–1138) had recognized the rights of the landed class in his kingdom to the disadvantage of the Polish peasantry; the peasantry throughout Eastern Europe emerged from the High Middle Ages in a much worse position than their Western European counterparts. The position of the monarchies in Poland and Hungary was weakened in the thirteenth century by the Mongol invasions of their lands, which produced depopulation and forced the kings to look for additional support from the cities and landowners in their kingdoms in exchange for still further concessions.

The tendency toward the establishment of new monarchies and the growth of royal power can be found in Scandinavia during this period as well. Norwegian and Swedish kings asserted their independence from Denmark in the eleventh century (though at the beginning of the twelfth century some parts of Sweden were not yet under royal control). As in Africa and Eastern Europe, religious conversion transformed these monarchies and gave them a new purpose and legitimacy. Paganism did not disappear overnight, especially among the common people, any more than did traditional African religions when their kings converted to Islam. But not for nothing did Harald Bluetooth (ca. 910–ca. 985), king of Denmark, erect a monument to himself celebrating his role in Christianizing the Danes. Norwegians continued to celebrate the accomplishments of their kings—Olav Tryggvason and Olav Haraldsson— who fostered the conversion of their country to Christianity more than those who actually made Norway independent. As in Eastern Europe, Christianity provided literate clerics to record written documents and laws and an effective model for organizing the kingdom; both Norway and Sweden were based on previous archbishoprics established by the Roman church. It seems that kings in Africa and Europe found Islam and Christianity, respectively, conducive to the establishment and success of royal power. Islam, however, had no central religious authority whose claims might compete with secular rulers. This was not the case in medieval Europe.

Church and State in the High Middle Ages

The origins of the conflict between church and state in the High Middle Ages can be directly traced to a new set of ideals and claims perpetuated by a group of churchmen centered on Rome during the mid-eleventh century. The reformers included a combination of political radicals and spiritual leaders who believed that the church had gone astray from many of its original ideals. They wanted to enforce clerical celibacy, restore ideals of sacrifice and humility among the clergy, end the buying and selling of church offices, and, most importantly, end the heavy influence exerted by lay rulers over church affairs. Their main objection was to the practice of lay investiture, in which laymen selected and bestowed spiritual authority upon church officials. When a fiery monk named

Hildebrand ascended the seat of St. Peter in 1073 as Pope Gregory VII, the reform faction had one of its most ardent disciples in the highest position of power within the church. Gregory shared with his fellow reformers the conviction that Rome needed to be at the center of the movement. They believed that the restoration of ancient Christianity included the primacy of Rome and a strong papal authority. Gregory set about to enforce his will on lay rulers and to reverse the long-standing practice of lay investiture, a change so radical that it is often referred to as the Gregorian Revolution. The main claims of Gregory involved the assertion of the primacy of papal power over both the church and over society as a whole. Gregory did not claim political jurisdiction over the Holy Roman Empire, but he did claim superiority over the Holy Roman Emperor, Henry IV (1050–1106).

Henry IV, however, defended his right to continue the practice of lay investiture. He ignored a letter that Gregory wrote to him in 1075 on the subject. Henry made no claims to ultimate authority over the church, but did believe that the practice of lay investiture fell within his rights as king. For Gregory to grant any validity to the imperial claim of authority to practice lay investiture, even over the papacy itself, would have meant acknowledging the complete failure of his own attempts to reform the church. Instead, Gregory made the radical move of issuing a letter of deposition against Henry, removing any obligations that his nobles or subjects had to obey him or recognize his authority. The threat of deposition galvanized Henry to travel south to meet Gregory in order to resolve the issue. Henry met the pope at the northern Italian fortress of Canossa, where he waited in the snow for Gregory's forgiveness. Although Henry felt compelled to submit to Gregory at the castle of Canossa in a humiliating fashion, he succeeded in forestalling Gregory from traveling northward and stirring up more trouble among the German princes. Canossa seemed at the time to represent a humiliating defeat for Henry and a moral victory for Gregory, but Henry soon regained the advantage and eventually invaded Rome with the intention of deposing Gregory.

It is easy to view Gregory as a zealot who sought great political power for the papacy. But Gregory was a sincere reformer with an idealistic vision for his church that he sought to implement. Gregory needed the support of the German bishops, yet he risked alienating them by insisting on the celibacy of the clergy, an important part of his reform plan. Though later popes cultivated an increase in the wealth and power of the papacy, Gregory indicated in his letters a desire to return the church to its original ideal of apostolic poverty. Still, the spiritual and moral prestige of the papacy was the strongest weapon in Gregory's arsenal, which was not enhanced by his political struggle with Henry IV.

A compromise was finally reached in the twelfth century between a more moderate pope—Calixtus II (r. 1119–1124)—and a more moderate emperor—Henry V (r. 1106–1125). The predecessor of Calixtus, Paschal II (r. 1099–1118), was more concerned with improving the quality of the clergy and the spiritual reputation of the church than with a political victory over the emperor. He offered to renounce ecclesiastical ownership of imperial lands in exchange for Henry's commitment to stop the practice of lay investiture. Failing to gain the support of his own cardinals for this proposal, Paschal could not follow through with a deal that Henry V found perfectly acceptable. It was left to Calixtus to negotiate a compromise with Henry that temporarily satisfied all parties. At the Concordat of Worms in 1122, the pope gained the right to appoint clerics and invest them with the spiritual symbols of their authority, and the emperor gained the right to approve or veto clerical appointments and to have his bishops continue to swear allegiance to him as their feudal lord. This compromise did not bring an end to disputes between church and state; popes and emperors continued to seek opportunities to extend their claims to power at the expense of the other.

Pope Innocent III (r. 1198–1216) had strong views about the power of the papacy and considered the pope to be the living representative of Christ on earth. The development of canon (or church) law during the twelfth century had added legal justifications for the power of the papacy, which now had a number of legal tools at its disposal in order to assert its claims of supremacy. Church leaders had long made a distinction between the "two swords" of spiritual and temporal power that God had given to his representatives on earth. Supporters of the papacy argued that the pope not only had authority over the spiritual realm, but also had the right to intervene in the affairs of secular rulers if those rulers became tyrants and alienated the leading nobles of their kingdom. Innocent III extended the papal claims to superiority over temporal rulers by claiming the right to depose kings and deprive them of their power *ratione peccati* ("by reason of sin"). Innocent argued that as the final moral arbiter over Christendom, he had authority over all laymen, including kings and emperors. As pope, he intervened in the domestic affairs of France, England, and the Holy Roman Empire; his support for Frederick II in 1214 helped to determine the outcome of the Battle of Bouvines and forced John to acquiesce and accept Innocent's candidate as his archbishop of Canterbury.

Thirteenth-century popes such as Gregory IX (1227–1241) and Innocent IV (1243–1254) continued to follow the doctrines of Innocent III and make strong claims for the authority of the papacy over secular rulers. They both contributed to the establishment of a papal monarchy. Gregory IX forced Frederick II to fulfill his vow to go on a Crusade by threatening him with excommunication. In 1233 Gregory started the Inquisition as a force against heretics, particularly the recalcitrant Albigensians in southern France. In 1234 Gregory promulgated a new set of papal laws in a book called the *Decretals*; these laws formalized the legal judicial authority of the pope over the church and helped to make Rome the center for appeals from all over Europe. Both Gregory and Innocent also contributed to the growing financial resources of the papacy, providing a more tangible foundation for papal power. Perhaps most importantly, they continued to assert papal control over appointments to church offices, setting up a new round of conflicts between the papacy and secular rulers of England and France later in the thirteenth century. Unfortunately for the papacy, one of the major enterprises intended to enhance papal prestige and authority had disintegrated into a dismal failure—the Crusades to recover the Holy Land for Christianity from Muslim rule.

Historical Relations with the East—The Crusades

In 1091 the Byzantine emperor, Alexis I, requested assistance from Pope Urban II for the protection of Christians in the Holy Land. Alexis was concerned as well with the safety of his own empire and wanted whatever military assistance he could get from Western Europe. Urban could not miss this opportunity to come to the aid of the Byzantine Empire because of the potential to claim Roman superiority over the Eastern Church and end the schism between the two churches that had occurred earlier in the century. (He could not have anticipated that the Crusades would only further increase hostility between eastern and western Christians and thus the two churches.) Urban also viewed a Crusade as an opportunity to strengthen the papacy and to affirm his political leadership of Europe in the midst of the investiture controversy. If the temporal rulers of Europe joined in such a large military initiative under the auspices of the papacy, that would support papal claims to supremacy.

But the call of the papacy for a Crusade to kill the infidel represented a significant departure from the teachings of Christ found in the New Testament. The papacy had to find a way to justify its support for open warfare. When Urban issued his call for the First Crusade, he specifically targeted Islam as the enemy of Christianity. According to the account by the chronicler Fulcher of Chartres of Urban's 1095 speech at Clermont announcing the First Crusade, the pope castigated the Muslims' evil ways and represented them as a threat to Christianity. This gave the whole enterprise the aura of a holy war. Urban painted an inaccurate picture of Muslims slaughtering Christians (the invading Turks had expanded mainly at the expense of Muslim Arabs) in order to convince European Christians that God wanted them to kill.

The Crusades harked back to the Old Testament and its ideal of a God who blessed his chosen people with military victories over their enemy. Urban further strengthened the religious dimension of the Crusade by granting an indulgence for all those who would die in battle, guaranteeing them forgiveness of sins and entry into heaven. Crusaders took a vow that opened them up to excommunication if they deserted. But religious passions were so high that the First Crusade would have had a strong religious dimension rooted in contemporary practices of popular piety anyway. The opportunities to turn the Crusade into a pilgrimage, the chance to look for holy relics, and the possibility of enhancing one's chances of salvation provided the Crusaders with powerful spiritual incentives that intermingled with the larger objectives of the papacy.

Prior to the Crusades, European Christians did not possess such an intense hatred of Muslims, mainly because most had never seen or encountered one. Jews were more likely to be seen as the enemy, which explains why the first targets of the Crusaders were actually Jews in Bohemia and Germany who were brutally attacked by those on route to the Holy Land. The exception to Christian ignorance of Muslims was in Spain, where Christians and Muslims had lived in close proximity and fought each other intermittently for several centuries. Later Europeans looked back to Spanish history to find the roots of their hatred of the Muslims as a result of the Crusades. The story of El Cid, Rodrigo Díaz de Vivar, an eleventh-century Spanish warrior, was immortalized in a twelfth-century epic poem that reflected the new crusading mentality brought on by the First Crusade more than the historical reality of Christian-Muslim relations during the eleventh century. The Crusades intensified the fear and hatred that Christians felt toward Muslims. That hatred made possible the slaughter of about 40,000 Muslims when the Crusaders captured Jerusalem in July 1099. After the Muslims rallied to retake land from the Europeans during the Second Crusade, hatred became intermingled with fear and a certain amount of respect. Still, of the twelfth-century Crusade led by Louis VII of France, the chronicler Odo of Deuil wrote that the intention was to "wipe out our sins with the blood or the conversion of the infidels" (1948, 71).

Just as the Crusades intensified Christian hatred of Muslims, so they also exacerbated Muslim hostility toward Christians and Christianity, despite the fact that once they settled in the Holy Land, Christians did not force Muslim conversion and generally did not interfere with Muslim practice of their religion or their laws. For their part, Islamic rulers had tended not to persecute Christians either, as long as they posed no threat to their power and obeyed the laws of their state. (A period of persecution under Caliph Hakim in the early eleventh century stood out as a notable exception that proved the rule.) But, as converts, the Seljuk Turks were much more fanatical than those Islamic rulers in Baghdad, Jerusalem, and Cairo whose families had a tradition of moderate rule over Christians and Jews. The Turks tended to view the conflict with Christian Europeans as a holy war as well.

The First Crusade enlisted the support of Europeans from virtually every country and of every social class. After 15,000 Europeans embarked for the Holy Land without adequate training or provisions in the ill-fated "Peasants' Crusade," the real military initiative got under way when nobles, mainly French, put together a legitimate feudal army under the leadership of Raymond of Toulouse and Godfrey of Lorraine. Once the Crusaders took the cities of Nicaea, Edessa, and Antioch, they captured Jerusalem from the Egyptians in 1099 and set about to establish a permanent presence in the midst of their Muslim enemies. The Europeans divided their conquests in the Holy Land into four separate principalities—the counties of Edessa, Antioch, and Tripoli and the kingdom of Jerusalem—modeled on European feudal principles.

The Second Crusade came as a response to a successful attempt made by the Turks to take back Edessa in the 1140s. This time the Europeans did not meet with military success, despite the religious inspiration provided by Bernard of Clairvaux, the most prestigious monk in Europe and a great champion of Roman Christianity. The failure of the Second Crusade fundamentally altered the nature of the crusading movement. Later Crusaders went east with a greater mixture of motives, though always under the guise of doing the will of God and defending the interests of the church. During the Third Crusade, after being abandoned by Philip II of France and the drowning death of Frederick Barbarossa en route to the Holy Land, Richard the Lionhearted of England ended up negotiating a treaty with the Muslim king Saladin to allow Christians to visit the holy shrines in Jerusalem. The sack of Christian Constantinople during the Fourth Crusade in 1204 demonstrates just how far the Crusades had come from their original mission. Other crusades followed in the thirteenth century in an attempt to prop up the fragile hold that the Europeans still had in the Holy Land. Louis IX of France led a crusade that lasted from 1248 to 1254 and another one in 1270, convinced that God would bless his holy cause, but his efforts failed to reverse the fortunes of the Europeans who remained in the Holy Land; their last stronghold of Acre fell to the Muslims in 1291.

Although the Crusades by no means brought about an improvement in Christian-Muslim relations overall, they did bring Christians and Muslims into much greater contact with each other. Not all of that contact involved violence and warfare. Christians became aware of products available in the East and engaged Muslims in trade. European Christians also became much more aware of Islamic culture, which exerted its own influence in European art, architecture, music, learning, and technology. The Syrian Muslim chronicler Usamah ibn Munqidh (1095–1188) noted that the more recently Europeans had arrived in the Holy Land, the more rude and uncivilized they were, implying that Islam had a civilizing influence on these barbarians from the north.

Some socialization occurred among Christians and Muslims; some Christians and Muslims intermarried. Still, the Crusades generally intensified religious hatred, fanaticism, and intolerance—on both sides of the religious divide between Christians and Muslims. Despite examples of tolerance displayed by Christians toward Muslims and vice versa during the period of the Crusades, each regarded the other as inferior and enemies of God.

Medieval Thought and Philosophy

One of the important consequences of the economic and social changes of the eleventh century was an increased emphasis on learning and intellectual discourse. As European agriculture expanded, population grew, trade revived, and towns and cities emerged, a smaller proportion of the population needed to engage in agricultural pursuits and more people could afford to pursue intellectual and cultural interests. As merchants and pilgrims traveled more in an increasingly peaceful Europe, ideas spread and people became exposed to different ways of thinking and different cultural practices. The church provided the opportunities for education in monastic and cathedral schools, which eventually gave way to the rise of universities during the twelfth century. Since religion and theology were regarded as subjects of paramount importance in a society that was dominated by the church and Christianity, many of the most brilliant thinkers of the age were drawn to theology and philosophy in order to support the Christian faith. With an increase in intellectual activity, however, there also came new ideas and potential challenges to the prevailing notions of religious orthodoxy.

Medieval philosophy—within Christianity, Islam, and Judaism—attempted to strike a balance between the truths taught by revelation and those taught by Aristotle and the classical philosophers who bequeathed their intellectual heritage to the Middle Ages. Since early church fathers—especially St. Augustine—had fused classical learning so thoroughly with their understanding of Christianity, it was difficult for later medieval thinkers to separate philosophy from theology or to know where one left off and the other began. Prior to the twelfth century, Islamic thinkers had contributed to the preservation of classical philosophy, especially the ideas of Aristotle. An Islamic adherent of Aristotelian philosophy, Averroës (1126–1198) angered Islamic authorities in Spain by equating Aristotle's writings with truth. The influence of Aristotle and classical philosophy on Jewish thought appears most prominently in the work of Moses Maimonides (1135–1204), a Spanish Jew who applied Aristotelian philosophy to his interpretation of the Old Testament.

The attempt to balance faith and reason dominated the philosophy of Anselm of Bec (1033–1109), a teacher who served as archbishop of Canterbury during the late eleventh and early twelfth centuries. Anselm believed, as did most medieval philosophers, that reason and faith were both gifts from God and that it was perfectly legitimate to use reason in defense of faith. Anselm used reason and logic to formulate his original and highly influential proof for the existence of God. Anselm argued that since God, by definition, was the greatest being that could possibly exist and since a being that does or must exist is, by definition, greater than a being that does not or might exist, then God must exist. Anselm's argument might not convince nonbelievers, but it was never intended to; he wrote to strengthen people in their faith rather than to convince those who had none. Nonetheless, his use of reason in support of the Christian faith opened the door to further debate about the relationship between faith and reason.

In the twelfth century those with concerns about the use of reason to justify the Christian faith had them reinforced by the thought of Peter Abelard (1079–1142), a teacher in Paris who attracted students from all over Europe. Abelard became famous partly as a result of his own autobiography, *A History of My Misfortunes*, in which he detailed his tragic love affair with his female student, Heloise, which ended in Abelard's castration on orders from Heloise's furious uncle. In his book *Yes and No*, which consisted of 156 theological questions on which he presented conflicting viewpoints drawing on the Bible and the writings of the Church, he wanted his students or his readers to draw their own conclusions—to use reason in order to understand their Christian faith. Abelard's opponents, led by the prominent Cistercian monk Bernard of Clairvaux (1090–1153), who had become one of the most powerful leaders of the church in Europe, saw him as leading his readers into doubt and thus potentially into heresy. Bernard took exception to Abelard's logical attempts to penetrate such Christian mysteries as the Trinity; Abelard died in 1142, begging the forgiveness of Bernard and seeking reconciliation with the church.

Similarly, Islamic authorities thought that Averroës had gone too far in his use of reason and his estimation of Aristotle. Averroës believed in the possibility of a complete reconciliation between faith and reason, since God was the sole author of all truth. Averroës was so convinced of the importance of reason that he believed that certain truths were prerequisites for salvation, contradicting previous Islamic teachings on the subject. His ideas had a great influence at the University of Paris in the thirteenth century, where his followers became known as Latin Averroists.

The Jewish thinker Maimonides was also strongly influenced by the writings of Averroës, whose works were quickly translated into Hebrew. Both Averroës and Maimonides were from the city of Córdoba, the center of Muslim power in Spain. Maimonides became a prominent official in Egypt, where he served as physician to the Egyptian sultan. In his most famous work, *A Guide for the Perplexed*, Maimonides produced the most systematic attempt to combine

Judaism with classical philosophy. He saw no contradiction between reason and Judaism. He believed that philosophy was a necessary aid to anyone seeking a true understanding of God. Maimonides argued that true faith came only after understanding, because only then could one speak with any confidence about what it is that one believed. But he never insisted that human beings were capable of a complete understanding of God. Although Maimonides, like Anselm and Abelard, used reason to understand his faith, he deferred to the Bible on any issues that seemed to defy rational philosophy. Still, by insisting upon the absolute necessity of certain philosophical and religious truths, Maimonides advocated a form of Judaism that was more rigid, less tolerant, and less open to mystical avenues toward the divine. His ideas represented an important strain in Jewish thought, but never became accepted as completely orthodox. Maimonides upset conservative Jewish leaders just as Averroës had provoked a hostile reaction from conservatives in the Islamic world.

In the Christian West, the philosophy of Thomas Aquinas (ca. 1225–1274) marked a culmination of the trend toward the harmonizing of faith and reason. He achieved his synthesis mainly by applying the teachings of Aristotle to Christian teachings. Like Averroës, Thomas believed that all truth could be reconciled since God was responsible for both the truths of faith and those conveyed by reason. He appropriated from Aristotle the proof for the existence of God as a first cause or a prime mover necessary for all other aspects of creation. Thomas was also influenced by the Aristotelian ideal of the state as a product of nature with the purpose of existing for the common good. But he continued to adhere to the main points of Christianity even as he used the ideas and arguments of Aristotle in support of the Christian faith. In 1277 the Bishop of Paris, Etienne Tempier, issued a list of 219 propositions, whose teaching would henceforth be prohibited, including some of the ideas of Thomas Aquinas. Tempier was part of a conservative reaction at Paris that opposed the attempt of philosophers to integrate Christian thought and non-Christian ideas, such as Aristotle's view that the world was eternal, a concept that contradicted the Christian theology of creation. Thomas's ideas, though they met with some opposition from the church, greatly influenced the future direction of Christian thought. Thomas was a product of the new universities at Naples and Paris, which provided an institutional framework for free inquiry in the medieval world, but many of the cultural achievements of the period occurred outside that framework in the fields of art and literature.

Medieval Art and Literature

The prosperity of the High Middle Ages resulted in a huge expansion in the number of churches throughout Christendom, as well as the building of ever larger and more expensive cathedrals in major towns and religious centers. The soaring spires, pointed arches, and brilliant stained glass windows of the Gothic cathedrals reflected a new sense of optimism and a vision of Christianity that found inspiration in divine light.

Whereas Romanesque churches had thick walls that supported rounded arches and symmetry based on classical ideals of harmony and proportion, Gothic cathedrals deflected weight away from the walls through flying buttresses, ribbed vaults, and pointed arches that allowed for higher constructions and for more space for windows. The builders of the Gothic cathedrals produced a vision that inspired medieval people who would never have witnessed any other constructions that even approximated the size of these stone monuments to light, God, and Christianity. The massive amounts of stone required for their construction would also have awed people who lived in dwellings constructed of wood or thatch. Medieval people had no other buildings with which to compare these miraculously soaring edifices. The effect of the stained glass windows was heightened by the location of the apse and the choir at the east end of the building—which the parishioners faced during services—allowing the morning light to illuminate the stained glass images in front of them. Light, as the least material aspect of the earthly realm, seemed to the medieval mind the closest approximation to God that could be found on earth.

The incorporation of human and mythological figures played a much greater role in Gothic architecture than it did in Romanesque. The angels, saints, prophets, and Biblical figures whose statues and images could be found throughout these cathedrals reinforced or taught basic Christian belief and at the same time offered protection against the devil and his forces of darkness. Gothic architects sought to harmonize sculpture with their buildings and make it an integral part of the cathedral design. Carved figures stood out from the walls in a way that Romanesque sculptures did not. They were also more realistic and depicted human figures as unique individuals rather than as merely symbolic representations. In creating these figures, sculptors displayed a new, positive attitude that emphasized the salvation of humanity through God, Jesus, and the intercession of the Virgin Mary.

Another major change in medieval culture that occurred from the eleventh to the thirteenth centuries was the emergence of vernacular literatures, especially in French, German, and Spanish. Epic poems celebrated the continued value placed upon the military capabilities of the nobility, but also they reflected the growing importance of feudal relationships and Christianity. The most famous and most popular French epic was the *Song of Roland*, based on an obscure historical incident when the rear of Charlemagne's army came under attack from Basques while crossing the Pyrenees after an invasion into Muslim Spain.

Nave of Chartres Cathedral. Begun in 1194, the nave displays some of the characteristic features of Gothic architecture, including ribbed vaults, pointed arches, vast open spaces, and the penetration of light. *(Photograph by David Merrett)*

Roland is depicted as a Christian knight who sacrifices his life out of devotion to his king, secure in the knowledge of his own salvation.

The German *Nibelungenlied*, or "Story of the Nibelungs," was the most popular epic written in German during the twelfth century. The poem reflects some of the brutality, violence, and warrior ethos of the early Middle Ages, but combines those features with the courtly values and expectations of the twelfth-century nobility. The main figure of the poem is Siegfried, who embodied many of the virtues of a feudal warrior at the same time that he gave the Germans their own heroic figure comparable to Roland. In Spain, the legend of the famous warrior Rodrigo Díaz de Vivar (ca. 1043–1099) became immortalized in the epic poem *El Cid*—the first poem written in the Spanish language. Although the historical Rodrigo performed military service in the armies of both Muslim and Christian rulers in Spain, the poem portrays him as the definitive Crusader helping to liberate Spain from Muslim control.

The creation of the medieval romance reflects the tempering of the warrior ethos of the nobility with the virtues of civilization and culture. As wealth increased and living conditions improved, medieval writers increasingly concentrated on the potential for happiness and enjoyment of life in this world. An increasingly literate and educated population provided an audience for this new kind of literature. Andreas Capellanus wrote *The Art of Courtly Love*, based largely on Ovid's *Art of Love*, codifying many of the conventions that were celebrated in medieval romances. Andreas stressed that true love was only possible between a man and a woman who were not married to each other. Courtly love could be sexual or not—its defining characteristic was the purity of a man's love for a woman and the ennobling effect that such sentiments had upon him. The troubadour poets, mainly from southern France, and German *minnesängers* contributed to the tradition with their lyrics celebrating love. After the beginning of the Crusades, a number of songs voiced the laments of lovers separated by the departure of a knight for the Holy Land.

Most medieval romances centered on the legends of King Arthur and his court. Though based on a historical ruler in Britain during the period of the Anglo-Saxon invasions, these stories reflected the values of the twelfth century and bore little resemblance to the historical period they were supposed to

For information and views of another famous Gothic cathedral, Notre Dame of Paris, visit www.notredamedeparis.fr/-English-.

The Song of Roland

Roland looks abroad over hill and heath and sees the great multitude of the Frankish dead, and he weeps for them as beseems a gentle knight, saying: "Lord and barons now may God have mercy upon you, and grant Paradise to all your souls, that ye may rest among the blessed flowers. Man never saw better men of arms than ye were. Long and well, year in and year out, have ye served me, and many wide lands have ye won for the glory of Charles. Was it to such an end that he nourished you? O France, fair land, today art thou made desolate by rude slaughter. Ye Frankish barons, I see ye die through me, yet can I do naught to save or defend you. May God, who knows no lie, aid you! Oliver, brother, I must not fail thee; yet I shall die of grief, and I be not slain by the sword. Sir comrade, let us get into battle."

So Count Roland falls a-smiting again. He holds Durendal in his hand, and lays on right valiantly, that he cleaves in twain Faldron de Pui, and slays four and twenty of the most worshipful of the paynims. Never shall ye see man more desirous to revenge himself. And even as the hart flies before the hounds, so flee the heathen from before Roland. "Thou dost rightly," then said the Archbishop; "such valor well beseems a knight who bears arms and sits a good horse; in battle such a one should be fell and mighty, or he is not worth four deniers, and it behooves him to turn monk and get him into a monastery to pray the livelong day for our sins." And Roland answered him, saying: "Smite and spare not." And at these words the Franks go into battle again: but great is the slaughter of the Christians.

—Translated by Isabel Butler

Source: Charles W. Jones, ed., *Medieval Literature in Translation* (New York: David McKay, 1950), p. 546.

What message is this passage meant to convey? What emotions is it meant to stir? Why does Roland determine to keep fighting? How might literary works such as this have contributed to support for the Crusades in the twelfth century?

represent. The late twelfth-century French author Chrétien de Troyes wrote the most popular Arthurian romances. They depict ideal courtiers who possessed a combination of beauty, humility, gentle manners, social graces, discretion, physical strength, and martial skills that could be used in the service of their king. They lived according to a code of chivalry, which encouraged them to be loyal and brave in service to their lord, fair and generous in their treatment of both friends and enemies, and respectful, even devout, in their attitude toward women of the nobility.

One of the most popular medieval romances, judging by the number of surviving manuscripts, was *The Romance of the Rose*, the first part written by Guillaume de Lorris prior to 1237, the second part completed by Jean de Meun much later in the thirteenth century. The poem is an allegory on the theme of love. Even in the Arthurian romances, romantic love could be taken as an allegory for a higher spiritual quest. The search for the Holy Grail, best exemplified in the story of *Parzival* by Wolfram von Eschenbach, is an example of how the romance morphed into a spiritual quest. In *The Romance of the Rose*, the courtier searches for a beloved rose, symbolizing the perfect lady. The first part is more sentimental and in keeping with the medieval traditions of courtly love. Jean de Meun injects a new spirit into the poem, containing more social criticism and taking a less favorable position toward women.

The theme of courtly love also appears in the writings of Dante Alighieri (1265–1321), a Florentine poet, philosopher, and political theorist. In 1290 Dante's beloved, Beatrice, died. Dante married the following year and in 1292 wrote in the Italian vernacular *La Vita Nuova (The New Life)*, a work that alternates prose and verse. Dante writes here of a love so strong that it has completely overwhelmed and subdued him to the point where passion is unchecked by reason. In this work, as in his life, Dante uses Beatrice as an inspiration to lead him to a loftier goal. He worships her from afar and loses himself in something larger than himself. Although *The New Life* deals with the theme of courtly love, Dante stresses the divine nature of love, which he ultimately directs toward God.

In Dante's poetic masterpiece, *The Divine Comedy*, he embarks on a journey through the circles of hell, purgatory, and heaven, allowing him to reveal his cosmological vision of spiritual reality. The Roman poet Virgil guides Dante through the circles of hell, which descend according to the seriousness of the sins that had placed the individuals there. In the first circle, for example, Dante encounters individuals such as Aristotle, Plato, and Cicero, who had led virtuous lives but could not enter heaven because they were not Christian. He depicts St. Francis of Assisi (ca. 1181–1226), who had committed his life to the ideal of apostolic poverty, as representative of the new spirit of Christ on earth—a striking contrast to the numerous popes and clerics that Dante places in hell and purgatory. Dante also has high praise for St. Dominic (ca. 1170–1221), the founder of the Dominican order, which placed a greater stress on preaching and learning. In his vision of paradise, Dante portrays heaven as containing two circles of love and learning existing in perfect conformity and symmetry, symbolizing the harmony between the ideals of these two orders working together in their service to God and the church. Finally, in this poem Beatrice's physical beauty only serves as a prelude to her ability to lead Dante to contemplation of a higher beauty and eventually to the beatific vision (the direct encounter with God) in paradise itself.

Conclusion

During the twelfth and thirteenth centuries, Europeans created a vibrant and flourishing civilization that was marked by such achievements as the rise of universities, an increased output of literature in a variety of forms and on a variety of topics, the construction of the Gothic cathedrals, and a thriving economy characterized by agricultural expansion. The church, despite the continuation of flaws associated with any human institution, provided a sense of unity and religious authority, even as it tolerated a wide range of intellectual discourse and encouraged philosophical reflection. Women benefited from opportunities in the towns to participate in the guilds as wives and widows, while the ideals of courtly love and the veneration of the Virgin Mary softened men's attitudes toward women as worthy of respect and honor. These centuries were generally characterized by peace, order, and political stability, with kings generally containing potential threats from the nobility and supporting the economic activities of merchants and townspeople. The Crusades contributed to the consolidation of the power of national monarchies by reinforcing their leadership mission and allowing them to send off potentially troublesome nobles to satisfy their aggressions in the Holy Land.

These centuries had their darker side, however. Jews experienced a growth of anti-Semitism that was sometimes encouraged by the church and that resulted partly from the Christian fanaticism associated with the Crusades and partly from increased resentment at their economic success as moneylenders. The Crusades bred increased intolerance between Christians and Muslims and brought turmoil to the Middle East, even as they diverted violent activity away from Europe. They also contributed to the deteriorating relations between the Roman and the Byzantine churches. The sometimes bitter rivalry between popes and temporal rulers led both to seek increased power and revenues. Many people began to feel that this led the church far away from its true spiritual mission. By the end of the thirteenth century, the church-state conflict was again intensifying. Pope Boniface VIII (r. 1294–1303) would assert even stronger claims for papal prerogatives at the expense of temporal rulers, only to face opposition from the kings of France and England that was just as hostile and determined as that offered by Henry IV to Gregory VII in the eleventh century. The church was on the verge of a number of crises that did not erode Christian piety but did detract from the hierarchy's role as the inspiration for it. Europe started to experience a decline in the economy during the early fourteenth century, concomitant with frequent agricultural depressions and a general decline in population that became catastrophic when the bubonic plague swept through Europe at mid-century. In the face of a series of crises in church, state, and society, Europeans became even more intolerant of outsiders and nonconformists as they searched for scapegoats on which to blame their problems. For these and other reasons, historians often refer to the fourteenth century as a period of crisis in the late Middle Ages.

1. How did the expansion of population in Europe contribute to some of the other important developments in European society during the High Middle Ages?
2. What led to the development of new political monarchies in Europe and Africa during this period? Discuss the similarities between European and African monarchies.
3. What impact did the Crusades have on Christian-Muslim relations? Were the results uniformly negative?
4. What were the main goals of medieval philosophers and theologians? Were they successful in achieving those goals?
5. How did medieval literature reflect medieval society?

Suggestions for Further Reading

Barber, Malcolm. 2004. *The Two Cities: Medieval Europe, 1050–1320*. 2nd ed. London: Routledge.

Cahill, Thomas. 2006. *Mysteries of the Middle Ages: The Rise of Feminism, Science, and the Arts from the Cults of Catholic Europe*. New York: Nan A. Talese.

Jordan, William Chester. 2004. *Europe in the High Middle Ages*. New York: Penguin.

Morris, Colin. 1987. *The Discovery of the Individual, 1050–1200*. Toronto: University of Toronto Press.

Odo of Deuil. 1948. *The Journey of Louis VII to the East*. Edited and translated by Virginia Gingerick Berry. New York: W.W. Norton.

Rubenstein, Richard E. 2003. *Aristotle's Children: How Christians, Muslims, and Jews Rediscovered Ancient Wisdom and Illuminated the Dark Ages*. Orlando: Harcourt.

Suggested Websites

www.fordham.edu/halsall/sbook.html

This website contains the Internet Medieval Sourcebook on Fordham University's excellent web page.

http://labyrinth.georgetown.edu

This website directs readers to numerous resources related to medieval history and contains information on a wide variety of topics.

www.medieval-life.net/life_main.htm

This is a good introductory website that contains general overviews of a variety of topics related to the period, including Africa.

http://omacl.org

This online medieval and classical library provides access to numerous texts and literary works from the period.

http://the-orb.net

This is an online reference work for medieval studies.

8 The Crises of the Late Middle Ages, ca. 1300–1500

In the fourteenth and fifteenth centuries, Europe experienced a series of problems and catastrophes that challenged the confidence in God's goodness and the harmony of faith and reason that were the hallmarks of the medieval era. Frequent warfare and popular unrest created turbulence and distress for many people. Climatic disaster led to poor harvests and epidemics that affected both people and livestock. The population declined as agricultural shortages led to malnutrition, which increased susceptibility to disease.

The social and economic changes of the fourteenth century undermined the faith, confidence, and stability of European society. The most dramatic challenge of the period was the Black Death, a plague that struck Europe in 1348 and over the course of a two-year period killed as much as 45 percent of the population. The move of the papacy from Rome to the French city of Avignon and the appearance of rival claimants for the papal seat shook people's confidence in the church and its leadership. Their faith and confidence shaken, people sought new approaches to religion and explored ways to reform the church itself, from within and without.

These interlocking occurrences contributed to the political and social developments that unfolded during the fourteenth and fifteenth centuries. They contributed to challenges to political authority and crises of leadership in the state, the church, and society. Women played a significant role in the religious and economic life of the period, as they responded to the crises in their own way. As for a global perspective, the impact of the plague outside of Europe and peasant unrest and social upheaval in China offer opportunities for a useful comparison with developments in Europe.

The Black Death

In 1348 a bacterial germ that has now been identified as *Yersinia pestis* caused what became known in Europe as the Black Death, otherwise known as the bubonic plague, so-called because of the telltale signs of swelling or "buboes"

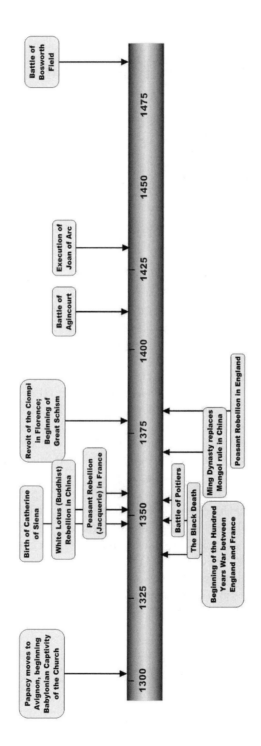

in the lymph nodes of the groin and armpits. The germ traveled to Europe on ships from the Black Sea area via infected rats. Fleas spread the disease from rats to humans. Even though people at the time did not understand the biological origins of the Black Death, they quickly became aware that it was contagious, even if they did not know exactly how the disease was carried. Italians learned the concept of quarantine from Muslims in North Africa and took steps to isolate those afflicted with the plague. People transported corpses to common graves and spread lye over them to contain the disease as best they could. Others burned scented wood in an attempt to purify what they believed to be the corrupted air, but to no avail; none of these measures prevented the heavy loss of life caused by the plague.

Recent estimates of the death rate in Europe from the plague usually range between 35 and 45 percent, though the lack of knowledge of pre-plague population levels makes determining exact numbers difficult. One thing is certain: the psychological effect on the people who experienced such shocking mortality rates must have made it seem even more severe. A poem popular in fourteenth-century England stated:

> In thirteen hundred and forty-eight
> Of every hundred there lived but eight.
> In thirteen hundred and forty-nine
> Of every hundred there lived but nine.

The French chronicler Jean de Venette reported that 500 dead were carried from the Hôtel-Dieu (one of the charitable foundations established in the High Middle Ages to provide care for the sick and dying) in Paris to the cemetery of the Holy Innocents every day at the height of the plague. The sheer numbers of the afflicted overwhelmed the ability of these charitable institutions to cope with the crisis, and overcrowding led to a serious deterioration in the care that infected individuals received. Many contemporary reports refer to large numbers of the dead remaining unburied because not enough people lived to bury all the corpses.

The church, whose clergy was already beginning to acquire a reputation for greed and immorality, lost many of its dedicated and selfless members who devoted themselves to tending to the sick and dying. Physicians, like the clergy, died in greater proportion to the rest of the population because of increased exposure to the ill. In addition to the loss of the most altruistic members of society, other consequences of the plague included rising crime rates, rampant immorality, and changing attitudes toward death, which was no longer viewed as a natural transition to the afterlife but as a cruel and indifferent master who called all to join him in a macabre dance.

The high death rates associated with the Black Death and the other problems facing society at this time affected the position of women as well. More
men died of the plague than did women, perhaps as a result of men's greater
interaction with others. In urban areas, women, although they remained a
minority of the workforce, became increasingly involved in a number of economic endeavors—making yarn and silk, spinning and weaving in the growing
textile industries, inn-keeping, and selling wine, food, and household items
such as kitchen utensils, tools, and leather or metal boxes at markets. Many
women were widowed at a relatively young age, sometimes more than once
if they remarried quickly after the death of their first husband. Fortunately
for widows, they retained the property that they brought as the dowry to their
marriages; however, the unfortunate widow who possessed few resources after
her husband's death might be expelled from her husband's family, unwelcome
in her own, and forced to scratch out a living as best she could.

This plague did not affect only Europe. Merchant ships that brought the
disease to Europe, beginning with its arrival in Sicily in October 1347, carried it
to Africa and the Middle East as well. By 1347 the plague appeared in Alexandria and spread from there throughout all of Egypt. In 1348 it devastated Gaza
in Palestine before reaching the Muslim holy city of Mecca. Islamic medical
authorities had no better explanation for the plague than did European Christian
physicians. The most common natural explanation in both cultures centered
on climatic changes, material decay, astrological factors, or some combination of the three factors polluting the air. But most Islamic writers, like their
Christian counterparts, attributed the plague to the will of God. The Muslim
poet Abu l-Qasim ar Rahawi saw the plague as evidence of God's displeasure
with humanity. The noted historian Ibn Khaldun, whose parents perished from
the Black Death when he was only seventeen, observed that the plague had led
to a general decline in civilization and an erosion of political authority in the
Islamic world, in addition to the dramatic decrease in population. He pointed
to the weakening of dynasties; the plague attacked the Mamluk army in Egypt
and helped to prepare the way for the eventual fall of Egypt to the Ottoman
Turks in the sixteenth century. Some Muslims, however, refused to believe that
the God they worshipped would visit such a horrible disease upon his people
as a punishment for their sins. Their belief in a merciful and compassionate
God led them to view the plague as an opportunity for martyrdom that would
bring the members of the faithful who died of the disease an earlier entry into
the pleasures of paradise. Whereas Christians believed that the plague was
indicative of God's displeasure or the power of Satan, or both, some Islamic
theologians retained an optimistic viewpoint about the relationship between
Allah and his Muslim followers.

As people in Europe struggled with the meaning of the Black Death, they looked for scapegoats to blame in an effort to exert some control over this devastating plague. The crisis caused by the Black Death, which reappeared at frequent intervals in Europe for the next several centuries, created an atmosphere of fear and terror that lingered in the minds of Europeans, who became more vigilant against those who might not only be hostile toward Christians but even, Christians thought, be in league with Satan. Jews were the most easily recognizable group of outsiders in a society that was overwhelmingly Christian. During the fourteenth century, pogroms against Jews increased along with Christian resentment toward them. In addition, the pursuit of witches began in the fourteenth century, intensified in the fifteenth, and became commonplace in the sixteenth and early seventeenth centuries in many parts of Europe. Those accused of witchcraft tended to be women and poor men who were marginalized and deemed expendable by society.

Social Upheaval and Peasant Rebellion in Europe and China

The Black Death transformed European society in the fourteenth century. The deaths of so many people created huge labor shortages as fewer peasants and workers were available to work the land or staff urban shops. Many members of the aristocracy struggled financially, faced with labor shortages, low rents, and increasing employment opportunities for peasants in the towns. Landowners generally had no choice but to commute labor services in exchange for rents, since they had no hope of reaping a profit from the labors of the peasants on their land. Social unrest manifested itself not long after the appearance of the Black Death, when the upper classes began to conspire against the peasants and workers to reverse the advantages that the lower classes had recently gained. Before the Black Death transformed their world, peasants and workers maintained traditional attitudes of obedience toward authority. In the aftermath of the Black Death, the peasants and workers began to view social inequality not as a preordained and fixed condition of society but as a historical development that could be challenged and changed. Rather than accepting their position at the bottom of the social hierarchy, they asked in a contemporary rhyme, "When Adam delved and Eve span, who was then the gentleman?" A whole generation of workers lost their faith in the ability of political authorities to look after them, learned to question the church and their faith in God, and were now prepared to look after themselves.

The labor shortages resulting from the population decline caused by the Black Death gave urban workers hope that they could improve their lives. A rebellion occurred in Paris in 1358, sparked by the hanging of an accused murderer without a trial. Workers revolted in Paris in 1378 to oppose the levying of new taxes. Insurrections in Rome led to the overthrow of the government there in 1347 and 1353. The revolt of the *ciompi*, or wool workers, in Florence in 1378 was probably most indicative of the changing attitudes of a new generation. Urban laborers—particularly the *ciompi*—demanded the right to take part in the Florentine government, to form unions, and to gain entry to the guilds. After some initial success when the government of Florence bowed to popular pressure and agreed to their demands, these workers failed to achieve any lasting gains once the authorities regained control of the situation.

In 1358 peasants throughout northern France revolted in an uprising known as *jacquerie* (from Jacques, a common name for French peasants). French peasants had endured a number of catastrophes: the Black Death, the devastation of their land in the Hundred Years War with England, and the oppressive taxes levied to pay for the war. Peasants engaged in random, sporadic violence and seizure of property and livestock; in one case the pregnant wife of a knight and her daughter were repeatedly raped while her husband was tied to a stake and forced to watch. The revolt, which lasted a little over a month, ended with the nobles rampaging through the countryside wreaking havoc on the peasants and their homes and fields; about 20,000 peasants of an estimated 100,000 participants died in the debacle, while others suffered imprisonment or had their homes burned. Despite this ignominious outcome, the *jacquerie* reveals that times had changed and that peasants would no longer accept their lot without question.

In response to the labor shortage, the English Parliament passed on February 9, 1351, the Statute of Laborers, which set a fixed schedule of wage rates in various occupations. The Statute of Laborers caused a great deal of resentment among the English peasants, which reached new heights when Parliament imposed a new poll tax on the peasants in 1380. Discontent and expectations for further change in England led to the Peasants' Revolt in 1381. Some 60,000 rebels from Kent, as well as from the counties of Essex, Sussex, and Bedford, marched on London, where many Londoners joined them. Once the peasant rebellion in England had ended, the nobility reacted with a vengeance. King Richard II had resisted the temptation to order a massive slaughter of the rebel mobs, but had allowed a more deliberate and methodical punishment of those considered the ringleaders; the leaders of the rebellion and more than 1,500 others were beheaded or hanged. The failure of these rebellions, however, could easily mask the changes that had occurred in society, changes impossible to reverse.

Just as in Europe, peasants did not occupy a particularly valued position in China. They were generally seen as expendable to the larger interests of the kingdom or ruling dynasty. In both Europe and China, peasants tended to accept the prevailing worldview that emphasized stability, tradition, the importance of family relationships, and acceptance of one's place in the universe. In Chinese cosmology, human society occupied a position between heaven and earth; any disruption of its fundamental order would disrupt the cosmos as a whole. But the status of the peasant in China was not altogether clear because of the complicated nature of obligations and payments owed by the peasants and the variety of tenant-landlord relationships. Furthermore, many landowners in China did not possess much land and had to rent out a good portion of it to meet their own subsistence needs, blurring the lines on occasion between landlord and peasant. In the countryside, China essentially had a society of free landowners who did not face the same restrictions as the majority of people who worked the land in medieval Europe. A marked gap still existed, however, between the more prosperous landowners (or gentry) and those who would have been considered peasants.

In the late fourteenth century, China, like Europe, experienced a wave of peasant rebellions, reflecting some similarities and differences with Europe during this period. The peasant rebellions in China contributed to the collapse of the Mongol Yuan dynasty (1271–1368) and the rise of the new Ming dynasty (1368–1644). But the weakening of central authority led to further instability in the countryside, as regional military governors known as warlords emerged and gained control, oppressing or taking advantage of the peasantry at will. Chinese peasants became increasingly frustrated with the inability of the weak central government to maintain order and protect them from their oppressors. French peasants who participated in the *jacquerie* voiced similar complaints in the midst of the chaos of the Hundred Years War.

Peasant rebellion in both Europe and China was also motivated by a combination of social grievances and religious ideology. English peasants were inspired by the criticism of the church offered by the Oxford thinker John Wycliffe (ca. 1330–1384), whose followers among the common people became known as Lollards. In the rebellion of 1381, peasants committed numerous acts of violence directed at the church, including the murders of the archbishop of Canterbury and the abbot of Bury St. Edmunds. In 1351 religious dissidents

For more on Asian history visit the Asia for Educators website, sponsored by the Weatherhead East Asian Institute at Columbia University, at http://afe.easia.columbia.edu/tps/1000ce.htm#order.

Primary sources related to state and society in Europe during the late Middle Ages are available at Fordham University's Medieval Sourcebook at www.fordham.edu/halsall/sbook1w.html#Late%20 Medieval%20Governments.

in northern China who opposed Mongol rule rose up in what became known as the Red Turban rebellions; by 1361 the Red Turbans had seized control of the northern half of Korea. The White Lotus Rebellion in 1352 in the southern province of Guangzhou was named for the Buddhist sect that agitated for it and contributed to the downfall of the Yuan dynasty.

Finally, although China did not experience anything as devastating as the Black Death at that time, the country did experience in the mid-fourteenth century a succession of natural disasters. Droughts, famines, floods, and earthquakes undermined people's confidence that the government possessed the Mandate of Heaven, the concept that the rule of whoever governed at a particular time was sanctioned by a higher power. Beginning in the 1330s, recurring famines in northern China prepared the way for a wave of epidemics that thrived on a weakened or malnourished population, much as similar conditions had prepared the way for the impact of the Black Death in Europe. These deteriorating conditions in the country made the Mongol rulers, who had never won complete acceptance by the Chinese, increasingly vulnerable to rebellion. The dynasty collapsed in 1368 with little resistance, having previously lost control of the country. No such disaster befell any of the ruling dynasties of Europe at the time, but Europe did experience fundamental social and political changes that were as shaped by war as they were by the Black Death or any other factor.

The Shaping of the Past: Military Transformation and the Hundred Years War

The Hundred Years War (1337–1453) between England and France actually lasted 116 years and technically was not a single war, as it involved long periods of peace between the conflicting powers. The very name suggests, however, the prolonged nature of conflict and violence, which in turn had longer and more significant effects than previous conflicts between the two countries. During the Hundred Years War, English kings brought armies to France and raised troops there to strengthen their position and, at times, to enforce their claim to the French throne. They created a great deal of political instability and uncertainty in the process. The English forces had the upper hand in the early stages of the war, marauding and wreaking havoc in the western part of France and winning the few major battles. The English armies were smaller than the French, but the superior numbers of the French army proved insignificant in the major battles. On August 26, 1346, the English king, Edward III (r. 1327–1377), located his troops on a sloping hill between the Maie River and the woods of Crécy. He prepared to face a force three times larger than his, a French army of roughly 20,000 armored knights and 10,000 men-at-arms on foot. Taking advantage of the high ground and the superior weaponry

The Mandate of Heaven

China   If you dare to have constant dancing in your palaces, and drunken singing in your chambers,—that is called the fashion of sorcerers; if you dare to set your hearts on wealth and women, and abandon yourselves to wandering about or to the chase,—that is called the fashion of extravagance; if you dare to despise sage words, to resist the loyal and upright, to put far from you the aged and virtuous, and to seek the company of youths,—that is called the fashion of disorder. Now if a high noble or officer be addicted to one of these three fashions with their ten evil ways, his family will surely come to ruin; if the prince of a country be so addicted, his state will surely come to ruin. The minister who does not try to correct such vices in the sovereign shall be punished with branding.

Oh! Do you, who now succeed to the throne, revere these warnings in your person. Think of them!—sacred councils of vast importance, admirable words forcibly set forth! The ways of Heaven are not invariable: on the good-doer it sends down all blessings, on the evil-doer it sends down all miseries. Do you but be virtuous, be it in small things, or in large, and the myriad regions will have cause for rejoicing. If you not be virtuous, be it in large things or in small, it will bring the ruin of your ancestral temple.

Source: James Legge, trans., *The Sacred Books of China: The Texts of Confucianism,* in F. Max Mueller, ed., *The Sacred Books of the East,* 50 vols. (Oxford: Clarendon Press, 1879–1910), vol. 3, pp. 92–95.

France   Albeit the king can make new establishments, he must take care that he makes them for a reasonable cause and for the common profit and by great counsel, and especially so that they be not made against God nor against good customs; for if he did so (which, God willing, will never happen) his subjects would not have to suffer it because each one above all else must love and fear God with all his heart and for the honor of Holy Church, and, after, his earthly lord.

—Philippe de Beaumanoir

Source: Philippe de Beaumanoir, *Coutumes de Beauvaisis,* ed. Amadée Salmon, 2 vols. (Paris, 1889–1900), quoted in Charles T. Wood, *Joan of Arc and Richard III: Sex, Saints, and Government in the Middle Ages* (New York: Oxford University Press, 1988), p. 122.

What are the main ideas involved in the Chinese concept of the Mandate of Heaven? What limitations does Beaumanoir place on the ruler? How closely do the views of Beaumanoir from fourteenth-century France approximate the Chinese concept of the Mandate of Heaven?

of their archers, the English won an overwhelming victory. Ten years later, at the Battle of Poitiers, a vastly outnumbered English army used the same tactics as at Crécy to decimate a much larger French force. According to the chronicler Jean de Froissart, the French had more than 60,000 troops to the 8,000 of the English.

These battles did not prove decisive by any means (the military campaigns continued, with both monarchies strained by the escalating costs of the war), but they do illustrate the changing nature of warfare in the fourteenth century. Froissart's description of the Battle of Poitiers illustrates the manner in which skillful English archers used their longbows to overcome the larger, heavily armored French cavalry:

> The engagement now began on both sides; and the battalion of the [French] marshals was advancing before those who were intended to break the battalion of the [English] archers, and had entered the lane, where the hedges on both sides were lined by the archers, who, as soon as they saw them fairly entered, began shooting in such excellent manner from each side of the hedge, that the horses smarting under the pain of the wounds made by their bearded arrows would not advance, but turned about, and by their unruliness threw their riders, and caused the greatest confusion, so that the battalion of the marshals could never approach that of the prince. (Froissart 1961, 58)

The longbow, which was capable of piercing metal armor, brought about a new direction in warfare that featured heavy casualties and a huge advantage to an infantry consisting of dismounted knights and other men-at-arms supported by skilled longbow-men. Heavier armor, which changed from mail to plate in this period, gave knights on horseback additional protection but made them less mobile and less effective. The cavalry remained an essential component of warfare in this period, and some innovations, such as the replacement of a shield by a lance in the left hand of a cavalryman, enhanced his fighting capabilities. But the introduction of cannons, the superweapons of the early modern age, further decreased the importance of mounted cavalry. The size of the armies contributed to the declining role of the aristocracy in warfare as well. During the Hundred Years War, kings began to institute permanent standing armies, consisting primarily of peasants, on which they could rely to meet any challenge that might arise. While chivalrous courage and individual displays of skill and strength remained appropriate for tournaments, they no longer played a decisive role in battle.

Unable to distinguish themselves on the field of battle through individual feats of heroism because of the new weaponry, nobles found other ways to make themselves valuable to kings. In some cases, they even stooped to hire themselves out as mercenaries to raise armies. The prevalence of warfare continued to provide opportunities for members of the nobility to have military success, which was still their currency in trade. Nobles remained leaders in the military and society, even if their overall importance as fighters had decreased. Kings continued to award their nobles important commands, based largely upon their prominence at court. In general, however, the changes in warfare strengthened the position of the king and the peasantry at the expense of the nobility, the dominant class of the preceding period. In the most important battles of the period, the kings themselves assumed command of their armies.

This trend tied the fortunes of each country increasingly to the success or failure of its monarchs in war. The Battle of Poitiers resulted in the capture of the French king, John II, in addition to the deaths of leading French noblemen and thousands of soldiers and the confiscation of huge amounts of French gold, silver, and jewelry by the English. With the French government in chaos, John agreed to the Treaty of Bretigny (1360), which recognized English control over a large portion of France. French fortunes revived under King Charles the Wise (r. 1364–1380), who rebuilt the French army and recovered much of the territory the French monarchy had lost. England then went through a period of political instability, caused by the growing unpopularity of Richard II (r. 1377–99). Richard opposed the war, which had brought money and employment to many in England but cost the monarchy a fortune. Richard executed or exiled leading nobles who opposed him. In 1399 one such noble, Henry of Bolingbroke, dethroned Richard and took the crown for himself as King Henry IV (r. 1399–1413), thus establishing the new ruling dynasty of the House of Lancaster.

Soon internal warfare between rival factions in France provided the English with a new opportunity. The second Lancastrian king, Henry V (r. 1413–1422), resumed the conflict in France and achieved spectacular success, most notably at the Battle of Agincourt in 1415, in which an outnumbered English army again decimated a much larger French force.

If Edward III had begun the Hundred Years War with the only intention of solidifying his hold over English lands in France, Henry V made the claims of the English king to the French throne a realistic possibility. But Henry died at age thirty-five in 1422, and the English throne went to his infant son who ruled as Henry VI until 1461. The absence of a strong English monarch allowed for a revival of French power, sparked by Joan of Arc, one of the most interesting and enigmatic figures of the period.

Born in Domrémy-la-Pucelle, a village in a border province away from the center of the French monarchy, the teenage Joan of Arc (1412–1431) provided a new wave of inspiration for France. Voices told her, she said, to lead Charles, the French dauphin, or heir to the throne, to his coronation at Rheims. When she left home to offer her services to Charles in 1428, few French people had any hope that Charles could defeat the seemingly indestructible English

Battle of Agincourt, 1415. This fifteenth-century miniature reveals much about early perceptions of warfare.

forces. Charles and his advisers realized that they could use Joan to their political advantage by promoting her as the fulfillment of a prophecy that foretold that a virgin from Lorraine would save France. Joan, wearing male clothing and armor and leading an army of 4,000 men, successfully ended the English siege of Orleáns in May 1429. That victory paved the way for Charles to proceed through English territory to Rheims for his coronation in July. But when Charles realized that he had more to gain by making peace with the English—even though Joan wanted the English driven completely out of France—he betrayed her. Convicted of heresy by the church, she was handed over to the English authorities for punishment; they burned her at the stake at the age of nineteen. Yet Joan had rallied French morale at a particularly bleak time and made it more difficult for the French to ever accept an accommodation with the English. She helped to transform the war from a territorial and dynastic struggle between the English and French monarchs into a nationalistic crusade by the French people to oust a foreign invader from their lands.

Warfare and Political Change in the Fourteenth and Fifteenth Centuries

The Hundred Years War had a profound impact on the monarchies and the political futures of both England and France. During the war, the English nobility supported the monarchy, believing that they had much to gain from supporting their king because of the opportunities for wealth and status that fighting in France provided. In France, the nobility was divided, with the powerful dukes of Burgundy allying with the English for most of the war to prevent the further strengthening of their royal rivals. Only when Joan of Arc rallied the people to the support of the Valois claimant to the throne, Charles VII, did the French nobility begin to unite behind the monarch.

After Joan's death in 1431 the war continued until 1444, when the two sides reached a truce that lasted until 1449. Until 1444 the English had continued their policy of aggression in France despite the indifference of the weak and mentally limited Henry VI (r. 1422–1461, 1470–1471). Henry had bouts of insanity, but even at his most lucid he was incapable of providing the leadership expected of a monarch. Charles VII (r. 1422–1461) was almost as disappointing to the French in the early years of his reign, a weak military leader who proved incapable of uniting his own court, much less the country. More concerned with the trappings of power than the work required of an effective monarch, he allowed selfish power-seekers who could not get along with one another to govern in his stead. But when the war resumed in 1449, the French gained the upper hand. Charles began to take more responsibility and finally to provide effective leadership at organizing military forces, gaining additional prestige by personally leading his armies into combat.

By 1451 the French had regained control of all English possessions in France, with the exception of the port of Calais on the English Channel. By 1453 the English had virtually conceded defeat. England's defeat combined with the further mental deterioration of Henry VI led to a power struggle among the nobility known as the War of the Roses. Rivalry among the nobles as they took advantage of a weak centralized government to increase their own power

For primary sources related to the Hundred Years War in France, see www.fordham.edu/halsall/sbook1m.html#The%20Hundred%20Years%20War.

More on Joan of Arc can be found on the website of the museum in Rouen dedicated to her life: http://musee.jeannedarc.pagesperso-orange.fr/indexanglais.htm.

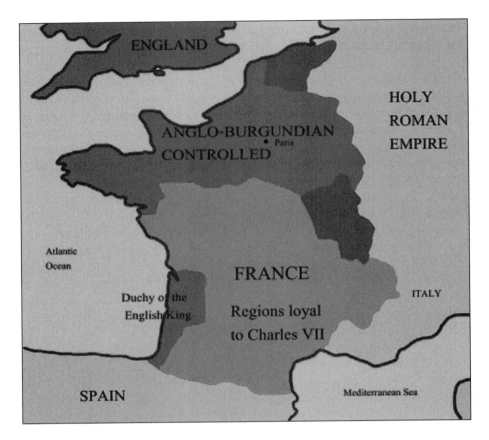

English possessions in France, 1435

led to chaos. Nobles employed private armies in a system often referred to as bastard feudalism, whereby men gave their allegiance in exchange for money rather than land, making them little more than mercenary soldiers. Edward IV (r. 1461–1470, 1471–1483), the son of Henry's greatest rival, Richard, duke of York, assumed the throne on the death of Henry VI. He had to contract with specific individuals to control local violence. When Edward died in 1483, his oldest son was not of age to take control and Edward's brother, Richard, duke of Gloucester, took the throne as Richard III. The upstart Henry Tudor, of distant Lancastrian heritage, challenged Richard for the throne and defeated him at the Battle of Bosworth Field on August 22, 1485. Henry married Elizabeth of York, the daughter of Edward IV, thus uniting the two feuding royal families and establishing the Tudor dynasty.

As the founder of a new dynasty, Henry could hardly afford to alienate the nobility. But they no longer formed the backbone of support for the monarchy.

The nobility had contributed to the cause of the monarchy in the Hundred Years War both through personal service and as representatives of the kingdom in Parliament, where they traditionally granted taxation rights to the king and enacted legislation for the good of the realm. The English nobility emerged from the Wars of the Roses considerably weakened, partly because of the casualties they suffered in the wars of this violent period and partly because the English monarchs allowed the diminution in the ranks of the nobility. In 1453 forty-four barons had been summoned to Parliament. King Edward IV summoned forty-one barons to his first Parliament in 1461. In 1484 Richard III summoned just twenty-six. Henry VII, continuing a trend of reducing their numbers, developed a loyal core of supporters, mostly with legal backgrounds, who depended entirely upon him for their positions. He established new courts capable of curbing the nobles' power and he suppressed private armies, convincing Parliament to outlaw them in 1504. He did not legislate without Parliament but he called Parliament infrequently, thus decreasing the opportunities for conflict. Henry also arranged a number of family marriages to tie his new dynasty to other European ruling families. He sought more to strengthen his position at home than to seek conquest and territorial expansion. By the end of Henry's reign in 1509, he had strengthened the monarchy and secured his family on the throne.

After the Hundred Years War, by contrast the French monarchy looked for new conquests. France's victory in the war had strengthened the French monarchy. The French king retained the right to collect the *taille*, a tax on land and wealth, without the consent of the Estates General, thus enhancing the royal authority and financial position of the monarchy of Louis XI (r. 1461–1483) and his successors. By the time of his death in 1483, Louis XI had established royal control over most of France. When his son and successor Charles VIII invaded Italy in 1494, he set off a new period of conflict in Europe as monarchs vied for land in Italy and elsewhere to maintain their prestige and thwart their rivals. Louis XII (r. 1498–1515), who succeeded Charles, launched another invasion of Italy in an attempt to conquer Milan. Louis also sought favor from the French populace by reducing taxes.

At the end of the fifteenth century, several other monarchs pursued similar policies and strengthened the prestige of monarchy in Europe. In Spain, the marriage of Ferdinand and Isabella in 1469 brought together the two most powerful kingdoms in the Iberian Peninsula, Aragon and Castile. Although they did not create a completely unified nation-state, the two monarchs did undertake several initiatives to enhance their power at the expense of the nobility. For example, in Castile Isabella relied on town militias, the *Hermandades*, to enforce royal policy. The reconquest of Spanish territory from the Muslims greatly enhanced the prestige of these two rulers. In the Holy

Roman Empire, Maximilian I (r. 1493–1519) annexed Bohemia, Moravia, and land in Hungary to his own holdings in Austria. He joined with Ferdinand of Aragon, Pope Alexander VI, the duchy of Milan, and the Venetian republic to resist French expansion in the Mediterranean. Maximilian's marriage to Mary of Burgundy gave him claims to lands in the Low Countries, in addition to Alsace-Lorraine and the Franche-Comte on the Swiss border. His son, Philip, married Joanna, the eldest daughter of Ferdinand and Isabella, and heiress to their vast possessions.

In Russia, Ivan III (r. 1462–1535), also known as Ivan the Great, began to forge Russia into a powerful early modern state. He wanted first and foremost to unify all Russian-speaking people under his rule, centered on Moscow. He largely succeeded in doing so. The country more than tripled in size between the beginning of Ivan's reign and 1533. Russian expansionist policy, like the expansionist policies of Spain, found justification in a religious mission. The importance of religion had not waned in the fourteenth and fifteenth centuries, but the authority of the western Christian church showed serious symptoms of decline.

Symptoms of Waning Authority in the Western Christian Church

The story of medieval Christianity largely involved the triumph of the western church in Rome as the dominant and unifying religious institution for most of Europe. It also involved the increasing power and authority of the papacy over that church. The popes in the thirteenth century, beginning with Innocent III (r. 1198–1216), asserted their power more successfully than at any other period in the history of the papacy. In the fourteenth century, however, the papacy began to lose some of its privileged position. As the power of the papacy declined, so too did the authority of the church. That decline began in 1294 when a canon (church) lawyer who had spent most of his life in Rome ascended the papal throne as Pope Boniface VIII (r. 1294–1303).

Already in his late seventies when he ascended the papal throne, Boniface sought to resolve some of the issues that still confronted the papacy after its long but intermittent struggle for power with the secular monarchs of Europe. In particular, Boniface wished to defend papal authority over lay rulers and the clergy serving in their lands. In 1296 he issued a papal bull (document) titled *Clericis Laicos*, which stated that the clergy had no obligation to provide money to secular rulers. This decree affected particularly Philip IV (the Fair) of France (r. 1285–1314) and Edward I of England (r. 1272–1307), who were engaged in war against each other and desperately needed revenue. Both Philip and Edward defended their right to collect money from the church with thinly veiled threats that they could not protect the clergy if they did not derive enough revenue from the church.

After thousands of pilgrims (and the revenue they brought) poured into Rome during the Jubilee Year of 1300, a reinvigorated Boniface renewed his attack on the secular rulers with a letter of reprimand to Philip the Fair over the arrest of a French bishop by the secular authorities. Philip had charged the bishop with heresy and treason, a direct affront to Boniface, who had appointed the individual in question. Boniface, addressing Philip in a haughty and patronizing tone, attempted to make clear papal jurisdiction in this matter. In 1302 Philip, objecting to Boniface's claim to temporal authority in France, summoned for the first time a representative body known as the Estates General to consent to taxation and to approve the king's position against Boniface. In turn Boniface issued another bull, *Unam Sanctam*, in response to the poor attendance of the French bishops at an assembly that he had called in Rome. *Unam Sanctam* proclaimed that salvation did not exist outside the western Christian church under the leadership of the papacy. Though this was hardly a revolutionary statement, Philip had had enough of Boniface's arrogance. In response, Philip sent a band of soldiers into Italy to confront the pope, perhaps intending to bully him into resigning or to capture him and bring him to France to face trial for heresy. The king's henchmen seized and imprisoned the pope. When Boniface died in 1303, the papacy was at its lowest point in centuries. He had failed in his primary objective of defending papal authority over lay rulers and the clergy in their realms.

In 1304 the College of Cardinals elected as pope a French archbishop who took the name of Clement V (r. 1305–1314). Although he had spent his early career in Rome, Clement did not have a personal attachment to the city, which he regarded as disorderly and unsavory. In 1309 he moved the seat of the papacy from Rome to Avignon, where it remained until 1377. The period during which the papacy resided at Avignon became known as the Babylonian Captivity of the Church, a reference to the period of Old Testament History when the Hebrew elite were taken into Babylon away from the holy city of Jerusalem. Since Avignon (now within the modern borders of France) was not legally a part of the French kingdom at that time, the popes retained their independence from the French monarchy, but the papacy lost much of its prestige.

Contemporaries and historians alike have criticized the popes who resided at Avignon, though, individually considered, most of the popes in this period proved quite capable administrators and organizers. The papacy flourished as an institution while in Avignon, establishing firm control over church revenues and an efficient administrative bureaucracy. But prominent lay people and clergy alike continued to clamor for returning the papacy to Rome, which they were long accustomed to considering the holy city. No amount of organizational ability would have appeased people like the renowned mystic Catherine of Siena (1347–1380), who looked to the papacy for spiritual leadership rather than administrative skills.

In 1377 Pope Gregory XI returned the papacy to Rome, but he died shortly thereafter. The Roman people then demanded the election of an Italian pope, who they believed would keep the papacy in Rome where it belonged. Bowing to this request, the College of Cardinals elected an Italian archbishop who became Pope Urban VI. Urban wanted to reform the church and he started by trying to prevent cardinals from accepting pensions or money and gifts for clerical business. Before long thirteen of sixteen cardinals declared the election invalid on the grounds that its outcome had been determined by popular pressure.

The thirteen left Rome and elected a French cleric as Pope Clement VII, who set up his papacy in Avignon. Now there were two popes in Europe, Urban VI in Rome and Clement VII in Avignon. The election of Clement as pope introduced one of the most troubling episodes in the history of the papacy and the western church, known as the Great Schism. Between 1378 and 1417, England, Germany, and Italy supported the Roman popes, while France, Castile, Aragon, and Scotland supported the popes in France. The schism further damaged the prestige of the papacy and called into question the legitimacy of the sacraments since both popes placed areas that did not support them under the interdict, which forbade sacraments from being performed. Given the dubious position of both popes, no Christians could be sure that the sacraments they received had the approval of the rightful pope. During the fourteenth century, the deteriorating condition of the church inspired reform movements and new attitudes that would begin to challenge the central authority of the church.

Reform Ideas, the Conciliar Movement, and Popular Christianity

In response to the papacy's waning prestige, supporters of the secular monarchies called for the state to assume increasing control over the church. At the beginning of the fourteenth century, before the papacy even moved to Avignon, a Dominican student of Thomas Aquinas, John of Paris (ca. 1250–1306) wrote a treatise titled *On Papal and Royal Power*.

John had become concerned about the controversy that embroiled Philip IV with the papacy. In this treatise, he maintained that since in the Bible kingship preceded true priesthood as a historical development, kingship did not derive its authority from the spiritual realm. John also suggested that popes had no right to the goods of the laity, except in cases of extreme necessity for the good of

John of Paris on the Relationship Between Church and State

And therefore we say that priestly power is greater than royal power and surpasses it in dignity, because we always perceive that whatever pertains to the ultimate end is more perfect and better, and it directs whatever pertains to an inferior end. . . . And therefore priestly power is of greater dignity than secular power, and this is commonly conceded: "As lead is not as precious as gold, so the priestly order is higher than the royal power.". . .

And yet, if the dignity of the priest is ultimately greater than that of the ruler it is not necessarily that it is greater in all ways. For the lesser, secular realm does not hold its power from the greater, spiritual realm in such a manner that the former originates in or was derived from the latter, as in the case of the power which a proconsul holds from the emperor who is greater in all matters, since the proconsul's power is derived from him; but secular power is held in the manner of the head of the household in relation to that of the commander of an army, since one is not derived from the other, but both are given from some superior power. . . .

—John of Paris, *Of Royal and Papal Power*, 1303
Translated by Cary J. Nederman

Source: Cary J. Nederman and Kate Langdon Forhan, eds., *Medieval Political Theory: A Reader: The Quest for the Body Politic, 1100–1400* (London: Routledge, 1993), pp. 164–165.

This treatise was developed during the controversy between Philip IV of France and Pope Boniface VIII. What is John's main argument here? Does he regard the king or the pope as having the greater authority? How does he qualify his answer to that question? What is the significance of this passage as it relates to the authority of the papacy in the early fourteenth century?

the community. Dante Alighieri (1265–1321), the great Italian poet, criticized the papacy and the Roman Catholic clergy for numerous abuses, including simony (the buying and selling of church positions), the excessive concern with wealth, and nepotism (placing family members into church offices). In *The Divine Comedy*, he made Pope Boniface VIII a symbol for everything that he considered wrong with the church, including simony, hypocrisy, pride, the clergy's desire for wealth, and the intervention of the church in politics. In his political work, *On Monarchy* (ca. 1313), Dante called for the papacy to yield to the German emperor in political authority and to renounce its worldly authority and possessions.

Later in the fourteenth century, the English scholar and Oxford professor of philosophy John Wycliffe (ca. 1329–1384) defended the political authority of the English king over the English church. Claiming that wealth had corrupted the church, he called for the church to relinquish its property and return to the ideal of apostolic poverty; he also suggested that the pope could err on matters of faith. But Wycliffe, going beyond a critique of the administrative structure and political authority of the church, called into question some of the church's seven sacraments and challenged the church's interpretation of Holy Communion or the Eucharist, which was that the bread and wine actually changed substances and become the body and blood of Christ.

In Bohemia, a priest and professor named John Huss (ca. 1369–1415) drew on Wycliffe's views to launch his own reform movement. Huss emphasized belief in the Bible as the only guide to faith. He argued that Christ—not the pope—was the true head of the church. He proclaimed that people achieved salvation from God rather than from a corrupt priesthood or through the ceremonies of the church. This direct attack on the authority and the sacraments of the church led to the branding of Huss as a heretic by 1411. By 1414 the Catholic Church had excommunicated Huss and condemned his ideas.

The church sought to resolve the divisions resulting from Huss's criticisms and the Great Schism by summoning a series of church councils. The early church had developed its doctrine through such councils, and reformers believed that councils might still carry enough authority to help the church out of the dilemma posed by the rivalry of two competing popes. In 1409 the Council of Pisa—a gathering of cardinals, archbishops, bishops, abbots, leaders of the different monastic orders, canon lawyers, and representatives from universities and most European countries—made the first attempt to resolve the question of papal legitimacy. But when the cardinals elected a new pope and called for the popes at Rome and Avignon to resign, both refused; instead of resolving the issue of who was the rightful pope, the church now had three rival claimants. Finally, after five years in which there were three popes, the Holy Roman Emperor Sigismund forced the pope at Pisa to summon another council to meet at Constance. The Council of Constance finally resolved the Great Schism by forcing the resignation of the Roman pope and, with some difficulty, deposing the popes at Pisa and Avignon. The council decreed that church councils meet at regular intervals (one in five years, the next in seven, and then every ten years) from that point forward, marking a temporary victory for the conciliar movement. The Council of Constance appeared to have resolved the church's problems and reaffirmed its role as spiritual guide, defender of religious orthodoxy, and an authoritative force in European politics; however, the conciliar movement further eroded the prestige of the papacy by challenging its supremacy in the church, thus creating the seeds for further internal conflict.

During this period there was a pronounced rise in women's spirituality, as evidenced by the growing numbers of women who joined religious associations and of women mystics, many of whom were later canonized as saints. Unlike the male flagellants who responded to the Black Death with self-punishment to atone for the sins of a depraved society, women mystics and ascetics fasted and denied themselves comfort in an attempt to attain a greater level of spiritual closeness with God. Female visionaries and prophets presented an alternative route to the word of God from that offered by ordained clergy. The prestige of a woman such as Catherine of Siena (1347–1380) in the fourteenth century and the success of Joan of Arc prior to her execution in the fifteenth indicate some level of acceptance of women in authoritative roles.

The second youngest of twenty-five children, Catherine of Siena began to see visions of Jesus at an early age and decided to devote her life to him. Catherine joined a female branch of the Dominican order and developed a strong desire to become the mystical bride of Christ. She whipped herself and became ill by depriving herself of food, sleep, and all bodily comfort. She fasted for long periods of time, during which she ate only the communion bread she received at church. Catherine devoted her life to helping the poor and the sick, prior to achieving an international reputation that allowed her to intervene at the highest level of papal politics, as she did in her calls for the return of the papacy to Rome from Avignon. Before she died she is said to have received the stigmata, the miraculous appearance of the wounds of Christ on her own body. She died at the age of thirty-three, the same age at which Christ had died, even denying herself water near the end to hasten her demise so that she might imitate Jesus even in her age at death. In 1461 the church made Catherine the patron saint of Italy.

In addition to such devout religiosity, many in society responded to the spiritual crisis with a commitment to and enthusiasm for popular Catholicism, which flourished at a local level in many parts of Europe, including countries as diverse as England and Spain. Many people continued to rely on the services of their own parish priest and held him in high esteem, despite the disrepute in which the clergy as a whole were generally held. In a world that took very seriously the existence of the devil and demons and the threat that they posed, people looked to the church and its sacraments as a practical shield against the misfortunes that these evil beings could cause. People undertook pilgrimages, purchased relics, and made promises to saints in exchange for the saint's intervention to forestall storms, crop failures, and livestock disease. Christians attended mass on Sunday; did not eat meat on Fridays, during Lent, or at certain other appointed times in the church calendar; and confessed their sins to a priest at least once a year. People flocked to religious processions such as those held on the feast of Corpus Christi, which celebrated the communion wafer as the body of Christ in an event that united the entire community around a common symbol. Such observances and activities indicate that Catholicism was a living, vibrant religion, with both strengths and weaknesses, in the late medieval period.

However, in the fifteenth century some educated Christians began taking a new approach to the Christian life and wondered if the activities of most Christians really fit the definition of a good Christian. Christian humanism was a movement that combined an interest in the classical learning of Greece and Rome with an emphasis on the Christian faith in an effort to teach people how to be "good Christians." An association of devout laymen known as the Brethren of the Common Life committed itself to founding schools and improving education in order to spread the message of Christian humanism throughout northern Europe. The Brethren were connected to a larger movement known as the *Devotio Moderna* or "modern devotion," which produced many of the most noted Christian humanists.

The *Devotio Moderna* stressed the importance of living the Christian faith as part of the world, not in isolation from it. Geert Grote (or Groote) (1340–1384), considered by many the founder of the *Devotio Moderna*, came from the Netherlands and studied medicine, theology, and law before he decided to commit himself to a life of spiritual asceticism outside the framework of the institutional church. He stated that Christians should give money where it is most needed, specifically to those who are poverty-stricken. Women mystics in Belgium formed their own lay order called the Béguines, which performed charitable works in the service of those in need. The Béguines had a difficult time gaining acceptance from the male clergy, who disapproved of their avoidance of marriage without joining an established religious order, but they persisted in living a life devoted to asceticism and service. A leading figure of the *Devotio Moderna*, Thomas à Kempis (ca. 1380–1471), came from a peasant background but managed to receive an education that prepared him both to live and write about religious life as a devout layman. In his influential book, *The Imitation of Christ* (1425), Thomas encouraged people to imitate Christ completely in their lives, even if doing so meant enduring hardship and suffering.

Conclusion

The crises of the late Middle Ages changed Europe irrevocably. The outbreak of the Black Death in Europe in 1348, during the period of the Avignon papacy, provoked a spiritual crisis that added to the problems and the waning prestige of the late medieval church. In society at large, the fourteenth and fifteenth centuries witnessed a frequent preoccupation with death and increased questioning, skepticism about God and the church, and a search for meaning and a new understanding of people's relationship with God. The long period during the fourteenth century during which the papacy resided in Avignon and the following period during which rival popes claimed the right to occupy the throne of St. Peter led increasing numbers of Christians to stop viewing the papacy as the impartial representative of Christ on earth. Reformers such as John Wycliffe and John Huss challenged some of the sacraments and the church's fundamental teachings about them. The Hundred Years War, which had begun with the English king seeking increased power and control of additional land in France, ended with dynastic instability and political chaos in England and with the French monarchy enhanced in status and poised to become a more dominant power in France and Europe. But by the end of the fifteenth century a new dynasty had become established in England that would not only revive the authority of the monarch but also provide the leadership to transform England into a formidable power capable of challenging the authority of the Roman church and the dominant European powers of France and Spain.

European society as a whole emerged from the crises of the late Middle Ages to pursue new directions in territorial expansion, learning, art, culture, and religion. The expansion of European interests to other parts of the globe would dramatically affect other civilizations, which in turn affected European civilization. The Islamic world, also recovered from the onslaught of the Black Death, continued to rival Europe for power in the Mediterranean for the next several centuries. China recovered from its period of instability to flourish again during the Ming period. These developments of the early modern period form the subjects of the next three chapters, dealing with the Renaissance, the beginnings of European expansion, and the Reformation.

1. What were the psychological and social consequences of the Black Death?
2. How did the Hundred Years War represent a force for change? What was the significance of the conflict beyond the amount of territory controlled by the kings of France and England?
3. How were politics and religion intertwined in the fourteenth and fifteenth centuries? Who held the upper hand in the relationship between church and state during this period?
4. How did the religious beliefs of people in the early modern period relate to their everyday lives?
5. What major problems and challenges confronted the Roman Catholic Church in the fourteenth and fifteenth centuries? Did these problems and challenges make the Protestant Reformation inevitable?

Suggestions for Further Reading

Bossy, John. 1985. *Christianity in the West, 1400–1700*. Oxford: Oxford University Press.

Froissart, Sir John. 1961. *The Chronicles of England, France and Spain*. H.P. Dunster's condensation of the Thomas Johnes translation. Introduction by Charles W. Dunn. New York: E.P. Dutton.

Jones, Michael K. 2003. *Bosworth: Psychology of a Battle*. Stroud, England: Tempus.

Tong, James W. 1991. *Disorder Under Heaven: Collective Violence in the Ming Dynasty*. Stanford, CA: Stanford University Press.

Tuchman, Barbara. 1978. *A Distant Mirror: The Calamitous 14th Century*. New York: Ballantine Books.

Wood, Charles T. 1988. *Joan of Arc and Richard III: Sex, Saints, and Government in the Middle Ages*. New York: Oxford University Press.

Suggested Websites

www.bbc.co.uk/history/british/middle_ages/black_impact_01.shtml

From the BBC website on British history, this site includes analysis, information, contemporary accounts, and external links to other sites dealing with the Black Death.

http://ehistory.osu.edu/osu/archive/hundredyearswar.cfm

This website contains maps, translations from Froissart's chronicle, a timeline, a bibliography, and additional information and features related to the Hundred Years War.

www.fordham.edu/halsall/source/anon1381.html

This website contains a contemporary chronicler's account of the Peasants' Rebellion in England in 1381.

www.travelchinaguide.com/intro/history/yuan/decline.htm

This website, intended to promote travel in China, contains information about the fall of the Yuan dynasty and the transition to the Ming dynasty, as well as other topics of Chinese history.

www.warsoftheroses.com

This website is intended to facilitate a detailed understanding of the Wars of the Roses in England through biographies of major figures at the time, a timeline of battles, and some historical analysis.

9   The Renaissance, ca. 1350–1517

The Italian town of Lucca, having survived an attempt at annexation by neighboring Florence, fell to Pisa in 1341. Thus began a decade marked largely by the rise of the Visconti rulers of Milan, who threatened Florentine power and independence from the 1340s until the end of the fourteenth century. In 1343 Florence was moved to adopt a new constitution, restricting political office to those who belonged to one of the twenty-one most prominent guilds in the city. Then, in the last two years of the decade, Italy, like the rest of Europe, suffered enormously from the calamity of the Black Death.

These seemingly disparate developments all contributed to the enormous changes that occurred in Italy during the period that we know as the Italian Renaissance, although none of them seem to be harbingers of any kind of rebirth, which the word *renaissance* implies. Rivalry and warfare characterized much of the history of Renaissance Italy, particularly from the mid-fourteenth to the mid-fifteenth century. The frequent troubles of the city-states led to the emergence of powerful authoritarian leaders or princes (known in Italy as *signori*) capable of defending their territory and of ruling with a strong hand so as to crush internal dissent. Florence ostensibly remained a republic and proud of its republican institutions, the representative nature of which, however, became increasingly limited until the Medici family gained power in the fifteenth century. The Black Death contributed to an economic downturn in a society already marked by social and psychological depression and more fascinated with death than with any kind of birth.

Thus, we must look for those factors that might have contributed to the cultural and intellectual predominance associated with Italy during the fourteenth and fifteenth centuries if we are to account for the cultural phenomenon of the Renaissance. Indeed, Italy did have several advantages over the rest of Europe, despite its problems and internal divisions. Economically, Mediterranean trade centered on Italy. When trade between Europe and the Near East increased during the Crusades, Italian commercial centers, particularly Venice and Genoa, capitalized on their geographical locations. Italian merchants and bankers played a prominent role in the long-distance trade and financial affairs

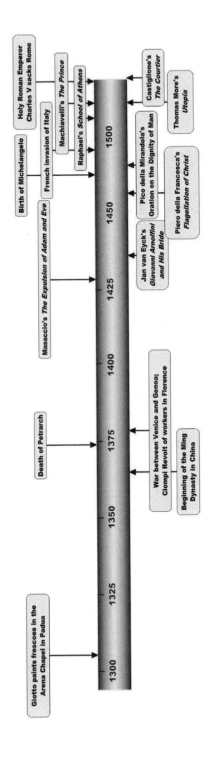

of Europe as a whole. To a large extent, the Renaissance in Italy derived from the economic success enjoyed by the Italian city-states in the late Middle Ages, during which Italian merchants took advantage of increased long-distance trade in the Mediterranean region and Europe's growing demand for goods from the East. Venice, in particular, had become a significant maritime power by the fourteenth century and acquired a territorial empire that extended well beyond the Italian peninsula to Greece and eventually Cyprus. The Italian Renaissance flourished primarily in an urban environment and incorporated the values of merchants and urban dwellers, which frequently contradicted those of the nobility who had dominated the Middle Ages from their castles and manorial estates.

By 1300 Italian towns had successfully resisted the encroachment attempted by the Holy Roman Emperors from the eleventh to the thirteenth century. During the Renaissance, Italy consisted of a number of independent kingdoms, principalities, and city-states, where central issues of political authority and the relationship between the state and the individual constantly arose and received different interpretations. Social change and political independence also led to new ideas about social organization that affected the position of women and the everyday life of residents of the city-states. Shifts in cultural, aesthetic, and religious beliefs and values followed as well. Developments in Italy transcended regional significance because of the special position that Italy occupied for the rest of Europe—religiously, intellectually, politically, culturally, and economically. But the political divisions within Italy made it vulnerable to foreign attack. The interest that the German emperors displayed in Italy provoked the attention of other European rulers, such as the French king, Charles VIII, who invaded Italy in 1494.

Thus, throughout this period the governments of the Italian city-states had to be continually alert to possible attacks, either from rival city-states within Italy or from invasion by foreign powers. Venice fought a war with Genoa from 1378 to 1381 in order to consolidate its position in the Mediterranean. Venice won a clear victory and emerged in a much stronger commercial position, even though in the short run Venice sacrificed men and money and renounced its territorial gains. In the early fifteenth century Venice expanded its territory in Italy, annexing the cities of Padua, Vicenza, and Verona. In the mid-fifteenth century the city-states of Florence, Milan, and Venice agreed to end their quarrels in the Peace of Lodi of 1454, soon thereafter expanded into the Treaty of Venice. For a time, even Naples and the Papal States joined the alliance to form the Most Holy League, an expanded peace agreement. But warfare in Renaissance Italy did not end; Pope Sixtus IV (r. 1471–1484) was the first of several popes who sought to expand papal territories and influence throughout central Italy at the expense of rival powers. The frequent rivalry

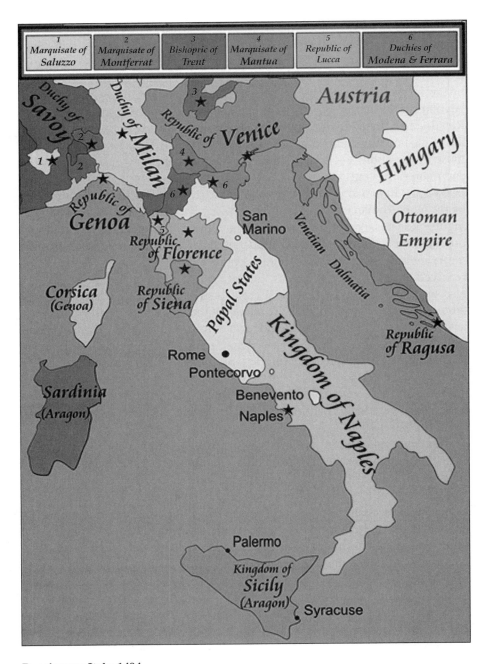

1	2	3	4	5	6
Marquisate of Saluzzo	Marquisate of Montferrat	Bishopric of Trent	Marquisate of Mantua	Republic of Lucca	Duchies of Modena & Ferrara

Renaissance Italy, 1494

and warfare of the period prevented the formation of a unified Italy or even a unified state in northern Italy that would have been able to protect the peninsula from foreign invasion.

Signorial Rule in Milan and Northern Italy

Throughout this period Milan was a major force to be reckoned with under the powerful but despotic rule of the Visconti family (r. 1287–1447) and then that of the Sforzas (1450–1500)—after Francesco Sforza joined the Visconti family through marriage. Milan flourished under its hereditary princes, prospering both from trade and from its fertile agricultural lands. But the rulers benefited even more than the people, using their immense resources to pursue a policy of military expansion, especially under the most powerful of the Visconti rulers, Giangaleazzo, between 1385 and 1402. The Viscontis encouraged prosperity both as a way of keeping the people happy and to increase their own tax base, which they fully exploited.

The Milanese rulers were representative of a trend toward signorial rule in Italy, in which despots imposed their will on the state and ruled in their own self-interest. City-states frequently invited individuals to come in from outside to take over the reins, overcome local factionalism, and bring order to city government. Known in Italy as a *podestà*, such an individual might lack the base of support available to a local prince, but he could acquire sufficient power to essentially take over the government. *Podestàs* had the advantage of not being aligned with a particular group or class, making them potentially acceptable to everyone, even though they usually upheld the interests of the elite. By 1450 Florence, Venice, and Siena were the only major city-states that had preserved a republican form of government.

Political success in such an unstable environment depended on equal measures of skill, art, and luck; many regimes were extremely short-lived. Two rulers of the city-state of Genoa, for example, lasted less than a day in power. Political factionalism in Italy took two forms: rival noble families or factions competing against one another for political power, and popular factions representing the common people attempting to wrest control of city government away from the nobility. An example of the latter occurred in Genoa in 1383 when the common people—led by the butchers—became tired of aristocratic tyranny and revolted, successfully forcing concessions that included lower taxes and a prohibition on the nobles' participation in government. The Genoese went through an extremely unstable period in the early 1390s before turning to the French to protect them from Milanese expansion. The Genoese ousted the French after only two years in 1398 amid massive destruction of property in a huge uprising. Even in relatively stable city-states, such as

Florence, conspiracies and coup d'états were frequent threats. In April 1478, the Florentines discovered the involvement of the papacy and the kingdom of Naples in a failed plot to assassinate Lorenzo and Giuliano de' Medici, the two leaders of Florence's most prominent political family. This plot was once known as the Pazzi Conspiracy after the rival Florentine banking family that stood to gain the most from the demise of the Medici. However, an Italian historian named Marcello Simonetta has now shown the plot to have been engineered by a former ally of the Medici, the humanist prince Federigo da Montefeltro (1422–1482). Simonetta discovered secret correspondence between Federigo and his own ancestor, Cicco Simonetta, the de facto head of the Milanese government. Their encrypted messages show the plot to have been much more widespread than anyone had imagined. The main goal of the plot was to end Medici rule in Florence and prevent Florentine power from becoming too dominant in central Italy. The plot was also supposed to pave the way for a republican government that would be less willing to intervene in the expansionist designs Pope Sixtus IV (r. 1471–1484) and King Ferrante of Naples. The failure of the plot strengthened the position of the Medici, who joined the ranks of princely rulers that increasingly dominated the Italian city-states.

Signorial rule had its benefits, as despots poured resources into public works, supported the local church, and attempted to foster a prosperous economy and to provide relief when the economy lagged, all in order to justify their rule in the eyes of the people. Among the most prominent *signori* outside of Milan were the Este dynasty in Modena and the Gonzaga family in Mantua. In the case of Modena, the Este family resided forty miles away in Ferrara, making their presence in the city felt mainly on ceremonial occasions rather than on a daily basis, though they did have a governor that resided in the city. Of course, Modena paid its taxes to the Este duke and had to answer to ducal authority in legal matters, as well as provide soldiers for the ducal army. The Gonzagas enjoyed a harmonious rule without internecine strife or much popular opposition. However, most Italian despots, having no legitimate claims to authority, constantly had to look over their shoulders and increase their power to deal with the challenges that others might pose to their claims. The more power these despots acquired at home, the more tempted they were to expand the territories under their control, a temptation, however, that did not apply to despots alone.

The Most Serene Republic of Venice

In 1543 Cardinal Gasparo Contarini of Venice wrote a book titled *Commonwealth and Government*, which celebrated the city's stability and reflected the pride that Venetians took in their government. Venice, known as the "most serene republic," had become a symbol of political stability, liberty, and harmonious government in other parts of Europe, including England. But by the seventeenth century a counter-myth had developed—in England in particular—that challenged the serenity of Venetian history and took note of its economic decline that began in the sixteenth century. Furthermore, because wealthy nobles and merchants dominated the government, many people in Venice itself would have regarded its reputation for freedom as a myth. However, during the height of the Renaissance, Venice seemed to flourish. It also seemed to have developed a political system that worked effectively, if not always as harmoniously as Venetian propaganda would claim. While government in Florence wavered between republicanism and reliance on the leadership of a single family, Venice maintained a single form of government throughout the Renaissance period. Although relations were not always harmonious among the various constituents of the Venetian government, Venice achieved a level of political stability unmatched by other Italian city-states.

At the head of the government was the doge, who played the monarchical role. The doge had a life appointment in order to provide a measure of stability to Venetian government, but exercised his authority more through his personal prestige and influence than through formal constitutional powers. The Great Council, representing both the nobility and the common people, controlled the executive, legislative, and judicial branches of the Venetian government. A senate of sixty leading members of the Venetian aristocracy implemented the decisions of the Great Council. However, the Great Council did not play a large role in the major decisions of state, which fell to relatively few individuals of the Venetian aristocracy who rotated positions within government. The real center of power was invisible to those outside the governing structure.

Venetian merchants helped maintain this stability by exercising tightfisted control over the commercial interests of the city. Venice's unique position among the Italian city-states derived not only from its political stability, but also from its status as a maritime power. Venice benefited from its ideal geographical location on the Adriatic with easy access to the Po and other rivers, while the surrounding swampland protected it from invasion. Venice used its location to establish sea routes to the Mediterranean, trade routes from Italy to Germany and Austria, and a monopoly on salt in northern Italy. A powerful Venetian navy protected Venice's merchants, who maintained trading contacts throughout the Mediterranean and the Middle East. Foreign merchants from all over Europe came to Venice to trade and conduct business. Venetian ships transported silks, spices, and luxury goods from India and the East. Venice also benefited from the traffic of pilgrims who made Venice an important stop on their travels from the late fourteenth century.

The wealth that Venice acquired from trade allowed the city to acquire an empire, with territories along the Adriatic coast and in the Aegean and Mediterranean Seas, including control over the island of Crete. Venice thus became a republic within a larger empire. While other Italian states were overrun or conquered by foreign invaders, Venice maintained its independence. With some exceptions like the war with Genoa, the government kept Venice relatively free from embroilment in the clashes that wasted the men, money, and efforts of other city-states and free from permanent alliances that could have led Venice into actions not central to its own self-interest. The Venetians knew that their city was virtually immune from attack, which gave them a status not shared by any other city-state. For example, Venice even held aloof from the papacy, with which the city frequently quarreled. Its independence made Venice few friends among the other city-states and, in fact, led to a certain suspicion, if not hatred, on the part of its Italian rivals. To this, the Venetians responded with either disdain or indifference, reinforcing their own sense of pride in their independence and their accomplishments.

Venice's imperial status and mercantile character did much to shape the city's social relationships. There was less distinction between the merchant class and the aristocracy than in other city-states, even Florence. There were fewer social distinctions within the Venetian merchant class, as well, because of a sense of participating in a common enterprise for the good of the city. In addition, foreign merchants established communities in Venice during this period, giving it a strong international flavor. The religious confraternities known as the *scuole* were wealthy and powerful organizations that brought people together and played a prominent role in Venetian society and government. Commitment to a common enterprise softened the relations among classes as well, encouraging frequent intermingling, especially in the houses of wealthy citizens. People from different social classes did not live in isolation from each other, but all lived close to their trading or economic interests. Venetian merchants had such far-flung interests that they relied on a number and a range of employees of lesser social status whom it would not be in their interest to alienate. Trade enriched the city and of course made the merchants more powerful, but it contributed as well to the common welfare and in this case promoted better social relations among classes.

Florence and Renaissance Society

In 1378, when the Florentine government had to suppress the working-class uprising known as the *ciompi* revolt, social relations in Florence did not appear nearly as harmonious as those in Venice. Florence was already one of the largest and most important cities in Europe, with a population approaching 100,000. But the failure of Florence's two largest commercial banking families, the Bardi and the Peruzzi, and the onset of the bubonic plague in the mid-fourteenth century had plunged Florence into a major depression. Guilds became more restrictive and the transition from journeyman to guild master more difficult. Established merchants and bankers enjoyed significant advantages, such as trading contacts, experience, capital accumulation, and, most importantly, political clout over newcomers to trade and commerce. Social groups tended to become more rigid and closed to outside members, in large part because of a decline in the Italian economy that stemmed from bank failures and a declining population in the rest of Europe. All of these factors created social tensions and class division. The *ciompi* revolt occurred at a time of high unemployment in the city that resulted from a decline in the production of woolen cloth on which the prosperity of the city largely depended. For a brief time it appeared as though the *ciompi*, or wool-carders, would gain admission to the city's guild system, which dominated the government. The government not only successfully crushed the revolt but, afterward, managed to prevent future uprisings and kept the working classes under control by fostering pride among all the citizens, making sure they all were fed, and overseeing an efficient justice system. Florence also evolved a form of government that allowed for a certain amount of representation and popular participation, while still safely dominated by the wealthier merchants, bankers, manufacturers, and professionals (e.g., lawyers, judges, physicians). Meanwhile, guild organization continued to exercise a strong influence over the divisions and regulation of Italian society.

Government in Florence consisted of an executive body called the *signoria* and two legislative bodies, the Council of the People and the Council of the Commune. The *signoria* held nine members, who had their candidacy validated by a commission before they served for an exceptionally brief two-month term. The *signoria* proposed legislation to the two legislative councils and administered the affairs of the city. Florentine political institutions distributed political influence somewhat broadly among the leading citizens instead of vesting political power in the hands of a single ruler or even a select few. The merchant class largely excluded the hereditary nobility from positions of real political authority. Meanwhile, the government drew support from the lesser merchants and artisans by allowing their guilds representation in the *signoria*. Florence's more open political system—compared with states ruled by hereditary monarchs or princes—increased the possibility for individuals to enhance their political stature while also intensifying competition within social groups such as the nobility or the merchant class.

Thus, Florentine merchants competed with one another and with older noble families for political, economic, and social status. The wealthy merchants became an elite aristocratic class of their own, a new nobility whose prestige eclipsed the rest of the mercantile and professional classes of guild masters, lesser merchants, shopkeepers, artisans, lawyers, and bankers. The more traditional landed aristocracy still had prestige, but social status increasingly depended on wealth in addition to birth. The greatest guilds in Florence were the two wool guilds, the *Arte della Lama*, which consisted of the cloth manufacturers, and the *Calimala*, which prepared the finished products for sale, including the highly specialized art of dyeing the cloth. Florentine guild communities further broke down into seven major guilds known as the *arti maggiori* and fourteen lesser guilds known as the *arti minori*. The major guilds consisted of cloth, wool, and silk manufacturers, bankers, physicians, and fur merchants, as well as one of miscellaneous judges and merchants. Butchers, bakers, cobblers, blacksmiths, and carpenters were included among the more numerous minor guilds.

What was the role of women in this burgeoning and competitive society? Social prescriptions limited expectations and opportunities for women of all classes during the Renaissance. Yet women of all classes often bore huge family responsibilities, both inside and outside the home. Francesco Datini spent most of his time in Florence and Pisa while his wife Margherita supervised her husband's estate in Prato and helped manage his business. The widow Alessandra Strozzi managed her family's properties from the death of her husband in 1435 to her own death in 1471 without remarrying. Women frequently worked outside the home in the workshops of male family members, even if they did not always receive pay for their work.

The pressure to have large families had a significant impact on the position of women in Florentine society. Ensuring a sufficient number of children to provide heirs to perpetuate the family line stands out as one of the paramount social concerns of this period. Marriage at all levels of society during the Renaissance was influenced as well by concerns to promote the interests of individual families. Florence even established a special fund in 1425 to assist families unable to provide dowries for their daughters, a prerequisite to an advantageous match. Families deposited money when their daughters were infants and after a set term received an increased amount to be used for their daughter's marriage. Alessandra Strozzi received 500 florins from the fund that she used to supplement the 1,000 florins that she was able to provide for the marriage of her oldest daughter, Caterina; she justified the decision to spend 1,000 florins in a letter to her son by saying that she could not have procured a match for her daughter otherwise. Women without adequate dowries either had to marry beneath their social class, enter a nunnery, become domestic servants, or even resort to prostitution. Women frequently had little or no say in the selection of their marriage partner.

The conferral of a dowry symbolized the legal transfer of authority over a woman from her father to a husband. Women could inherit property in Renaissance Italy, but seldom did; they even had difficulty reclaiming property that they brought into a marriage as part of their dowry if their husbands predeceased them. If her husband died, a woman would often return to her father's house. Italian Renaissance society had little place for a single, independent woman and little regard for a woman's identity beyond her male associations. Girls from aristocratic or wealthy merchant families frequently married at fifteen or sixteen; poorer girls had to wait a few extra years until their fathers could provide a proper dowry. Alessandra Strozzi, a member of a prominent merchant family, married her twenty-five-year-old husband when she was fourteen. But women of all classes tended to marry in their teens, prolonging their childbearing years and making them an average of eight years younger than their husbands—more in aristocratic marriages. The age difference between spouses reinforced the power of the male in the marriage and emphasized the reproductive purposes of the union as opposed to an ideal of mutual companionship. Women of the noble and merchant classes enjoyed a relatively high standard of living, but generally were expected to spend little on themselves and to put the interests of the family ahead of their own. In such a society, one of the main opportunities for women to find personal fulfillment was to join a religious order; behind the walls of an abbey some women took up such activities as writing and painting with oils, thus participating in the intellectual and artistic developments of the Renaissance.

The Shaping of the Past: Petrarch and the Origins of Renaissance Humanism

A woman named Laura (possibly Laura de Noves) contributed to the life of the Renaissance in a different way: she inspired the poetry of Francesco Petrarch (1304–1374), who is usually considered the founder of Renaissance humanism. Petrarch was a law student who abandoned legal studies to pursue his interest in classical literature before moving from Florence to Avignon, the temporary residence of the papacy for much of the fourteenth century and the site where he first laid eyes on Laura in 1327. (Alas, Laura was already married and so Petrarch entered the clergy.) Petrarch's works, such as *Africa* and *Letters to Illustrious Men*, earned him popularity among educated readers throughout Europe. He combined his reverence for the classics with his own creative genius and a philosophical outlook that embraced the human experience in the here and now. What sets Petrarch apart from those medieval thinkers who preceded him is primarily his emphatic insistence on the importance of classical culture as a guide for human learning, understanding, and behavior.

Scholars throughout the Middle Ages had long attempted to synthesize classical and Christian learning and tended to take the importance of the classical tradition somewhat for granted. Petrarch—believing that his medieval predecessors lacked appreciation for that tradition—embarked on a literary campaign to glorify the achievements and relevance of the classical world. Petrarch and subsequent Renaissance humanists viewed the philosophical works of Plato and Aristotle, the historical accounts of Livy, Caesar, Plutarch, and Suetonius, the political ideas of Cicero, and the poetry of Homer, Virgil, and Ovid all as having practical value in the new social and economic world of the Renaissance. The Romans especially had much to teach about effective communication, rhetoric, and skills of verbal persuasion. The educated classes of the Renaissance had an interest in Latin authors that was more than merely academic in nature.

People during the Renaissance did not use the term *humanism*, but did refer to the *studia humanitatis*, or "study of the humanities." Renaissance humanists generally valued learning applied in the service of society rather than the search for abstract truth, as in the scholastic tradition. During the Renaissance, educational emphasis shifted away from logic and toward rhetoric and other applied skills necessary for effective communication, important ingredients for success in a more commercial society. But humanism—and sometimes individual humanists—came to embody many trends and to encompass a variety of viewpoints on diverse topics, making it a movement that historians struggle to define and understand. Throughout the Renaissance, for example, humanists debated which was superior: the contemplative life or the active life. Was a life of quiet thought and study preferable to a life of activity and service in the public world? Petrarch, although he believed in the application of knowledge to everyday life, still preferred the contemplative to the active life.

Many of his successors, however, especially those associated with Florence, found the active life more valuable and became strong advocates of political participation and service in the public arena. These "civic humanists" created a myth of a historically independent Florentine republic and stressed the importance of individuals subordinating their needs to those of the republic. In Florence the idea of civic humanism represented to some degree a response to the expansion of the city-state's influence over its surrounding territories, some of which occasionally revolted or expressed displeasure with Florentine rule. Civic humanism also received a boost from the attack on Florence in 1402 by Giangaleazzo Visconti, who had launched Milan on an aggressive foreign policy that was mainly directed against Florence. Civic humanists such as Leonardo Bruni (1369–1444) found their inspiration for republican ideals in the writings of Cicero, who had praised the Roman Republic as the ideal state

Petrarch's Letter
to Boccaccio, ca. 1366

You see that I cannot speak of these matters without the greatest irritation and indignation. There has arisen of late a set of dialecticians, who are not only ignorant but demented. Like a black army of ants from some rotten old oak, they swarm forth from their hiding places and devastate the fields of sound learning. They condemn Plato and Aristotle, and laugh at Socrates and Pythagoras. And, good God! Under what silly and incompetent leaders these opinions are put forth! I should prefer not to give a name to this group of men. They have done nothing to merit one, though their folly has made them famous. I do not wish to place among the greatest of mankind those whom I see consorting with the most abject. These fellows have deserted all trustworthy leaders, and glory in the name of those who, whatever they may learn after death, exhibited in this world no trace of power, or knowledge, or reputation for knowledge. What shall we say of men who scorn Marcus Tullius Cicero, the bright sun of eloquence? Of those who scoff at Varro and Seneca, and are scandalized at what they choose to call the crude, unfinished style of Livy and Sallust? And all this in obedience to leaders of whom no one has ever heard, and for whom their followers ought to blush! Once I happened to be present when Virgil's style was the subject of their scornful criticism. Astonished at their crazy outbreak, I turned to a person of some cultivation and asked what he had detected in this famous man to rouse such a storm of reproach. Listen to the reply he gave me, with a contemptuous shrug of the shoulders: "He is too fond of conjunctions." Arise, O Virgil, and polish the verses that, with the aid of the Muses, thou didst snatch from heaven, in order that they may be fit into hands like these!

How shall I deal with the other monstrous kind of pedant, who wears a religious garb, but is most profane in heart and conduct; who would have us believe that Ambrose, Augustine, and Jerome were ignoramuses, for all their elaborate treatises? . . . They will soon turn their impudent tongues even against Christ, unless he, whose cause is at stake, interferes and curbs the raging beasts. . . .

Source: James Harvey Robinson and Henry Winchester Rolfe, *Petrarch: The First Modern Scholar and Man of Letters* (New York: G.P. Putnam's Sons, 1898), pp. 210–211.

How does this letter reflect Petrarch's humanism? How does it reflect the Renaissance attitude toward learning and education? What does it reveal about Petrarch as an individual and his relationship to his own age?

because it coordinated its laws and institutions with the interests and activities of its citizens. In Cicero and the works of other classical authors, Bruni found justification for Florence's political system and its superiority over that of belligerent Milan. Following Florence's survival after the military threat from Milan, humanists in Florence took a more active role in the political life of their city-state.

Humanism and the Dignity and Nobility of Humanity

The fifteenth century brought an important change in the direction of humanism. In the fourteenth century, Renaissance society had produced the need for a newer, more pragmatic approach to political realities and called for more practical skills that could be applied to that society. In the fifteenth, the legacy of Petrarch continued with a reconsideration of human nature and humanity's relationship with God. A major turning point was a work by Count Giovanni Pico della Mirandola (1463–1494) titled *Oration on the Dignity of Man* (1486). In this treatise Pico explains his view that humanity occupies a unique position on the Great Chain of Being—the philosophical concept that everything created existed in an ordered hierarchy—because human beings alone possess the freedom to choose their own destiny. By their choice, humans can ascend to the level of angels or descend to the level of beasts. Elsewhere, Pico explored mystical and magical connections between earth and the heavens, between philosophy and Christian theology, in a search for truth. Like his older friend, the neo-Platonist philosopher Marsilio Ficino (1433–1499), Pico believed that the quest for truth could not be achieved through narrow dogmatism and adherence to a single philosophical or spiritual approach. He contradicted church doctrine by stating that no act—no matter how much a sin—deserved eternal damnation. Although he was a Christian and a student of canon law, Pico's quest for universal truth caused him a great deal of trouble with the church. Pico's view of humanity, his search for truth, and his openness to diverse spiritual traditions, including Christianity, Judaism, Zoroastrianism, Islam, and Platonism, transcend his own age.

While Pico defended the dignity of man, an earlier writer and poet named Christine de Pisan (1364–1429) had already defended the status and dignity of women. Christine's husband of ten years, a French royal official, died when she was twenty-five, leaving her at the French court with three young children and no means of support. Her literary skills brought her patronage from the French court, which she used to advocate for peace in Europe (she lived during the Hundred Years War between England and France) and to compose poems and treatises on a wide range of subjects. These subjects included religion, government, and history, but her two most famous works, *The City of Women* and *Epistle to the God of Love*, deal with the subjects of women's lives and reputations. Christine's own success led her to emphasize women's capabilities and achievements, making her an early advocate for women's equality with men. She cited examples of women who had disproved the view that women should not be educated, such as the daughter of a Bolognese law professor who gave lectures from behind a curtain in her father's absence.

Support for women's education appears as well in the work of Baldasare Castiglione (1478–1529), a highly cultured gentleman from Mantua with both a strong scholarly background and practical experience as an administrator. In his famous work *The Courtier* (1528), Castiglione portrays his ideal female courtier as one who gives equal attention to learning and leisure activities, while also cultivating her beauty and grace. She should strive for a balance between wisdom, generosity, morality, and kindness; she should be neither too outgoing nor too shy. The court lady, however, should avoid masculine activities that would detract from her lovely, graceful, and delicate nature. The ideal female courtier, therefore, provides pleasant company for men, but otherwise serves no practical purpose. By comparison, the ideal male courtier should be courageous and skillful in combat and the use of arms, as well as loyal and faithful, charming and sincere, generous and discreet. He should be confident of his abilities but at the same time humble and modest. The ideal courtier differed from the medieval knight, being at once more well-rounded and more individualistic than the knight, who was expected to subordinate himself more completely to his lady and his lord. For Castiglione, the ideal courtier sought perfection in order to reflect well on his prince.

Castiglione based his portrait of the courtier on his study of the classics as well as his own experience, especially his years at the court of Urbino between 1504 and 1508. Federigo da Montefeltro—who established the court of Urbino in 1444 and reigned until 1482—provided much of the inspiration and served as something of a model. A skilled military leader, Federigo valued learning and philosophy, patronized artists, appreciated ancient art, and established an excellent library at his court. By the early sixteenth century, however, Italy seemed in need of more than a society of well-rounded, educated, and brave courtiers such as Federigo and those envisioned by Castiglione. The French had already invaded Italy in 1494; in 1527 the emperor Charles V invaded and sacked Rome. The dire political situation called for a new kind of leader who would unify Italy and rescue it from foreign invasion.

The Florentine statesman and diplomat Niccolò Machiavelli (1469–1527) called for such a leader in his best-known work, *The Prince* (1513). Machiavelli lived at a time of political crisis that informed his thoughts and writings about politics. A victim of factional politics in Florence, he sought to ingratiate himself with the dominant Medici family that ruled the city in order to regain a position in government. Machiavelli sought to establish the basis for legitimate political authority. He defended republican government in his *Discourses upon the First Ten Books of Titus Livius*, in which he viewed a republic as having certain inherent advantages, including the commitment of the citizens to its preservation. But Machiavelli concerned himself less with abstract political theory than with the practical political situation of his own age.

In the writing of *The Prince*, Machiavelli's personal interests coincided with his desire to see a strong ruler capable of defending his native land, despite his statement of republican views in the *Discourses*. In *The Prince*, Machiavelli recommends strategies that would enable a prince to consolidate his power, crush his opposition, and manipulate the populace to ensure its obedience, if not support. Machiavelli has frequently been criticized for his amoral view of politics, associated with the principle that the end justifies the means. For example, Machiavelli advises that, once in power, a prince ought to rely more on his enemies than his friends, since an enemy will have to work hard to gain the new ruler's approval. Machiavelli warns that a prince cannot always practice virtue in a world in which so many people are not virtuous. A prince who hopes to rule successfully, Machiavelli says, must learn how *not* to be virtuous.

However, Machiavelli's true views are perhaps most discernible in his *History of Florence* (1525). In this work he argues that Florence needed strong and enlightened leadership combined with a virtuous and active citizenry. He attributes Florence's problems to political faction and the pursuit of private gain by both leaders and citizens. Furthermore, Machiavelli's ideal prince does bear some resemblances to Castiglione's ideal courtier. For example, Machiavelli urges the ideal prince to cultivate and encourage excellence in all human endeavors. He calls on princes to patronize the arts and support learning and the acquisition of knowledge. Many princes in the sixteenth century did support these endeavors, including the founding of early museums. But a greater number of princes and kings of the sixteenth century seemed to follow his advice to learn how not to be virtuous, forever tarnishing Machiavelli's reputation by association with them—more than on the basis of his works themselves.

Humanism and the Northern Renaissance

At the same time that Machiavelli was composing *The Prince*, the English lawyer and humanist Sir Thomas More (1478–1535) was writing a small treatise about an imaginary land named Utopia. In the first part of this treatise, More renews the debate that had preoccupied Petrarch over the merits of the contemplative life versus those of the active life in a consideration of whether philosophers should give service to the state if they do not approve of the policies of the prince. More, a close personal friend of King Henry VIII and later his chancellor, ultimately concludes that—though philosophers may not correct all the flaws of the ruler—they can do more good by serving the ruler than by withdrawing from the public arena. The second part of the treatise provides a description of Utopia, a place meant to demonstrate that human beings could create an ideal society on earth. (*Utopia* was a Greek word that could be interpreted as "ideal place" or "no place" depending on a slight variation of the Greek spelling.) More did not seriously advocate that England completely imitate Utopia, but his positive outlook on human nature seemed to indicate his belief in the potential for improving society. More cleverly located his society on an island in the south Atlantic at a time when overseas explorations were in fact discovering fantastic places, making More's tale believable to some readers who thought that Utopia was a real place.

More uses his ideal society as a means to criticize his existing one. For example, Utopian society features communal ownership, which acts as a deterrent against capitalist competition and the striving after wealth that seemed to create so many new problems in early sixteenth-century society. More criticizes kings for fighting wars to gain new territories instead of concentrating on governing the ones they had properly. Interestingly, More stresses the relative equality of men and women, who receive the same education in his Utopia. He states that education serves a woman better than either wealth or beauty and urges women to base their actions on what they know to be right rather than on the opinion of men.

More was just one example of a group of northern humanists who were influenced by the Italian Renaissance but who developed their own ideas. The Renaissance in northern Europe retained a more specifically Christian context, although the Italian Renaissance must not be thought of as anti-Christian, particularly given the numerous art works from the period on Christian subjects. In fact, northern humanists are often referred to as Christian humanists, although they saw value in the moral teachings of pagan authors as well. Christian humanists sought a reconciliation of the New Testament and the literature of classical antiquity and believed that both could contribute to knowledge of how to lead a moral, Christian life. Christian humanism, with its emphasis on how to bring individuals closer to God and how to live as a good Christian within the world, reflected many of the trends of early modern society. Religion became something to be lived in the here and now in addition to providing preparation for the afterlife.

In his *Handbook of a Christian Knight* (1501), the Dutch humanist Desiderius Erasmus (ca. 1466–1536) advocated an ethic based on love rather than on church dogma and observations of church ritual. Erasmus was a teacher, a tutor, a priest, and a scholar who continually advocated for the reform of the church and the ideals of the *Devotio Moderna*. Although Erasmus never abandoned the Catholic Church, he did criticize the church and its abuses, most notably in his entertaining and satirical work *The Praise of Folly* (1509), which he addressed to Sir Thomas More, in whose house it was written. The work is an open satire, praising many of the (to him) foolish practices associated with late medieval Catholicism. Erasmus criticizes not just the most obvious abuses, such as simony, nepotism, and the greed and immorality of the clergy, but also some of the most widespread manifestations of popular Christianity. For example, he places among the regiment of fools those who believe stories of incredible miracles and those who pray to various saints, believing that saints will protect them. But Erasmus did not merely criticize the late medieval church; he also sought to strengthen Christianity through scholarship, producing a critical edition of the Greek New Testament and a new Latin translation (1516) while also editing and composing commentaries on the writings of the early church fathers.

The German humanist Johannes Reuchlin (1455–1522), who like Erasmus was educated by the Brethren of the Common Life, also sought to instill new life into Christianity through study and learning. Although he understood Latin and Greek, he regarded the neglected Hebrew language as the most powerful and important language for religious inspiration. The author of a book of Hebrew grammar, Reuchlin saw Hebrew as the language of God, one with a great power of expression and spiritual insight. He became interested in Jewish mysticism. Reuchlin believed that the Jewish Kabbalah, a collection of teachings based on Jewish mystical traditions found outside the Old Testament, and the ideas of the Greek mathematician and philosopher Pythagoras, who believed in a reality shaped by mathematical relationships, both confirmed the truth of Christianity. Reuchlin advocated personal and religious freedom for Jews, although he supported their segregation from Christians. Few at the time shared Reuchlin's views; in 1510 a Christian convert from Judaism named Johannes Pfefferkorn called for the confiscation and burning of all Hebrew literature as being offensive to Christ. Reuchlin had to defend himself (both in print and in court over a ten-year period) from the charge of demonstrating too much sympathy to Jews; he had only limited success as he was forced to retract one of his pamphlets and pay court costs.

The Social Transformation of Art in Renaissance Italy

Three interests of Renaissance artists connect their work to the ideas of the humanists: their interest in new ideas about humanity that emphasized human dignity and possibility, their interest in the revival of classical antiquity, and their interest in nature and the things of this world. The use of classical models and the desire to imitate classical antiquity characteristic of the Renaissance as a whole became more pronounced in the art of the fifteenth century. But this trend did not involve a rejection of Christianity: the church remained a major patron of artworks during the Renaissance while secular merchants and princes also commissioned a large number of religious works. Throughout Italy, wealthy benefactors, guilds, princes, and prelates provided patronage for Renaissance artists, who produced numerous religious paintings for the interiors of churches, sculptures for the exteriors, and portraits of many of their famous patrons. However, those artists in highest demand were valued because of their creative innovations that did much to shape the development of art and the values of society in conjunction with the tastes of their patrons.

Giotto di Bondone (1266–1336) of Florence usually receives much of the credit for the beginnings of Renaissance art in Italy. Giotto created a new style and imbued his art with drama and a heightened sense of the importance of humanity unseen in other artists of his time. Contemporary viewers of Giotto's art would have learned the religious stories related through his paintings and identified with the anguish or joy that they saw in his very human figures; his art reflected a society of individuals who had become increasingly comfortable with their own humanity.

Art in fourteenth- and fifteenth-century Italy flourished for a variety of reasons, including the availability of surplus wealth for patronage, the discovery of hundreds of ancient statues and monuments that provided models for the great artists of the period, and the fierce competition among skilled artists—and among the courts, city-states, and wealthy patrons vying for their talents—to enhance their reputation and status by raising the level of their work. But the contributions of individual artists cannot be minimized just because they lived in a society that placed such a high value on their work; artists, not the age, produced art. In other words, Renaissance art was great because Renaissance artists made it so. For example, Giotto's style influenced the development of Italian art for the remainder of the Renaissance. Masaccio (1401–1428) was one of the most important artists of the early fifteenth century because he most clearly created a new style with his use of space, light, shade, and dramatic expression. Masaccio also based his figures clearly on classical models and gave them an elegant form. If Renaissance artists reflected some of the ideals of humanism, they did so in an aesthetic style and a language that they created. Masaccio mastered a technique known as chiaroscuro, the use of light and shade to create a gradual transition from light to dark that gives to his paintings a sense of three-dimensionality. He

Raphael, *The School of Athens***, 1510–1511**

also provided for future Renaissance artists an excellent example of the use of perspective in painting in *The Trinity* (1425), a fresco painting in the church of Santa Maria Novella in Florence. The painter Piero della Francesca (ca. 14201492) wrote treatises on perspective and geometry and used mathematical principles in the execution of paintings such as his *Madonna of the Misericordia* (1445) and *The Flagellation of Christ* (ca. 1456), furthering the trend set by Masaccio.

Gradually, Renaissance artists began to turn to classical motifs and mythology for the subject matter of their painting, although they never abandoned their attention to religious themes. Raphael (1483–1520) displayed his fascination with classical antiquity in *The School of Athens* (1512), in which he included great individuals from the past such as Plato and Aristotle in the same scene with his own contemporaries such as Leonardo da Vinci and Michelangelo. This work achieves the classical goal of balance in its overall composition and sets the compelling human portraits within an architectural setting. Sandro Botticelli (ca. 1445–1510) took classical subjects for the inspiration of such paintings as *The Birth of Venus* and *Primavera*. But he combined them with Christian motifs to harmonize disparate trends of the period, including the glorification of the nude. Giorgione (ca. 1477–1510), a prominent Venetian painter, took a mythological story from Ovid and rendered a dynamic and balanced painting called *The Concert*. The Venetian Titian (ca. 1490–1576)

Piero della Francesca, *The Madonna of Mercy,* **1445.** This central panel of the Misericordia altarpiece is one of Piero's earliest works, and demonstrates his artistic virtuosity and mastery of the application of mathematical principles to art even as he departs from the realism of the period in his depiction of Mary as towering over her supplicants. This painting—commissioned by a group of laymen dedicated to performing acts of mercy—reflects the importance of the relationship between patrons and artists, since Piero did not select the arrangement of the figures or the gold color of the background. Piero displays some progressive aspects of his painting here, however, including his creative use of light and the sculpture-like modeling of the Madonna's face, neck, and hands.

produced paintings that combined classical themes with elaborate landscapes, such as *Bacchus and Ariadne* (1522).

It makes sense that in an age in which humanist writers stressed the dignity of humanity, artists would take a great interest in the human body, which they even used as a measure of architectural proportions. In their striving for a perfect imitation of nature and a greater realism, Renaissance artists became especially interested in the various manifestations and movements of the human body. But they displayed an almost equal interest in conveying individuality and emotionalism, beginning, again, with Giotto. Like Giotto, Masaccio conveyed strong emotions in his paintings, using bodily postures as well as facial expressions to do so. In *The Expulsion of Adam and Eve* (ca. 1427), for example, the two subjects depart paradise in utter agony and shame. In sculpture, Donatello (1386–1466) seemed to bring stone to life in his *St. George*, while his *David* is a testament to physical grace and beauty. Michelangelo Buonarotti (1475–1564) could equally use a single figure to display his skill and such human attributes as grace, beauty, confidence (*David*) and wisdom, stability, and power (*Moses*.) Michelangelo also perfected a technique known as *contrapposto*, defined by the positioning of opposite figures in a dramatic tension that indicated movement through the relationship of each person and the action anticipated from it. Michelangelo portrayed *contrapposto* in his *Pietà*, a common subject for sculptors but one elevated by Michelangelo from a religious symbol to a real scene of human drama and emotion. Leonardo da Vinci (1452–1519) provided another excellent example of *contrapposto* in his *Last Supper*, a static painting depicting a scene of action, tension, and emotion all created by the relationships of the individuals portrayed. Artists such as Michelangelo and Leonardo displayed an interest in science and mathematics, seeking to understand nature in order to further their attempts to inject realism into their art. Both Leonardo and Michelangelo were interested in human anatomy and sought to create images of human movement that were technically correct down to the ways that each muscle would be positioned in a particular pose. The influence of mathematics and science on art, however, never superseded the concern of Renaissance artists with beauty.

Explore the especially rich collection of Renaissance art at the National Gallery in London at www.nationalgallery.org.uk/paintings/explore-the-paintings/browse-by-century/*/Module%5B495%5D%5Bchoos eSecond%5D/1500.

The Social Transformation of Art in Northern Europe

Northern European society shared in the same trends that shaped art and society in the Italian Renaissance, but had a more ambiguous relationship to the legacy of classical antiquity and the secularization of society. Northern artists did not ignore the artistic achievements taking place in Italy during the High Renaissance. Italian artists working in northern cities, such as Bruges, brought with them an appreciation for ancient models, while northern artists such as Albrecht Dürer (1471–1528) traveled to Italy for education and inspiration. But Dürer remained a German artist and his distinctive style reflects some of the differences between northern European and Italian society.

Northern artists, including Dürer, retained a mystical approach to religion that contrasts with the worldly atmosphere and stress on humanity found even in the religious art of the Italian Renaissance. Works such as *Knight, Death, and the Devil* display a dark sense of brooding about the human condition. Most of the religious art of northern Europe in the fourteenth and fifteenth centuries reflects a society that was enjoying new material success, but still had deep concerns with religion and the afterlife. Northern art, like the society that produced it, seemed uneasily poised between the advances of a thriving commercial, increasingly urban society and the late medieval emphasis on death, pestilence, and the end of time.

Thus, even as northern artists incorporated elements of Italian art—use of perspective, color, shading, and the application of classical principles of geometric balance and proportion—into their compositions, their works retained a distinctive spirit. Beginning in the fifteenth century, northern artists reproduced the humanity and the material surroundings of their patrons with increasing accuracy. The art of painters like Jan van Eyck (1390–1441) and Rogier van der Weyden (1399–1464), both from the Netherlands, reflected the realities of the urban world of the bourgeoisie and their increasingly prosperous society. Filled with the clothing and everyday accoutrements of the middle class, northern painters depicted and thus appealed to the merchant classes and leaders of society who were their patrons. For example, van Eyck's *Giovanni Arnolfini and His Bride* (1434) portrays the Italian financier who worked in Bruges in a way that truly reflected the world of the patron. But whereas Italian artists glorified the human body and used art to reflect the dignity of human beings, northern artists depicted even serious bodily flaws; their art reflected the imperfection of humanity, which was related to the constant need for spiritual redemption. The lack of idealism in northern art can be seen as much in the portraits of van Eyck as in the grotesque images found in the paintings of Hieronymous Bosch (ca. 1450–1516), including his *Garden of Earthly Delights*. The Isenheim altarpiece by the German painter Matthias Grünewald (ca. 1475–1528) demonstrates this juxtaposition of earthly and spiritual realities, as it includes an extremely realistic and gory portrayal of the dead Christ upon the cross and supernatural depictions of demons. Northern art reflected a society that retained a larger sense of pessimism about the human condition and placed a greater emphasis on faith than Italy, with its optimistic humanist philosophies and its glorification of the ancient past.

Ming China

While the Renaissance flourished in Europe, the rise, establishment, and then the early stages of decline of a new dynasty forged an equally significant—and in many ways comparable—period in the history of China. China already possessed some advantages that prepared it for the great achievements of the Ming dynasty (1368–1644), including a system of canals and advanced irrigation techniques that sustained China's flourishing agricultural economy. By the fifteenth century, China had a population of over 100 million people, about twice that of all of Europe. China also possessed a stable bureaucracy and a system of state examinations that produced educated, competent employees and allowed the government to function effectively even in periods of dynastic instability and civil war. Finally, artistic, philosophical, and religious traditions founded in antiquity provided a basis for continued creativity and the cultural unity of Chinese civilization.

During the period of instability and peasant unrest that plagued China from the mid- to late fourteenth century (see Chapter 8 in this volume), people recognized the need for a new authority worthy to assume the Mandate of Heaven, the concept by which the Chinese measured the legitimacy of their emperors. Such a figure emerged in the person of Chu Yüan-chang (1328–1398), who came from the peasant class. After capturing Beijing (Peking) in 1368, he announced the beginning of a new "brilliant" (Ming) dynasty and changed his imperial name to Hung-wu, meaning "great military power." Hung-wu bears a number of similarities to his later English counterpart, Henry VII (r. 1485–1509), whose triumph in the Wars of the Roses was discussed in Chapter 8. Like Henry, Hung-wu had come from an obscure background, risen to power through military victory, and lacked a dynamic or charismatic personality. Both leaders consolidated their power slowly and carefully, relying greatly on their own counsel and initiative. Both men understood that money provided an important basis for the stability of their rule. Finally, both Henry and Hung-wu benefited from people's longing for an end to violence, war, and political instability and their eagerness to accept the military victors, regardless of background or personal charisma.

After the initial foundation of the dynasty by Hung-wu, however, it was primarily the well-developed bureaucracy that kept the government functioning effectively and maintained the emperor's authority throughout the kingdom during the Ming dynasty. The central bureaucracy in Beijing consisted of over 20,000 men who maintained authority over a vast network of administrators and minor officials that extended throughout the country. Traveling officials who reported directly to the central government oversaw the general functioning of local government in order to address incompetence or corruption. A conservative populace that seldom questioned the workings of the government or the authority of the emperor kept that authority from crumbling. Of course, as long as the military retained its allegiance to the emperor, his authority had a source of backing that would make it difficult, if not impossible, to overthrow. Finally, the Ming adhered strictly to the practice of primogeniture by which the eldest son of the emperor inherited the throne. Therefore, rarely were there any problems in the imperial succession. Such a centralized administration was in direct contrast to the political divisions in Italy at this time, though other European rulers would strive to develop similar methods of administration in early modern Europe.

Like the European economy, that of Ming China was predominantly agricultural. At the beginning of the dynasty, Hung-wu deliberately chose to support agriculture in an attempt to restore the countryside that had been devastated during the previous civil wars and to distinguish his rule from that of the previous Mongol emperors, who had focused on foreign trade. But Ming prosperity rested not just on the successful cultivation of rice and other crops, but on a flourishing market economy in which goods from one region were exchanged for goods from other regions. An efficient system of water transport, in which man-made canals supplemented China's many natural waterways, enhanced internal trade and contributed to the success of the country's market economy. Organizations of particular crafts and manufactures resembled the guild system of medieval Europe in that they were organized by merchants within distinct regions or cities and provided a system of mutual support for their members. As was often the case in Europe, particular manufactures came to be associated with particular towns in China—for example, porcelain with Jingdezhen, silk weaving with Suzhou, and cotton cloth with the area outside Shanghai. A market town economy provides a balance between diverse regions and decreases regional rivalry by a mutual dependence based on the exchange of goods and services. Thriving market towns offered more wealth, goods, and services to their residents and to travelers passing through the towns than small rural villages could provide. Such an economy strengthened the bonds of social organization. The vast majority of the Chinese population, probably around 90 percent, however, continued to live in small rural villages.

As in Renaissance Italy, Chinese society placed a strong emphasis on family ties, which were reinforced by the intricate trading network that flourished in the Ming period. The Chinese emphasis on family and lineage enhanced the position of elite families the longer they held land or influence at the local level. Furthermore, these prominent families possessed the wealth and leisure to allow their sons to study and take the examinations required for appointment to the state bureaucracy. Unlike medieval European society, distinctions in Chinese society were based on transient factors like wealth, land, and education, which could change from generation to generation, rather than blood or inherited noble status. The possibility of social mobility there mirrored the increasing opportunities brought by the Renaissance, first in Italy and then elsewhere in Europe. In China, the main social distinction at the local level was between government officials, including members of the state bureaucracy, and the rest of the population. In addition, age has historically been more respected in Chinese society than in the West, so elders in the villages possessed a good deal of authority, frequently acting as judges in quarrels between neighbors about property or family disputes over inheritances and the like. Aside from the authority of state officials and village elders, there was a fair amount of social and political equality among the Chinese, even though a complex system of classification determined the amount of taxation or labor service owed by each particular household. This equality did not extend to women, however. China remained a patriarchal society under the Ming, bearing some resemblances to Renaissance Italy in this regard. Because Ming society, like that of Renaissance Italy, valued family lineage, men sought to control women in order to arrange marriages that would benefit the entire family. The subordination of women to family interests contributed to the Chinese practice of foot-binding young girls, which made them more attractive and desirable to potential suitors. Foot-binding—crushing the bones of the feet, leaving the girl deformed and unable to walk or stand without pain or difficulty—demonstrated that the father had enough wealth and status so his daughter did not have to work in the fields or home. A husband who married a woman who had had her feet bound as a girl displayed his own means and status.

Just as Europe was experiencing its Renaissance of learning and culture from the fourteenth to the sixteenth century, culture flourished in Ming China as well. Shen Zhou (1427–1509) founded the so-called Southern School of painting, emphasizing landscape painting and exploring humanity's relationship with nature at the same time that many Renaissance artists were exploring the same theme; Shen and his student, Wen Zhenming (1470–1559), were members of the literati class of scholars who took up painting almost as an afterthought to their intellectual pursuits and careers as government officials.

The history of art in Ming China is dominated by the practice of a variety of different arts by members of the literati, demonstrating the value placed on the ideal of a well-rounded, cultured, and creative person that in some ways approximated the Renaissance concept of the ideal courtier. Chinese authors—like their European counterparts of the Renaissance period—sought understanding of human nature through an exploration of the human condition. The plays of Tang Xianzu (1550–1617) in the late sixteenth century address some of the same themes explored in Shakespeare's works. In *The Peony Pavilion* of 1598, Tang introduced ideas about the nature of happiness that transcended the world inhabited by most of his readers: the story, which deals with a young woman who dies of depression and later comes back to life to find her dream lover, seems to suggest that humans cannot expect to find perfection in this life, but may one day attain true happiness outside of the confines of everyday reality. While most European authors still wrote primarily for an elite audience, the best Chinese novelists, poets, and dramatists of the same period had more popular appeal; *The Pearl-Sewn Shirt* by Ling Meng-tsu explores the effects of marital infidelity and jealousy. *The Golden Lotus*, by Lai Wang, the raciest of Chinese novels from the period because of its detailed and graphic accounts of sexual encounters, was considered indecent by the conservative Confucian establishment. The hero of Shui Hu Chuan's famous novel, *All Men Are Brothers*, closely resembles the English folk-hero Robin Hood; the novel suggests that human beings need to eschew traditional morality in order to thrive in a world that rewards emperors for doing the same thing. In many ways the novel *Monkey* by Wu Cheng resembles the picaresque novels of early modern Spain, the tradition that influenced Cervantes's great Spanish adventure novel, *Don Quixote*. Finally, the Ming period also witnessed achievements in craftsmanship, particularly the creation of the distinctive style of Ming porcelain and the decoration of bronze ware with enamels of various colors to produce patterns of flowers and leaves in a practice known as *jingtailan* (known to us by the French word *cloisonné* for the particularly high quality of clay found in China that could withstand extremely high temperatures).

Additional images of artistic objects and paintings from Ming China are available at www.metmuseum.org/toah/hd/ming/hd_ming.htm.

In 2006 the J. Paul Getty Museum in Los Angeles hosted an exhibition dedicated to Renaissance landscape painting. See the website for this exhibition at www.getty.edu/art/exhibitions/landscape_renaissance.

272

Artistic Landscapes from
Ming China and Renaissance Italy

Tang Yin, *Mount Hua*, 1506

Tang Yin and Pietro Perugino are almost exact contemporaries. Tang Yin's art reflects the ancient tradition of Chinese landscape painting called *shan shui hua* (from the Chinese words for mountains and water), dating to the third century and largely influenced by Daoist ideas on the haromony of the natural world.

Renaissance landscapes such as this one by Perugino reveal a growing appreciation for nature, but, as was typical of such paintings, the landscape is merely a backdrop for human activity.

In these two paintings, what is the relationship of the human viewer to the image? What do the styles and contents of these wroks reveal about the differences between Chinese and Western civilization?

Pietro Perugino, *Resurrection of Christ*, 1496–1498 *(By permission of the Cleveland Museum of Art)*

Conclusion

The term *Renaissance* has been designated at times to refer to a cultural and artistic movement that drew its inspiration largely from cultural antiquity and at other times to refer to a period of history that began in Italy around the beginning of the fourteenth century and lasted until the Counter-Reformation of the mid-sixteenth century in northern Europe. This chapter has been based on a combination of these two definitions, viewing the Renaissance both as a cultural phenomenon and as a period in European history. On the one hand, Renaissance thinkers contributed to an important reevaluation of human nature best reflected in Pico's *Oration on the Dignity of Man.* On the other hand, the period was characterized, at least in Italy, by political authority that derived increasingly from either military power or the support of significant sections of the social elite rather than on any principles of legitimate rule. The political schizophrenia of the Italian city-states was reflected in the political writings of Machiavelli, who wrote one work in support of republican ideals and another that recognized the harsh realities of practical politics.

The *signori* sought to bolster their support and their claims to authority through measures and public works that benefited their subjects, through patronage of art that served political purposes, and through simple displays of force. Their claims to power were practical, not theoretical. The situation was a little different in Florence and Venice, where elite rulers claimed to still cling to Roman republican ideals. Powerful Venetian doges from the social elite still claimed to rule as part of a balanced constitution. Until the sixteenth century, the Medici rulers in Florence preserved the outward forms of the republic.

Despite controversies over the meaning of terms like *Renaissance* and *humanism*, there was a greater emphasis in this period on learning in the service of humanity and optimism about the potential for human achievement with the proper education and training. Erasmus stressed this ideal in his *Handbook of a Christian Knight*, while Castiglione provided the definitive portrait of the Renaissance ideal for men and women in *The Courtier*. Erasmus also played a critical role by beginning to question the practices of the church that did not lead to the betterment of society or individuals, in his opinion. Individuals such as Martin Luther in the period after 1517 built on those criticisms—and on humanist learning and scholarship—to challenge prevailing ideas about religion in the movement known as the Reformation. In the meantime, Europeans, in addition to looking inward, had begun to look outward. For Europeans also began a significant period of global expansion during the fifteenth and sixteenth centuries.

1. Describe the main political characteristics of the Italian city-states. How did politics differ in some of the principal city-states? Why were Italian politics so unstable during the Renaissance?
2. How would you define Renaissance humanism? What is civic humanism? What do these movements reveal about Renaissance society and politics?
3. What accounted for the flourishing of art and the number of great artists in Renaissance Italy? What were some of the ways that art was shaped by society during this period? To what extent did art help to shape society during this period?
4. Discuss the similarities and differences in humanism in Italy and northern Europe. What common threads unify humanism as a movement?
5. In what ways are the major political and social characteristics of Ming China similar to those of Renaissance Europe? In what significant ways do they differ? How would you compare the position of women in each society?

Suggestions for Further Reading

Brotton, Jerry. 2006. *The Renaissance: A Very Short Introduction*. Oxford: Oxford University Press.

Burckhardt, Jacob. 1999. *The Civilization of the Renaissance in Italy*. Translated by S.G. Middlemore. New York: Barnes and Noble.

Huang, Ray. 1981. *1587: A Year of No Significance: The Ming Dynasty in Decline*. New Haven: Yale University Press.

Jardine, Lisa. 1996. *Wordly Goods: A New History of the Renaissance*. New York: W.W. Norton.

Machiavelli, Niccolò. 1516. *The Prince*. Various Editions.

Marcello Simonetta. 2008. *The Montefeltro Conspiracy: A Renaissance Mystery Decoded*. New York: Doubleday.

Suggested Websites

www.fordham.edu/halsall/sbook1x.htmil

This website contains a good selection of primary sources from Renaissance writers such as Petrarch, Boccaccio, Vasari, Machiavelli, and Castiglione.

http://history.hanover.edu/early/italren.htm

This website contains texts from primary sources related to the Italian Renaissance, including works by Petrarch, Lorenzo de Medici, Pico della Mirandola, Leonardo Bruni, and Marsiglio Ficino.

www.idbsu.edu/courses/hy309/docs/burckhardt/burckhardt.html

This site contains the famous work by Jacob Burckhardt, *The Civilization of the Renaissance in Italy*, which has been so influential in Western thinking about the period since the second half of the nineteenth century.

www.learner.org/exhibits/renaissance/resources.html

This website provides links to additional websites, as well as basic information about a variety of topics related to the Renaissance period, including a special section devoted to Florence.

http://library.thinkquest.org/3588/Renaissance/?tqskip1=1&tqtime-0604

Called the Virtual Renaissance, this website provides access to maps, links, chronologies, and resources available on the topic.

10   The Beginnings of European Expansion, ca. 1400–1540

In 1453 the Ottoman Empire took control of Constantinople and became a serious threat to European political and economic interests in the Mediterranean world. This Ottoman expansion occurred at the same time that Europeans were also beginning to expand their horizons for a variety of reasons. Monarchs and rulers viewed expansion of territory as a means to increased wealth, prestige, and political authority. European society during the Renaissance produced an increasing number of individuals who sought personal riches, glory, or simply adventure through voyages of discovery and exploration. The impulse to expand Christianity and conquer the infidels did not die with the failure of the Crusades to the Holy Land. Christian Europeans transferred their military and religious zeal to other outlets, such as Africa and, after Columbus, the Americas. The rise of the Ottomans as a Mediterranean power particularly benefited Portugal, which rose to greatness as an Atlantic sea power and took the initiative in cultivating a lucrative trade in slaves with African principalities. Europeans' growing interest in overseas trade brought them into increasing contact with distant and in some cases previously unknown civilizations. To trace these world-shaping developments, we begin—again—in Italy.

The Rise of Capitalism

Even though Europe experienced a decline in population during the fourteenth century, European commerce continued to expand, perhaps because people who survived the plague had more money to spend. To take advantage of increased economic opportunities and a growing demand for luxury goods, European merchants developed new methods of mobilizing money for large-scale business enterprises. Merchants devised the practice of holding large amounts of money in bulk while they regulated the relationship between creditors and debtors by maintaining records of who owed what to whom and allowing transfer of money to occur on paper rather than through actual physical exchanges; in other words, they established banks.

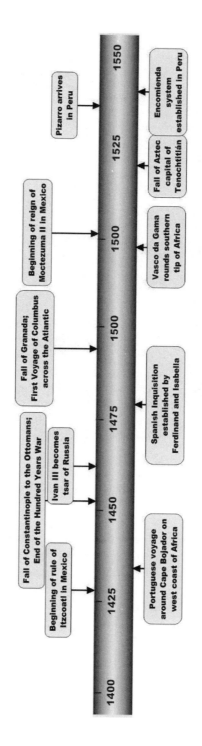

1400　1425　1450　1475　1500　1500　1525　1550

Beginning of rule of Itzcoatl in Mexico

Fall of Constantinople to the Ottomans; End of the Hundred Years War

Ivan III becomes tsar of Russia

Fall of Granada; First Voyage of Columbus across the Atlantic

Beginning of reign of Moctezuma II in Mexico

Pizarro arrives in Peru

Portuguese voyage around Cape Bojador on west coast of Africa

Spanish Inquisition established by Ferdinand and Isabella

Vasco da Gama rounds southern tip of Africa

Fall of Aztec capital of Tenochtitlán

Encomienda system established in Peru

Quentin Massys, *The Money Lender and His Wife*, 1514. The couple portrayed in this painting reveal much about the European merchant class of the early sixteenth century through their clothing and the distinctive objects adorning the table and shelves.

In the first half of the fourteenth century Italian bankers began to engage in money lending, a business previously reserved for Jews because of the medieval church's prohibition of usury, or charging interest on loans.

The church did not abandon its position on usury, but Italian bankers began to circumvent the prohibition by claiming increased risks with the advent of

Read a brief biography of Quentin Massys and view additional works by him at www.wga.hu/frames-e.html?/bio/m/massys/quentin/biograph.html.

long-distance trade and fluctuating rates of exchange. (Wills from this period indicate, however, that many bankers still feared danger to their souls from having disobeyed the church.) Florence became the main center of a flourishing international trade and of Italian and European banking, including the administration of the finances of the church. The two most prominent banking families in Florence were the Bardi and the Peruzzi, who represented only the most successful and dominant companies among those that numbered in the hundreds at a time when growing opportunities seemed limitless. The story of the growth of Italian banking and commerce was not one of uninterrupted success, however. The banks of the Peruzzi and the Bardi failed when they could not collect on huge loans granted to Edward III of England.

Even a series of disasters that included the Bardi and Peruzzi bankruptcies, the Black Death, and the territorial expansion of Pisa and Milan (Florence's main rivals) did not spell the end of Italian or Florentine success in commerce and banking, however, as subsequent bankers and merchants would learn from the mistakes of these early firms. Italy was also well positioned to take advantage of the growing demand for goods and luxuries because of its position on the Mediterranean and the seafaring traditions of its coastal cities. Furthermore, Italian merchants had created enough momentum for commerce that bankruptcies, plague, and the increased warfare of the fourteenth and fifteenth centuries could only slow, but not stop, the economic success that they had created. By the first half of the fourteenth century Venetian merchants alone transported to Europe a wide range of products, including pepper, quicksilver, ginger, a variety of sugars, indigo, fruits, plant-derived medicines, and incense, from Tunis, Baghdad, Cyprus, and elsewhere. In exchange, the Venetians offered a variety of specialized goods, including both artistic and functional objects produced by local artists and craftsmen. The Venetians were renowned glassmakers, producing mirrors, windowpanes, glass beads, and other glass items, both clear and colored. In the interior of the peninsula Italian weavers contributed to a flourishing textile industry, which, along with that of Flanders and later England, served much of Europe. Italians learned to build ships of all shapes and sizes to accommodate different cargoes and to allow for different speeds, depending on the needs of the merchants who required them. For example, the "thin galley" was fast and easy to maneuver, giving it advantages in naval battles but making it suitable for transporting only valuable goods that required little space, such as spices, dyes, or gold. Larger vessels weighing between 120 and 500 tons and unequipped for battle or precision sailing transported products such as salt and timber. The typical merchant ship of the period fell between these two extremes; the Italians called it a *galia grosa*, or "fat galley." The merchants of northern Italy often recorded what they learned from their experience for the benefit of prospective merchants; the *Zibaldone da*

Canal, an educational manual from Venice in the 1320s, contains the kind of complicated mathematical calculations and problems that merchants would be required to make, as well as information about currency exchanges in different places in the Mediterranean region and the appropriate units of measurement for commodities such as pepper, ginger, and elephant tusks.

In the meantime, a group of cities located on the fringes of the Baltic Sea in northern Europe formed an alliance that proved fruitful in both power and money far from Italy and the Mediterranean. In the early thirteenth century, merchants in several northern European towns, including Bremen, Cologne, Hamburg, and Lübeck, had decided to organize to protect their common commercial interests from pirates, the Swedes, and particularly the Danes. The merchants convinced their towns to cooperate in the enforcement of contracts, alliances, and law enforcement. This alliance, known as the Hanseatic League, comprised about fifty towns by the middle of the fourteenth century and more than eighty by 1400, extending as far east as the Russian city of Novgorod. By the fourteenth century, Hanseatic League merchants had gained control of the Flemish cloth trade and enjoyed special privileges in the English wool trade. Northern merchants supplied much of Europe with fish, timber, furs, seal oil, hemp, iron, cattle, grain, amber, and wild honey, all natural resources unavailable in abundance in many other parts of Europe. They brought back to the Baltic regions finished and unfinished textiles and a variety of luxury and everyday items produced by European craftsmen, artists, and metalworkers. The league operated in much the same way as a national government, using force to protect its member towns and its monopoly on northern trade routes and fishing grounds. A formal decree dating back to the 1260s required each city in the league to assist in making the Baltic Sea a pirate-free zone. As league towns grew wealthier, they also grew more powerful and capable of defending their autonomy from foreign powers. As a result of the Hanseatic League, trade in the Baltic Sea region of northern Europe was just as active and nearly as lucrative as Italy's Mediterranean trade.

Throughout Europe, notably in Italy, France, and the German states of the Holy Roman Empire, merchant princes accumulated vast fortunes and came to exercise a considerable degree of political power and influence. Some individual merchants became so successful and enormously wealthy that they began to live—and sometimes act—as if they belonged to the aristocracy or even royalty. For merchants, who were expected to tend to their business affairs and lead a humble and devout home life, to emulate the aristocracy represented a profound shift in European social, economic, and political history. The emergence of the merchant princes demonstrated in visible fashion the social implications of the expansion of the European economy in the fourteenth and fifteenth centuries. Cosimo de Medici (1389–1464) made his family the most important political force in Florence and used his vast wealth to shape Florentine politics to his own objectives. Pierre and Martin des Essars, members of the bourgeoisie in Rouen, became so wealthy that they rose to the level of nobility through their relationship with the French monarch, Philip IV, whom they supplied with money, art, jewelry, tapestries, books, and other goods and services. France's most successful merchant, Jacques Coeur, headed a large commercial enterprise and had trading contacts throughout Europe and the Islamic world; in addition to his trading interests, Coeur owned a silk factory in Florence, a paper mill in Bourges, and lead, silver, and copper mines near Lyons. He accumulated so much wealth that he became paymaster for the royal household of Charles VII during the later stages of the Hundred Years War. The German Fugger family maintained a string of banks with each one independent of the other, protecting the central enterprise in their native Augsburg from the failure of any one of its parts. Jakob Fugger II (1459–1525), who entered business at the age of fourteen at the family's Venetian warehouse, laid the foundations for the family's enormous success by expanding its interests beyond the spice, silk, and wool trade into the even more profitable enterprises of banking and mining.

In 1453 the Hundred Years War ended and Jacques Coeur found himself facing charges of corruption undoubtedly related to the vast sums of money owed to him and the desire of the French authorities to rid themselves of those debts. In the same year merchants throughout Europe felt the reverberations of the fall of Constantinople to the Ottoman Turks. Not that any European states rushed to the rescue of the eastern capital. The Italian city-states were divided and mainly interested in trade (with Christians or Muslims); England and France had been entirely preoccupied with the conclusion of the Hundred Years War; Spain had not yet completed the *reconquista*, the reconquest of the peninsula from the Moors. Still, when Constantinople fell to Mehmet II (the Conqueror), the Ottomans solidified their position as the dominant political power in the Muslim world and a new potential threat to Christian Europe and a hindrance to European trade in the Mediterranean.

Fortuitously, new economic possibilities arose when changes in shipping technology and patterns opened up the Atlantic as a third arena where commerce could compete with, and then eclipse, the Mediterranean and Baltic trades. The Italian city-states took the lead in the shift of trade to the Atlantic seaboard, which was made possible by the construction of large ships with ocean-going capabilities. Venice, which established trading connections with England and the Netherlands, pioneered the construction of great galley ships, with carrying capacities of over 200 tons, powered by both oars and sails. To put this figure in perspective, at the beginning of the fifteenth century most Hanseatic ships could carry about 75 tons, while English ships generally could not carry more than 100 tons. European mariners began to acquire a vast knowledge of the seas as cartographers began producing maps depicting European coastlines in extremely precise detail. New technological devices further contributed to the Atlantic trade. Since the thirteenth century, seamen had been using the compass to steer their course. The portolan was a chart that ship captains could use in conjunction with the compass to chart their course in advance without relying on landmarks, thus allowing them to sail confidently on the open sea away from land. A device called a lead enabled sailors to navigate through the dark waters of the Atlantic without destroying their ship on unseen shoals. Sailors would swing the lead, a hollow piece of metal weighing between seven and fourteen pounds attached to a rope marked in fathoms, to touch and bring up matter from the floor of the sea to give them an idea of the depth and nature of the ocean floor in murky waters. With the increase in the Atlantic trade, sailors and merchants from southern Europe encountered merchants and residents of northern Europe. At the same time that trade in the Mediterranean, the Baltic, and the Atlantic was bringing the regions of Europe into closer contact, the lucrative prospects of the trade in spices attracted European interest in commerce with far distant parts of the world.

The demand for spices in Europe in the medieval and early modern periods resulted from certain agricultural realities that affected the daily lives of everyone from king to peasant. Farmers simply could not afford to keep much of their livestock alive throughout the winter, so every autumn thousands of animals went to slaughter. Pickling, salting, or smoking the meat helped it last throughout the winter, but even with the best preservatives, meat would become unappetizing at best and rancid at worst. Concerns for both taste and health led to increasing demands for spices that could obscure the taste of the often unpleasant (and sometimes deadly) fare served at mealtime. These preservative spices (cinnamon, nutmeg, mace, ginger, cloves, cumin, aniseed, and, of greatest importance, pepper), however, could be found only outside of Europe, mostly in Asia and the East Indies. High prices for small amounts made the spice trade especially appealing for adventurous merchants for whom tremendous profits outweighed such risks as shipwreck and piracy.

The Rise of Portugal and Spain

The Portuguese had already begun explorations down the west coast of Africa in an effort to find a shorter route to the Indies, the source of those spices high in demand. The rise of the Ottomans further encouraged the search for new routes to the East. Isolated by geography and its large Spanish neighbor from the rest of Europe, Portugal turned a liability into an asset by turning toward the sea, eventually establishing an enormously successful trade with India and the East that made Portugal one of the wealthiest and most powerful countries in Europe. Portuguese exploration started under Prince Henry the Navigator (1394–1460), the third son of King John I. The gold trade of Africa provided him with an opportunity to gain the wealth that would satisfy this younger son's ambitious nature and serve as his main motivation in sponsoring expeditions down the West African coast. Although he is widely celebrated for the establishment of a scientific school of navigation and for sponsoring a voyage that rounded Cape Bojador on the west coast of Saharan Africa in 1434, Henry's primary objective was the acquisition of the Canary Islands. Although he failed in his personal objectives, Henry began a tradition of Portuguese exploration that bore fruit later in the century when the Portuguese navigator Vasco da Gama (ca. 1469–1525) captained a voyage that rounded the Cape of Good Hope and discovered the sea route to India in 1498. Two years later his countryman, Pedro Alvarez Cabral (ca. 1467–ca. 1520), accidentally discovered Brazil when his voyage destined for the East Indies ran off course, claiming for Portugal the territory that would become central to its empire in the early modern period.

As important as was the rise of Portugal, its overseas success paled in comparison with that of its larger Iberian neighbor, Spain, which was not precisely a unified country even at the end of the fifteenth century. But Spain took much longer than Portugal to take an interest in overseas trade and exploration, partly because of civil wars and succession disputes that created internal anarchy and partly because Spaniards were still struggling to conquer the remaining Muslim territories on the peninsula. A turning point for both these difficulties occurred with the marriage of Ferdinand of Aragon to Isabella of Castile, heirs to the two principle Spanish Christian kingdoms, in 1469. Isabella assumed the throne of Castile in 1474; Ferdinand became king of Aragon five years later. At first they had to overcome a tradition of civil violence, as well as some questions about Ferdinand's rightful inheritance of his throne. The latter goal they achieved by claiming that Juana, the daughter of the previous king, was illegitimate and packing her off to a Portuguese nunnery. The civil violence they overcame with the support of nobles who desired a measure of stability and by directing those with violent tendencies in the direction of the last great Muslim stronghold on the peninsula—Granada. They had prepared the way for this success by introducing the Spanish Inquisition in 1478. The Inquisition was directed against Jewish and Muslim converts to Christianity suspected of continuing to observe the traditions of their former faiths. In this endeavor it was all too successful.

The reigns of Ferdinand and Isabella did much to provide an imagined unity in Spain before formal unification of the country took place. The king and queen are widely known and remembered for completing the *reconquista*, capturing Granada from the Moors in 1492 after a lengthy struggle that began in 1481. Of course, Jews and Muslims remember them differently and viewed them differently at the time. Isabella, on the advice of Tomás de Torquemada (1420–1498), the Grand Inquisitor of the Inquisition, violated her promise that the surrender of Granada would be accompanied by a grant of religious toleration. Both Jews and Muslims were now required to convert to Christianity or leave the country. The approximately 20,000 Sephardic Jews who left the country took with them a new messianic form of Judaism, expecting their recent tribulations to foreshadow their imminent deliverance. One Jewish writer referred to Isabella as "the wicked Queen" who had initiated forty-five years of suffering and affliction. Spanish Muslims who chose to leave were welcomed in Istanbul and the Ottoman Empire. Thus, the conquest of Granada and the year 1492—like most historical events—had not just a single meaning. European Christians outside of Spain viewed it as revenge for the fall of Constantinople and as part of a larger struggle against Islam. The stage was set for continued warfare between Spain and the Ottoman Empire that would extend into the seventeenth century. But for Spain it marked an occasion of great celebration that commemorated the successful conclusion of a centuries-long struggle and anticipated the future greatness of a unified nation.

The Spain of 1492 had a fairly sound economy based on the thriving wool industry in Toledo and Seville and the silk industry of Andalusia, a newly reformed and centralized governmental administration carried out by the ministers of Ferdinand and Isabella, a tradition of commitment to Christianity and the crusading mentality, and an elite class of warrior nobles available for new opportunities to fight. The king and queen, like other monarchs of the period, needed to search for new sources of revenue to finance their ambitions at home and abroad. All these factors prepared the way for the rise of a wider Spanish empire in the sixteenth century. But until Granada fell Ferdinand and Isabella could not afford to divert their resources to a proposed expedition to the Indies by a Genoese mariner named Christopher Columbus (1451–1506), who intended to sail westward across the Atlantic instead of around the southern tip of Africa. After the fall of Granada they were persuaded to support this visionary, completely unaware that his voyages would soon bring Spain into contact with two advanced civilizations that no one in Europe knew existed or could have imagined in their wildest dreams.

Mesoamerican Civilizations: The Aztecs and the Incas

The Aztec Empire in Mexico and the Inca Empire in Peru had complex political and social structures and religious beliefs that would challenge the preconcep-

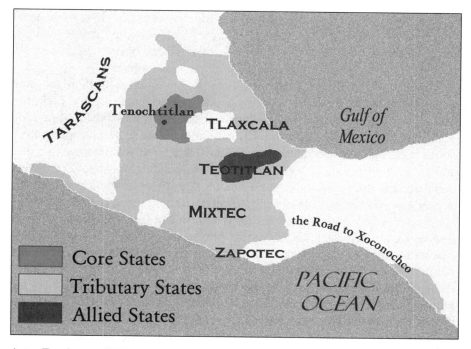

Aztec Empire, ca. 1519

tions of the Europeans who encountered them. When Columbus sailed across the Atlantic under the Spanish flag in 1492 in search of a westward course for the Indies, no one considered what Spanish policy would be if Columbus were to discover lands and people hitherto unknown to Europeans. Before considering the encounter between the Spanish and these Mesoamerican civilizations and the Spanish conquest itself, however, it is useful to understand something of the nature of these civilizations and to compare them to early modern Spain.

In the two centuries prior to Columbus's voyages across the Atlantic, a tribe known as the Mexica, known to us as the Aztecs, was rising to power and dominance in the valley that now bears its name. Once the Aztecs established their own state in the valley, they greatly enlarged their territory through warfare, treaties, and alliances with neighboring states. In 1372 the Aztecs selected their own king to legitimize their position and soon the Aztec kingdom became the dominant one in the region. The Aztecs benefited from the leadership of their first two kings, Acamapichtli (r. 1372–1391) and Huitzilihuitl (r. 1391–1418), under whom their capital of Tenochtitlán became a great metropolis that was a magnet for people throughout the valley. During the rule of Itzcoatl (r. 1428–1440) Tenochtitlán became the center of the wealthiest and most militarily powerful kingdom in Mexico. As in Europe, most of the people still lived in smaller villages and the city's economy depended upon the agricultural land outside of it, land that the Aztecs lacked. Land shortage, however, was not the main reason for their frequent wars.

The Aztecs' belief in their own greatness combined with their religious views to reinforce the notion that they had to expand their territory. Elaborate religious and political ceremonies, formal institutions, massive building projects, artistic sensibility, and a thriving economy characterized a sophisticated civilization that included as an integral part of it large-scale human sacrifice and an indifference to, if not a celebration of, human bloodshed. The Aztecs believed that the sun god required human blood for survival, since all life depended upon blood. This belief gave them further incentive to wage war to ensure a steady supply of captives for their sacrifices, especially the massive ones associated with significant events for the state, such as the elevation of a new king or the dedication of a new temple. The Great Temple in Tenochtitlán had two staircases of 113 steps leading at a forty-five-degree angle to a stone platform that contained shrines to the god of the sun and the god of the rain. Thousands of wretched and foredoomed victims, resigned to their fates, made the somber trek up the steps of the pyramids. In a ceremony known as the heart sacrifice, the live victim lay stretched out with arms and legs held by four men; the priest slashed open the chest and grabbed the heart, ripping it out of the body and dedicating it to the sun god, while the victim's body tumbled down the steps of the temple. In addition to the sacrifices carried out in association with their religious beliefs, the Aztecs exercised capital punishment on crimes ranging from adultery to repeated drunkenness. A prominent priestly class oversaw the calendar, the temple complexes, and both the formal and informal religious rites and practices of the people.

Aztec society featured a social organization based on kinship units that extended over several domiciles and a fair amount of social mobility within the two broad classes of nobles and the common people. By the time the Spanish arrived, however, Aztec society had become increasingly stratified, thanks in part to the intermarriage between the Aztecs and the nobility of other tribes. The kinship units lived on communally owned land and comprised specific tribal clans whose identities were based on particular locations within Tenochtitlán. At its height the city boasted 200,000 residents and was maintained in a surprisingly orderly fashion given the teeming activity that occurred there on a daily basis. Marketplaces were thronged with people, many of whom arrived via canoe along the canals lined with stone that facilitated traveling throughout the city. The markets featured an enormous diversity of goods for sale or exchange, ranging from abundant foods—meat from a variety of animals (e.g., venison, rabbit, turkey, and hairless dogs), innumerable fruits and vegetables, and the mainstays of maize and beans—to textiles, dyes, furniture, household items, valuable jewelry of gold, silver, and precious stones, and a wide array of other supplies and consumer goods that must have made the city a shopper's paradise. Independent farmers made up their own class and provided many of these goods, making slavery primarily an urban phenomenon among the Aztecs. Slavery was on the rise in the fifteenth and early sixteenth centuries. The two main categories of slaves were those captured in war, who were liable to end up as human sacrifices, and people of Mexica descent who could have become slaves in a variety of ways (because of unpaid debts, as punishment for crimes, or as children sold by their indigent parents). Slavery in Aztec society was not hereditary; like indentured servants, slaves retained some rights that gave them an accepted status as human beings; in other words, they were not merely treated as property. To the contrary, slaves could own property and, if wealthy enough, could own other slaves as well.

Women played important roles in Aztec society even though, as in Europe, political and military leadership came almost exclusively from men. As in medieval Europe, Aztec women sometimes functioned as merchants and when necessary substituted for their husbands (with no disadvantage vis-à-vis other male merchants) to ensure that goods reached the marketplace. Wives were essentially partners in their husbands' businesses, as symbolized by their participation in rituals associated with religious festivals. In some instances, Aztec women controlled religious rituals, which enhanced their authority and prestige in society. Aztec women of the nobility, like their European counterparts, had more limited opportunities than the rest of their gender. Their families viewed them as marriageable commodities whose honor needed protection and preservation, best accomplished through seclusion in the Aztec equivalent of an abbey school where girls primarily learned the art of embroidery. The Aztecs placed a high premium on embroidery as a decorative art, which gave considerable value to the work that noblewomen performed; however, the women of the nobility were still mainly valued as the means to an attractive marriage arrangement that would benefit their family as a whole. On the positive side, noble Aztec women could inherit land, receive tribute from vassals, and serve as regents during the minority of a male heir.

One thousand miles south of Tenochtitlán, the equally powerful Incas of Peru had also developed an effective and efficient administrative system and a successful economy. Like the Aztecs, the Incas had established their empire through a combination of alliances and military victories. The Incas began to expand for several reasons that probably included lack of land for a growing population, the need to build up their military to defeat enemies that threatened their lands around their capital of Cuzco, a simple desire for greater wealth and resources, and the premium that the Incas placed upon military virtues and the ability of their leaders to defend and expand their territory. The Incas, like the Aztecs, relied heavily on the political and military success of their kings. Thus they could not afford the luxury of a purely hereditary monarchy; they needed a ruler who could demonstrate dynamic, effective leadership. Regents were appointed to rule for young or weak kings; internal conflicts between those in or close to the royal family occurred frequently. Once the Incas had begun the impetus of expansion, it became its own dynamic as more resources were necessary to support the increasingly luxurious lifestyle of the royal family and Cuzco nobility. Administratively, the Incas divided their empire into four areas or *suyus*, corresponding to the northern, southern, eastern, and western regions, each of which they further subdivided into provinces of roughly 20,000 households. The Incas integrated conquered regions into their economy and made sure that they had access to all the same products and services as the rest of the empire. Unlike the Aztecs, Inca chiefs maintained more than a thousand government warehouses, tied into an elaborate, sophisticated system of production and distribution. The Incas also differed from the Aztecs in that they frequently retained the services of the leaders of people whom they conquered. The Incas even used captives for agricultural labor rather than as human sacrifices. In general, the Incas treated their conquered peoples much better than did the Aztecs, allowing them to maintain their own local leadership and their own gods in addition to bringing them the economic benefits of Inca rule. But the Incas made it clear that submission was required, and they appropriated sacred objects from conquered peoples with the implied threat of destruction should they revolt against Inca rule.

Incan society was based on household units, known as *ayllus*, which consisted of families and extended relations and which performed tasks related to agricultural production. The leaders of the *ayllus* possessed limited authority, including the right to oversee marriage and ritual. The most important households were those most closely related to the Inca king. The more closely related to the monarch, the more influential the family, with blood an important determining factor for noble status. Immediately below these households were those of the Incan nobility, a strong and influential class whose interests were closely tied to those of the king, probably even more than was the case in Europe, where the monarchy and nobility clashed so frequently. (An important exception in Europe was the Spain of Ferdinand and Isabella, where the monarchs succeeded in tying the interests of the nobility to the expansion of their own power.) Noblemen wore silver or gold crowns and specialized designs on their tunics indicating their noble status and lineage. Lower nobility among the Incas, known as *curacas*, oversaw the smaller administrative units of 5,000 households and below. Below them were the workers who farmed the land, built the cities, and wove the cloth. Division of labor among the Incas was sometimes based on entire villages that specialized in certain manufactures, such as pottery and cloth.

In Peru women became increasingly subordinate to the needs of the Incan empire during the period of expansion. Women of conquered tribes did much of the weaving required by the needs of the Incan state. The emperor assumed control over the marriage destinies of all conquered female subjects, a right that emphasized his power over the subject people as a whole. Many women from conquered tribes had their lives and destinies completely controlled by the emperor and his officials, who selected on the basis of their physical beauty girls around the age of ten to serve as "chosen women" or *agllakuna*, who were then educated at special schools in domestic crafts such as spinning, weaving, and cooking. The use of gender relations as one of the major strategies to further consolidate the power of Inca rule clearly put women in an inferior position vis-à-vis their male counterparts. However, women could and did exercise power and women of the nobility had the right to inherit property, a circumstance that was recognized by the Spanish when they assigned personal property to members of the Incan nobility after the conquest. The most powerful Incan woman was the Incan ruler's primary wife, known as the *coya*, who exercised important political power and influence as the mother of the heir to the throne.

The Incas apparently had gods devoted to almost everything, including those specific to individual *ayllus*. The Incas believed that gods, spirits, and ghosts permeated the world around them. Major gods included the thunder god, Illapa; the moon goddess, Mana-Quilla; the earth goddess, Pacha Mama; and the sun god, Inti, who was the main focus of the official religion. Ritual was very important in Inca society, symbolizing significant life passages such as puberty, marriage, and death and helping people to keep misfortunes or evil spirits at bay. Rituals usually involved either animal sacrifice or leaving food at sacred places; human sacrifice was rare but not altogether unknown. The Incas used prayer as well as ritual to propitiate the gods and spirits around them, but also believed that they could take other actions to prevent gods or spirits from harming them or bringing them misfortune. They were mostly concerned with ensuring agricultural success or healing and preventing illness. Despite their belief in multiple deities, the Incas also had a concept that they called *wak'a* that represented the belief in a transcendent divine presence behind all of its multiple manifestations.

Despite their obvious differences, some religious beliefs of the Aztecs and Incas could be related to Christianity and thus helped to prepare them for the teachings of Christian missionaries. The Incas believed in a creator-god called Viracocha, who later became a man and performed many wondrous acts on earth, though they did not regard the creator as an exclusively male figure. To the Incas, Viracocha was a remote god that did not attend as closely to human affairs as the multitude of gods that they made of more immediate concern. This belief mirrors that of Spanish Catholics, who venerated and prayed to saints or the Virgin Mary (usually a localized vision of her) instead of praying directly to God or Jesus for assistance with mundane matters and obsessed about the presence of demons instead of trusting the omnipotent power of a universal, transcendent God. Spanish rituals to celebrate saints' feast days or to ward off demonic influence are not far removed from the ritualistic activities of the Incas. The Aztecs too had a variety of gods, including a sun god, Tonatiuh, to whom Aztec warriors had a particular devotion; a fire god, Huehueteotl, to whom sacred fires were kept burning in designated temples; a rain god, Tlaloc, of particular importance in the land of Mexico; and a fertility earth goddess, Chalchiuhtlicue, associated with underground springs. The veneration of the Virgin Mary took root in Latin America perhaps because she could easily be reconciled with the notion of a female fertility goddess who had a maternal influence on her children. The Spanish later built a shrine to the Virgin of Guadalupe on the site of a temple dedicated to the Aztec earth goddess. The Aztecs also had a supreme deity that they called Tezcatlipoca, which meant "Smoking Mirror," who they believed had control over fate or human destiny. This is the closest they came to the belief in a ubiquitous, transcendent divinity that was present in every facet of the universe. One final comparison is noteworthy: while the Aztecs were justifying human sacrifice as central to their religious beliefs, the Spanish Inquisition had just been established on the principle that God demanded the death of heretics who did not accept the religious doctrines of the Catholic Church.

The First Encounters of Columbus with Native Americans

When Columbus proposed his imaginative venture to sail west from Spain to find a shorter and more direct trade route to the East Indies and Asia, the pious Isabella in particular welcomed the possibility of converting heathens in the East to Christianity. Ferdinand and Isabella granted Columbus—and his heirs—the titles of "Admiral, Vice-Roy, and Governor" of any islands or lands that he would discover. The Spanish sovereigns also granted Columbus the authority to "freely decide all causes, civil and criminal" as he saw fit. In 1492 Columbus set sail from Palos with his three small ships, the *Niña*, the *Pinta*, and the *Santa Maria*. After sixty-nine days the ships reached land—in the Bahamas on an island that would be named San Salvador (currently known as Watling's Island). When Columbus died in 1506, he still believed that the lands he had "discovered" were off the coast of Asia.

Columbus's first encounter with Native Americans was friendly enough; some of them guided him toward Cuba. The first comments on the natives that Columbus recorded in his journal and his first letter back to Ferdinand reveal a favorable impression. Columbus was struck by their nudity, but also by their modesty, their physical appearance, their meekness, their tranquility, and their receptivity to the Europeans and Christianity. He noted that none of the natives looked more than thirty years old and that they had no weapons whatsoever except wooden spears tipped with fish teeth. On the larger island of Hispaniola, Columbus enjoyed the hospitality and warmth of the Taino Indians, but found the Carib Indians fiercer, based on his first hostile encounter in this unfamiliar part of the world. When Columbus returned to Spain, he took six Lucayo Indians with him.

Whereas Columbus's first expedition had been modest, his second voyage, launched from Seville in September 1493, comprised seventeen ships, 1,500 men (1,200 of whom were soldiers), horses, and several varieties of European livestock, plants, and grains. Columbus had proposed establishing a Spanish settlement, but the makeup of his entourage indicated conquest as a more prominent goal. After his first landing on the island now known as Puerto Rico, Columbus arrived back on the island of Hispaniola to discover that the Spanish contingent he had left behind had all but vanished, some having been killed in internal fighting and some by natives incensed at the Spaniards' pillaging of the island and their appropriation of native women. A second group of colonists treated the natives just as badly, enslaving some of the younger natives before meeting the same fate as the first group.

Columbus wrote to the king and queen explaining what he hoped to accomplish on the island of Hispaniola. He wished to establish several permanent settlements in areas suitable for farming and to colonize the island quickly in order to establish an orderly society. To appeal to Ferdinand, Columbus exaggerated the amount of gold that he expected to find on the island. He urged that only approved colonists on the island should be free to collect gold in order to prevent it from falling into the hands of mere fortune-hunters; the colonists were to receive licenses to look for gold and to make monthly or even weekly reports on the amounts taken. Columbus wanted to protect the interests of the monarchy, and probably his own as well, by keeping an accurate account of the wealth of the island and ensuring that all gold was smelted quickly with a minimum of exchanges taking place before the authorities received their proper share. The natives, however, became increasingly suspicious of the Europeans and opposed Columbus's desire to search the island for gold. He agreed not to dig mines on the island as long as the natives provided him with a hawk's bell half-full of gold per person every four moons.

From here the situation of the natives deteriorated completely. Columbus shipped 500 Arawak Indians to Spain to be sold as slaves in February 1495. The Spanish conclusively defeated the Indians of Hispaniola in a battle that resulted in the capture of their chief, Caonabo, who died as a prisoner on route to Spain. Columbus conquered the entire island, enslaved much of the population, and doubled the gold tax to a full hawk's bell per person. Failure to comply with the tax, which few Indians could meet, carried the death penalty. Upon arriving in Santo Domingo on Hispaniola during his third expedition of 1498, Columbus dealt with a rebellion among the settlers by illegally granting them permission to use entire communities of natives as forced laborers without wages. This system, called the *encomienda*, became sanctioned by Spain in an attempt to ensure the profitability and success of the colonial enterprise. Even this did not allow Columbus to reassert his control, however, leading to his arrest on charges that all related to his abuse of power. A newly appointed Spanish commissioner imprisoned Columbus and sent him back to Spain in chains and disgrace.

Recovering politically once in Spain, Columbus in 1502 made a fourth and final Atlantic voyage that carried him to the Central American isthmus, where he continued to seek the elusive passage to Asia. In the course of Columbus's voyages, the original enterprise in search of trade with the East Indies took on a number of additional dimensions related to conversion, exploration, settlement, colonization, and conquest. Isabella died in 1504 and Ferdinand, who was less sensitive than his wife to the freedom of his new subjects, allowed them to be forced to work in mines and to be transported as slaves from island to island depending on the labor demands of the Spanish. In 1512 Ferdinand approved of the Laws of Burgos, which were designed to mitigate the harsh treatment of the natives and to place some restrictions on the actions of Spanish settlers. But Ferdinand cared more about gold than souls. The Laws of Burgos had little impact. Meanwhile, the combination of forced labor and exposure to European diseases, against which the natives had no immunity, had all but wiped out the Taino, the people first encountered by Columbus. They had inhabited for a thousand years the islands today known as Cuba, Puerto Rico, the Virgin Islands, and the Greater and Lesser Antilles. Archaeologists have only recently begun to learn more about a civilization that left few traces because of the impermanent nature of the materials that they used for their buildings and artifacts. The same cannot be said for the two major civilizations that the Europeans encountered in the Americas—the Aztecs and the Incas—whose magnificent civilizations remained much in evidence long after the arrival of the Spaniards who conquered them. These two civilizations bore little resemblance to the simpler tribes first encountered by Columbus. They represented major obstacles to the further extension of Spanish power in the New World. But Spanish conquistadors like Hernán Cortés (1485–1547) and Francisco Pizarro (ca. 1475–1541) were not easily deterred.

The Shaping of the Past: Cortés and the Conquest of Mexico

The Spanish conquistadors did not go to America with peaceful intentions but with visions of wealth, military success, and conquest. Religion, or the goal of converting more people to Christianity, they frequently employed to justify their expeditions. Hernán Cortés, the man who conquered the Aztec empire, came from the small town of Medellín in a region of Spain called Extremadura. After a troublesome youth, Cortés rejected a career in law and set sail for the "New World" in 1504 at the age of nineteen—motivated by a combination of desire for personal glory and fortune, religious fervor, and intense loyalty and devotion to Spain and its king, Charles I. In Cuba he achieved some success and political prominence. He eventually ran afoul of the ruling authorities there; he quarreled with Governor Diego Velásquez over the assignment of native Indians to Spanish settlers and again over his failure to marry a girl whom he had seduced who came from a family favored by the governor. Thus, after years in Cuba and the Caribbean, Cortés was not in particularly good favor when he landed on the shores of Mexico in 1519.

The emperor of Mexico since 1502 had been Moctezuma II, the son of a previous emperor, the nephew of his predecessor, and the eighth ruler of his dynasty. Since his dynasty dated back only to the late fourteenth century, Moctezuma looked back to the Toltecs—from whom the Aztecs probably derived many of their beliefs and ideas—for a link to the greatness of past civilizations in the region. One belief associated with the Toltecs involved the story of Quetzalcóatl, the plumed serpent who was predicted to return someday from the east to reestablish his earthly kingdom; the year for this anticipated event just happened to coincide with the news of the arrival of a bearded, white man (or god?) arriving from the east.

Cortés and his men landed on the island of Cozumel off the coast of the Yucatan peninsula, where their first encounter with the natives was amicable. Moctezuma and the Aztecs treated this news with a certain amount of fear and anxiety because only the legend of Quetzalcóatl could account for the arrival of men so different from themselves; they had no other framework for understanding this event. Soon after the Spaniards arrived on the Yucatan mainland, natives there launched a fierce attack; the Spaniards dealt them a decisive defeat, beginning a legend that the Spanish soldiers were invulnerable to harm (only two Spaniards had died in this initial confrontation). A second battle resulted in the deaths of thirty-five Spaniards, but another Spanish victory convinced the local Mayan inhabitants to make peace and appease the Spanish with gifts and women. Hearing of the far-off Aztec capital of Tenochtitlán, Cortés determined to march toward the Mexican interior, making friends with as many native groups as possible in order to conserve men and supplies and fighting only when he found it necessary.

The Spaniards had several advantages in their march through Mexico and their eventual struggle with the Aztecs. Alliances with tribes that had suffered under the Aztecs provided Cortés with strategic advantages, including materials to replenish weapons and supplies. Tribes such as the Totonacs had given their allegiance to the mighty Aztecs because they had no choice, but with the arrival of the Spaniards a new balance of power suddenly seemed possible. Cortés benefited as well from his translators, especially the Spaniard Jerónimo de Aguilar, a shipwreck survivor who had learned to speak Mayan before Cortés arrived, and a native woman named Malintzin (or Malinche), who spoke both Mayan and Nahuatl, the language of the Aztecs. Technologically, the Aztecs were hindered by a dearth of arms and by swords of a shorter length and poorer quality than the steel swords used by the Spanish, which were more capable of a deadly thrust at the enemy. The use of cavalry also gave the Spaniards a huge advantage, a force in battle for which the enemies of the Spaniards had no answer. The Aztecs lacked guns and gunpowder as well and still fought with Bronze Age weapons. But given his numerical disadvantage, Cortés could not have hoped to conquer the Aztecs without the support of other native tribes and he knew it.

Moctezuma had sent the newcomers gifts of tribute and at first had attempted to persuade them to leave Mexico and to stay away from Tenochtitlán. Once Cortés reached Tenochtitlán, relations with Moctezuma broke down fairly quickly, resulting in the emperor's arrest by the Spaniards. The Aztecs regrouped and expelled the Spaniards from the city temporarily, but on September 30, 1520, the Spaniards placed Tenochtitlán under siege, occupying the main avenues into the city. The Aztecs then enticed the Spanish to places where they would be vulnerable to attack from Aztec warriors in armored canoes that could repel the Spanish gunfire. Aztec warriors triumphed over the Spanish on several occasions, including an incident in which fifteen Spaniards were captured and sacrificed in view of other Spanish soldiers.

Ultimately, however, the Aztecs failed to destroy the intruders. What finally tipped the scales in favor of the Spanish were neither superior arms nor military strategy. Rather it was a disease—smallpox. A smallpox epidemic erupting in late September lasted for more than two months, ravaging the bodies and the spirits of the native inhabitants of the Aztec capital. The Spaniards had a greater degree of immunity to the disease and experience and knowledge that helped them cope with the threat of it, all of which the Aztecs completely lacked. According to native accounts, those stricken with the plague could not move from their beds and few were healthy enough to care for the sick, so that those of the ill who did not die of the disease starved to death. The chronicler Bernal Díaz described the houses as full of corpses and said that the Spanish could not walk in Tenochtitlán or in Tlatelolco either without stepping on the bodies of dead natives. With so many people sick, fields went untended, food shortages became severe, and the social order began to crumble. Showing no mercy, the Spanish stepped up their blockade and completely isolated the starving and dying population, now powerless to resist a Spanish onslaught. The invaders prevented the importation of food, destroyed an aqueduct that carried fresh water into the capital, and destroyed and ravaged much of the rest of the city, leading to the collapse of the mighty Aztec empire.

Pizarro and the Conquest of Peru

Francisco Pizarro, whose origins are even more obscure than those of Cortés, led the conquest of the great Inca Empire. Pizarro had every intention of conquering Peru, having received a royal license in 1529 to do exactly that. He associated his personal ambitions with the expansion of the Spanish empire and the goals of the monarchy. Those goals included the conversion of the Peruvian inhabitants to Christianity, and enough representatives of the church went to Peru to accomplish that purpose. It is difficult, however, to discern much hint of religious sentiment in Pizarro's conduct or personal objectives for the enterprise, which chiefly seemed to be to overthrow the Incas and establish his own private kingdom. Within a few years of their arrival in 1532, Pizarro and his brothers had laid the foundation for Spanish rule in Peru and shamelessly enriched themselves.

As in the conquest of Mexico, in Peru the Spaniards were initially welcomed by natives dissatisfied with the ruling dynasty. Some of the chiefs of oppressed tribes provided the invaders with the supplies that they needed, including maize, firewood, and sheep. Like the Aztecs, the Incas failed to recognize the discontent of peoples they had conquered, and internal dissension further weakened the empire. The timing of Pizarro's arrival in Peru in 1532 was crucial, for a recent civil war had divided the empire because of the unpopularity of a new ruler, Atahuallpa. Pizarro had other advantages

Explore the following website—designed to accompany a PBS documentary series on the conquistadors—for images and information about Cortés, Pizarro, and the empires that they overthrew: www.pbs. org/conquistadors/cortes/cortes_flat.html.

Rival Images of the Spanish
Defeat of the Aztecs

Different societies in conflict will provide different interpretations of the same series of events, both in writing and in visual representations. Compare the Aztec representation of the war with the Spaniards in this illustration of the massacre in the main temple from the *Codex Duran* with the painting of *The Taking of Tenochtitlan by Cortés*.

What messages are both images meant to convey? What story do they tell? Why did the artists select these particular incidents for depiction?

Massacre of the Mexicans *(Courtesy of Getty Images)*

The Taking of Tenochtitlan by Cortes, 1521 *(Courtesy of Getty Images)*

▲▼ ▲▼ ▲▼ ▲▼ ▲▼ ▲▼ ▲▼ ▲▼ ▲▼ ▲▼ ▲▼ ▲▼ ▲▼ ▲▼

possessed by Cortés, including technological superiority over a Bronze Age civilization, the use of cavalry, employed in much the same way as it had been in Mexico, and the prior exposure of many of his men to smallpox. The Spanish had the advantages of superior arms and armor. The Incas used stones as their main projectile and the thick cotton tunics that they wore as body armor offered little protection against Spanish guns. Pizarro had one new advantage, however: that of learning from the experience of Cortés in bringing down a powerful empire. Another difference was that the Inca did not at first take the Spaniards seriously enough, whereas the Aztecs perhaps took the Spaniards too seriously by initially viewing them as potential gods.

By 1536 Inca forces had acquired guns and the knowledge of how to use them and had become capable of confronting the Spaniards on equal technological terms. Yet the Spanish defeated the Incas for a combination of reasons, just as they had the Aztecs. The native leadership lost its nerve after Pizarro captured the emperor, Atahuallpa, who was murdered in July 1533. The Spanish employed terror, using surprise to slaughter unarmed people in taking control of cities. In military engagements, even when the Spaniards

Spanish Investment in the Indies

Below is an account of a conversation between two Spaniards, Almagro and Pedrarias, in which Pedrarias agrees to be bought out of his investment in the enterprise associated with the discovery and conquest of Peru. The conversation was recorded by Fernández de Oviedo (1478–1557), a Spanish historian whose *General History of the Indies* is an invaluable account of Spanish conquest and colonization in the Americas.

———————

In February, 1527, I had some accounts to settle with Pedrarias, and was frequently at his house for the purpose. While there one day, Almagro came in and said to him, "Your Excellency is of course aware that you contracted with Francisco Pizarro, Don Fernando de Luque, the schoolmaster, and myself, to fit out an expedition for the discovery of Peru. You have contributed nothing for the enterprise, while we have sunk both fortune and credit; for our expenses have already amounted to about fifteen thousand *castellanos de oro*. Pizarro and his followers are now in the greatest distress, and require a supply of provisions, with a reinforcement of brave recruits. Unless these are promptly raised, we shall be wholly ruined, and our glorious enterprise, from which the most brilliant results have been justly anticipated, will fall to the ground. An exact account will be kept of our expenses, that each may share the profits of the discovery in proportion to the amount of his contribution towards the outfit. You have connected yourself with us in the adventure, and, from the terms of our contract, have no right to waste our time and involve us in ruin. But if you no longer wish to be a member of the partnership, pay down your share of what has already been advanced, and leave the affair to us."

To this proposal Pedrarias replied with indignation, "One would really think, from the lofty tone you take, that my power was at an end; but, if I have not been degraded from my office, you shall be punished for your insolence. You shall be made to answer for the lives of the Christians who have perished through Pizarro's obstinacy and your own. A day of reckoning will come for all these disturbances and murders, as you shall see, and that before you leave Panama."

Source: William H. Prescott, *History of the Conquest of Peru*, vol. 2, edited by John Foster Kirk (Philadelphia: J.P. Lippincott, 1902), pp. 459–460.

Almagro eventually agrees to release Pedrarias from his obligation at the cost of 1,000 pesos. Oviedo goes on to say that "by this act [he deserted] the enterprise, and, by his littleness of soul [forfeited] the rich treasures which it is well known he might have acquired from the golden empire of the Incas." Why, according to Oviedo's account, does Pedrarias say that he wants to abandon his share of the enterprise? What general attitudes are exhibited toward the project on both sides of the conversation? What is Oviedo's attitude toward it?

were grossly outnumbered, they fought with an utter determination born of the knowledge that they had no choice in a hostile land but to fight or die. They made use of auxiliary Indian troops to take control of the Inca capital of Cuzco, cutting off the lines of supply much as the Spanish had done in taking Tenochtitlán. In taking Cuzco, Pizarro ordered his soldiers to refrain from destroying the residences, mostly in order to preserve them for the Spanish, but his men wantonly looted the temples and palaces. Once Pizarro entered Cuzco, bringing a civil war to an end, he sought to rule with the cooperation of Inca leadership. Peaceful relations between the Spanish and the Incas did not last long, however. Manco Inca, a prominent leader whom Pizarro had actually placed in authority, revolted in 1535, was captured, and then escaped in April 1536; in the war that followed, the Spanish turned against the natives, raping many of the Inca women and burning alive the leaders of the resistance.

In Peru the Spanish did not scruple to seize the best lands and richest mines for themselves or even to resort to pilfering from the tombs of the Inca. They established in Peru the *encomienda* system, in which Spanish soldiers received grants of substantial amounts of land on which the natives would be forced to labor. As early as 1534 Pizarro began this practice, thus beginning the transformation of a land and a people whose language he did not speak and of whose society he was basically ignorant. The *encomienda* system did become modified as the sixteenth century wore on, with the crown becoming more involved and taking over most of the private units, but it played an important role in the early stages of the conquest of both Peru and Mexico.

The Spanish left a complex legacy in America. The demographic impact of the introduction of European diseases such as smallpox was perhaps the greatest immediate result, but this could have been avoided only if the Spanish had never left Europe to cross the Atlantic. Politically, two great empires collapsed, while the civilizations and religious beliefs associated with them became subsumed under the influence of Spanish and European civilization.

Other Examples of Expansion

Two other examples further illustrate the role that expansion played in European history in the early modern period. English interest in Ireland dated to the twelfth century, but efforts to colonize and consolidate their power there intensified in the fifteenth and sixteenth centuries. English colonization of Ireland followed what became a familiar pattern of European expansion, combining an attempt to establish new settlements with the formation of alliances with powerful local rulers. Frontier settlements always offer new opportunities, and English merchants and craftsmen migrated to Ireland to take advantage of them. Russian expansion had to await the decline in the power of the Mongols and the emergence of Muscovy as a leading power under a stable dynasty in the mid-fifteenth century. The Muscovite state of Russia expanded on a number of fronts during the fifteenth and sixteenth centuries, the most dramatic period of expansion occurring during the reign of Ivan III (r. 1462–1505). The Russian occupation of Novgorod during his reign followed a familiar expansionist pattern of settlement combined with harsh treatment of the native population.

In Ireland English colonists settled mainly in towns, but elsewhere the English relied on alliances that they made with the Irish earls of Kildare, Desmond, and Ormond. The Black Death of 1348 took a heavy toll on the urban population in Ireland and lessened the English presence there. The English retained their local alliances, but after the mid-fourteenth century their control over the country "beyond the Pale" (the name of the area near Dublin where the English had direct control) diminished considerably. English rule in Ireland received a serious challenge from the Kildare Rebellion in the 1530s. Coinciding with the English Reformation and Henry VIII's break with the Catholic Church (see Chapter 11 in this volume), the rebellion provoked a renewed interest in England in the colonization of Ireland. In the 1560s under Elizabeth I, the English began to create a plantation system that created an English landlord class in the countryside. During the sixteenth century, the prospect of land in Ireland attracted English settlers, especially among the younger sons of nobility who would not inherit property because of the English system of primogeniture. A stronger landlord class with larger estates was created after another major rebellion in 1598.

As Henry VIII did in Ireland following the Kildare rebellion, Ivan III redistributed properties around Novgorod to those who he knew would remain loyal to him, especially poorer members of the noble Muscovite nobility (though some properties were given to the former slaves of prominent local families). But Russian expansionist policy also reflected the expansionist policies of England, Spain, and other European countries in the justification found in a religious mission. As with the Spanish, tsarist religious and political objectives were inseparable. Ivan III and the Russian tsars sought to unify Russia under the Russian Orthodox Church and to expand into areas controlled by Muslims and pagans to the south and east. Throughout this early period of expansion, though, Russia's claims to territory did not always match its ability to control local populations. Russia had a huge frontier with scattered military garrisons that enforced Muscovite authority as best they could. But many people nominally under Russian control were not, in fact, at all. Russian authorities often contented themselves with verbal statements of loyalty without pressing their luck too far.

Conclusion

At the beginning of the fourteenth century, Europeans had only begun to expand their horizons beyond their own continent. Trade flourished in the Mediterranean and then in the Baltic and North Seas, and the search for new opportunities and further profits led to refinements in banking and finance, improvements in nautical technology, and bold new enterprises in overseas commerce. These developments set the stage for the beginnings of European expansion and increasing contact and conflict with other parts of the world. Over the course of the fourteenth and fifteenth centuries, the Ottomans challenged Europeans for the control of the Mediterranean, spurring expansion. The Portuguese sent numerous expeditions down the west coast of Africa and began to explore the interior of the continent as well. The Spanish expelled the Muslims from Spain, then financed Columbus's voyage to search for new trade routes to the east. But expansion overseas was only part of a general drive by rulers and countries determined to increase their wealth and power, as reflected by attempts to expand closer to home, exemplified by the English colonization of Ireland and by Russian expansion.

When he landed on the island of San Salvador, Columbus opened a new era in Western civilization and world history by bringing Europeans and Native Americans into contact. Much of the history of the world for the past 500 years has revolved around the continued expansion of European influence on the rest of the world, a story that will occupy a position of prominence in the chapters to come. And the shift from the Mediterranean to the Atlantic economy intensified rivalries between northern and southern merchants that were exacerbated in the sixteenth century by the division of Europe into two rival religious creeds—Catholic and Protestant—as a result of the Reformation of the sixteenth century.

1. What major economic changes accompanied the rise of capitalism in Europe during the fourteenth and fifteenth centuries? How were these changes related to one another?
2. What factors contributed to European expansion to other areas of the world by the end of the fifteenth century? What drew European merchants and rulers to specific areas of expansion?
3. Why did Spain and Portugal play such an important role in the expansion of Europe during this period?
4. How did Aztec and Incan civilizations differ from each other? In what ways were they similar? How would you compare them to European civilization?
5. What factors contributed to the fall of both of these civilizations to the European conquerors?

Suggestions for Further Reading

Braudel, Fernand. 1982. *Civilization and Capitalism, 15th–18th Century,* Volume II: *The Wheels of Commerce.* New York: Harper and Row.

Clendinnen, Inga. 1991. *Aztecs: An Interpretation.* Cambridge: Cambridge University Press.

Cobo, Father Bernabe. 1990. *Inca Religion and Customs.* Translated and edited by Roland Hamilton. Austin: University of Texas Press.

Davidson, Miles H. 1997. *Columbus Then and Now: A Life Reexamined.* Norman: University of Oklahoma Press.

Fernández-Armesto, Felipe. 2006. *Pathfinders: A Global History of Exploration.* New York: W.W. Norton.

Wood, Michael. 2000. *Conquistadors.* Berkeley: University of California Press.

Suggested Websites

www.fordham.edu/halsall/sbook1z.html

This website offers access to a number of primary sources dealing with European expansion in the period covered by this chapter, including documents on Portuguese exploration and selected letters and documents related to Christopher Columbus, as well as links to other sites and sources associated with the Spanish *reconquista*.

www.indians.org/welker/aztec.htm

This website is very useful and informative for students wishing to explore information about various aspects of Aztec culture and civilization in a well-organized and accessible format.

http://loki.stockton.edu/~gilmorew/consorti/1fcenso.htm

This website provides some general information about the Incas, with access to photos, maps, and additional sources of information.

www.win.tue.nl/cs/fm/engels/discovery/columbus.html

This is a Columbus navigation page that provides links to a variety of sources related to different aspects of Columbus's life and each of his voyages.

11   The Protestant and Catholic Reformations

In early modern Europe, every Christian from princes to paupers viewed religion as central to their thoughts and experiences, partly because their faith emphasized that each Christian had the duty to love others and partly because of the power and control exercised by the institutional church. Most people, including Jews and Muslims, believed in God and God's ultimate control over life and death. Many Christians believed that saints could and did aid them in successfully completing their daily tasks, in preserving them from danger, or in helping them to convalesce after an accident or illness. Religious images and symbols confronted people everywhere they went. Yet even in the Middle Ages, the potential for division among Christians existed, despite the church's concerns with preserving a level of conformity and extirpating heresy by whatever means necessary. The social and economic changes of the late medieval world prepared the way for the acceptance of new ideas, new attitudes toward the church, and new institutional realities.

The Reformation of the sixteenth century was a religious movement that challenged the abuses, practices, and certain doctrines of the established church. It also promoted the search for a more personal faith in the context of a reformed church believed to coincide more closely with that of the first Christians. Early reformers such as Martin Luther, Huldrych Zwingli, and John Calvin concluded that the church failed to provide meaning to their personal understanding of Christianity. Many Europeans proved open to reform ideas and would reject Catholicism for a reformed faith that offered a different path to God and a different interpretation of the Christian experience. The Reformation ended up creating a complex legacy that divided Europe into rival religious camps, leading to a further intertwining of politics and religion and more than a century of religious strife and warfare.

The Catholic Church experienced its own Reformation that also sparked the spiritual renewal of individuals and the bonding of communities. Some historians prefer the term *Catholic Reformation* instead of *Counter-Reformation* in recognition of the reforming movement that existed within the Catholic Church before the Protestant Reformation and that continued throughout the era. Originating with the Christian humanism of individuals such as Erasmus,

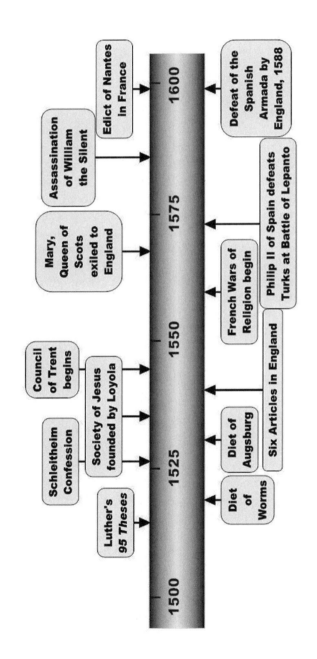

a faction within the church wished to reform church abuses and to modify the church's religious teachings in much the same direction as Luther had. The Oratories of Divine Love in sixteenth-century Italy and the work of Cardinal Francisco Ximenez de Cisneros (1436–1517) in Spain provide two examples of reform movements that did not derive their impetus from the Protestant Reformation. Cisneros attacked clerical abuses vigorously and laid the groundwork for Spain's relative immunity from the appeal that the Protestant Reformation had elsewhere in Europe.

The history of Christianity in Russia in the sixteenth and seventeenth centuries offers some compelling comparisons with the religious history of Western Europe at the time of the Reformation. Behind the divisions that occurred in both churches lay a conflict characterized by alternative approaches to spirituality and differing views about God, humanity, and the nature of religious experience. The experience of the Russian Orthodox Church suggests some important similarities in religious reform movements, as well as some striking dissimilarities that highlight the enduring differences between two distinct cultures.

The Shaping of the Past: Martin Luther's Break with the Church

Martin Luther (1483–1546), an obscure professor of theology at the University of Wittenberg in Saxony, conceived of Christianity in a new way. He did not set out to change the world, nor did he intend to lead or establish a rival church and religious movement that would divide Europe religiously and lead to 150 years of religious strife, warfare, and persecution. Yet his challenges to the belief system and the religious institution that had dominated European history for the previous 1,000 years led to precisely those results.

The second of eight children of Hans and Margaretta Luther, Martin Luther grew up in a fairly prosperous German family. In 1501, at the age of eighteen, he matriculated at the University of Erfurt to prepare for a career in law. By 1505 he had earned his master's degree and entered law school, as planned. Then his career took a dramatic and unexpected turn that led him away from the law and into the church. Fulfilling a vow made to St. Anne in the midst of a tremendous thunderstorm, Luther entered the strict Augustinian monastery at Erfurt, where he was ordained a priest in 1506. In 1510 he traveled to Rome but was disgusted by the extent to which the Eternal City failed to correspond to his idea of a pious, serious atmosphere befitting the position that the city occupied at the center of western Christianity.

Upon returning to Germany, Luther enrolled in the recently founded University of Wittenberg in Saxony, from which he received his doctorate in theology in 1512. Both as a student and as a professor there, he was plagued by constant doubts about how he could know for certain that he had achieved salvation. This central question of Luther's life, which had also troubled him during his time as a monk, became the focal point of the theology that characterized the entire Reformation movement. How, Luther questioned, could individual Christians, aware of their own sinfulness and immoral impulses, know that they had done enough good works to earn salvation from a God who, according to the church, demanded "righteousness" as a precondition for salvation? After years of agonizing over this question, Luther came to some resolution of his spiritual crisis around the year 1515. He concluded from his study of the Bible, particularly the book of Psalms and Paul's Letter to the Romans, that God did not demand righteousness or good works as a condition for salvation, as the church taught. Rather, God, by his grace, "justified" those who simply had faith. Luther came to believe that Christ had sacrificed himself on the cross for all Christians, who, to be saved, had only to accept this gift of salvation.

Until October 1517 Luther did not realize the potential significance of this understanding, nor did he intend to start a conflict with the church. Then he heard about the campaign of Johann Tetzel (ca. 1465–1519), a Dominican representing the papacy, to sell indulgences in the vicinity of Saxony to finance the building of St. Peter's Cathedral in Rome. Indulgences were documents provided by the church that absolved the sins of either the purchaser or a departed loved one. They were based on the claim of the church that it possessed a "treasury of merits" accumulated from the innumerable good works performed by Christ and the saints beyond what they needed to achieve salvation. Luther reacted to Tetzel's campaign by posting his Ninety-Five Theses on the door of the church next to Wittenberg Castle on October 31, 1517. Luther intended his theses as an invitation to further debate and discussion in his own theological circle. Within no time, however, his theses had been published without his knowledge and began circulating widely amid much public controversy.

Luther had previously discovered in Erasmus's new critical translation of the New Testament that John the Baptist had told the Jews not to perform acts of penance but rather to change their way of thinking. Translating the Greek as "be penitent" in opposition to the Latin "do penance," he accordingly denied that the pope had the authority to remit punishments or to forgive sins. Luther stressed that every Christian who truly repented would have complete forgiveness from both guilt and punishment, rendering indulgences totally superfluous. The church accused Luther of heresy and sent the theologian Johann Eck (1486–1543) to debate him. When Eck accused Luther of reprising the heresies of John Wycliffe and John Huss, Luther acknowledged that he believed in the truth of some of the teachings of Huss and stated his position that church

From Luther's *Ninety-Five Theses*

13. The dying are freed by death from all penalties, are already dead as far as the canon laws are concerned, and have a right to be released from them.

15. The fear or horror is sufficient in itself, to say nothing of other things, to constitute the penalty of purgatory, since it is very near the horror of despair.

16. Hell, purgatory, and heaven seem to differ the same as despair, fear, and assurance of salvation.

20. Therefore the pope, when he uses the words "plenary remission of all penalties," does not actually mean "all penalties," but only those imposed by himself.

21. Thus those indulgence preachers are in error who say that a man is absolved from every penalty and saved by papal indulgences.

26. The pope does very well when he grants remission to souls in purgatory, not by the power of the keys, which he does not have, but by way of intercession for them.

36. Any truly repentant Christian has a right to full remission of penalty and guilt, even without indulgence letters.

38. Nevertheless, papal remission and blessing are by no means to be disregarded, for they are, as I have said the proclamation of the divine remission.

40. A Christian who is truly contrite seeks and loves to pay penalties for his sins; the bounty of indulgences, however, relaxes penalties and causes men to hate them—at least it furnishes them occasion for hating them.

43. Christians are to be taught that he who gives to the poor or lends to the needy does a better deed than he who buys indulgences.

47. Christians are to be taught that the buying of indulgences is a matter of free choice, not commanded.

54. Injury is done the word of God when, in the same sermon, an equal or larger amount of time is devoted to indulgences than to the Word.

81. This unbridled preaching of indulgences makes it difficult even for learned men to rescue the reverence which is due the pope from slander or from the shrewd questions of the laity.

84. Again, What is this new piety of God and the pope that for a consideration of money they permit a man who is impious and their enemy to buy out of purgatory the pious soul of a friend of God and do not rather, because of the need of that pious and beloved soul, free it for pure love's sake?

Source: Harold J. Grimm, ed., *Career of the Reformer: I, Luther's Works,* 31 (Philadelphia: Fortress Press, 1957), 25–33.

What do the above theses reveal about the basis for Luther's attack on indulgences? How far does he carry that attack? What is his attitude toward purgatory? What is his attitude toward the pope? Do these theses deserve the attention they are given for initiating the Reformation?

councils were no more infallible than the pope. He later came to conclude that he had a great deal in common with Huss, while saying of Wycliffe in 1520 that "if Wycliffe was a heretic in one degree, they [Luther's opponents in the church] are such in ten degrees" (Dillenberger 1961, 266).

By 1520 Luther had abandoned hope that the spiritual renewal of the church could come from Rome and he appealed to the German princes to take the lead in reforming the church. The princes had some long-standing grievances against the papacy based on money collected by the church that ended up in Rome and papal interference in the appointment of bishops and archbishops within their realms. When Luther called upon the German princes to summon a council to lead a reform of the church in 1520, he established a potential basis for German nationalism and unification against the foreign tyranny of the papacy. Emperor Charles V summoned an imperial assembly of secular and ecclesiastical representatives from the German territories and cities to meet in the city of Worms in 1521 to consider a variety of issues, including the Turkish threat, his need for assistance in his conflict with France, and the possibility of religious reform. Charles invited Luther, who had several months earlier been excommunicated by the church, to attend the assembly to answer questions regarding his writings and ideas. If Luther traveled to Worms thinking that he would receive a fair hearing for those ideas, he soon discovered that Charles's main goal was to affirm the religious unity of his realm. When Luther refused to recant his views at Worms, Charles placed him under an imperial ban. Charles forbade anyone to give Luther food or drink and instead ordered that "wherever you meet him, if you have sufficient force, you shall take him prisoner and deliver . . . to us in close custody."

Once the church had excommunicated him, Luther became free to further develop his own theology. He translated the Bible into German. He got married to a former nun. He started his own church. His ideas spread across the continent. He had started a movement that changed people's lives and ways of thinking, that divided European Christendom, that produced civil wars and new international rivalries between Protestant and Catholic nations, and that contributed to the social and economic upheaval and instability that accompanied the transition from the medieval to the modern world.

Critical to Luther's attack on the sacramental system was his doctrine of

Besides information about modern Lutheranism, this Lutheran website contains sixteenth-century writings by and about Luther, as well as other related sources such as the Augsburg Confession: www.iclnet.org/pub/resources/text/wittenberg/wittenberg-home.html.

Lucas Cranach the Younger, *Martin Luther and the Wittenberg Reformers,* **ca. 1543.** Luther, the initiator of the Protestant Reformation, is portrayed by Cranach (1515–1586) among fellow German reformation leaders. This oil on panel is in the Toledo, Ohio, Museum of Art.

the "priesthood of all believers." Luther believed that Christ had called all believers equally and that they existed as members of an invisible church distinct from that governed by the Catholic hierarchy. Part of the appeal that this message had for many people lay in the relative simplicity of the message and the ease with which even the uneducated might understand the basic concept. Although the Reformation benefited from the printing press, sermons in parish churches and woodcuts or illustrations in pamphlets played a more significant role among the masses than the actual written word. Lutheranism benefited in particular from the combination of popular support and the protection of powerful German princes, such as Frederick the Wise in Saxony and Philip of Hesse.

The Further Shaping of the Protestant Reformation

It did not take long for the Reformation to spread from Germany to Switzerland, France, and England. The reform initiatives of Huldrych Zwingli (1484–1531) in Zurich and John Calvin (1509–1564) in Geneva strengthened the Reformation as a whole, even as differences among the individual reformers began to divide the movement. Zwingli took an even stronger stand against Catholic practices than did Luther. Luther, for example, accepted art and music as aids to the worship and contemplation of God, as long as they did not become a substitute for prayer, whereas Zwingli saw no place for them in church or worship services. Calvin tried to provide a scriptural basis for Genevan laws and society, which he helped to transform into a state characterized by a distinctly Protestant civic piety. In his 1536 book *The Institutes of the Christian Religion*, Calvin explained Protestantism in a systematic, organized, and comprehensive manner. His main message centered on the power and magnificence of God and the sinfulness of humanity, making God's decision to save anyone all the more impressive and generous. But Calvin did not intend the *Institutes* to serve as a replacement for the Bible, which, he emphasized, was the main source for knowledge about God. The doctrine most closely associated with Calvin is predestination. Calvin argued that because God was all-powerful and all knowing, God must have preordained or predestined who would be saved and who would be damned even before their birth. He held that God had chosen in his mercy to save people who could never achieve perfection and escape the taint of original sin, thus proving His love for humanity. People should trust in God's mercy and live a life of profound gratitude for predestination, which lifted an impossible burden from their shoulders.

Calvin provided the Protestant Reformation with a coherent and systematic theology that gave it an international appeal and allowed Protestantism to compete more effectively with the Catholic Church. He provided a model of church organization that involved the laity and provided a standard against which each church could be measured. His views allowed for social and political rebellion against any magistrate that prevented what he regarded as the true worship of God. But Calvin also sanctioned the persecution of heretics and witches and contributed to the religiously intolerant atmosphere of sixteenth-century Europe. Calvinism would become the major religious creed of the Huguenots in France, the Reformed churches in the Netherlands and in much of Germany, the English and American Puritans, and the Presbyterians in Scotland.

Table 11.1

Main Differences Between Protestantism and Catholicism

Protestantism	Catholicism
Two sacraments, baptism and communion	Seven sacraments
Priesthood of all believers	Hierarchical priesthood, headed by pope
Justification by faith alone	Justification by faith and works
Sole authority of the scriptures	Authority of scriptures and church tradition
Bread and wine do not change their substance during communion	Bread and wine transformed into body and blood of Christ during communion
Marriage of the clergy permitted	Celibacy of the priesthood
Church services in the vernacular	Church services in Latin
No belief in purgatory or masses for the dead	Belief in purgatory and masses for the dead

Table 11.2

Main Differences Among the Major Protestant Reformers

Luther	Zwingli	Calvin
Humans justified by grace of God through faith	Humans must make decision to have faith and obey moral laws of scripture	Humans reunite with Christ through faith
God made decision to justify; no emphasis on predestination	God has total power; humanity completely dependent on God for salvation	God predestines individuals for heaven or hell even before birth
Baptism symbolic of God's free gift of grace	Baptism a symbol of human faith, made by the community on behalf of the infant	Baptism a sign of forgiveness of sins, reuniting infant with Christ
Consubstantiation: Christ present with the bread and the wine	Eucharist is a memorial service commemorating Last Supper; Christ not physically present	Eucharist a symbol, but Christians also receive body and blood of Christ with the bread and the wine
Church based on history, contains both saved and sinners	Church identical with Christian community, contains both saved and sinners	Distinction between visible and invisible church: visible church contains saved and sinners, invisible church only the saved

The greatest challenge to the contemporary political and social structure came from a diverse group of Protestants known as the radical reformers. The radicals sought to restore primitive Christianity as closely as possible to its original form. The early Christians had been martyrs; the radicals sought to be martyrs. The early Christians had consisted only of true believers; the radicals wanted their churches to consist only of true believers. The early Christians had no official connection with the state; the radicals sought to sever any ties with secular authority. Early Christians did not participate in warfare; radicals such as Conrad Grebel (1448–1526) attacked Zwingli for supporting warfare. Early Christians did not own property; some radicals believed in communal ownership of property. Such positions earned the radicals the distrust of the authorities and did, indeed, lead to frequent persecution.

The main group of radicals was known as the Anabaptists, chiefly identified by their belief in adult baptism. Anabaptists believed that, since their church should consist only of true believers, their members should come to the church of their own free will as adults; the group thus rejected infant baptism. The Anabaptists were centered in Switzerland and southern Germany, where they drew on the discontent that arose after the defeat of a peasant rebellion that broke out in 1525. Because many Anabaptists were forced to flee persecution to other lands, the history of the movement lacks structure or coherence. Michael Sattler wrote the Schleitheim Confession in 1527, one of the few definitive statements of radical beliefs, emphasizing voluntary baptism, the symbolic nature of baptism and communion, pacifism, the approaching end of time, and the forbidding of oaths.

The historical significance of the radical reformation outweighed the actual number of radicals or their lack of political influence. The divisions among the radicals and even among the Anabaptists further contributed to the divisions within reformed Christianity and a process known as denominationalism. Some people became increasingly attracted to even more radical ideas, including the rise of Unitarianism, which rejected the fundamental Christian concept of the Trinity. The Bohemian nobleman Kaspar von Schwenkfeld (1489–1561) went so far as to question whether a visible church was even necessary, heralding the concept of religious toleration and the denial of the state's right to persecute people for their religious beliefs.

Thomas Cranmer, Henry VIII, and the English Reformation

The Protestant Reformation in England initially resulted from the desire of Henry VIII (1491–1547) to divorce his wife and marry another woman with whom he had fallen in love and with whom he hoped to produce a male heir. Around 1525 Henry became troubled because he and his wife, Catherine of Aragon, had produced only one surviving child—a daughter, Mary—during their sixteen-year marriage, despite several pregnancies. Since Catherine had originally been wed to Henry's brother, Arthur, the king asked Cardinal Thomas Wolsey, his archbishop of York and chief political minister, to petition the pope to grant an annulment on the basis of a church law that prohibited marriage to a deceased brother's widow. Henry's desire for a divorce increased significantly when he fell in love with Anne Boleyn, one of Queen Catherine's ladies-in-waiting. Unfortunately for Henry and for Wolsey, Catherine's nephew, the Holy Roman Emperor, Charles V, attacked Rome in 1527 so Pope Clement VII was in no position to offend Charles and grant the divorce. Undeterred, Henry then dismissed Wolsey and summoned the English Parliament, which during the next seven years approved a succession of more than thirty acts that collectively established royal control over the church in England. The most significant of these acts was the Act in Restraint of Appeals (1532), which asserted the principle of royal control over the English church. The Act of Supremacy, passed in 1533, declared Henry the "supreme head" of the Church of England, formalizing the break with Rome and the papacy. Then, in 1534, the first Act of Succession legalized Henry's marriage to Anne and placed Anne's children in line to succeed to the throne of England, disinheriting Catherine's daughter, Mary. This act would have made Elizabeth, the daughter of Anne and Henry, next in line to the throne. Elizabeth would have succeeded Henry had Anne remained his queen. But Anne lost favor with the king, was charged with adultery, convicted, and beheaded in 1536.

Henry's main objectives in breaking with the Catholic Church and the papacy seem to have been political, but the English Reformation had an ecclesiastical leader as well—Thomas Cranmer, whom the king appointed archbishop of Canterbury in 1532.

Cranmer studied divinity at the University of Cambridge and in 1529 attracted the attention of religious advisers close to the king when he suggested that the king seek the opinion of the English universities on the matter of his divorce. Cranmer possessed a deep familiarity with the writings of the continental reformers and the theologians of the early Christian church, as well as with the Bible. He believed strongly in the Protestant doctrines of justification by faith, the priesthood of all believers, and the sole authority of the scriptures. He thus had no qualms about the idea that the English clergy could oversee the matter of the king's divorce or about the possible religious consequences of a break from Rome.

Steering a middle course between the temperamental king and the pious archbishop was Thomas Cromwell (ca. 1485–1540), an ex-soldier who had risen to prominence under Wolsey and replaced him as the king's leading minister after the cardinal failed to procure Henry's divorce. In her 2009 biographical novel, *Wolf Hall*, Hillary Mantel explores the 1530s from Cromwell's perspective, providing some sense of how this enigmatic figure managed to accomplish so much in such a short amount of time despite enormous pressures from the king and various domestic and foreign factions surrounding the court. Cromwell accumulated almost a dozen titles and offices as a reward for his loyal service and providing the king what he wanted, but he was a critical figure in shaping the political and religious history of sixteenth-century England. He contributed to the growth in the political power of the monarch and the state, while also taking measures to make sure that England would remain a Protestant nation.

Soon after the beheading of Anne Boleyn, Cromwell began abolishing the English monasteries, whose lands were sold to enhance the treasury and create a class of landowners loyal to the Crown and the Reformation. Henry supported this measure, but had never completely converted to the new theology of the Reformation. In 1539 he decided to reinforce certain aspects of Catholic doctrine in the Six Articles, to which Protestants derisively referred as the "whip with six strings." The Six Articles reaffirmed the Catholic doctrine of transubstantiation, the practice of auricular confession, the custom of distributing only the bread and not the wine to the laity during communion, the celibacy of the priesthood, and the legitimacy of vows of chastity and private masses. Anyone contradicting these articles could be sentenced to death. Cromwell did not openly challenge the Six Articles, but he did attempt to reinforce England's commitment to Protestantism in a different way—by arranging an alliance with the German Protestant duchy of Cleves through the marriage of Henry VIII and the duke's daughter, Anne. The move backfired. Henry felt no attraction for Anne of Cleves and, having lost confidence in Cromwell, had his former minister beheaded in 1540. It was left to Cranmer to foil the Catholic sympathies of most English bishops and to defend the remnants of Protestantism left in the English church until Henry's death in 1547.

Cranmer continued to guide the English church, steering it in a clearly Protestant direction during the reign of Edward VI (r. 1547–1553), who was ten years old when he succeeded to the throne following his father's death. Yet as late as 1549, Cranmer still proceeded slowly in abolishing traditional ceremonies, fearing that excessive innovation would prevent people who did not understand the reformed faith from embracing it. Cranmer's reservations notwithstanding, Parliament repealed the Catholic Six Articles, authorized the marriage of the clergy, and approved of Cranmer's first and second *Book of Common Prayer* in 1549 and 1552. English replaced Latin in religious services throughout the country and the doctrine of the English church became more clearly Protestant in the Forty-Two Articles, a new official creed. Before Protestantism could become firmly established, however, Edward succumbed to tuberculosis in 1553 at the age of sixteen and was succeeded by his very Catholic half-sister, Mary.

Mary (r. 1553–1558) convinced Parliament to repeal the Protestant legislation of the reigns of Henry and Edward, but Parliament refused to restore the lands that had been confiscated from the church. Many people, however, were unprepared for the extent of Mary's commitment to Catholicism. Against the advice of Parliament and without the approval of her subjects, Mary married Philip, the son of Emperor Charles V and heir to the Spanish throne. Philip took advantage of the marriage to draw Mary and England into his war with France, resulting in the loss of the French port of Calais, the last English possession on the European continent. Approximately 300 Protestant martyrs were executed during Mary's reign, and many more escaped persecution by fleeing to Germany and Switzerland. Cranmer, burned at the stake in 1556, was one of the martyrs. When Mary died in 1558 at the age of forty-two, she left no Catholic heir to the throne and a country that may have been better prepared than ever for the Protestantism that she and her religious advisers had tried to eradicate.

In England in 1558, the religious direction of the country was in question because no one knew for sure where lay the sympathies of the new queen, Elizabeth I. Elizabeth would ultimately oversee the establishment of a church that retained some elements of Catholicism and some of Protestantism. In 1559 Parliament reestablished Elizabeth's supremacy over the English church by designating her "supreme governor," a term a little less blatant and controversial than Henry's title of "supreme head." An Act of Uniformity in that same year authorized a moderate version of Cranmer's *Book of Common Prayer.* The Thirty-Nine Articles of 1563 left doctrines of special sensitivity, such as predestination and the presence of Christ in the Eucharist, undefined or vaguely worded so that they could be accepted by a majority of people in England. However, during Elizabeth's reign English Protestants became increasingly divided over the future of the English Reformation, many drawing their inspiration from the ideas of Calvin as well as from the radical Reformation.

Social Consequences of the Reformation

Protestantism challenged a social order that valued family, community, and social groups such as guilds above the concerns or interests of specific individuals. Protestantism placed more emphasis on the direct relationship between an individual and God. Salvation became an intensely personal matter. This emphasis on spiritual individualism carried over to other aspects of people's lives.

Among the social consequences of the Reformation affecting the everyday lives of the people were new attitudes toward marriage and sexuality. Luther rejected marriage as a sacrament because he did not regard the ceremony as one of divine origin. Luther particularly opposed the practice in the Catholic Church of refusing or allowing annulments on the basis of the ability of the couple to pay. But Luther, who married a former nun, Katherine von Bora, in 1525, upheld the dignity of marriage, writing that "the union of man and wife is in accordance with the divine law" and that marriage "is incomparably superior to any laws, so that it ought not to be broken for the sake of laws, but laws for its sake" (Dillenberger 1961, 332–333). Calvin and Luther had similar views on marriage and sexuality. Both denied that marriage served the sole function of procreation and that celibacy represented a higher spiritual state, views traditionally associated with Catholicism. They argued instead that marriage provided both partners with companionship and that sex within marriage was something to be celebrated, not denigrated. Calvin accepted and even glorified the human body, rejecting anything that would harm it or cause it to suffer. Protestants, then, did not regard marriage as a sacrament and believed that marriage served the purposes of companionship and sexual comfort. These beliefs help to explain a law passed by the city of Geneva in 1545, stating that a woman who was abandoned by her husband for no fault of her own could after one year obtain a divorce and permission to remarry. The Catholic Church emphasizes that marriage is for life; in the sixteenth century annulments were much harder to come by, except perhaps for royalty and the very wealthy, than they are today. Even today many lay Catholics still oppose the church's strict views prohibiting divorce. Protestant views on marriage could account in part for the appeal of reformed faith to many women.

Protestantism has also been associated with a renewed emphasis on the importance of education for the laity because of its doctrine of the priesthood of all believers and its emphasis on scripture reading. Arguing for the importance of education, Luther complained in the *Address to the Christian Nobility* about "how unwisely we deal with our poor young folk, whom we are commanded to train and instruct." He even went so far as to state the wish, "Would to God also that each town had a girls' school, where day by day, the girls might have a lesson on the gospel, whether in German or Latin" (Dillenberger 1961, 475). Luther's primary disciple, Phillip Melanchthon (1497–1560), and Martin Bucer (1491–1551) in Strasbourg, among other reformers, strongly supported public primary education for boys and girls alike. In Calvin's Geneva, it was compulsory after 1536 for all children to attend primary school, where they studied reading, writing, arithmetic, and the catechism. However, secondary schools were not provided for girls and, thus, true educational equality did not exist.

Despite his arguments in favor of the education of girls, Luther did not call for equality for women in all spheres of public life. However and perhaps most significantly, Luther believed that women possessed spiritual equality with men; his doctrine of the "priesthood of all believers" extended to women as well as men. Calvin also agreed with the subordination of women to men in political organization, but believed that both stood before Christ as spiritual equals.

Many Protestant churches had a significantly larger percentage of women as members, and women played a variety of roles in the establishment of new churches in England and on the European continent in the late sixteenth and seventeenth centuries. Although, at that time, the notion of spiritual equality did not extend to women preachers in the mainstream Protestant churches, later offshoots such as the Quakers did allow women to preach. In an age in which religion was so important, any religious change in the attitudes toward women surely represented a significant change in society as a whole.

Another societal change in the sixteenth century involved the harsh economic circumstances brought on by inflation that made poor relief a major topic of concern. The Catholic Church considered almsgiving or donations for the poor as a good work that would help a person achieve salvation. Although the Reformation stressed faith and downplayed the significance of good works as contributing to salvation, Protestant communities did not ignore the need to provide assistance to the unfortunate. Thesis 43 of Luther's *Ninety-Five Theses* stated that "Christians should be taught that one who gives to the poor, or lends to the needy, does a better action than if he purchases pardons." Legislation in Luther's Wittenberg in 1522 provided for a community chest to finance assistance to the poor, education for poor children, dowries for daughters of the poor, and low-interest loans for workers and artisans. Many Protestant communities imitated this example as they abandoned traditional Catholic avenues for poor relief.

The Reformation and the Jews

Protestantism did not inherently increase or decrease hostility to Jews, but the Reformation called more attention to the Jews because of the heightening of religious passions and the central role that religious identity started to play in European society.

In the sixteenth century, attitudes of animosity and of tolerance toward Jews could be found among both Protestants and Catholics. Luther believed that Jews could be excused for not converting to Catholicism but had no excuse once he had shown them the light of true Christianity. Under Luther's influence, the princes of Saxony and Brandenburg took action to exile Jews from their lands. But not all Lutheran princes followed suit, and the prince of Brandenburg later softened his position. While Luther railed against Jews and called for their expulsion from Germany and the destruction of their homes, his disciple Urbanus Rhegius (1489–1541) became an advocate for a tolerant policy toward them. Rhegius hoped for Jewish conversion no less than Luther, but he adopted an approach of friendly debate and encouragement instead of persecution. He studied the teachings of Jewish scholars as much as he could to better prepare himself for a dialogue with them. In 1540 Rhegius advocated for the Jewish community in the town of Braunschweig and attempted to persuade the Lutheran ministers there to desist from anti-Semitic messages in their sermons.

While the Catholic monarchs of Spain expelled the Jews from their territories and prohibited them from migrating to the New World, Catholic territories in Italy and Eastern Europe, especially Poland and Lithuania, welcomed Jews and gave them a measure of toleration. The Spanish Inquisition forced Jews and Muslims to convert to Christianity, but elsewhere in the church an attitude of tolerance prevailed on the basis of respect for free will. Many of the sixteenth-century popes tolerated Jewish immigration to Rome, which derived much of its Jewish population at that time from Spanish, Portuguese, and Sicilian refugees. For example, Pope Paul III allowed Jews to arrive in Italy via the papal port of Ancona, where many of them chose to settle. Catholic authorities generally condemned pogroms and any outbreak of violence against Jews. However, the position of Jews was always subject to a change in political ruler or the whims of the populace. For example, Pope Paul V was an exception to papal tolerance of Jews, restricting them to a ghetto in Rome and allowing for a measure of persecution against them throughout the Papal States. Many Jews also migrated to the Balkan territories of the Ottoman Empire, preferring to take their chances with the Muslim Turks rather than to remain in Christian Europe.

Eventually, Jews found safe havens in Protestant states as well as Catholic. The Netherlands became a popular destination for European Jews by the late sixteenth century because of economic opportunities and the tolerant religious policies of the Dutch Protestants. The newcomers found already established communities of Jews who had fled there because of Spanish persecution. In the seventeenth century, the English Puritan ruler Oliver Cromwell permitted Jews, who had been banished by Edward I in 1290, to return to England and granted them religious toleration, though he hoped that by doing so he would hasten their conversion to Christianity. One English Puritan writer of the 1640s even referred to the Jews as "the apple of God's eye." Wherever they settled, Jews attempted to keep their community together, unified by their religion and symbolized by the synagogue where they went to pray and receive instruction from their rabbi in the Hebrew scriptures.

The Inquisition and the Religious Legacy of Sixteenth-Century Spain

In the fifteenth century the Spanish revived the medieval institution known as the Inquisition, a special church court created by the thirteenth-century papacy to deal with the heretics who strayed from the orthodox doctrine of the church. The Inquisition set neighbor against neighbor in an attempt to exploit fear and to encourage denunciations lest one be denounced first, and then made arrests without charges, confiscating the property of its prisoners. The Inquisition of the fifteenth century targeted mainly those Moors and Jews who had converted to Christianity to force them to remain committed to the Catholic faith. When Spanish Muslims and Jews who had remained true to their faith revolted against the intimidating tactics employed to encourage their conversion to Christianity, Spanish authorities responded with a royal decree in March 1492 that all Jews and Muslims must either convert or face expulsion from the country. That decree led to the outward conversion of many Spanish Jews and Muslims, many of whom continued to practice their birth religion in secret. About 150,000 Jews left Spain for North Africa, Turkey, and the Balkans.

The Spanish monarchs used the Inquisition to deal with anyone who posed a threat to their political sovereignty or who represented any form of deviance in Spanish society. The Spanish Inquisition stepped up its efforts after the Reformation to ensure that Protestantism did not gain a foothold in the Iberian Peninsula. The Inquisition did great harm to the Spanish church because it inhibited the mystical tradition that had provided so much of the strength of late medieval Christianity. The Inquisition distrusted people who sought spiritual experience outside the traditional confines of the church; its learned inquisitors especially were suspicious of women's mystical experiences and sought to prohibit their free expression of prayer and their religious message. In Spain, Christian mystics such as Teresa of Avila (d. 1582) and John of the Cross (d. 1591) stand out as all the more exceptional because of their ability to overcome the suspicions of the Inquisitors. These individuals fulfilled their personal quests for religious experience within the local monastic settings of Spain where personal religiosity flourished in the sixteenth century. They sought a direct connection with God through prayer, contemplation, and living a virtuous life. Teresa entered the Carmelite convent in Avila in her early twenties as, to her, a slightly more preferable alternative to marriage. She almost killed herself by the age of twenty-four, exacerbating her poor health by her monastic regimen and attempted cures that did more harm than good. By the age of thirty, she adopted a more sensible and, for her, rewarding spiritual routine that focused on prayer and mystical contemplation of the interconnectedness of all things, of which she came to feel a part. Teresa felt very strongly that one could only find God internally rather than by looking outside of oneself. She tried to show others the path that she had taken to spiritual bliss in her books, *The Mansions* and *Book of Her Life*. Her follower, St. John of the Cross, wrote his *Ascent of Mount Carmel* in the same tradition. Teresa also founded a reformed branch of the Carmelites, one of the orders associated with the movement known as the Catholic Reformation.

The Catholic Counter-Reformation

Although there was a separate and independent reform movement within the Catholic Church, the Reformation did produce a reaction and response from the Catholic Church. One development that contributed significantly to the success of that response was the establishment of a new religious order called the Society of Jesus, founded by a former Spanish soldier named Ignatius Loyola (1491–1556). Loyola underwent a sudden conversion in 1522, when, having sustained a serious injury ten months earlier, he prayed to St. Peter to intervene on his behalf. Despite being administered last rites, Loyola made a miraculous recovery for which he held St. Peter responsible. In 1522–1523 he isolated himself at Manresa near Barcelona, followed by a pilgrimage to the Holy Land in 1524. Ten more years of spiritual commitment, including theological study at the University of Paris, culminated in the formation of the Society of Jesus in 1534, dedicated to reform through social aid and purging the church of corruption and heresy. Loyola provided the members of his order with a model for spiritual development in his *Spiritual Exercises*, which sought to guide the Christian through an examination of one's life, a renunciation of sin, the achievement of spiritual enlightenment, and finally union with God. He and six other members of the new group took vows of poverty and chastity, originally intending to engage in missionary activity in the Holy Land. Instead, Loyola received formal approval from Pope Paul III in 1540 to use his Society of Jesus, whose members became known as Jesuits, to combat Protestantism. The Jesuits initiated their first phase of reform mainly through ministering to the disadvantaged in society—the sick, the destitute, prisoners, and women, especially prostitutes—while they also expanded their order. The Catholic Church had found a reformer and a spiritual leader to rival any that had converted to Protestantism. Equally significant was the devotion and obedience that the Society of Jesus professed to the papacy, which it served with unquestioning loyalty as the Society's main mission and defining purpose.

Catholic reform and even a possible reunification with Protestant churches had seemed possible when Alexander Farnese became Pope Paul III in 1534. He elevated a number of humanists to the rank of cardinal and supported further communication between Protestant and Catholic reformers. A report by a papal commission in 1537 detailed the numerous abuses that still plagued the church. In 1541, Cardinal Contarini, one of the leaders of a group that became known as "Italian evangelicals" because of their commitment to renewing the church through an emphasis on the message of the gospels, was invited by Emperor Charles V to meet selected Protestant representatives at Regensburg in southern Germany. However, even though some Catholics (including Contarini) were willing to listen to arguments on the doctrine of justification by faith, they could not hope to gain papal approval for the rejection of the Catholic interpretation of the Eucharist or the rejection of papal authority.

In 1545, at the beautiful city of Trent in northern Italy, a church council authorized by Paul III convened under the auspices of the papacy to deal with the divisions that had torn Europe apart at its religious seams. The two main purposes of the Council of Trent were to be a redefinition of Catholic doctrines and a plan for reforming the church. Meeting intermittently from 1545 to 1563, the Council of Trent in many ways marked the beginning of the Counter-Reformation and a new era in the history of the papacy. The pope agreed to give more autonomy to lower church officials while remaining the official head of the church and the final arbiter of any disputes within the church. The pope retained the right to appoint bishops, but the council insisted that the pope select them more carefully with regard to their character and qualifications. In general, the papacy retained its authority, but the days of a strong secular papal monarchy were over. The major decision made at the Council of Trent was to accord equal importance to scripture and tradition, while affirming that only the Roman Catholic Church had the authority to interpret scripture. This decision, which denied the Protestant beliefs in the sole authority of the scriptures and the priesthood of all believers, undermined any immediate hope for reconciliation between Protestants and Catholics. The council also reaffirmed the seven sacraments, the role of the priesthood in administering those sacraments, the validity of indulgences, and the importance of good works in addition to faith for salvation. In order to strengthen respect for the priesthood, the council insisted that the clergy live up to their vows and put an end to church abuses.

Two additional responses to Protestantism came in the form of the Roman Inquisition and the decision of the papacy to impose censorship through the Index of Prohibited Books. In 1542 Pope Paul III organized the Roman Inquisition and used it to attack heresy and Protestantism in Italy. Cardinal Giampietro Caraffa had pressured Paul III to establish the Inquisition in Italy and served as its first Inquisitor General. Caraffa even set up instruments of torture in his own house in anticipation of his new responsibilities. He is said to have remarked that "even if my own father were a heretic, we would gather the wood to burn him!" (MacCulloch 2005, 231) The Roman Inquisition had the authority to arrest and imprison suspected heretics and seize their property and possessions, while the state assisted in extracting confessions and meting out punishments. The dukes of Milan allowed the Inquisition to operate in their territory from 1542, while Cosimo I, the grand duke of Florence, sanctioned the activities of the Inquisition throughout Tuscany. When Paul III died in 1549 the Council of Trent was a long way from finishing its wok and the issue of reform and the future of the Catholic Church were still quite uncertain. When the College of Cardinals elected Caraffa as Pope Paul IV in 1555, however, it signaled a commitment to this new direction of the Catholic Church and ensured that the Counter-Reformation papacy would play a key role in the reviving fortunes of Catholicism in the second half of the sixteenth century. Paul IV issued the first complete list of banned books in 1559, which included the works of Erasmus and great literary works such as Boccaccio's *Decameron.*

Politics and Religion in the Sixteenth Century

During the sixteenth century few people in positions of authority had any notion that people of different faiths, even under the broad umbrella of Christianity, could peacefully coexist in the same country or territory. The decentralized nature of political authority in the German lands of the Holy Roman Empire thwarted any easy solution to the religious divisions caused by the Reformation. Princes and independent cities sought both religious and political autonomy and resisted the emperor's interference in either realm. Of course, the emperor did not accept this view nor did Catholic princes support the rights of their Protestant counterparts to break from the Roman church. The Diet of Speyer in 1529 imposed restrictions on the spread of reformed doctrines, leading a group of Protestant princes to protest officially, leading to the term "Protestant" and its association with the Reformation. The Diet of Augsburg in 1530 began as an attempt to find a compromise solution between Charles V and the German princes and ended with a condemnation of Protestantism. In response, the Lutheran princes, determined to protect both their autonomy and their new faith, organized the League of Schmalkalden for defensive purposes. The conflict between Charles V and the Protestants ended in 1555 with the Peace of Augsburg, which established the principle that would guide not only German but European politics for the foreseeable future, expressed in Latin as *cuius regio, eius religio*, meaning that the religion of the prince would be the religion of his region.

For the French Protestants, known as Huguenots, the Calvinist doctrine of predestination, with its notion of the existence of a special elect chosen by God, suited well a religious minority that was often persecuted. Despite persecution, Protestantism spread throughout the kingdom, even attracting the support of many nobles and members of the bourgeoisie. In 1562 the first of eight identifiable wars of religion began when Henry, the Catholic duke of Guise, and his retainers attacked a Huguenot congregation at Vassy, east of Paris. The Treaty of St. Germain in 1570 restored religious freedom for the Huguenots in most of France and allowed them to worship in specified locations, but the peace was short-lived. The wars resumed shortly thereafter and lasted into the 1590s, largely because, although France was still overwhelmingly Catholic, the Huguenots had strong leadership and seemed to threaten the interests of powerful noble and ruling families. After the Treaty of St. Germain, the queen mother and de facto ruler Catherine de Medici (1519–1589) allied the French monarchy with the forces of the duke of Guise. In the St. Bartholomew's Day massacre of August 23–24, 1572, the Catholic forces murdered the Protestant Lord Admiral of France, Gaspard de Coligny (1519–1572) and about 3,000 others in Paris alone and slaughtered another 10,000 to 20,000 in the French provinces. The massacre renewed the French wars of religion. After the assassination of Catherine's son, Henry III in 1589, the Protestant King Henry of Navarre (1553–1610) claimed the French throne as Henry IV, having been previously designated by Henry III as his successor. After four more years of war, Henry IV converted to Catholicism. Then, in an attempt to resolve the religious dispute in France once and for all, in 1598, he issued the Edict of Nantes, which recognized the Huguenots as a legal minority and affirmed their control of a number of towns and cities. In addition, the Huguenots received religious freedom outside of Paris and eligibility for all civil rights and public offices. The Edict of Nantes finally brought peace to France after decades of civil war.

In the Netherlands, religion provided a motivating and unifying factor in opposition to domination by the Spanish. Opposition to the Spanish was so widespread that Catholics often hated their rule as much as Protestants did. The provinces of the southern Netherlands valued their independence, but supported Charles V, who had been raised there. The provinces regarded the new Spanish king, Philip II (r. 1556–1598), as an outsider. Their opposition to his policies led him to fear loss of control over an important territory, while the spread of the Reformation in the Netherlands offended his Catholic sensibilities. Philip's decision to station a large number of troops in the Netherlands further antagonized the native population. Open rebellion in the 1560s provoked additional retaliatory and oppressive measures from Philip. When the Spanish sacked a number of peaceful towns in 1576, all seventeen provinces of the Netherlands united behind the Protestant leader, William the Silent of Orange (1533–1584), in an agreement known as the Pacification of Ghent. All the provinces agreed to expel the Spanish. But in 1579, Philip's skillful diplomat, the Duke of Parma, persuaded the ten southern provinces, still predominantly Catholic, to abandon their commitment to the Pacification. Undeterred, the seven predominantly Protestant northern provinces formed the Union of Utrecht under William's leadership and declared their independence from Spain, in 1581. The Protestants became even more determined in

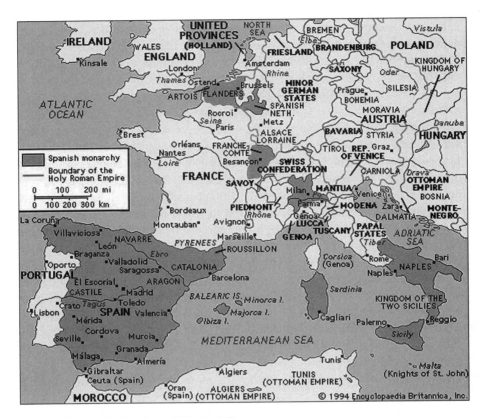

Western Europe in the time of Elizabeth I

their struggle to fight after the assassination of William, who fell permanently silent in 1584. In 1609, the Dutch and the Spanish consented to a truce that lasted twelve years until 1621, when the Netherlands became involved in the cataclysm known as the Thirty Years War.

Philip II of Spain became the monarch most committed to preserving the Catholic Church against Protestantism. Philip began his reign with the added benefit of a Catholic wife, Mary I, upon the throne of England. Mary's death in 1558 effectively ended the Anglo-Spanish alliance, although Philip still entertained hopes of a friendly relationship with her successor, Elizabeth (r. 1558–1603), the daughter of Henry VIII and Anne Boleyn. However, the end of the English alliance came back to haunt Philip when the English came to the support of the Netherlands just when he was trying to restore order in his rebellious Dutch provinces. Increasing tension between England and Spain dominated European diplomacy in the 1570s and early 1580s. Philip bided his time in the hope that Elizabeth would die or be overthrown by Catholic plotters in England and be succeeded by her Catholic cousin, Mary Queen of Scots. Mary spent almost twenty years, from 1568 to 1587, under house arrest in England, where she became the focus of a number of plots to assassinate Elizabeth, some of which had Mary's knowledge and support. In 1587, Elizabeth's ministers confronted her with indisputable proof that Mary was plotting with Philip II to eliminate her and convinced the queen to sign a death warrant, which was hastily carried out. Mary's execution provided Philip with both the excuse and the final motivation for an invasion of England. He organized the Spanish Armada for that purpose, sending 130 ships to pick up troops in the Spanish Netherlands and transport them for a land invasion and assault on London. When the enormous fleet delayed to wait for the troops and tried to anchor in the turbulent English Channel, English seamen sent small fire-ships toward the huge Spanish vessels. The Spanish ships pulled up anchors, leaving them to the mercy of the winds and the currents, which scattered them and forced them to sail in the treacherous waters of the North Sea. Many of the ships that successfully circumnavigated Britain wrecked along the coasts of Ireland; few made it back to Spain. When Philip died in 1598 at the age of seventy-two, Spain was still a great power, but England and the Netherlands had successfully defended the Protestant cause and demonstrated that Protestantism would remain a major factor in European life.

Russia and the Eastern Orthodox Church

After the capture of Constantinople by the Ottoman Turks in 1453, the decline of Constantinople as the center of the Greek Orthodox Church gave greater significance to the leadership of the Russian Orthodox Church in Moscow. The Russian Church continued to take its main theological and spiritual approach to Christianity from the Greek tradition, however. This gave Russian Orthodoxy both a different look and a different orientation than western Christianity.

Beginning in the sixteenth century, some Russians began to take an interest in religious reform in ways parallel to the reform movement in Western Europe that preceded the Protestant Reformation. Criticisms of Russian monasticism became more frequent in the fifteenth and sixteenth centuries, especially resentment about the amount of land that monasteries owned. In addition, Russians became aware of some inaccuracies in the translations of ecclesiastical documents from the original Greek texts. This mirrored the interest in new translations of the Bible by scholars such as Erasmus and the "back to the sources" mentality of European humanists and reformers alike. Whereas Luther's revisiting of the Greek New Testament had helped to inspire his new Reformation theology, however, Russian reformers focused more on how new translations of Greek sources affected external religious activities

▲▼ ▲▼ ▲▼ ▲▼ ▲▼ ▲▼ ▲▼ ▲▼ ▲▼ ▲▼ ▲▼ ▲▼ ▲▼ ▲▼

Religious Architecture—Catholic, Protestant, and Russian Orthodox

The Eastern Orthodox Church shared with the Catholic Church an appreciation for the value of art in the service of religion, best represented by the construction of elaborate cathedrals and frequent use of religious icons in public worship and private devotion. Following are photographs of church architecture representing the three main religious traditions discussed in this chapter: Roman Catholic, Protestant, and Russian Orthodox.

The first photo shows St. Basil's Cathedral in Moscow, built from 1555 to 1561 by Ivan IV (Ivan the Terrible). The second photo shows St. Peter's Basilica in Rome, built in the early sixteenth century around the beginning of the Reformation. In fact, the profits from the indulgences sold by Tetzel in Germany were intended to help finance the construction of St. Peter's. Tetzel's campaign prompted Luther to write his *Ninety-Five Theses*. The third photo, from a later period, is a good example of Protestant architecture: eighteenth-century John Wesley's Chapel in Bristol, England.

Describe the differences in architectural style of these three structures. What does the architecture of each tradition reveal about the religious or spiritual vision that inspired it? Can one draw conclusions about the differences among the three religions and their approach to the sacred by a comparison of church architecture as represented by these three examples?

St. Basil's Cathedral, Mosow *(Photograph by Thomas S. Pearson)*

St. Peter's Basilica, Rome (*Photograph by Pasquale Simonelli*)

John Wesley's Chapel, Bristol, England *(Photograph Kenneth L. Campbell)*

For more information about St. Basil's Cathedral and other historical sites in Moscow, visit www.moscow.info/red-square/st-basils-cathedral.aspx.

Additional views of St. Peter's Basilica in Rome can be seen at http://saintpetersbasilica.org.

For interior views and more information about John Wesley's Chapel in Bristol, go to www.newroombristol.org.uk.

such as ritual, ceremony, and how many fingers one used when making the sign of the cross.

Both western and Russian Christianity experienced a transition in the early modern period from communal religion toward faith as a more personal and private matter. Russians inspired by the reform movement shared with European Protestants and reform-minded Catholics a belief in a practical form of Christianity that placed a greater emphasis on how one lived and treated others than on specific forms of worship and ritual behavior. Protestant reforms had already been adopted by a number of powerful nobles in the neighboring kingdom of Poland-Lithuania; by mid-century reform ideas were appearing in Moscow. Russian church councils met four times from 1547 to 1554 to consider possible reforms and different ideas for ending church abuses. Some heretics condemned by the 1554 council may have been influenced by Protestant ideas.

Much sixteenth-century reform focused on strengthening the prestige of priests and bishops to compensate for the declining reputation of Orthodox monks. The major initiative for change, however, did not occur until a new patriarch of the Russian Orthodox Church named Nikon (1605–1681) committed to the reform cause in 1652. Nikon wished to restore Russian conformity with Greek Orthodox observances and to reduce the extent of state control over the church. It was as if Pope Leo X had written the *Ninety-Five Theses* and played the role of Martin Luther in the Catholic Church in 1517. In Europe, Protestants regarded the pope as the Antichrist; in Russia, conservative Christians saw the Antichrist in the reformer, Nikon. In Europe, reformers challenged and then broke with the establishment; in Russia, reformers were the establishment.

Nikon was responding in part to the concerns and direction of Tsar Alexis, who particularly objected to the practice at Orthodox services of different priests reciting separate parts of the liturgy at the same time as a way of shortening the service, which they otherwise rushed through, reading the words so fast that no one could understand what they were saying. Alexis wanted a dignified, orderly service that would reflect the grandeur of the religious vision for which it stood. He did not care if the service were longer; in fact, he saw that as one of the potential benefits of reform. The tsar left it entirely to Nikon to introduce his reforms in a timely manner. Nikon launched a wave of liturgical reforms from 1652 to 1658. He introduced a revised psalter in 1652 and mandated a series of changes in church ritual that included folding three fingers instead of two when making the sign of the cross and altering the number of alleluias sung before the reading of the gospel. Behind the concern for ritual, however, lay a desire to make the Russians better Christians and to introduce a reformed Christianity that stressed piety and morality.

Nikon's dedication to reform provoked a hostile reaction from other leading members of the church, including the archpriest Avvakum (ca. 1620–1682), who became the leader of an opposition movement of "Old Believers." Avvakum had joined a conservative movement when he was young that convinced him of the need to renew Russian spirituality and morality through stricter observance of ecclesiastical ritual. Avvakum and his supporters regarded Nikon as a heretic and said so in 1653. Avvakum believed that any change in the church would undermine traditional Russian society and Russian autocracy, all of which he saw as integrated into a coherent organic whole. To Avvakum, the church had already been permeated by too many Western European influences and become too subordinate to the Russian state. For him, orthodoxy gave meaning and order to the lives of the Russian people. It no longer mattered if translations were correct or incorrect—what mattered was not upsetting the faith that people placed in the traditions of the church and the mystical role that it played in their lives. Change could be seen as calling into question the salvation of all those who had worshipped under the old system. The Old Believers regarded these changes as nothing short of apocalyptic.

Some of the arguments and concerns of the Old Believers echoed those that Catholics had directed at the Protestant Reformation in sixteenth-century Europe. Both groups saw themselves as the defenders of true Christianity, even though the religious cultures that both represented had themselves evolved and changed over time. Catholic apologists continually stressed the importance of church tradition and encouraged believers to put their trust in an institution that had survived for over a thousand years. The Catholic Church had provided a sense of meaning and order to the lives of its parishioners through an annual cycle of holy days and a ritualistic set of ceremonies and observances. If anything, the Russian Orthodox religion permeated all aspects of thought and belief to an even greater extent than the Catholic Church did in Europe. The western Christian church cut across national boundaries throughout Europe—in fact, nationalist sentiment contributed in some places to the desire or willingness to break with Rome. The Russian Orthodox Church had become thoroughly entangled with what it meant to be Russian. Furthermore, Russia had no secular culture that corresponded to that of Western Europe or even the Byzantine Empire before 1453.

In Russia religious conflict took the form of a schism in the Russian Orthodox Church, known as the *raskol*. Avvakum and the Old Believers left the church rather than worship according to new service books. (Many English Catholics had the same reaction when the government of Edward VI instituted the Book of Common Prayer in the mid-sixteenth century.)

Although Nikon was deposed in 1666, his reforms became a part of Russian Orthodoxy and the Old Believers were declared heretics the following year. Just as much as the Catholic leaders in the west, the Russian authorities regarded schism as dangerous, treasonous, and heretical. Some leading members of the Old Believers had their tongues cut out prior to execution. Others, including Avvakum, languished in prison in the frozen north beyond the Arctic Circle. More than 20,000 fanatical sectarians died between 1672 and 1691, including many of self-immolation in churches that they had set on fire in the hopes that they could be with Christ before the final judgment. Many left Russia to escape persecution; Siberia, China, and the Americas were among their destinations.

By the end of the seventeenth century, reform had taken root in the Russian Orthodox Church, which came to be governed by a Holy Synod instead of the pope-like patriarch. The *raskol* officially ended in 1690, but the Old Believers, or variants thereof, remained a strong sectarian force into the nineteenth century and persisted into the twentieth. Not all Old Believers were superstitious fanatics blindly adhering to past traditions. They continued to provide an alternative approach to spirituality than that offered by the dominant clerical and political elite.

Conclusion

The religious reformation that began in Europe in the sixteenth century can be considered one of the most significant events that shaped world religious history. The Reformation was a series of movements that differed significantly from each other, but, when taken together, resulted in the sudden and rapid polarization of the monolithic Christian church into two distinct groups–the Roman Catholic and the Protestant. But Protestant and Catholic political leaders shared some important commonalities. For all their differences, Protestants and Catholics still worshipped the same God, regarded the Bible as their primary religious source, held the same conception of fallen humanity contaminated by original sin and needing the intercession of Christ as redeemer, and believed in the competing forces of good and evil in the world. These beliefs manifested themselves in the sixteenth and seventeenth centuries in the European-wide persecution of people believed to be witches in league with the devil (see Chapter 4 in Volume II). Both Catholics and Protestants relied heavily on logic and rational argument to defend their positions, regarding God as a being whose existence could be proved and demonstrated. Many Catholics and Protestants believed that two religions could not coexist within the same state, although in practice Catholics and Protestants in a number of local communities across Europe found a way to do just that. Both Catholic and Protestant rulers regarded religious uniformity as a prerequisite for political loyalty. Both persecuted religious minorities and feared countries with a different religion as real or potential enemies. Thus religion came to shape much of the political discourse that followed the Reformation.

The Reformation had a number of social consequences, although these have been widely debated among historians. The Reformation was in some ways related to the development of a more individualistic society, though which was the cause and which the effect is a complicated matter. The Reformation offered alternative views on marriage, sexuality, education, the role of women in society, and poor relief. If the period did not fundamentally alter the patriarchal and hierarchical nature of European society, it both reflected and contributed to social changes that did affect the lives of individual men and women, especially in those lands most affected by the Reformation. Finally, because the Reformation movement coincided with a period of European exploration and overseas travel, the religious controversies of Europe were transported to the far corners of the globe within a relatively short period of time.

1. What were the decisive factors and events leading to Martin Luther's break with the Roman church?
2. Discuss the social consequences of the Reformation. In particular, what impact did the Reformation have on women? Would attitudes have changed in this period independent of the religious changes that were occurring?
3. Describe the response of the Roman Catholic Church to the challenge of the Reformation. Which specific responses were most effective? Least effective? Why?
4. Why were politics and religion so closely intertwined during the sixteenth century? How did this relationship differ in different countries? What accounted for these differences?
5. How did the reform movement in Russia compare to the European Reformation? How was the schism in Russian Orthodox Christianity similar to and different from the schism between the Protestant and Catholic churches?

Suggestions for Further Reading

Dillenberger, John, ed. 1961. *Martin Luther: Selections from His Writings*. Garden City, NY: Anchor Books.

Gregory, Brad S. 1999. *Salvation at Stake: Christian Martyrdom in Early Modern Europe*. Cambridge, MA: Harvard University Press.

Kaplan, Benjamin. 2007. *Divided by Faith: Religious Conflict and the Practice of Toleration in Early Modern Europe*. Cambridge, MA: Belknap Press of Harvard University Press.

Lindberg, Carter, ed. 2000. *The European Reformations Sourcebook*. Oxford: Wiley-Blackwell.

MacCulloch, Diarmaid. 2005. *The Reformation: A History*. New York: Penguin Books.

Mantel, Hillary. 2009. *Wolf Hall*. New York: Henry Holt.

Naphy, William G. 2003. *Calvin and the Consolidation of the Genevan Reformation*. Louisville, KY: Westminster John Knox Press.

Suggested Websites

http://englishhistory.net/tudor/primary.html

This website contains a good sampling of primary source documents from sixteenth-century England, many of which relate to the Reformation and the developments discussed in this chapter.

www.fordham.edu/halsall/sbook1y.html

This website contains a selection of primary sources from Luther, Calvin, and the English Reformation, as well as a section devoted to the Catholic Reformation.

www.mun.ca/rels/reform/index.html

This website also contains a selection of important documents related to the Reformation, as well as a collection of pictures connected to the topic.

www.tudorhistory.org

This website contains many features related to sixteenth-century English history, including brief biographies of all the rulers of the period and the wives of Henry VIII, primary sources, and a guide to films.

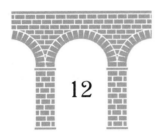

12   The Age of European
      Expansion, ca. 1550–1650

In the second half of the sixteenth century, the rivalry between Catholicism and Protestantism extended overseas. In the initial push toward overseas expansion, both the Portuguese and the Spanish officially proclaimed the spread of Christianity their top priority. A dozen members each from the Franciscan and Dominican orders followed Cortés to Mexico in the 1520s intent on ensuring the conversion of the Indians and defending them from oppressive treatment. With the spread of the Reformation in Europe, Catholic orders made a great effort to increase the number of Catholics worldwide. The Jesuits concentrated their efforts on Asia precisely because of the large population there that offered the possibility of increasing the numerical superiority of Catholics over Protestants. Protestant missionary efforts did not approach the scale of the Catholics in this period, partly because Protestants had their hands full defending their interests in Europe and in part because they lacked the religious orders that played such an important role in Catholic missions.

However, the continuation of European exploration and expansion after 1550 was mainly carried out under the auspices of the national states for political and economic reasons. The English and the French focused their efforts primarily upon North America beginning in the 1530s and intensifying around the beginning of the seventeenth century, though both hoped to find new passages to the East with an eye toward the lucrative spice trade. In the early seventeenth century the newly independent Dutch succeeded in gaining a significant portion of the spice trade and emerged as a commercial power in the East Indies. European influence was felt throughout the Americas and significant parts of Africa and Asia, including increased contact with China, India, and Japan.

Japan provides a good basis for cross-cultural comparisons with Europe during this period. Contemporary developments in Japan greatly affected that country's response to Western contact. Japanese society was undergoing considerable change at the time when it first came into contact with Europeans. The case of Japan illustrates the ways in which the response to European contact and cross-cultural interaction depended largely on internal factors within an individual society. The internal changes in sixteenth-century Japan

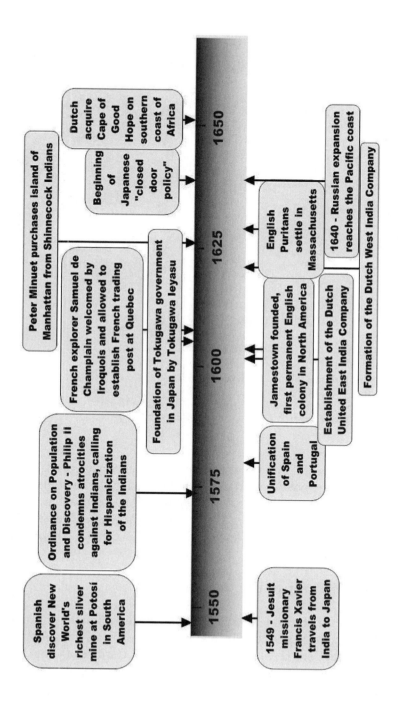

Spanish discover New World's richest silver mine at Potosi in South America

Ordinance on Population and Discovery - Philip II condemns atrocities against Indians, calling for Hispanicization of the Indians

Peter Minuet purchases Island of Manhattan from Shinnecock Indians

French explorer Samuel de Champlain welcomed by Iroquois and allowed to establish French trading post at Quebec

Foundation of Tokugawa government in Japan by Tokugawa Ieyasu

Beginning of Japanese "closed door policy"

Dutch acquire Cape of Good Hope on southern coast of Africa

1549 - Jesuit missionary Francis Xavier travels from India to Japan

Unification of Spain and Portugal

Jamestown founded, first permanent English colony in North America

Establishment of the Dutch United East India Company

English Puritans settle in Massachusetts

1640 - Russian expansion reaches the Pacific coast

Formation of the Dutch West India Company

1550   1575   1600   1625   1650

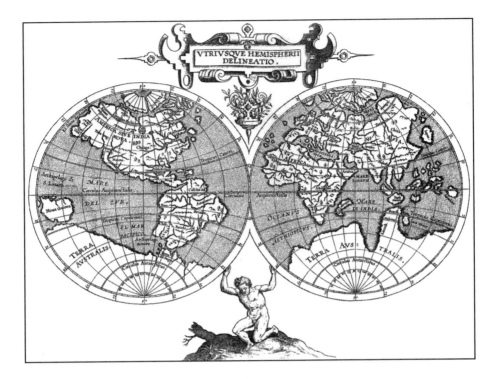

Wytfliet's Map of the World, 1598. This map illustrates the vast portion of the globe that had been discovered by the close of the sixteenth century. Colonization of the New World was well under way. From *The Scottish Geographical Magazine* 16, no. 1 (1900). (*Courtesy of the University of Texas Libraries, The University of Texas at Austin*)

also provide a useful basis of comparison with the changes experienced in European society, politics, and the economy during the same period. In the century following 1550, a world network of trade developed and patterns of cross-cultural interaction emerged that significantly influenced the future of both the West and all areas with which it came into contact. This chapter tells the story of those influences.

The Iberian Empires in Latin America

In the course of the sixteenth century Spain incorporated most of Latin America—the areas collectively colonized by the Spanish and Portuguese in South America, Central America, Mexico, and the Caribbean—into its empire and developed a bureaucracy and an imperial system to govern its American colonies. The Spanish government in the New World during the post-conquest period concentrated on ruling the Indians through law rather than military force, making this period very different from the early stages of Spanish presence in the Americas (see Chapter 10 in this volume). Representatives of the colonial governments also developed closer relationships with the natives through intermarriage and unofficial ties such as becoming godparents. Colonial officials, therefore, although they surely profited from their positions, frequently governed in such a way that took native interests into account. As early as 1512 in the Laws of Burgos, King Ferdinand had attempted to restrict exploitation of the Indians, but these laws had little impact. Indians continued to suffer under Spanish rule because of the continued expectation that they would pay tribute to the Spanish. In 1573 the Spanish government issued the Ordinance on Discovery and Population, which outlawed further colonial conquests in the Americas and proclaimed that the main goals of Spain there were to promote Christianity and to protect the natives.

Economically, the Spaniards who immigrated to the New World dominated the natives. Spanish colonists exploited the resources of Latin America, including sugar, gold, silver, mercury, coffee, and cacao, without offering much in return. In the 1530s and 1540s the Spaniards began exploiting several gold-fields and silver mines in South America; the richest silver mine was located at Potosí in what is now south-central Bolivia, discovered by the Spaniards in 1545. The Spanish colonies served a critical function in the Spanish economy by contributing bullion that was available for trade with other nations, which in turn produced taxes and revenues for the monarchy. Spanish colonial authorities did not encourage the development of native industry. Instead, they insisted that the colonies fulfill their economic function as a market for European goods. Spanish colonists shipped raw materials from the colonies to Spain where they were exchanged for manufactured goods, especially weapons and textiles, to be sold in the colonies.

The Spanish forced the native populations of their colonies to work in the goldfields, silver mines, and other enterprises—with brutal consequences for the everyday life of the natives. In Peru, for example, the Spanish adapted the native practice of work rotation (called a *mit'a*) to their own purposes, assigning workers to places where colonial landowners needed labor. Three-thousand such *mitayos* worked in the mercury mines in Huancavelica, enduring long hours, harsh working conditions, and additional health risks—particularly pneumonia and respiratory problems—attendant to the handling of a toxic substance. The practice of bringing their families along with them to retain some semblance of a normal life away from their homes subjected children to work at an early age and exposed women to the threat of rape by Spanish colonists. In Brazil and other colonies, native women were sometimes forced to become prostitutes.

Cross-cultural interaction between Indians and Spaniards occurred most frequently in the work that Indians did for the Spanish on their farms, ranches, and various enterprises. Traditional village life became interrupted when Indians relocated closer to Spanish settlements and sources of employment. New employment patterns and geographical mobility weakened traditional social structures in Indian villages. The Indians ended up assimilating to Spanish ways simply because of wider exposure to them; even those who never left their villages became influenced by those who had. Intermarriage did occur between Europeans and the natives; as a general rule, those with the most European blood had a higher position in society than those with less European blood. When more Spanish women started to arrive in the colonies, Spanish men became less likely to marry Indian women though they did not hesitate to have sexual relationships with them. Those of mixed blood were called *mestizos*, who had a higher position than full-blooded Indians, who in turn ranked higher than Africans. In general, Indian lords and nobles assimilated more rapidly and to a greater degree than the common people.

Many Indians, including the lords, retained some commitment to their native culture and way of life, even as they adapted to some of the new ways brought by the Spanish. For example, native religion did not disappear entirely, but it survived only surreptitiously. Christianity dominated and most people adopted it, but nonetheless preserved some of their ancient traditions. For example, the Mayans retained a belief that Mayan lords would rule as vassals of Jesus after the Second Coming. The Spanish and the Portuguese both did their best to Christianize the Indians, especially those who lived closest to European settlements, but never fully succeeded in eradicating traditional influences. The unchristian nature of many aspects of Spanish and Portuguese rule in the colonies actually encouraged the Indians to retain traditional elements of both native and African religions in the colonies, including the practice of sorcery as a means of gaining some control over their lives. In general, religious leaders tended to defend the rights of the natives. In 1567, the bishop of Yucatan, Francisco de Toral, wrote to the monarch, "It is a great weight on the conscience to see the helpless natives so vexed: I have seen a daughter taken from her mother to serve blacks and mestizos, and a wife from her husband, and other hardships with the tributes, so that the natives are at the point of despair."

The Erosion of Spanish Commercial Power and the Rise of the Dutch

The expansion of Spain in the Americas coincided with a period of dramatic inflation in Europe that has become known as the price revolution. Even in the sixteenth century, a popular theory attributed the rise in prices to the increase in gold and silver bullion imported into Europe from America by Spain. It appears, however, that the increased circulation of bullion only contributed to a trend caused primarily by the rise in population. More people meant increased competition for land, goods, and resources. The growing military and administrative needs of most European states, themselves affected by rising prices, meant increased taxation, which in turn led to even higher prices in an inflationary spiral. Prices increased throughout the sixteenth century, despite the actions of European governments to control inflation, primarily by debasing their coinage (a step that was usually unpopular because it devalued money). The resulting social hardships owing to the failure of wages to keep pace with prices were exacerbated by the bullion imported from the New World, while interest in importing more riches as a solution to inflation only continued to grow.

The discovery of the Americas and the riches found there in the form of gold and silver, especially silver, both encouraged additional participants in the process of European expansion and facilitated European trade with Asia. Europeans now had an abundance of precious metals to exchange for highly valued Asian goods and spices or African slaves. Thus, economic motivations remained paramount for many interested in overseas enterprises; the only way to get an expedition financed was to offer hope of sufficient returns on the investment.

American silver and gold did not make Spain a wealthy country compared to her European competitors. As early as 1551, the Spanish monarchy permitted Spanish bullion to leave the country in exchange for goods or loans. The bullion imported by the Spanish ended up contributing to the wealth of other Europeans, including the Dutch, who had significantly more shipping capacity than the Spanish. Spain did not even dominate trade in the Atlantic, where other nations had more shipping tonnage. Spain's competitors were even controlling most of the silver trade by the end of the sixteenth century, a fact not lost on contemporaries who alluded to the amount of Spanish silver going to England and the Low Countries.

The Spanish blamed many of their problems on the Jews or New Christians (converts to Christianity from Judaism) and stepped up persecution at home even as Jews received a measure of tolerance in the empire. Alternatively, the Spanish blamed foreign merchants and bankers who they believed were taking advantage of the Spanish by charging high prices or interest rates on loans. This tendency to look for scapegoats prevented the Spanish from taking steps such as reinvesting money in Spanish industries and businesses to rectify an unfavorable balance of trade caused by the fact that Spain simply used its wealth from America to purchase goods and weapons that were being manufactured elsewhere.

The Dutch were the main beneficiaries of the erosion of Spanish commercial power. They had the advantage of a relatively advanced economy that depended heavily on their role in redistributing goods throughout Europe. The entrepôt economy in which the Dutch stored and then reshipped commodities such as sugar greatly increased the wealth that became a basis of the country's power. Because the Netherlands had no state church, the country followed a policy of religious tolerance, attracting Jewish exiles from Spain and Portugal who made significant contributions to the Dutch economy. The Netherlands was also one of the most heavily urbanized countries in early modern Europe; its merchant class was highly motivated and accomplished in commerce and shipbuilding, providing an infrastructure that the government of the new nation could use to encourage expansion. Although the Netherlands was a small nation, the Dutch recognized that international trade could lead to great wealth.

Dutch trade with the East Indies became the single most important source of wealth that made the Netherlands such a prosperous and successful country in the seventeenth century. The United East India Company—known by its Dutch initials of VOC—benefited from the support of the Dutch government, which chartered the company in 1602 and allied itself with the rising and ambitious merchant elite. The VOC was an innovative company that retained a steady base of capital reserves, while simultaneously reinvesting in the company and dispersing some of the profits to individual investors. The income of the company's managers depended on their ability to increase the total volume of the company's trade since their commissions were based on a combination of profits, revenue, and investments. These factors contributed to the spectacular growth of the company and the competitive spirit that drove it. The Dutch shared with other European nations a mercantilist approach to trade, meaning that they believed that they could increase their trade only at the expense of their competitors. For that reason, the Dutch government granted the VOC military powers as well. The Dutch entered into negotiations for a monopoly of the spice trade in return for protection of the natives of the Spice Islands of the East Indies. The Dutch made alliances with some native rulers and forced others to acquiesce to their presence and control. To defend their trading areas from intruders and to organize their own trade, the Dutch began building fortresses and trading posts throughout the Spice Islands. The Dutch became the dominant power in the region by controlling key points and dealing, ruthlessly when necessary, with uncooperative islanders or their European rivals. They forcefully expelled the Portuguese from Amboina and the Spice Islands in 1605. They eliminated a British garrison from Amboina in 1623 and took Malacca from the Portuguese in 1641. The Dutch had become unrivalled and unchallenged in their position in the East Indies, strengthening their position still further by the acquisition of the Cape of Good Hope on the southern tip of Africa in 1652. Possession of the cape gave ships traveling between the Netherlands and the East Indies a place to stop for supplies, which greatly enhanced the chances of survival on those lengthy voyages.

English Exploration and Expansion

Although the English lost interest in colonization after some ill-fated adventures in the 1530s, their interest in the Americas picked up again during the reign of Elizabeth I for several reasons. First, England needed money and its rulers could not help but notice the hordes of gold and silver steadily sailing across the Atlantic on Spanish ships. Elizabeth, like other monarchs of the period, needed money for defense, administration, and maintenance of a lavish court that would earn the respect of her subjects and foreign ambassadors alike. Second, Spain represented a political threat to Elizabeth and to England, so any inroads the English made into Spain's source of treasure would be desirable (see Chapter 11 in this volume). In response to the Spanish threat, Queen Elizabeth at first gave unofficial support through members of her Privy Council to pirates such as John Hawkins (1532–1595) and Francis Drake (ca. 1540–1596) to raid Spanish ships sailing from the Caribbean to Spain and seize their cargoes of gold and silver. Although the pirates profited individually from the raids, plenty of Spanish bullion ended up in the English treasury. Third, England sought a new and shorter trade route to Asia in order to participate in the lucrative eastern trade in spices and other goods. More than 200 London merchants and government officials founded the Muscovy Company in 1553 for the express purpose of discovering just such a route.

In addition, ships in search of a northwest passage to Asia attempted to circumvent the North American landmass by sailing north of Canada. Although the search for a northwest passage was no more successful in reaching Asia than was the search for a northeastern route, the northwestern route did lead the English to Hudson Bay and the St. Lawrence River. Thus began English interest in the land that would become known as Canada, starting with the failed efforts of some Congregationalists to make a living out of catching walrus. Even if these discoveries brought no immediate benefit, they furthered the discussion in England of future plans for North America. Sir Humphrey Gilbert (ca. 1539–1583), the half-brother of Elizabeth's famous courtier, Sir Walter Raleigh (1552–1618), organized expeditions to North America in 1578 and 1583. Gilbert hoped to find a northwest passage to Asia, but he quickly turned his interest to colonization. Although the 1583 expedition ended in mutiny, shipwreck, and Gilbert's disappearance, Gilbert had helped to shift English policy regarding North America in the direction of colonization.

In 1607, Jamestown, Virginia, became the first English colony in North

William Bradford on Life and Farming in Early Massachusetts, ca. 1623

All this while no supply was heard of, neither knew they when they might expecte any. So they begane to thinke how they might raise as much tome [corn] as they could, and obtain a better crope then [sic] they had done, that they might not still thus languish in misery. At length, after much debate of things, the Govr (with the advice of the cheefest amongest them) gave way that they should set corve [corn] every man for his owne perticular, and in that regard trust to them selves; in all other thing to goe on in the general way as before. And so assigned to every family a parcel of land, according to the proportion of their number, for that end, only for present use (but made no devission for inheritance) and ranged all boys and youth under some familie. This had very good success, for it made all hands very industrious, so as much more torne [corn] was planted then [sic] other waise would have bene by any means the Govr or any other could use, and saved him a great deal of trouble, and gave farr better contente. The women now wente willingly into the feild, and tooke their litle-ons with them to set torne [corn]; which before would aleeg weaknes and inabilitie; whom to have compelled would have bene thought great tiranie [tyranny] and oppression.

The experience that was had in this commone course and condition, tried sundrie years and that amongst godly and sober men, may well evince the vanitie of that conceite of Plato's and other ancients applauded by some of [l]ater times; and that the taking away of propertie and bringing in communitie into a comone wealth would make them happy and [fl]ourishing; as if they were wiser than God. For this comunitie (so far as it was) was found to breed much confusion and discontent and retard much imployment that would have been to their benefite and comforte. For the young men, that were most able and fitte for labour and servise, did repine that they should spend their time and streingth to work for other men's wives and children without any recompense. The strong, or man of parts, had no more in devission of victails and cloaths then [sic] he that was weake and not able to doe a quarter the other could; this was thought injuestice. The aged and graver men to be ranked and equalised in labours and victails, cloaths etc., with the meaner and yonger sort, thought it some indignite and disrespect unto them. And for men's wives to be commanded to doe servise for other men, as dresing their meate, washing their cloaths, etc., they deemd it a kind of slaverie, neither could many husbands well brooke it. Upon the poynte all being to have alike, and all to doe alike, they thought them selves in the like condition, and [one] as good as another; and so, if it did not cut off those relations that God hath set amongst men, yet it did at least much diminish and take off the mutuall respects that should be preserved amongst them. And would have bene worse if they had been men of another condition. Let [n]one objecte this is men's corruption, and nothing to the course it selfe. I answer, seeing all men have this corruption in them, God in his wisdome saw another course fiter for them.

> *Source:* William Bradford, *History of Plymouth Plantation*, ca. 1650, edited by William T. Davis (New York: Charles Scribner's Sons, 1908), pp. 216–217.
>
> **What does this passage reveal about life for the English colonists in the early years of their settlement in North America? What does it reveal about women's work and gender relations in the colony? Why does Bradford suggest that communal farming would not work? Do you agree with his assessment?**

America, not counting the "lost colony" of Roanoke off the coast of what is now North Carolina, which was founded in 1585 but abandoned within two years. The Jamestown settlers, of course, faced numerous obstacles. They had to familiarize themselves with the land and its inhabitants, on whom they initially depended for their survival. Disease, cold, and hunger took their toll in lives in the early years of the colony. The colonists faced internal divisions. The seemingly friendly Indians soon turned aggressive under their domineering ruler, Powhatan, who did not like the English infringing upon his empire and wished to see them dead or gone. The colony survived but floundered until the 1630s, when the colonists learned to grow a better quality of tobacco that could compete with that raised in Spanish territories.

The survival of the Jamestown colony proved that the English were in North America to stay. In 1620 the Pilgrim settlers, who sailed from England aboard the *Mayflower* in search of a place where they could worship as they pleased without government interference, established their colony at Plymouth, Massachusetts, having missed their intended destination of the island of Manhattan on the lower Hudson River. More Puritan immigrants followed them to Massachusetts in 1629. English Puritans disillusioned with the Personal Rule of Charles I (see Chapter 13 in this volume)—during which the king ruled for eleven years without calling Parliament—continued to leave for North America throughout the 1630s. Not everyone who left England did so for religious reasons; even in Massachusetts a large proportion of the settlers came for economic or personal reasons. The Catholic colony of Maryland, founded under the auspices of Charles I, depended on tobacco for its economic prosperity, as did Virginia. By 1650 about 50,000 Englishmen resided in the American colonies.

Life in the early years of the English colonies in North America was extremely harsh, especially in the earliest settlements of Jamestown and Plymouth. A high percentage of the early settlers died, and new immigrants continued to die at a high rate even after the initial founding. Illness stalked the colonists; women died at an especially high rate as the caretakers of their children when they became ill. In Plymouth, thirteen of the eighteen adult women among the original settlers died within six weeks of arriving, including the wife of the future governor William Bradford, Dorothy, who drowned by the *Mayflower*. The Pilgrims in the Plymouth colony struggled until about 1625.

Had it not been for the assistance and support of friendly Indians in both places, it is doubtful whether either colony would have survived at all. In Jamestown, colonists invited Indians to dine with them, sleep in their homes, and even to live with them in order to introduce them to English manners and lifestyles. In Plymouth, the Indians taught the colonists much about survival and the new land where they had decided to settle.

French Exploration and Expansion

French exploration in the Americas began with the efforts of the Florentine navigator Giovanni da Verrazano (1485–1528), who in 1523–1524 while searching for a passage to Asia sailed the length of the North American coast from Carolina in the south to Nova Scotia in the north. One of the first French explorers to follow Verrazano was Jacques Cartier (1491–1557), who in 1534 made the first of his three voyages to America, sailing to Newfoundland and exploring some of the Canadian interior via the St. Lawrence River. Although no permanent French settlement resulted from these early explorations, they did stimulate further French interest in the New World.

Civil wars of religion that tore France apart in the second half of the sixteenth century postponed further French ventures in North America. Interest in exploring and colonizing the New World revived when France began to recover during the reign of Henry IV (1589–1610). A group of investors that included merchants from Rouen and prominent members of the French court successfully petitioned Henry IV for exclusive rights to the fur trade with the Indians in North America. In 1601 they asked Samuel de Champlain (1567–1635), who had just returned from an expedition to the West Indies, to explore the lands near the mouth of the St. Lawrence River to find a suitable site for a trading colony. Like many other European explorers, Champlain was also motivated by a sense of religious calling to bring Christianity to the natives.

But when Champlain reached the area, he discovered that the rich fishing areas of the North Atlantic were crowded with fishermen from other European countries. These Europeans had already established a rudimentary trade with the natives, making huge profits by exchanging everyday goods such as combs, copper brooches, toys, hatchets, axes, iron pots, and fishhooks for the Indians' pelts and furs. Furs, especially beaver skins, were in great demand in Europe and could be sold for as much as twenty times what they cost. Such profits had attracted French interests in Canada in the first place.

Seeking uncharted territory on which he could set up a trading post and establish a colony, Champlain sailed further inland up the St. Lawrence. He founded the first permanent and successful French settlements in North America at Port Royal in 1605 and at Quebec in 1608. Champlain's—and the French government's—interest in exploration, however, extended beyond establishing New World colonies and trading with the native inhabitants. The search for a northwest passage to the East Indies and its lucrative spice trade continued. No one yet knew the size of the North American landmass or how far beyond it lay Asia and its treasures.

Champlain encouraged the French government to send settlers to the New World even as he continued to explore the interior of the continent, never abandoning hope of finding a passage to Asia. But Frenchmen did not emigrate in the same numbers as the English prior to 1650. French Protestants, known as Huguenots, faced persecution at home, but French settlements in the New World offered them no safe haven. When the Huguenots did leave France in the seventeenth century, they went to the Dutch colony of New Amsterdam (later New York) rather than to French Canada.

The Effects of European Colonization in North America

The effects of European colonization in North America varied by region because of the varying nature of the settlers from different countries and the Native American tribes who already resided there. For example, in the Pimería Alta, which comprised what is now northern Mexico and southern Arizona, tribes such as the Pueblos—who had lived in the region for centuries—generally resided in permanent settlements along rivers, possessed an agrarian economy, and had a more structured social organization than some other tribes. The economy of these southwestern tribes depended on raising crops, maintaining livestock, cultivating gardens and orchards, and making textiles and pottery for interregional trade, though some groups in areas of higher elevation still supplemented farming with hunting and gathering. The Pueblo generally (but not always) accommodated themselves to the Spanish colonists, tolerating the construction of Catholic churches and learning to weave wool from the sheep that the foreigners had imported to the region. By contrast, the Navajos and Apaches, who moved into the southwest from the north only in the early sixteenth century, fiercely resisted Spanish control. These two tribes were more nomadic, hunting buffalo and using dogs to pull their possessions on travois. Northeastern tribes, conversely, relied on a combination of trade and agriculture, the Hurons, or Wyandots as they called themselves, being the most prolific traders. Trading largely in furs, they traveled frequently and spread out their settlements along what is now the border between the United States and Canada from Lake Michigan eastward.

Oftentimes relations were peaceful, but wars between Indians and Europeans represented one major effect of European colonization between 1550 and 1650. The Spanish fought the Apaches and the Pueblos in order to settle in northern New Mexico in the 1590s. The victorious Spanish treated their enemies harshly, forcing women between twelve and twenty-two into servitude, killing hundreds of male rebels, and cutting off the hands of two Hopi prisoners as a message to the Hopis about the futility of resistance. Indians continued to resist nonetheless. The Spanish fought the Navajos and Pueblos in New Mexico in 1606. A revolt by the Zunis against the Spaniards in 1633 in which a number of Spanish soldiers and two missionaries were killed demonstrated Spanish vulnerability, even though the Spanish did retaliate. War continued intermittently for years, as it did between English settlers and Indians in Virginia and Massachusetts. In Virginia war with the confederation of tribes known as the Powhatans broke out in 1609 and again in 1622, when a large-scale massacre by Indians took the lives of 347 colonists, more than 30 percent of the colonial population at that time. When news of this tragedy reached Massachusetts, the Pilgrims turned from pacifism to aggression toward the Massachusetts Indians, who became the victims of an attack led by Myles Standish (ca. 1584–1656).

Throughout North America from 1550 to 1650, Native Americans suffered a dramatic decline in their population from the combined effects of warfare and disease. Some of the highest mortality rates occurred among the Indian tribes that the Spanish encountered in Florida. European diseases that afflicted the Indians included chicken pox, measles, smallpox, scarlet fever, and typhoid. In the north both the Huron nation and the Iroquois suffered from regular epidemics that resulted from European contact in the first half of the seventeenth century. To take just one tribe as an example, historians estimate that the Huron Indians declined from a population of 32,000 to 10,000, mainly from exposure to European diseases, by the mid-seventeenth century. But the impact of disease went both ways; most scholars believe that Europeans first became exposed to syphilis in the New World and took it back home with them.

American Indians participated in a cross-cultural exchange with Europeans and were not easily subdued or merely the passive victims of European expansion. Indians preserved much of their heritage and tribal organization even in the face of the challenges and new realities presented by the European presence. They continued to shape the history of their native land, often in collaboration with the English, Spanish, French, and Dutch. Indians used the land productively for farming, growing tobacco, beans, maize, pumpkins, and squash, teaching many of their techniques to English settlers. They understood the necessity and principles of soil rejuvenation, planting different crops in the same fields in order to conserve the soil. They used fire to keep the woodlands under control.

As political instability and religious intolerance in England drove more settlers across the Atlantic to North America, however, the newcomers appropriated ever more land. The colonists justified their appropriation of the land by perpetuating the idea that the Indians were "savages" and that the English brought them the benefits of civilization. This argument contradicted earlier reports about the native people by such writers as Thomas Harriot (1560–1621), who had purposefully emphasized the friendly and peaceful, if somewhat exotic, nature of the Indians in order to encourage future settlement in the New World. Having accompanied two expeditions in 1585 and 1586, he based his information on firsthand knowledge of the native population, two members of which were brought back to England as living proof of Harriot's assessment. Before long, however, some English writers began to argue that the Indians did not possess the capacity for civilization, equating them with beasts or even demons. Convinced of their own superiority over the Indians, English settlers claimed that they would make better use of the land, even that they had a divine imperative for their "taming" of the land.

The relationship between Indians and French explorers and colonists differed significantly from that between Indians and English settlers. In the early seventeenth century Champlain negotiated with the Algonquin Indians in Quebec to allow the French to settle in their lands, convincing them that the French had come to assist them with their crops and in other ways. Relationships between the French and the native inhabitants were generally cordial, revolving primarily around the fur trade. The French did not come to North America in large numbers to establish their own settlements isolated from the natives. Since they were more interested in trade with the Indians or converting them to Christianity, the French established their posts and missions near the natives' established villages.

In 1609 the Dutch joined in the settlement of North America when the English explorer Henry Hudson claimed the territory that later became New York for the Netherlands. The Dutch opened trading relations with the various tribes inhabiting the lower Hudson River valley, including the Manhattans and the Mohicans. Before long the Dutch were trading with the Iroquois as well, offering knives, tools, and guns in exchange for furs and food. In 1626, Peter Minuit, the Dutch governor of the colony of New Netherlands, bought the island of Manhattan from the Shinnecock Indians. This sale was indicative of the attitude of the northeastern tribes toward land, which they did not think of in terms of permanent possession.

Whereas the first English settlers came to farm and the French and Dutch came to trade, the Spanish came to the southwest to establish huge estates that would enrich them and enhance their social status. Prior to 1650, relatively few Spaniards attempted to settle in the Pimería Alta; those who did differed significantly from the earlier conquistadores bent on conquest. The Spaniards did not attempt to push the Indians off their land, but rather to employ them as workers on their lands and estates. Indians assisted the Spaniards in all areas of the economy—working in their fields, constructing their homes and churches, producing their clothing, and transporting their goods. A process of assimilation occurred in the Americas during the post-conquest period that was encouraged by a 1573 Spanish ordinance calling for the Hispanicization of the Indians but also the preservation of Indian society. Indians adopted some Spanish ways (and vice versa) in the form of different tools, foods, clothing, and language. But not all tribes readily accepted Spanish influence. The Hopis, for example, were a Pueblo tribe that completely retained their native language and rituals that connected them to their gods. To aid in the process of assimilation, priests and members of religious orders established Catholic churches throughout the southwest, usually associated with established towns or estates rather than as separate missions, at least in this early period. The Catholic clergy provided education for children of prominent native families and provided religious training and services for the native population.

The French also actively sought the conversion of the Indians to Christianity. French Jesuit missionaries penetrated farther into the interior of the Huron nation than any other Europeans and achieved a high rate of conversion among the Hurons, especially during the 1640s. The Jesuits became more successful the more they learned to accept the (to them) strange ways of the Hurons and to refrain from imposing the same moral standards as they would expect of European Christians. As elsewhere, the Jesuits adopted a greater level of flexibility than might have other missionaries and here they reaped the dividends. The Jesuits were successful because they tried to bridge the two cultures instead of imposing one on the other. French missionaries also benefited from the war between the Algonquin-Huron alliance and the Iroquois, since French support made their allies more favorably disposed toward their Christian religion.

Meanwhile, back in Europe, expansion stimulated intellectual and scientific thought, technological development, and commercial initiative. The travels of Europeans and the expansion of European interests around the world opened up new horizons, even for those who remained at home. Thoughtful Europeans did not just assume their superiority over foreign cultures, but reexamined European society in light of the new knowledge that they gained from them. Travel literature flourished, especially in the seventeenth century. The chronicles of Bernal Diaz del Castillo were published in Spain for the first time in 1632, more than 100 years since he joined Cortés on his expedition to Mexico and over fifty years after his death. Europeans started to develop an interest not only in the experience of other Europeans but in the populations with which they came into contact. In 1642 Roger Williams's Algonquian-English dictionary became the first published dictionary of a Native American language.

European Expansion into Africa and the Slave Trade

The sixteenth and seventeenth centuries witnessed a vast increase in the amount of cross-cultural contact between Europeans and Africans, especially along the west coast of Africa, which the Portuguese began to explore and open up in the fifteenth century. Europeans and Africans traded a wide variety of commodities with each other. Both African and European merchants sought to maximize their profits and negotiate exchanges for goods that they could sell at much higher rates than they paid. Africans were interested in acquiring cloth and other goods that the Europeans could acquire in their growing trade with Asia, as well as European products, especially firearms, alcohol, fruits and vegetables, including eventually such American crops as cassava, maize, and sweet potatoes. European merchants discovered (or created) a demand in Europe for ivory, animal hides and pelts, and ostrich eggs and feathers, among other exotic items, in addition to their obvious interest in slaves, gems, gold, and other precious metals.

Slavery and the slave trade were not new to the African continent in the fifteenth century. A flourishing trade in slaves both in the Saharan and sub-Saharan regions had existed at least since the tenth century, part of a much larger trading network dominated largely by Arab merchants. Nor were African rulers and merchants averse to selling slaves to Europeans when they first became interested in the fifteenth century. In fact, the more interested the Europeans became in acquiring slaves, the more extensive became the search for slaves by African rulers in the interior of the continent.

A Portuguese sailor named Antam Gonçalves captured the first twelve African slaves to be imported into Portugal in 1441, only seven years after the first Portuguese journey around the coast of Guinea. Gonçalves had used force to capture his slaves, but the Africans had well developed defenses that prevented Europeans from taking slaves at will from coastal territories. The Portuguese then—partly by design but mainly out of necessity—sought friendly relations with the African leaders with whom they dealt and traded. Some Portuguese merchants began to station representatives in Africa in order to make arrangements with local merchants for subsequent shipments of slaves. By the late fifteenth century the Portuguese had concluded treaties and trade agreements with a number of African rulers, agreements that included the exchange of

European and Asian goods supplied by the Portuguese for slaves supplied by
the Africans. The Portuguese had also established a stronghold from which
they could manage and defend their African interests in their fortified castle
at São Jorga de Mina in present-day Ghana. African merchants, for their part,
began to install middlemen in coastal towns to negotiate and make deals with
the Portuguese. At first the Portuguese mainly took African slaves to Portugal
to supplement the local labor force, which already included slaves of Moor-
ish descent. But demand was limited and soon reached a saturation point
since Portuguese slave owners—who mainly employed slaves as domestic
servants—generally had no need for more than a dozen slaves at the most.

In 1515, with the first direct transport of African slaves from Africa to
America, a new chapter in the history of the slave trade began. The English
entered the slave trade in 1562, when John Hawkins obtained about 300 slaves
in Sierra Leone and transported them to Hispaniola to sell to his Spanish
enemies. Spain had become interested in buying slaves to compensate for a
labor shortage on its plantations and mines in the Americas. Estimates of the
numbers of slaves imported from Africa to the Atlantic islands and America
vary widely; the number was probably between 50,000 and 75,000 for the
sixteenth century (out of approximately 9.5 million in the entire history of
the Atlantic slave trade). The number of slaves imported to Spanish America
alone increased to about 125,000 in the first half of the seventeenth century.
While some Europeans and Africans expressed reservations even in this early
period about the moral validity of such an enterprise, those who were directly
involved showed little consideration for the humanity of the people they con-
signed to a life of servitude. Slaves transported to America had to endure the
horrid and unsanitary conditions of the voyage across the Atlantic known as
the "middle passage." Many died along the way from disease, ill-treatment, or
suicide. Prior to the journey, they were frequently held in cramped dungeons
in forts or castles built along the coast of West Africa.

African slaves did not meet their fate always with total resignation; recent
historians have cautioned against viewing them as merely passive victims
of this brutal enterprise. Some did try to escape during the boarding period,
preferring to risk drowning in the perilous Atlantic waters along the coasts
where this process took place than submit to being forcefully removed from
their home continent. Some jumped overboard while at sea, preferring death
to slavery. Ships transporting slaves had larger crews in order to prevent sui-
cides and rebellions. At home in Africa, vulnerable groups banded together
to relocate and build defenses to protect their freedom.

With the establishment of sugar plantations in America, the need for slaves
in the Spanish and Portuguese colonies increased exponentially. In addition,
the Spanish desperately needed slaves to fully exploit the Potosí silver mine

in Peru. The Spanish colonies had the greatest demand for slaves, as well as the money to be able to afford them. What they lacked was a trading presence along the African coasts. Since the Spanish did not have direct access to the African slave trade, which was dominated by the Portuguese along with Italian merchants and financiers, they granted licenses giving others the right to import slaves to the Spanish colonies in America. One could purchase a license from Spain in return for a flat sum and an agreement to pay a tax on each individual slave transported. Some in Spain objected to the harshness of the treatment accorded the Africans shipped to the Americas as slaves. Tomás de Mercado, a Dominican friar from Seville, had witnessed the conditions of slaves arriving in Mexico during the 1550s. In his *Practices and Contracts of Merchants* (1569), he described them as "cheated, violated, assaulted, and despoiled." But Mercado spoke only as an isolated individual; the Dominican order issued no formal condemnation of the slave trade or the licensing system.

The unification of Spain and Portugal under Philip II in 1580 gave the Portuguese merchants direct access to Spanish colonies until Portugal reasserted its independence in 1640. But Spain never succeeded in gaining complete control over the slave trade to its overseas dominions. Spanish colonists proved willing to pay lower prices to those willing to risk illegally selling slaves. Around the time that Portugal regained its independence (much to the chagrin of Portuguese slave merchants), the licensing system broke down. Spanish merchants could no longer afford the taxes or the risks associated with carrying slaves in seas increasingly frequented by pirates and foreigners. Although at first refusing to license further the upstart Portuguese, Spain eventually had to swallow its pride and use them, although it also granted an *asiento*—a long-term contract to import black slaves into Spanish America— to an Italian company from Genoa. But both the Portuguese and the Genoese had to subcontract their license to foreign ships. Spain now had to rely on the trading ships of its greatest enemies—the English and the Dutch—to meet the demand for slaves in its colonies.

The Shaping of the Past: The Formation of the Dutch West India Company

It did not take long for the Dutch after they proclaimed their independence from Spain to become involved in trade with Africa. Dutch merchants had successfully captured from the Portuguese the lion's share of the gold and ivory trade in West Africa by the end of the sixteenth century. In 1611, two years after the beginning of a twelve-year truce with Spain, the Dutch established Fort Nassau on the Gold Coast as a safe harbor for Dutch ships trading in West Africa. But they were excluded from the slave trade by Portugal's connection to Spain and their exclusion from Spain's colonial markets. This did not, however, dampen Dutch enthusiasm for exploiting commercial opportunities in the Caribbean and the American continents, and Dutch merchants soon began to penetrate Spanish waters across the Atlantic in search of trade.

In June 1621 Dutch merchants officially established the Dutch West India Company for the purpose of fostering the establishment of Dutch colonies across the Atlantic and collaborating in the triangular trade involving Europe, Africa, and the Americas. By 1622 the Dutch were building fifteen new ships a year to trade with Brazil and bring back enough sugar to keep the twenty-nine refineries then operating in the Netherlands in full operation. Still, profits were slow in coming for the new company. It tried and failed to take two prominent sugar provinces from the Portuguese in Brazil. Needing a permanent port from which to operate, the Dutch in 1628 took from the Spanish the port of Curaçao in the Antilles chain in the southern Caribbean. Two years later the situation changed when the Dutch finally succeeded in seizing a significant portion of northern Brazil from their Portuguese rivals. They now had their own sugar plantations in need of slaves and saw an opportunity to capture a portion of that lucrative trade at the expense of the fading Portuguese empire.

With this incentive, the West India Company in the late 1630s and early 1640s engineered a series of raids in which it took over virtually every important Portuguese settlement along the West African coast, beginning with the important fort of São Jorge de Mina in 1637. As a result of these conquests, the Dutch obtained much gold from the rich Gold Coast territory of Mina, so named because of its abundant mines. More importantly, the Dutch temporarily gained an almost complete domination of the slave trade, of which they retained a significant share well into the eighteenth century; their participation lasted even longer. At the height of this trade, in 1644, the Dutch bought almost 7,000 slaves in Africa for shipment to America. These raids did more to shape the history of this part of Africa and its relationship to the rest of the world than anything the Portuguese had done in the previous 200 years. Western Africa now permanently became part of a global economic system centered on Europe, linked through the Dutch not only to America and Europe but also to Southeast Asia, where the Dutch East India Company operated. One African historian has seen this as the beginning of the process that eventually led to European conquest of the entire continent.

The Dutch West India Company did not achieve any more significant successes after 1650. A revolt against Dutch rule in Brazil resulted by 1654 in the loss of all its territory there except for the relatively small territory of Suriname, which remained a colony of the Netherlands (Dutch Guiana) until 1975. The Portuguese regained their position in Angola in west-central Africa and islands in the Gulf of Guinea by 1648. Still, the activities of the Dutch West India

Company were of immense importance. It had established a permanent Dutch presence in Africa in its forts along the Gold Coast, where it remained the main trading partner of the Africans there until the eighteenth century. Dutch traders were instrumental in introducing sugar plantations in the Caribbean islands. They founded the Dutch colony of New Netherlands and had a significant impact on the commercial and cultural development of the part of North America that later became New York. The Dutch West India Company went out of business in 1794, but it had played a decisive role in shaping the history of the seventeenth century and of the triangular trade that defined the relationship between Europe, Africa, and the Americas for several hundred years.

European Missionary Activity in the Far East

Between 1550 and 1650 Europeans traveled eastward in increasing numbers, motivated by the same factors that motivated their expansion in the Americas and Africa: merchants' desire for new sources of greater profits, rulers' aspirations to increase their status and influence, and missionaries' longing to spread the Christian faith. The Society of Jesus (the Jesuits) and other orders of the Roman Catholic Church sent missionaries to Asia to gain converts. By the end of the sixteenth century, the economic goals of European expansion had merged with the agenda of the Counter-Reformation to gain as many adherents to the Catholic faith as possible. The large number of Catholic compared to Protestant missionaries allowed Catholics to claim that they did more to spread the gospel and bring more souls to Christ. The few Protestants who attempted to justify their lack of missionary activity could only muster lame excuses related to the Calvinist doctrine of predestination or the impending apocalypse. The Catholic missionary efforts of the late sixteenth and early seventeenth centuries in the Far East exposed to Christianity people who would otherwise have known little, if anything, about Western religion. But in the end the Chinese and Japanese proved much more receptive to trade and economic dealings with westerners—and they did not always accept those relations readily. Trade does not inherently challenge people's beliefs or the value of their cultural and philosophical heritage. The Tokugawa government in Japan outlawed Christian worship in 1614.

Francis Xavier (1506–1552), one of the first seven members of the Society of Jesus, began his missionary work in 1542 in the Portuguese-controlled city of Goa in southwest India. Achieving little success in India, Xavier moved on to the Spice Islands and in 1549 embarked for Japan. In 1551 he wrote to his order in Goa that he had converted over 100 Japanese to Christianity and encountered very little resistance in the process. Opposition, however, came from Japanese religious leaders, who tried to convince the local princes that they would lose power if they abandoned the native gods. The Jesuits depended on the sympathy of Japanese daimyo (nobles), finding several who supported the efforts of the society. Everywhere he went Xavier approached the task of conversion by learning the native language and translating basic Christian beliefs, prayers, and creeds to make Christianity accessible to the natives.

Cultural differences presented difficulties for Christian missionaries in Asia, particularly in China, the area to which the Jesuits turned their attention next. The Chinese attitude toward religion contrasted sharply with the rigid and generally intolerant European perspective. Chinese civilization had tolerated three major religious traditions—Confucianism, Daoism, and Buddhism—for centuries. Confucianism emphasizes social stability and the importance of the family, providing an underlying source of comfort and permanence in the face of political upheavals. Daoism emphasizes harmony with nature and allowing the cycles of nature, and history, to take their course without resisting them. Buddhism provides a sense of spirituality and indifference in the face of suffering. Chinese people commonly adhered to the beliefs of more than one religious tradition, not viewing them as mutually exclusive avenues to the truth.

Despite these differences, the Jesuits in particular encountered a friendly reception and provoked a good deal of interest from the Chinese, at least in the early stages of their mission. They tried to work with the Chinese and fit in, rather than present their ways as always superior. Knowing, for example, that the Chinese people viewed Buddhist monks with disdain, the Jesuits chose not to dress as priests or monks. Instead, they dressed in Chinese styles, wore expensive silk garments, and as early as 1592 allowed others to carry them in sedan chairs in order to gain the respect of the people. Their most prominent missionary in China, Matteo Ricci (1552–1610), studied Chinese assiduously and could speak it fluently by the time he settled in Nanchang in 1595, read Confucian literature, and studied Chinese philosophy. Jesuit missionaries such as Ricci achieved a high level of visibility in seventeenth-century China and won some converts, but not the mass conversions they might have hoped for. For all the efforts of the Jesuits to adapt themselves to Chinese culture, they did not succeed in undermining its underlying philosophical and religious foundation in the form of the three traditions of Confucianism, Daoism, and Buddhism. Furthermore, their adoption of Chinese styles and manners provoked criticism—and ultimately formal chastisement from the papacy for being too flexible.

Access more information and sources on the coming of Christianity to Asia at http://afe.easia.columbia.edu/tps/1450.htm#christianity.

Missionary Prospects for Converting
Asians to Christianity

The first excerpt is from the Jesuit missionary Francis Xavier, who assesses the problems in attempting to persuade the Indians to convert to Christianity. The second is from Hsu Kuang-chi, the Chinese tutor to the imperial household, who gives his explanation for giving Christianity a fair hearing. These excerpts make for two excellent comparisons: the first on why Asians would or would not have good potential for converting to Christianity, the second on how a European viewed Asians compared to how an Asian viewed Europeans.

In the first place, the whole race of Indians, as far as I have been able to see, is very barbarous; and it does not like to listen to anything that is not agreeable to its own manners and customs, which, as I say, are barbarous. It troubles itself very little to learn anything about divine things and things which concern salvation. Most of the Indians are of vicious disposition, and are adverse to virtue. Their instability, levity, and inconstancy of mind are incredible; they have hardly any honesty, so inveterate are their habits of sin and cheating. We have hard work here, both in keeping the Christians up to mark and in converting the heathen. And, as we are your children, it is fair that on this account you should take great care of us and help us continually by your prayers to God. You know very well what a hard business it is to teach people who neither have any knowledge of God nor follow reason, but think it a strange and intolerable thing to be told to give up their habits of sin, which have now gained all the force of nature by long possession.

The experience which I have of these countries makes me think that I can affirm with truth, that there is no prospect of perpetuating our Society out here by means of the natives themselves, and that the Christian religion will hardly survive us who are now in the country; so that it is continual supplies of ours should be sent out from Europe. . . .

The Portuguese in these countries are masters only of the sea and of the coast. On the mainland they have only the towns in which they live. The natives themselves are so enormously addicted to vice as to be little adapted to receive the Christian religion. They so dislike it that it is most difficult to get them to hear us if we begin to preach about it, and they think it like death to be asked to become Christians. So for the present we devote ourselves to keeping the Christians whom we have. Certainly, if the Portuguese were more remarkable for their kindness to the new converts, a great number would become Christians; as it is, the heathen see that the converts are despised and looked down upon by the Portuguese, and so, as is natural, they are unwilling to become converts themselves. For all these reasons there is no need for me to labor in these countries, and as I have learnt from good authorities that there is a country near China called Japan, the inhabitants of which are all heathen, quite untouched by Mussulmans or Jews, and very eager to learn what they do not know both in things divine and things natural, I have determined to go thither as soon as I can. . . .

—Francis Xavier, from India, to Ignatius Loyola, 1549

Source: From Henry James Coleridge, *The Life and Letters of St. Francis Xavier,* 2nd ed., 2 vols. (London: Burnes and Oates, 1890), 2:67–68, 70–71.

To what factors does Xavier attribute the difficulty of converting the Indians to Christianity? How accurate is his representation of the Indians likely to be? Why was he so quick to give up on the mission in India? Why did he decide to go to Japan instead?

———

Why then is it that during the eighteen hundred years since the Buddhistic religion came to the East, the ways of the world and the hearts of men have not been reformed, except it be because, though seeming to be true, that religion is false? . . .

If there be an absolute desire to have men do good in perfection, then the knowledge of serving Heaven, communicated by your majesty's courtiers, is truly competent to repair and augment the royal Institutes, to strengthen and maintain the arts of the literati, and to restore and correct the laws of Buddha. The proof of this is, that the nations of Europe which are contiguous to each other, and more than thirty in number, receiving and practicing this religion, during a thousand and some hundreds of years up to the present time, whether great or small, have alike been kind to each other; whether high or low, have alike enjoyed repose; their prescribed boundaries have required no guard; nor has their sovereignty been hereditary; throughout their whole domain, there have been no deceivers or liars; the vices of lewdness and theft from of old have never existed; no one would venture to take up an article dropped upon the highway; and even gates and doors of cities and houses it was not necessary to have closed by night. As to revolt and anarchy, rebels and insurgents, not only were there no such things and no such persons, but such terms and such names had no existence. . . .

Now with regard to all the writers of these two sects, the Buddhist and Rationalists [Neo-Confucianists], so imperfect are their doctrines and so incomplete their laws of instruction, that, during this long period of two hundred and fifty years (since the rise of our dynasty), they have not been able to realize the designs of our august sovereign in giving them his special countenance. . . .

If his sacred Intelligence would deign graciously to receive our apology, grant a manifesto, and for a short space of time, and on perfect equality with the disciples of Buddha and doctors of the Tao sect, allow these courtiers [Jesuits] to remain [in the empire] to promulgate their doctrines and urge on their reformation, it is humbly conceived that, ere many years have elapsed, the hearts of men and the ways of the world, will be seen to have undergone a steady and gradual change, progressing till at length there shall be one grand reformation, and perfect virtue become universal. . . .

—Hsu Kuang-chi, guardian and tutor
to the sons of the Imperial house,
memorial to Fra Matteo Ricci, 1617

Source: Chinese Repository 9 (March 1850), pp. 118–126; reprinted in William H. McNeil and Mitsuko Iriye, eds., *Modern Asia and Africa*, Readings in World History, vol. 9 (New York: Oxford University Press, 1971), pp. 31–42.

What rationale does Hsu provide for giving Christianity a hearing in China? What does he hope this will accomplish? Why is he disillusioned with Buddhism? How accurate is his portrayal of European Christian civilization? From where might he have gotten his ideas?

The Effects of European Expansion in China and India

China was neither conquered by the West nor particularly attracted to European influences, making the effects of European expansion less extensive in China than in other areas of the world. The effects of European expansion in China were most evident in the economic sphere. As China became more involved in the expanding global economy, Portuguese merchants imported more silver into the country. Taking silver from their mines in the Americas, the Portuguese brought the precious metal to China, where they exchanged it for the Chinese silks, porcelain, and tea that they then sold in Portugal. This influx of silver lessened the value of silver money within China at the same time that it stimulated particular industries and benefited Chinese merchants involved in trade with Japan or Portuguese merchants in the Philippines or Macao. Chinese agriculture and commerce became more specialized and more oriented toward the global market, with the silk and porcelain industries thriving in particular in response to market demand.

India was already involved in a thriving, international commercial economy when Portuguese mariners arrived there at the end of the fifteenth century. The further increase in European trade based on a growing home market for foreign goods affected the Indian economy in several ways. Indians relocated from the countryside to manufacturing centers such as Surat, which specialized in shipbuilding. Prior to the late sixteenth century, most villages in India were self-sufficient, combining agriculture with craftsmanship and manufacturing of cloth, pottery, and metal and wood products for the maker's own use or for local consumption. Market demand transformed textile weaving into India's main industry, and Indians began taking full-time employment in the textile industry. Kashmir and Bengal specialized in silk, while cotton thrived most in the Deccan plateau in south-central India. Indian merchants exported cotton textiles to Persia and the East Indies, importing carpets and horses from the former and spices and metals such as tin, copper, and mercury from the latter. European merchants also purchased their share of Indian cotton goods. The global economy stimulated employment and enriched individual merchants, but those who benefited from the economy generally did not put their money back into long-term investment or into agricultural improvement that would have benefited India's growing population.

European companies in India did not, in the seventeenth century, generally seek to establish political control over Indian rulers. After several unsuccessful attempts by Englishmen to negotiate trading rights with the ruling Mughal dynasty, the emperor Jahangir granted the English the right to trade and reside in Surat in 1616 at the behest of Sir Thomas Roe, who served as an ambassador for the English East India Company and James I (r. 1603–1625). Roe advised the English not to fortify their trading factories (posts) in India because the Mughals could always destroy them if they wanted and could protect them from other invaders. Indian and European merchants therefore operated and negotiated as equals, engaging in commercial activity that benefited both. The Mughal dynasty benefited from a larger tax base, which financed elaborate building projects and beautiful palaces. Indian temples benefited from more generous donations. European trade with India continued to increase throughout the seventeenth century and expanded to different coastal areas, leading to an increase in the quantity and variety of goods imported into India and the extent of European influence as well.

Muscovite Expansion Through Siberia

The spread of Muscovite influence and control in Siberia represented another example of European expansion into Asia in the late sixteenth and early seventeenth century. Russian exploration of Siberia had begun by the mid-sixteenth century. Siberia represented a real frontier for the Russians, who gradually extended their influence by building forts and trading posts, much as settlers of the American West would do in the nineteenth century. The main interest of the Russians in Siberia was economic. The wide-open spaces of Siberia provided an attractive draw for Russian peasants and Cossacks who yearned for a simple kind of freedom away from routine agricultural servitude.

Expansion was undertaken largely under the auspices of a powerful merchant family, the Stroganovs. The tsarist government was more than happy to leave the enterprise to private initiative to which it could lend support without becoming overcommitted. The tsar regarded the khan of Siberia as one of the several threats on his borders that he was all too willing to see brought down, if possible. Attracted by the possibility of extending the lucrative trade in salt, fur, and fish, the Stroganovs encouraged settlers to move east. But eventually Russian expansion drew the opposition of native tribes who united behind the khan. The Stroganovs, looking to protect their salt mines and the fur trade, financed a Cossack and volunteer army that defeated the native troops in 1581–1582, largely as a result of superior guns and military organization. Once in possession of hostile territory, however, the invading force needed additional military support from Ivan IV to make good its claims. By 1640 the Russians had expanded all the way to the Pacific coast. The Russian government benefited from increased revenues from timber and mineral ores, while the Stroganovs grew enormously rich from their Siberian salt mines. But their enterprising spirit did not carry over into the Russian economy as a whole, which still lagged far behind the rapidly advancing economy of Western Europe. One effect of the expansion was that the Chinese began to look askance at Russian expansion and a mutual distrust eventually developed between these two large empires.

Japan in the Age of European Expansion

In some ways Japanese society in 1550 resembled that which existed in fifteenth-century England under the system often referred to as "bastard feudalism," in which nobles hired private armies with monetary retainers instead of granting them territorial fiefs and reinforcing the values of the feudal system. In sixteenth-century Japan, feudal lords dominated the country with the assistance of samurai warriors whom they retained, only a few of whom received landed fiefs in exchange for their services.

Instead, samurai received monetary payment on which they depended to support their families. This worked against an extended family system for the samurai class, although their households might include elderly parents, unmarried adult children, and the nuclear family of the oldest son. These samurai protected their lords, known as daimyo, on their travels and helped them defend their castles, enforce order in their domains, and provide local administration or collection of revenues. There existed some diversity among the samurai, but they primarily remained a warrior class who shared many of the values inherent in European feudalism: bravery, loyalty, honor, and proficiency at martial skills. As a warrior class, they proved all too willing to defend the interests of their lords, leading to private warfare that frequently undermined order and social stability.

Among the rest of the population the main distinction was between the urban and rural classes. As in sixteenth-century Europe, the peasantry still greatly outnumbered the residents of towns and cities. The latter comprised two distinct groups of artisans and craftsmen on the one hand and merchants on the other, even though Japanese had a single word for urban dwellers (chōnin). Among all the classes in sixteenth-century Japan, the merchants had the least amount of respect.

Japanese society operated under a strict class structure that allowed for little

Columbia University's Asia for Educators website contains primary sources, videos, and access to a great deal of information related to Japanese history during this period: http://afe.easia.columbia.edu/tps/1450_jp.htm.

Kumamoto Castle, Japan *(Photo by Akira Kaede)*

social mobility. The primary distinction in Japanese society existed between samurai and commoners, any of whom could be killed by any samurai if the commoners did not show proper deference to their social superiors. Altogether the samurai class accounted for only about 5 percent of the Japanese population. By the end of the seventeenth century, samurai warriors were becoming increasingly obsolete as a result of important developments that brought peace, order, and stability to Japanese society. At the same time the government placed even greater restrictions upon social mobility as it attempted to strictly enforce the rigid class structure and protect the social status of the daimyo and samurai. Merchants, for example, had to openly display their subservience to the aristocratic classes by bowing. As in Elizabethan England, sumptuary laws designed to prevent extravagance and reinforce social distinctions reserved certain materials, for example, gold and silver jewelry, for the aristocracy.

Japanese commerce benefited from the political unification of the country and the stabilizing political force provided by the Tokugawa government, founded by Tokugawa Ieyasu (1542–1616), who was appointed shogun by the Japanese emperor in 1603. Japan mirrored Europe in gradually moving from a barter economy to one based more on currency. Increased amounts of money began to circulate in the country among a wider range of people. More widespread use of money encouraged merchants to trade throughout the entire country instead of restricting themselves to regional fairs. The tax policies of the shogunate, which concentrated on land as a source of revenue, had advantages for Japanese merchants as well. The growth of the Tokugawa capital of Edo (modern Tokyo) and the Tokugawa policy requiring daimyo to have residences there combined to create a boon for Japanese merchants who capitalized on this large, centralized market. Daimyo not only had to provide for the staff that maintained their residences at Edo, but also had large expenditures related to regular travel between Edo and their domains. A network of roads to facilitate such travel made trade easier as well. Eventually Nagasaki, Osaka, and Kyoto also grew into major urban centers and attracted a great deal of commerce. These cities enjoyed a moderate amount of autonomy within the general structure of Tokugawa government, similar to the privileges of self-government enjoyed by many European cities as a result of royal charters.

Although the Japanese economy generally prospered in the secure environment provided by the Tokugawa rulers, not everyone shared in that prosperity. Peasants, in particular, hard hit by famines and poor harvests, still battled constant poverty. The land tax affected them more severely than it did the merchants. Because of their general contempt for merchants, neither the shogunate nor the daimyo viewed the merchants as a threat and thus did not impede their activity. In fact, they both had incentive to encourage nationwide commerce in order to increase their tax base, even if they taxed commerce at a fairly low rate. Even agriculture was becoming commercialized, with landowners devoting their lands to lucrative commodities such as tobacco, cotton, tea, sugar, and silk. Small landowners could not compete against larger ones and often opted to live as tenants. In many respects, the Japanese economy closely resembled that of Europe during this period. While capitalism encouraged local and long-distant trade and raised the standard of living for many people in urban areas, the majority of the population still struggled against the forces of nature for survival in a traditional agricultural setting. Meanwhile, the Japanese nobles rejected trade as beneath them, as did many European aristocrats.

After taking complete control of the government in 1603, Tokugawa Ieyasu initiated a policy of seclusion (*sakoku*) that closed Japan to foreign influence. Ieyasu and his successors in the Tokugawa shogunate realized that foreign influence could undermine the political stability that they sought to foster. They forbade Japanese citizens to travel abroad and refused to permit foreign merchants and missionaries to enter the country. Japanese resistance to outside influence culminated in the "closed country" policy enacted in 1639 that significantly reduced, but did not eliminate, Japanese contact with the outside world.

The few westerners who managed to overcome the ban on foreigners and make it into Japan had little impact. Christian missionaries won some converts, but, by and large, Japan's religious traditions, primarily Buddhism and Shintoism, were unchanged. Shintoism, the native religion of Japan, generally involved the worship of natural forces and particular natural entities believed to contain divine spirits. Shintoism closely resembled the shamanistic European paganism that predated Christianity and was absorbed into the dominant religion in Europe. Shintoism remained popular, especially among Japanese peasants, long after Buddhism had gained widespread acceptance in Japan.

Perhaps the most widespread effect of European contact with Japan was the introduction of certain crops, including cotton in the sixteenth century and tobacco at the beginning of the seventeenth century. Europeans brought other crops to Japan, too, such as potatoes, sweet potatoes, pumpkins, and maize. European merchants transported these crops from America to Asia, in the process linking continents around the globe.

Conclusion

By 1650—for the first time in world history—the continents of Africa, Asia, Europe, and the Americas had become linked with one another in a complex web of trading relationships. Numerous people and vast quantities of goods and bullion flowed across oceans with great frequency. The emerging global economy affected people all over Europe. In general, Europeans enjoyed an ever-increasing range of products and foodstuffs. While northern Europeans wore fur obtained from America, the Portuguese elite preferred silk imported from China, while they also used Chinese porcelain in their homes and drank Chinese tea with increasing regularity. Even though expansion brought much wealth to Europe, it also brought inflation, social disruption and instability, and disease. Travel to India and Africa brought the Europeans into contact with malaria and yellow fever, while the introduction of new medicines derived from American plants brought some compensating benefits in the area of public health. The introduction of syphilis probably had the biggest impact on European society, leading Europeans to refrain from drinking from the same cup or glass, kissing their friends, or visiting public baths. Finally, expansion altered diplomacy and political relationships. Rivalries overseas exacerbated old ones or led to new rivalries in Europe. Competition for land and resources overseas complemented the traditional dynastic wars for land and power in Europe. By raising the economic and political stakes, expansion contributed to the increasing attempts by monarchs to gain absolute control over their people, which made the rise of absolute monarchies, and the political tensions thereby created, the dominant political theme of the seventeenth century.

1. What factors led to an erosion of Spanish commercial power by the early seventeenth century?
2. What factors contributed to the rise of an interlocking global economy by the early seventeenth century? How did the spice trade fit into the global economy?
3. What were the main effects of European expansion on the Americas?
4. What factors contributed to the rise of the Atlantic slave trade during the sixteenth and seventeenth centuries? How did the Dutch West India Company help to shape the course of history in the seventeenth century, particularly the history of the slave trade and European relations with Africa?
5. What were the main differences and similarities between Europe and Japan in the late sixteenth and early seventeenth centuries?

Suggestions for Further Reading

Beasley, W.G. 1999. *The Japanese Experience: A Short History of Japan.* Berkeley: University of California Press.

Klein, Herbert S. 1999. *The Atlantic Slave Trade.* Cambridge: Cambridge University Press.

Milton, Giles. 1999. *Nathaniel's Nutmeg: Or, the True and Incredible Adventures of the Spice Trader Who Changed the Course of History.* New York: Farrar, Straus and Giroux.

———. 2000. *Big Chief Elizabeth: The Adventures and Fate of the First English Colonists in America.* New York: Farrar, Straus and Giroux.

Pestana, Carla Gardina. 2010. *Protestant Empire: Religion and the Making of the British Atlantic World.* Philadelphia: University of Pennsylvania Press.

Spence, Jonathan D. 1985. *The Memory Palace of Matteo Ricci.* New York: Viking Penguin.

Suggested Websites

www.brown.edu/Departments/Anthropology/SIAP/home.html

This website of the Spice Islands Anthropology Project contains a great deal of information about the Spice Islands, including history and suggested readings, along with visual images.

www.brycchancarey.com/slavery/index.htm

Brycchan Carey, a senior lecturer at Kingston University, established as part of his outstanding website a chronology on the history of slavery that would provide a nice supplement to the discussion of the slave trade in this chapter.

www.emory.edu/ENGLISH/Bahri/Spice_Trade.html

This useful website prepared by Louise Marie Cornillez provides a history of the spice trade, a bibliography, and links to other sites related to the topic.

www.pch.gc.ca/csp-pec/english/about/multimedia/explorers

This website has information about John Cabot, Jacques Cartier, and Samuel de Champlain, in addition to other explorers related to the history of Canada, along with links to related CD-ROMS and websites.

www.tolatsga.org/Compacts.html

This website provides brief discussions of numerous Indian nations that resided in the eastern United States at the time of European colonization, with bibliographic and geographic links.

13   Absolutism and Political Revolution in the Seventeenth Century

The central question of political theory in the first half of the seventeenth century was whether kings held their authority directly from God by divine right and therefore were above the law or whether kings owed their authority to the consent of the people (an idea known as popular sovereignty) and therefore were below the law. Divine right theory provided a justification for political absolutism, the principle that a single ruler could make major decisions about state policy without consulting his or her subjects and without interference from a representative assembly. However, the success of absolute governments depended to a large degree on the individual leadership of particular rulers.

In reality, most European nations could be placed on a spectrum between the abstract poles of absolutism and popular sovereignty. In England, monarchical power depended on the support of royal ministers, judges, and justices of the peace, all of whom maintained some degree of autonomy. The French law courts, known as *parlements*, also operated independently of express royal control. By the seventeenth century, more people in Europe had become educated, especially in urban areas, and were as likely to question political authority as they were to challenge religious or intellectual authorities. During the sixteenth century, the Protestant Huguenots in France had developed theories of political resistance to justify their rebellion against the monarchy. Such theories became more widespread in the seventeenth century. But so did the theory of the divine right of kings and belief in absolute monarchy grow alongside and in response to resistance theories. The religious wars of the sixteenth century increasingly turned into political struggles in the course of the seventeenth.

By 1600 European expansion had exacerbated international tensions as well, further contributing to the trend toward absolute monarchy. France, ever jealous of the power and colonial wealth of Spain, began to seek territory abroad to counter the empire of its Habsburg rivals. Spain used the wealth that it acquired from its American colonies to finance its territorial wars in Europe—wealth that largely ended up in the hands of Dutch, German, and Italian merchants.

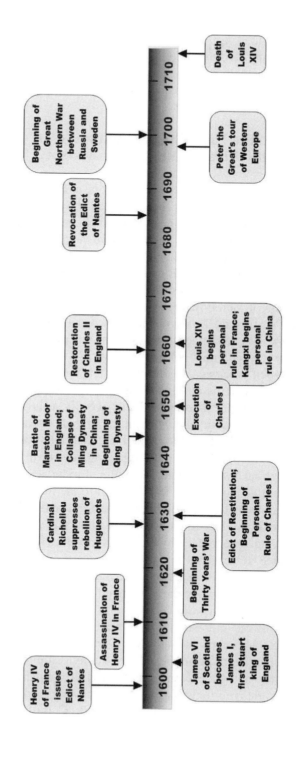

The French joined the English in attacking Spanish shipping in an attempt to cut off Spain's source of funds. The dynastic and territorial wars that spilled over into the seventeenth century and the increasing cost of those wars led European rulers to seek even greater authority over their subjects and the economic resources of their states.

The Shaping of the Past: The Assassination of Henry IV and the Rise of French Absolutism

When Henry of Navarre claimed the French throne as Henry IV (r. 1593–1610), he took control in a nation that had been weakened by thirty years of political division and religious warfare. The two most daunting tasks facing Henry were to resolve the religious crisis and to restore the prestige of the monarchy. To accomplish the first task, he issued the Edict of Nantes in 1598. The edict granted limited toleration to the Huguenots, allowing them all political rights and the freedom to worship in specified places. Although the measure did end the religious wars, it merely papered over the religious differences dividing Catholics and Protestants. To restore the power and prestige of the French monarchy, Henry took advantage of institutions and practices already in place rather than try to create a new political system. He used the royal council to overrule the French *parlements*, although when the council removed cases from the courts it created dissension among them. He reasserted the monarch's power to appoint ministers, naming the Duke of Sully, a Huguenot, as his chief minister. Henry did not radically overhaul the French system of taxation, but he and Sully introduced reforms to make tax collection more efficient.

In his exercise of royal authority, imposing rule on municipalities and provinces throughout France, Henry IV claimed to be acting in the interests of the French people. He placed officials loyal to the monarchy in important magisterial positions in the towns. Although he allowed the Huguenots control over 100 fortified towns, he still took an active interest in municipal posts there to ensure their allegiance to the Crown. By establishing royal clients in towns throughout France, Henry took a major step toward reviving and expanding royal authority. In the provinces, Henry won the allegiance of individual members of the nobility by awarding them financial grants. However, by imposing restraints on the political power of the nobility and dictating marriages based solely on the political interests of the monarchy, he alienated many of the nobles. Catholic nobles also resented Henry's heavy reliance upon Sully, who had remained a Huguenot even after Henry's conversion to Catholicism.

Although Henry had gone a long way toward strengthening the monarchy and bringing an end to religious warfare, the religious passions of the sixteenth century had not yet died in the early seventeenth. Catholics disapproved of the Edict of Nantes and some still distrusted their formerly Protestant king, who had not recognized the decrees of the Council of Trent as binding on the French church. Meanwhile, some Huguenots never forgave his conversion to Catholicism and were upset at some erosion of their privileges in the later years of Henry's reign. There were more than twenty plots against Henry's life between 1593 and 1604. Then, on May 14, 1610, in an apparent act of religious terrorism, a man named François Ravaillac stabbed Henry to death while the king was stuck in his coach because of some obstruction in the road. The suspicious circumstances of his death led to speculation about a conspiracy involving the Catholic Church, the Jesuits, and the king of Spain.

Henry IV left a strong legacy to France; his assassination left one almost as powerful. He had reaffirmed the ideology of sacred monarchy in France when he was alive; his death confirmed his status as a religious martyr who had sacrificed his life for the French nation. His assassination therefore strengthened his subjects' devotion to the monarchy. The French people longed for a strong, powerful monarch capable of maintaining peace in the kingdom. The assassination of Henry IV thus set the stage for the rise of absolute monarchy in France. In 1614 the Estates General—in its last session before 1789—proposed an article declaring that "the king of France receives his crown from God alone, and rules supreme within his kingdom." The French people had no desire to return to a state of civil war, such as they had known after the death of Henry III in the previous century.

Henry's son and heir, Louis XIII (1601–1643), was less than ten years old at the time of his father's death. Louis's mother, the Italian Maria de' Medici (1573–1642), acted as regent for her son, ruling France with the aid of Concino Concini (d. 1617), an Italian adventurer and a favored member of her entourage. Marie was a devoted Catholic with little sympathy for the French Huguenots, who viewed her as likely to revoke the privileges granted to them by the Edict of Nantes. A greater cause for their consternation occurred when, within a year of Henry's death, their supporter, the Duke of Sully, resigned as superintendent of finances as a result of his dissatisfaction with his treatment by Maria's royal council. Showing much greater deference to the church than her husband had, Maria supported efforts to introduce Catholic reform measures into France. Maria and Concini ignored the young king until 1617, when Louis became ready to assert himself. Upon taking control in France, Louis sanctioned the murder of Concini, had another government minister condemned to death, and may have considered having his mother killed before sending her into exile from the court.

The person who did the most to continue the efforts of Henry IV to strengthen the French monarchy, however, was Armand-Jean du Plessis, Cardinal Richelieu (1585–1642). Appointed chief of the royal council in 1624, Richelieu became chief minister for Louis XIII four years later. Although he virtually ruled the French government during the reign of Louis XIII, Richelieu always did what he believed to be in the king's best interests and thought of himself only as a servant of the Crown. Nor did he ever act without the support and the consent of the king, who took a more active role in government and the formation of royal policy than is usually portrayed. In fact, Louis retained Richelieu only because of his effectiveness in enhancing royal authority in the kingdom. He strengthened the royal navy financially, administratively, and militarily. He used royal officials known as *intendants* as a check on the power of the nobility and provincial governors. The *intendants* traveled throughout France as representatives of the Crown to see that the royal will was being followed, to ensure that taxes owed the Crown were collected, and to exercise general administrative functions related to provincial government.

Richelieu also stripped the Huguenots of their political and military power. He was not concerned with the religious views of the Huguenots; rather he objected to the share of political authority that they, along with the French nobility and provincial governors, enjoyed at the expense of the king. Richelieu repressed a Huguenot rebellion and in 1627 successfully besieged the Huguenot fortress at La Rochelle; following the victory, he rescinded many of the Huguenots' political and military privileges. Not wanting to make permanent enemies of the Huguenots, however, he left alone the provisions of the Edict of Nantes that called for religious tolerance.

Absolutism in France Under Louis XIV

The reign of Louis XIV (r. 1643–1715) in France is often taken as the epitome of absolute monarchy in Europe. When Louis XIV personally assumed the reins of power in 1661 at the age of twenty-three, he was filled with visions of royal glory and military triumph. He tried to foster a golden age of culture by sponsoring elaborate construction projects such as the immense royal palace at Versailles, patronizing artists and writers such as Molière and Racine, and establishing the French Academy of Sciences. Each of these undertakings was intended to reflect the glory of the "Sun King," as Louis was known in recognition of the central position of the sun in the new Copernican universe. As the sun was superior to all the planets, Louis was superior to all other monarchs—or so he wanted his subjects and the world to believe.

In addition to seeking to enhance his power and reputation through military victory and cultural enterprises, Louis XIV also tried to set a moral and religious tone for his kingdom under the guidance of Bishop Jacques-Bénigne Bossuet (1627–1704). Louis XIV represented the epitome of the divine right king and the absolute monarch in the seventeenth century. He reportedly said "I am the

Claude Lefebvre, portrait of Louis XIV, 1670

Visitors to the official website of the Chateau of Versailles—www.
chateauversailles.fr/en—can access some of the masterpieces located
there, learn more about the construction and the history of the palace,
and read about the life and reign of Louis XIV, and the ways in which
he used Versailles to symbolize and strengthen his monarchy.

state" and sincerely believed that his interests and France's interests perfectly coincided. After he revoked the Edict of Nantes in 1685 and expelled the Huguenots from France, he remained, like most other Frenchmen, impervious to the economic and intellectual resources that France lost. Bossuet praised this move by Louis, who was fulfilling the role of the monarchy favored by the bishop—ruling in the service of religion.

The emergence of France as a great military power, the flourishing of French culture, and the reputation of Louis as the Sun King represent the success of absolute monarchy in France. But absolute monarchy under Louis XIV did not come without cost. Absolute monarchy in France also involved stripping the nobility of their political rights and power, the growth of religious intolerance, as exemplified by the expulsion of the Huguenots, and the burdens borne by the common people—ever-increasing taxes and the sacrifice of sons, husbands, and fathers to the king's armies in his quest for glory. Louis's finance minister, Jean-Baptiste Colbert (1619–1683), had the thankless task of increasing royal revenues to feed the insatiable war machine necessitated by Louis's obsession for military glory. To raise money, Colbert levied new taxes on paper goods and granted a particularly unpopular extension of the salt monopoly that raised the price of a necessary commodity. Five out of six designated regions in France fell under the gabelle, or salt tax, which as a direct tax on consumers was already one of the most hated taxes in France.

How absolute was the monarchy of Louis XIV? Under Louis, the government had the power to tax without popular consent and to arrest people without charging them with crimes. The power of the state was perhaps best exemplified by lettres de cachet, sealed warrants issued by the king or an authorized royal official that could have anyone thrown in prison without recourse to the judicial system or due process of law. The warrants were not issued arbitrarily and were generally accompanied by some sort of police investigation; their purpose was detention, not punishment. That distinction, however, would have been small consolation to someone sitting in the Bastille, a large fortified prison in the heart of Paris.

The Habsburgs in Spain and Austria

A comparative analysis of the history of several absolute monarchies in seventeenth-century Europe reveals some common themes, but some differences as well. For example, the two branches of the Habsburg dynasty created absolute monarchies in Spain and Austria, but the history of those two countries differed considerably over the course of the century. The main distinction between the Spanish and Austrian Habsburgs was that in Spain the Habsburgs were a hereditary dynasty, whereas the Austrian Habsburgs depended on continued election to retain their hold on the imperial throne. The Spanish Habsburgs had no wish to see the Austrian Habsburgs lose the imperial crown and therefore threw their own weight into German politics. But the Spanish kings had to contend with problems of their own and by the end of the seventeenth century the Austrian Habsburgs had emerged as the stronger dynastic power of the two.

As Louis XIII had relied heavily on Richelieu to strengthen royal power, Philip III (r. 1598–1621) of Spain relied heavily on Francisco Gómez de Sandoval y Rojas, the Duke of Lerma, while Philip IV (r. 1621–1665) entrusted state affairs to Gaspar de Guzmán, the Count Duke of Olivares (1587–1645). Lerma was committed to strengthening or at least preserving the power of the Spanish Habsburgs, but financial pressures led him to negotiate peace with England in 1604 and a truce with the Dutch in 1609, bringing a temporary end to the Counter-Reformation crusade of the Spanish Habsburgs. Pressures on Lerma from opponents inside and outside Spain who began to see his conciliatory policies as damaging to Spanish prestige led to his downfall in 1618. Olivares fought to reverse the declining domestic and international fortunes of the Spanish Habsburgs, placing a greater priority on the former. Olivares was fully committed to his monarch and never lost confidence in the ability of Philip IV, under whom Madrid became a center of European civilization where the artist Diego de Velázquez (1599–1660) captured the dignity and formality of the royal court. Olivares had the new royal palace of Buen Retiro built to reflect the glory and power of the monarchy.

But a successful absolute monarchy depended above all on a strong army, and a strong army depended on people to serve in it and money to equip and pay them. Sixteenth-century wars with the English, Dutch, and French had drained Spain of the wealth it had imported from its New World colonies, while the attempt to compensate with increased taxes only hurt Spanish industry and agriculture. Wartime casualties and emigration to the New World resulted in a decline in the Spanish population. Spain's ill-fated decision to expel its Jewish and Muslim subjects in 1492 caused further population decline as well as severe economic depression.

Finally, the last of the Spanish Habsburgs, Charles II (r. 1665–1700), known as the Mad, was an ineffectual ruler, apparently suffering from mental weaknesses that were probably the result of Habsburg inbreeding.

The Austrian Habsburgs were more successful than the Spanish branch of the royal family in the seventeenth century. In Austria the Habsburgs ruled as absolute monarchs and used Roman Catholicism and allegiance to the dynasty to unify a number of territories that had little else in common besides Habsburg rule. The Habsburgs rewarded nobles loyal to the dynasty and dispossessed those who were not. Each Habsburg territory maintained an individual relationship with the empire and supported the Habsburg emperor but did not share interests in common with the rest of the imperial territories. Within each territory, the Habsburgs set up a separate government administration, overseen by an imperial governor appointed by the emperor from nominees put forth by the feudal estates (representing the nobility) for each territory. The representative assembly in each territory answered to the imperial governor rather than directly to the emperor and had the right to question imperial directives.

Changes within the empire brought about by the Thirty Years' War (1618–1648) affected the power of the Austrian Habsburgs. During the war, the Austrians relied heavily on mercenary generals such as Johann Tserclaes, better known as Graf von Tilly of Bavaria and Albrecht Wallenstein of Bohemia. Unable to pay these mercenaries in cash, the Habsburgs divided up their own lands to create huge estates for them. The Habsburgs gained Bohemia, but only by greatly expanding the lands of the Catholic nobility who had remained loyal to them and granting much of the remaining land to foreign mercenaries. Still, the Austrian Habsburgs emerged from the conflict in a stronger position than they had been, with the lands under their control now fully committed to Catholicism.

In what sense, then, could the Austrian Habsburgs be considered absolute monarchs? Absolute monarchy in the seventeenth century rested not just on military power, but on intangibles such as respect, even approaching worship, of the sovereign, intangibles that Emperor Leopold I (1640–1705) tried to cultivate. For example, pictures of Leopold were printed and priced to sell to all levels of the population. In the second half of the seventeenth century, the Habsburgs portrayed themselves as the rivals of French greatness as reflected in the court of Louis XIV. They did so through elaborate public ceremonies, such as the procession that accompanied the return of Leopold to Vienna after he had been elected emperor and the series of festivals in celebration of his 1662 marriage to Margareta Maria Theresa, the daughter of Philip IV of Spain. Such intangibles, however, did not help Leopold among his Hungarian subjects, many of whom were Protestant and demanded independence in part as a way of guaranteeing religious freedom. The Hungarians were caught between the Austrians and the Ottoman Turks, who continued to seek expansion in Europe, mainly at the expense of the Austrian empire.

Absolute Government in Prussia and Russia

In 1640, Frederick William (r. 1640–1688), known as the Great Elector, inherited the Hohenzollern lands of Brandenburg, which his family had ruled since 1415, and East Prussia, which they inherited in 1618. In 1648 Frederick William emerged from the Thirty Years' War in an enhanced position, but he had to create policies to increase his power within the state. Foreign armies had occupied the territory for much of the war, demanding food and housing from the inhabitants. Many residents died in battle while others were slaughtered by marauding armies or died of disease or hunger; the population of Brandenburg declined by as much as one-half to two-thirds during the course of the war. The terrible suffering that the people endured during the Thirty Years' War helped make them receptive to the idea of a strong monarch. The experience of the war also convinced Frederick William that military strength was the key to maintaining his lands. By guaranteeing the Brandenburg nobility that they would maintain their privileges over the rest of the population, Frederick William won approval for the taxation necessary to support a large army. In 1653 the Elector gained similar approval from the Junkers (the Prussian nobility) but at the price of conceding to the Junkers greater control over the peasantry on their lands, which helped to perpetuate serfdom in Prussia. Emboldened by his military power and the concessions of the nobility, Frederick William imposed on Brandenburg additional taxes—including an excise tax on manufactured and consumer goods in the towns—without the consent of the States-General, the assembly that had provided the nobility a voice in such matters. Frederick William extorted money from his other possessions in the Rhineland by threatening to use military force. Brandenburg-Prussia was being transformed into an absolute monarchy, governed by the will of the ruler with the support of the army.

Russia, which began the seventeenth century in chaos with weakened central authority, established a new dynasty that was to emerge 100 years later as a significant European power under Peter the Great. Russia's Time of Troubles began when Tsar Theodore of Russia, the son of Ivan the Terrible, died in 1598, leaving no heirs. Since no constitutional provision existed for the succession under such circumstances, a series of disputes among rival claimants resulted. The land assembly, or *zemskii sobor*—which included representatives of the nobility, clergy, townspeople, and even peasants—chose as tsar Boris Godunov (ca. 1552–1605), an experienced administrator who had served as Theodore's chief adviser. But the election of Boris Godunov as tsar did not end the Time of Troubles. Social upheaval caused by increases in taxation—which reduced growing numbers of peasants to serfdom—and attempts to modernize the Russian army exacerbated the crisis. A famine in 1602 caused further distress. Boris Godunov died suddenly in 1605, precipitating another dynastic and political crisis. Taking advantage of the chaos in Russia, both Poland and Sweden invaded the country in 1610. A Russian army managed to repulse the two invaders, but the military crisis led the nobility to call another meeting of the *zemskii sobor* to attempt to end the Time of Troubles. In 1613 the *zemskii sobor* elected sixteen-year-old Michael Romanov as tsar. The nobles chose him partly because they knew that he was too young and inexperienced to rule alone and would need to rely on the *zemskii sobor* for assistance. Nonetheless, Michael benefited from circumstances similar to those of Henry IV in France. Many Russians were eager for a strong monarch who would prevent a recurrence of the chaotic period they had just endured.

A major social problem during the Time of Troubles was the unrest and revolt of the peasants against the upper classes, who attempted to force stronger obligations and restrictions upon them. Hostility between peasants and landowners did not disappear during Michael's reign. Michael's son and successor, Alexis (r. 1645–1676) provoked a number of peasant uprisings by the imposition of new taxes in his attempt to solve the financial crisis of the monarchy. After the government suppressed the rebellions, Alexis introduced a new legal code in 1649 that institutionalized serfdom by ending the limitation on the right of landowners to reclaim runaway serfs and using a census to register serfs as belonging to specific estates. This code thus further restricted movements of peasants unless they were bought or sold.

Russian society was becoming more rigid and oppressive and Russian government more despotic, characterized increasingly by absolute rule at times bordering on tyranny. Unlike all other European rulers, the Russian tsars had no legal restrictions upon their authority. But the Russian monarchy depended heavily on the support of and the role played by the Russian Orthodox Church in state affairs. Tsars were still anointed by the patriarch (head) of the church at their succession to the throne. While elsewhere in Europe the church had increasingly come under secular control or clearly played a secondary role, in Russia the church operated as an almost equal partner with the tsar in the governance of the realm.

Financial problems, peasant uprisings, and religious divisions all threatened the position of the tsar during Alexis's reign, however. One of the largest peasant rebellions of the seventeenth century occurred in 1670–1671, led by Cossack Stepan Razin, who came from southern Russia where the Don Cossacks still had a great deal of military autonomy based on their willingness to serve as a line of defense on Russia's borders with Turkey. Divisions within the Russian Orthodox Church in the mid-seventeenth century threatened the stability of the government as the tsar was forced to cast his lot with one side or the other. A strong tsar was needed to succeed Alexis in order to solidify the monarchy and prevent a recurrence of the Time of Troubles. In 1689 Alexis's son, Peter, at the age of seventeen, seized control of the throne, which had fallen under the control of his older sister, Sophia, and her lover and chief minister, Prince Vasily Golitsyn. Thus began a reign that lasted until 1725 and that was arguably the most important in Russian history.

Peter instituted wholesale reforms that strengthened the monarchy and transformed Russia. He increased state control of the Russian Orthodox Church by placing it under a synod or council, abolishing the position of patriarch, and closing a number of monasteries while restricting the membership of those that remained. Starting in 1700, he forced all landowners to register with the government so they could be tapped for state service, extending that principle in 1714 with a further decree threatening nobles with loss of property if they did not enroll. In 1722 he created a Table of Ranks within the army, navy, and civil service that granted higher prestige to those nobles who through their talent rose to the upper echelons of the Russian military or bureaucracy. Administratively, Peter created new departments of the navy, artillery, and mines, used Western titles for positions like chancellor and agencies like the Privy Council, and divided Russia into separate districts to help systematize tax collection. Culturally, Peter became so enamored of the West that he forbade men to wear beards (following the style in the West), forced people to wear Western-style clothing, and adopted the Western Gregorian calendar, which lopped ten days off the older Julian calendar that Russia had followed. He encouraged Russian industries, especially in textiles, mining, and metallurgy, borrowing from the Western mercantilist philosophy of creating a favorable balance of trade of exports over imports. Even though Russia lacked secondary schools, Peter created a university, to force, as he said, his successors to address the country's educational deficiencies. The encouragement Peter gave to learning resulted in the publication of 700 books from 1682 to 1709, compared to 374 for the entire rest of the seventeenth century.

Absolute Government in East and West: Manchu China and Monarchical Europe

Despite some obvious differences, European and Chinese rulers faced many of the same problems; the histories of Europe and China in the seventeenth century have some important similarities that are as remarkable as their differences. Among the obvious differences, China was a large unified country, whereas Europe was divided into numerous separate states and kingdoms. The Chinese economy and society were largely agrarian, whereas commercial development and urban expansion had begun to transform the European society and economy. Even the most powerful European monarchs did not have the kind of absolute control over the life and death of their subjects as did the Qing emperor. Louis XIV vied with the pope for religious authority over French Catholics; Qing emperors confirmed the position of the religious leaders of each of the three major Chinese religions—Buddhism, Daoism, and Confucianism—and occupied a prominent symbolic place in each of them. Yet absolute government in China was based on many of the same foundations as absolute monarchy in Europe. The religious justification for political authority in China was similar to the European theory of divine right monarchy. As in Europe, imperial authority in China depended on military power. In the seventeenth century, war and revolution affected the population and economy of both Europe and China.

The Thirty Years War devastated the European economy, and the wars and rebellions that accompanied the collapse of the Ming dynasty in 1644 and the rise of the Manchus did the same in China. When starving peasants rose up against the increasingly weak Ming dynasty, Manchus from their northern homeland of Manchuria supported the peasant rebellions, seeing in them an opportunity to seize power. Ming supporters fled to the southeast as the Manchus gained control in the north. When the last Ming emperor died—by his own hand—in 1644, the Manchus rushed in. Conquering the Chinese capital of Beijing, they announced the beginning of a new dynasty, the Qing, or Pure, dynasty, which would rule China from 1644 until its collapse in 1912. But decades of war ruined much agriculturally productive land in China, as the Thirty Years War had in Europe. The population of central Europe declined dramatically during the Thirty Years War, probably more than 25 percent in the 1630s and 1640s alone. The number of Chinese may have declined by as many as 50 million between 1600 and 1670, falling from 150 million to 100 million as a result of wars, rebellions, plagues, natural disasters, and the failure of the Chinese irrigation system. The German lands did not recover economically from the destruction of the Thirty Years War until the eighteenth century; it took China at least that long for its agricultural production to recover from the wars that raged there.

Monarchs had ruled in Europe for 1,000 years before reaching the height of absolute rule achieved by Louis XIV; emperors had ruled China for a much longer period of time, but in many respects the Qing dynasty represented the epitome of absolute government there. The Qing emperors had absolute control over the state and those who served it. They had the power to control all government appointments and dismissals. They alone set domestic and foreign policy. No persons and no institutions had the authority to question imperial edicts.

The basic form of Chinese government did not change under the Qing dynasty. China remained an absolute monarchy with power residing in the emperor, whose authority was based ultimately on control of the army. In China the right to govern was known as the Mandate of Heaven, which heaven (an impersonal cosmic force) bestowed on a worthy individual who was then known as the Son of Heaven. As the intermediary between heaven and earth, the Son of Heaven had the duty to govern conscientiously, maintain order and harmony throughout the realm, stand as an example of moral correctness, patronize scholarship, and treat his subjects compassionately and protect them from disaster. The Qing emperors left the imperial bureaucracy intact and adapted existing Ming institutions to their rule. They maintained the imperial examination system that controlled entrance into the Chinese civil service.

In both Europe and China royal support for scholarship and the arts served the same general purpose: to place intellectual and cultural endeavors under state control. The emperor Xuanyue (better known as Kangxi, a posthumous name meaning "Lasting Peace") (r. 1661–1722), a scholar himself, studied astronomy, geography, mathematics, and music, in addition to classical Chinese literature and philosophy. As emperor, he placed a particular premium upon scholarship in the service of the state. Kangxi recruited Confucian scholars to the government service. He reinforced the importance of Confucian values such as thrift, filial piety, and obedience to the state in his Sacred Edicts of 1670.

He maintained the examination system and overcame the resistance of Chinese scholars to sit for the examinations by calling for nominations for a special national examination in 1679. He invited scholars to participate in the compilation of a Ming history. He supported other research projects as well, including a 40,000-character Kangxi dictionary, the authoritative Chinese dictionary until the twentieth century. An encyclopedia that he commissioned in 1700 was completed a few years after his death.

In China, the reign of the Kangxi emperor represents the height of Qing absolutism, as that of Louis XIV does for Europe. The reign of the Kangxi emperor bears several similarities to that of Louis XIV, including his inherit-

Additional primary source materials on Louis XIV, seventeenth-century France, and European absolutism are available at www.fordham. edu/halsall/mod/modsbook05.html.

For more about Chinese history and culture, including images of and additional information on Kangxi, visit the website sponsored by the People's Republic of China at www.chinaculture.org/gb/en_ aboutchina/2003-09/24/content_22914.htm.

The Sacred Edicts of Kangxi, 1670

1. Highly esteem filial piety and the proper relations among brothers in order to give due importance to social relations.
2. Give due weight to kinship in order to promote harmony and peace.
3. Maintain good relations within the neighborhood in order to prevent quarrels and lawsuits.
4. Give due importance to farming and the cultivation of mulberry trees in order to ensure sufficient clothing and food.
5. Be moderate and economical in order to avoid wasting away your livelihood.
6. Make the most of schools and academies in order to honor the ways of scholars.
7. Denounce strange beliefs in order to elevate the true doctrine [Confucianism].
8. Explain laws and regulations in order to warn the ignorant and obstinate.
9. Show propriety and courtesy to improve customs and manners.
10. Work hard in your professions in order to quiet your ambitions.
11. Instruct sons and younger brothers in order to prevent their committing any wrong.
12. Put a stop to false accusations in order to protect the good and honest.
13. Warn against giving shelter to deserters in order to avoid punishment with them.
14. Promptly and fully pay your taxes in order to avoid forced requisition.
15. Get together in groups of ten or a hundred in order to put an end to theft and robbery.
16. Free yourself from resentment and anger in order to show respect for your body and life.

—Translated by Lydia Gerber

Source: Reading About the World, vol. 2, edited by Paul Brians, Mary Gallwey, Douglas Hughes, Azfar Hussain, Richard Law, Michael Myers, Michael Neville, Roger Schlesinger, Alice Spitzer, and Susan Swan (San Diego: Harcourt Brace Custom Books, 1999). By permission of Lydia Gerber.

How do these edicts relate to strengthening support for the emperor and absolute monarchy in China? What values are emphasized? Are they different from Western values?

China and the West Compared

Historical Profile of China in Early Modern Times

1. Unified imperial system
2. Geographical isolation
3. Ideal of nature as a self-operating organism
4. Ideal of limited accumulation (landholding and agriculture)
5. Ideal of a morally evaluating mind (Confucianism)
6. Negative attitude toward change (stability, continuity, and tradition)

Historical Profile of the West in Early Modern Times

1. Pluralistic state system
2. Geographical openness
3. Ideal of nature as lawful
4. Ideal of unlimited accumulation (capitalism)
5. Ideal of an analytical mind (scientific rationality)
6. Positive attitude toward change (innovation and progress)

Source: Lists courtesy of Kenneth Stunkel.

How are these different characteristics of the two civilizations manifested in the history of Europe and China in the seventeenth century? Specifically, how do they relate to a comparison of the reigns of Louis XIV and Kangxi?

ing the throne at a young age and ruling as his own chief minister of state after dispensing with his regents. Kangxi also rivaled Louis XIV in his work habits and the numbers of reports and papers that he studied, annotated, and acted upon. Just as Louis had his new palace constructed at Versailles outside Paris, Kangxi had his summer palace built at Chengde, about 100 miles from Beijing. Louis had Versailles built partly to attract the prominent members of his nobility so he could monitor and control their behavior. Kangxi strengthened imperial authority in hostile regions by requiring all officials within a certain distance to present themselves to the emperor whenever he traveled. Failure to do so a first time would cost the offender a year's salary; a second offense meant transfer to a new post at a lower rank. Both Kangxi and Louis XIV sought to add lands to their empire for their own glory and that of their dynasty. Both Kangxi and Louis XIV found enough money to finance their wars, build their palaces, expand their territories, maintain their administrations, and sponsor a number of public works. However, both also left their successors with mounting problems that led to the progressive weakness of both dynasties in the eighteenth century.

The Shaping of the Past: The Execution of Charles I and the Struggle Against Absolute Government in Britain

English politics in the early seventeenth century revolved around two centers of power, the king and Parliament, but Parliament depended on the king for its very existence, since it met only at the monarch's behest. In 1603 James VI of Scotland inherited the throne of England, where he became known as James I (r. 1603–1625). James, the son and successor of Mary Queen of Scots, had ruled Scotland as a Protestant king for almost twenty years before assuming the English throne. He entered England seemingly unaware that there the roles of king and Parliament were well-defined by tradition or what the English referred to as the "ancient constitution." The monarch was a constant presence on the throne and, by tradition, held sole responsibility for certain aspects of governing, including foreign policy, overseas trade, minting of coins, and pardoning criminals. Parliament, though, controlled the power of the purse; extraordinary taxes or financial measures could not be leveled without parliamentary consent. Had both king and Parliament remained content with the rough division of powers as they were, English politics under the first Stuart monarchs would have been much more peaceful. In his coronation oath in 1603, James swore "to confirm to the people of England the laws and customs to them granted." Yet he had already developed his theory of the divine right of kings, which he outlined in the treatise *The Trew Law of Free Monarchies* (1598). In fact, during the reigns of James I and his son, Charles I, both king and Parliament seemed intent on expanding their powers at the expense of the other.

Within the first few years of his reign, James meddled with a disputed election to a seat in Parliament to have the matter resolved in his favor; he lectured Parliament on divine right and the respect owed to the monarch at all times; and he tested the limits of the king's right to tax by imposing new import duties, claiming that they were covered under the king's prerogative to control foreign policy. He convened a conference to consider the issue of religious reform, but refused to allow Parliament any say in the matter, instead relying on his conservative bishops to affirm the status quo despite numerous and vocal demands for change. Puritans continued to believe that the English Reformation had been only partially carried out. They feared God's displeasure because the English church still contained so many elements of "popery," such as a church hierarchy that contained bishops and archbishops as in the Roman Catholic Church, the elaborate vestments worn by Anglican clerics, and the use of the sign of the cross during baptism. Puritans also argued with James's decision to end war with Catholic Spain in 1604 because they viewed the struggle largely in religious terms, associating Spain with the forces of the devil and the papal Antichrist. Many English Protestants objected when James tried to negotiate a marriage alliance between his son Charles and a royal Spanish bride. Yet despite growing animosity between the king and Parliament, especially those members sympathetic to religious reform, James's reign ended peacefully, without any major political upheavals, while even the strongest advocates of a larger role for Parliament, religious reform, or limitations on the royal government did not challenge the right of the king to rule.

Although tensions continued to build between king and Parliament in the first fifteen years of the reign of Charles I (r. 1625–1649), followed by an increasingly revolutionary atmosphere in London after 1640, the civil war that began in 1642 came as a shock to the English people. For the next six years the English—as well as the subjects of the English king in Scotland and Ireland—were drawn into a bloody, violent conflict. After being drawn into war with Scotland in the late 1630s over his attempt to impose an Anglican prayer book there, Charles—who had ignored Parliament for eleven years—had to turn to Parliament for support in 1640, a decision that allowed his English subjects to express their grievances. During what became known as his Personal Rule, when the king ruled without Parliament from 1629 to 1640, Charles had avoided war so that he would not have to call on Parliament for money.

Much of the controversy and dissatisfaction with Charles's Personal Rule derived from his handling of religious matters. But in 1641 Parliament itself began to divide when Puritan members began to press for the abolition of all bishops in an effort to erase any traces of Catholicism from the Church of England. Gradually, Anglicans who wished to defend the Church of England against the Puritans joined with royalists who believed Parliament had become too radical in its challenge of royal authority to form a royalist party to support Charles.

In the Civil War, the royalist army at first fought its parliamentary adversary to a standstill, but at Marston Moor in 1644 and Naseby in 1646 royalist troops fell to Parliament's New Model Army headed by Oliver Cromwell

(1599–1658), a Puritan from the lower gentry who turned out to be an effective, persuasive military leader. Rather than surrender to such a zealot, Charles decided to take his chances with the Scots, to whom he capitulated in 1648—but only after reaching an agreement with several leading members of the Scottish nobility in December 1647 by which the king promised to establish Presbyterianism in England for three years, promote free trade between England and Scotland, and appoint Scots to his Privy Council, his household staff, and the staff of his son and heir, all in exchange for the Scots' support to help him regain control of England. Despite Charles's promises to transform England into a Presbyterian nation, English Presbyterians did not throw their allegiance to the king. In August 1648 Cromwell defeated the Scots at the Battle of Preston and captured Charles I. The execution of Charles on January 30, 1649, left England without a monarch, without the House of Lords, with a judiciary from which roughly half of the judges had resigned, and under the control of the Parliamentary army and a Rump Parliament that dismissed ninety-six Presbyterian members and was largely discredited. The future government of England was uncertain.

As some members of Parliament looked to enrich themselves, others turned to the leadership of the strongest man in the realm at that time—Cromwell. With the backing of the army, Cromwell could dictate the terms of government or change it at will whenever things did not go according to his plan. The English government under Oliver Cromwell in the 1650s was more absolute than that of any of the Stuart monarchs of the seventeenth century, even though Cromwell adopted the title of "Lord Protector" instead of "King."

Meanwhile, during the Civil War an inclination toward religious toleration and the autonomy of individual congregations began to spread throughout the parliamentary forces. In addition, religious radicals proposed new beliefs, including the idea that hell and sin did not exist but were only conventions used by the rich and powerful to keep the poor in their place. New religious sects like the Quakers and Ranters believed in direct personal inspiration from God. The Quakers believed that individuals had an "inner light" that reflected the divine spark within them. The Ranters argued that good and evil existed only in people's minds and that any action was good if one believed it to be so. Oliver Cromwell made Puritanism the dominant force in English religious and social life, but he personally favored religious toleration and did not persecute people for their private beliefs or practices. Even the Catholics enjoyed a measure of toleration under Cromwell, while Jews were legally permitted back into England for the first time since 1290. Puritans resented his lenient attitudes toward Catholics and questioned his decision to go to war against the Protestant Dutch.

For the time being, it appeared that the Stuarts' attempt to impose royal absolutism in England had failed, but Charles's execution aroused an immediate, strong public reaction that was sympathetic to the monarchy. Many began to view Charles as a religious martyr who had sacrificed his life to the religious principles of the Anglican Church. A ghost-written memoir titled *Eikon Basilike* contributed significantly to this upswell of support for the dead king. The decision to execute Charles thus set the tone for the succeeding ten years when England had no king but when support for the monarchy had never been stronger since the sixteenth century. Charles's execution paved the way in many respects for the restoration of the Stuart monarchy in 1660 on very favorable terms. His death, furthermore, helped to shape English history by contributing to a growing intolerance of religious fanaticism and a long-term skepticism toward political radicalism. Charles's execution also reverberated throughout the European continent for a long time. It taught a lesson to monarchs such as Louis XIV to take a hard line with their subjects and not to make concessions that might show a sign of weakness. Yet it also established an irreversible precedent in European history: subjects could not only rise up and overthrow a monarch but abolish a monarchy altogether. In less than a century, American revolutionaries would put an end to monarchical control of the English colonies. Finally, the fate of Charles set a precedent for the fates of Louis XVI in France in 1793 and Nicholas II in Russia in 1918.

In spite of growing opposition, Cromwell's control of the army maintained him in power until his death in 1658, when supporters of Charles, oldest son of Charles I, began to think about the restoration of the Stuart monarchy. Cromwell's son, Richard, succeeded his father as Lord Protector, but he could not control the army as his father had done. Within two years army leaders, led by General George Monck, began to negotiate with Charles Stuart for his return to England to assume the throne. In April 1660 the Long Parliament, which had met since November 1640, finally gave way to a new parliament that favored the restoration of the monarchy and in fact restored Charles II to the throne a few months later. Although the Restoration left unresolved some of the earlier issues related to the balance of power between king and parliament, it did entail the reestablishment of the House of Lords, the bishops' resumption of their positions in the Anglican Church, and an end to Puritan restrictions on dress and celebrations, including Christmas, which had been imposed during the Interregnum. In an effort to purge Puritan influences from the church, a new Uniformity Act in 1662 required Anglican clergy to use the Book of Common Prayer. The size of the army was reduced to 5,000 men and placed back under the control of the king, but—having witnessed the fate of his father—Charles did his best not to alienate his subjects for the rest of his reign, which lasted until 1685.

Political Conflict and Development in the Netherlands

In the late sixteenth century William of Orange (1533–1584), known as William the Silent, led the Dutch revolt against the political and religious absolutism of Philip II of Spain, who had been named ruler of the Netherlands by his father, Holy Roman Emperor Charles V. Philip had angered his Dutch subjects by refusing to compromise either on the issue of religious toleration or on the political position of the Spanish monarchy in the Netherlands. Although the Calvinist Reformation and opposition to Philip spread throughout both the northern and southern Netherlands, the Netherlands divided into two separate political entities after the revolt. The provinces of the southern Netherlands (the area that is today the country of Belgium), where the population was mostly Catholic, remained a Spanish dominion. The seven provinces of the northern Netherlands formed a new, independent political state officially known as the United Provinces of the Netherlands. By the end of the sixteenth century, the newly independent United Provinces was developing into a powerful commercial nation and an important financial center.

Having developed a tradition of challenging absolutism during the revolt against Spain in the sixteenth century, the United Provinces of the Netherlands continued in the seventeenth to symbolize that challenge first by sustaining resistance to Spanish authority and later by leading the opposition to the expansionist policies of the French absolutist, Louis XIV. In addition, the United Provinces devised a representative form of government that resisted the emergence of a single absolute ruler from within. In 1609 the Netherlands concluded a truce with Spain that lasted for twelve years. As in other European states, issues related to religion and foreign policy threatened the unity of the United Provinces. Preachers of the Dutch Reformed Church thought that the new government was too tolerant of other religions. Religious moderates wanted a permanent peace with Spain, while more adamant Calvinists within the Dutch Reformed Church opposed any kind of treaty with Catholic Spain, including the Twelve-Year Truce. The resumption of war with Spain in 1621 brought competing interests in the country together until the defeat of the Spanish Habsburgs in the Thirty Years War ended any threat to the independence of the Netherlands. But the Netherlands faced another political crisis that soon threatened the stability of the government.

Frederick Henry (1587–1647) and his son William II (1626–1650) of the House of Orange were the military commanders in chief of the United Provinces as well as stadtholders—leading officials charged with the enforcement of justice—in six of the seven provinces. At the end of the Thirty Years War in 1648, the Dutch Estates General ordered William to reduce the size of his army and lower taxes. With the army at his control, however, William refused to accede to these demands. William's refusal to obey the orders of the Estates General, along with his position as stadtholder in most of the provinces, suggested that he might easily become an absolute ruler. The crisis resolved itself when William died of smallpox in 1650, leaving only a one-year-old son. The following year the Estates General passed a resolution forbidding a stadtholder from ever holding office in every province at the same time. The United Provinces went without a stadtholder until Zeeland named William III to the position in 1672; within days, the 1651 edict was ignored and William became stadtholder in every province to unify the country for war with the French.

War and Political Consciousness in the Seventeenth Century

Throughout the European continent, war and politics were closely intertwined. When Henry IV ascended the throne at the conclusion of the French wars of religion, he inherited the French wars with the Habsburgs. Those wars halted temporarily at the end of the sixteenth century, but were revived by Henry's successor, Louis XIII, and his chief minister, Cardinal Richelieu. Religion and nationalist politics flared into a quarrel between the kingdom of Bohemia and the Habsburg emperors, which flared into the conflagration of the Thirty Years War in central Europe. War, religion, and political absolutism all seemed to combine to reinforce themselves in Europe during the first half of the seventeenth century.

The connection between war and the rise of political absolutism was reinforced by a series of changes and innovations in warfare that some historians have labeled a "military revolution." The major changes were a significant increase in the size of armies; the need for increased levels of administration and greater organization to supply, equip, and train larger armies; the adoption of new kinds of weapons, such as muskets and movable artillery; and novel strategies and tactics suited to these other changes. Stronger fortifications were also needed for defensive purposes against increased military firepower. Possession of larger armies and more efficient military bureaucracies gave the monarchs that controlled them greater power. The men who served in military units and administration displayed greater devotion to the state that they served; increasingly, military careers and promotions were opened up to talent instead of based on social rank or birth.

The Thirty Years' War, like the English Civil War, began as a struggle against absolutism and in its early stages involved a resumption of the religious wars of the sixteenth century. In 1617 the Holy Roman Emperor Matthias appointed his Catholic cousin, Ferdinand, as king of Protestant Bohemia. When

Ferdinand attempted to restore Catholicism in the kingdom, the Bohemian nobility protested. In a dramatic rejection of imperial authority, Bohemians threw two of Ferdinand's regents out of an upper-story window in the royal palace, an event that became known as the Defenestration of Prague from the Latin word for "window," *fenestra*. The Bohemian assembly then formed a provisional government and raised an army of 5,000 soldiers to liberate the country from imperial troops. The Protestant forces won some initial victories, but in 1619 Matthias died and Ferdinand, succeeding him as Holy Roman Emperor, found himself suddenly armed with vast resources to throw against his rebellious kingdom.

Alarmed by an overwhelming Catholic victory in Bohemia and fearing the spread of Catholicism to his own land, in 1625 King Christian IV brought Denmark into the war to prevent the collapse of Protestantism in northern Germany. By 1629, imperial forces, under the command of General Albrecht von Wallenstein, had defeated Christian's army and driven it out of German territory. The Edict of Restitution of 1629, which outlawed Calvinism in German lands and called for all lands that had become Protestant since 1552 to return to Catholicism, marked the highpoint for militant Catholics who hoped to reunite Europe under a single faith. But Christian's defeat led King Gustavus Aldolphus of Protestant Sweden—having concluded a treaty with Cardinal Richelieu that promised France's financial support—to invade Germany in 1630. Protestant forces were temporarily bolstered by Sweden's entry into the war. Swedish forces captured Munich and won the Battle of Lützen (1632), although Gustavus was killed in battle. The following year, imperial forces under Wallenstein won several victories over the Swedes. At this point, however, religious motivations among the leading participants soon became secondary to political and personal motivations. Wallenstein—on his own initiative—entered into secret peace negotiations with Saxony, Sweden, and France. (When Ferdinand learned of these negotiations, he removed Wallenstein from command of the imperial troops; the general was later assassinated.) In 1635 Holy Roman Emperor Ferdinand began negotiating with Brandenburg and Saxony in an attempt to exploit divisions in the Protestant alliance between those German states and Sweden, successfully convincing Brandenburg to ally itself with imperial forces. Brandenburg and Sweden were embroiled in a dispute over each other's claim to the territory of Pomerania. The shift away from religious motivations became even more evident when Catholic France entered the war on the side of the Protestants against the imperial Habsburgs in 1635.

It was only a matter of time before pure exhaustion brought an end to a devastating conflict that had destroyed entire towns, caused numerous civilian atrocities, and ravaged the German lands and economy. Civilians during the

---

Siege of Magdeburg

The following is an extract from a firsthand account of the aftermath of the siege of Magdeburg in 1631.

The number of those who were killed or died in the city—for not only the sword but also the fire swallowed up many people—cannot be accurately known. Soon after this appalling conflagration General Tilly had the corpses of those who had been burned or killed in other ways loaded from the streets, ramparts and elsewhere on to wagons and put into the waters of the Elbe, but for almost a full year afterwards many dead bodies were found—five, six, eight, ten or more at a time—in the ruined cellars where they had been overcome and had suffocated. Furthermore those who lay in the streets had been so consumed by the fire and shattered by the falling buildings that the pieces often had to be loaded up with pitchforks, with the result that no-one will be able to give the real number. By and large, however, it is thought that of the order of 20,000 people, adults and children, had to end their lives or suffered bodily injuries in such grim circumstances. This includes the two suburbs, and those of the Imperialist soldiers who died and were burned, for not only did many fall at various points in the assault but a good number were also late in leaving, spending too long searching houses or cellars or otherwise getting lost. The dead bodies which were put into the Elbe outside, in front of the Water Gate, were unable or unwilling to drift quickly away because at that point there is a whirlpool or eddy. Thus many floated about there for a long time, some with their heads out of the water and others with their hands outstretched as if to heaven, making a gruesome spectacle for onlookers. There was much prattle about this, folk saying that it was exactly as though these dead people were still praying, singing and crying out to heaven for vengeance.

—Otto von Guericke, Magdeburg council member

Source: Geoff Mortimer, *Eyewitness Accounts of the Thirty Years War, 1618–1648* (London: Palgrave, 2002), p. 70. Reprinted by permission of Palgrave Macmillan.

---

war commonly faced the threat of plunder and robbery; stories of rape and violence against civilians added to an atmosphere of fear. When General Tilly, commander of the forces of the Habsburg alliance, sacked Magdeburg in 1631, the city went up in flames and most of its citizens perished.

Military casualties were enormous, taking their worst toll on a country like Sweden, which had a relatively small population to begin with. Of 230 men recruited from one Swedish village during the war, 215 died; Sweden may have lost as many as 150,000 men during the course of the war. The overall population of Germany declined from 20 million in 1618 to perhaps as low as 16 million at the end of the war. In the 1648 Peace of Westphalia that ended the war, France, Sweden, and Brandenburg-Prussia each gained additional territory, prestige, and power. The big losers in the Thirty Years' War were the Holy Roman Empire, which lost many of its German lands, as well as considerable authority, and Spain, which continued to decline as a great power. Germany remained disunited for another two centuries, although within the empire, absolutism was strengthened in Brandenburg-Prussia and Austria, both of which would start to emerge as great powers in the succeeding period.

Louis XIV, however, was dissatisfied with the gains that France had made in the Thirty Years' War. (While Louis was still in his minority, France had continued fighting against Spain until the Treaty of the Pyrenees finally ended the conflict between those two rivals in 1659.) Assuming power for himself in 1661, Louis believed that military victories and territorial acquisition represented a major measure of his success as king. Throughout most of his reign he pursued war with an aggression that earned him the enmity of almost every other European nation. He began his military career on the attack, waging war against the United Provinces of the Netherlands in 1667 on specious grounds, but ended up struggling to maintain France's own territorial integrity against a coalition of every other major European power; other rulers, fearing Louis's apparently unlimited ambition, set aside their own differences to prevent France from dominating all of Europe. In his first war with the Dutch, Louis claimed that he was merely expanding French territory to its natural boundaries, but England, Sweden, and the United Provinces united against him and forced him to negotiate. However, after securing an alliance with England in 1670 based on a financial arrangement with the restored Stuart king, Charles II, Louis launched a second invasion in 1672. The Dutch barely survived, partly because of a decision to open the dikes and flood their own country to cut off Louis's army from the city of Amsterdam and the province of Holland and partly because of a second alliance organized by William of Orange (1650–1702), who was now determined to construct a permanent coalition capable of restraining French ambitions. Louis's continued aggressiveness pushed other nations into alliance with the Dutch. His claims to additional lands in western Germany in the 1680s led to a European-wide coalition called the League of Augsburg, which went to war with Louis in 1689. The two sides were well balanced and neither produced any great military leaders capable of producing a decisive victory. Louis kept Alsace and Strasbourg, but agreed to a commercial treaty with the United Provinces and accepted the claims of the Dutch William of Orange to the throne of England, which Louis had previously opposed. The constant combat caused a dramatic increase in the size of armies and took a

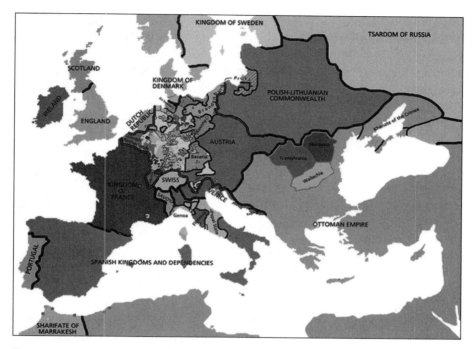

Europe after the Peace of Westphalia, 1648

heavy toll on the French population. Louis faced an allied army of 200,000 men in the War of the League of Augsburg (1689–1697), the largest to that date in European history. During the thirteen years of the War of the Spanish Succession (1701–1714), 455,000 men were inducted into the French army. By the end of that war, after nearly fifty years of continuous fighting, France was an exhausted and depressed nation—an ignominious conclusion to the reign of the Sun King.

Meanwhile, the Austrians had faced a great threat from the military expansion of the Ottoman Turks in their direction. The Habsburgs clashed with the Ottomans mainly over Hungary and Transylvania. The Ottomans invaded at times when the Austrians were preoccupied with fighting Louis XIV, while the Habsburgs initiated counterthrusts during lulls in the European wars. The Ottomans sought to stop Habsburg expansion rather than aiming at widespread conquest and domination in Europe. But other European powers—with the exception of Louis XIV, who actually made an alliance with the Turks—chose not to ignore the Ottoman threat and feared the implications of the fall of Austria to a Muslim power. Ever since the fall of Constantinople to the Turks in 1453, Europeans had engaged in an intermittent struggle against the Turks on land and sea, with neither side holding a significant advantage in arms or military technology. But after about seventy years of mostly truce—the Ottomans remaining neutral during the Thirty Years War—the Turks began a more aggressive offensive against Transylvania and Slovakia in the 1660s. As the Habsburgs were unprepared at that time to confront the Ottoman threat, they negotiated a treaty in 1664 that only encouraged the Turks to launch a series of additional wars in Hungary, Crete, Poland, and Russia over the next twenty years. During that period, political divisions and fighting among European powers made it difficult to stop the advancing borders of the Ottoman Empire. When the Turks placed Vienna itself under siege in 1683, however, a coalition of Venice, Poland, and Russia launched simultaneous attacks on the Ottomans and recaptured much of the territory that had been lost in the previous decades. Polish forces came to the rescue at Vienna, after which Austria went back on the offensive, driving the Ottoman army to the other side of the Danube River by 1697.

One of the best examples of the connection between war and absolutism was Russia under Peter the Great. Victory in wars against the Ottoman Empire and against Sweden gained Peter additional territory and enhanced the prestige of the Romanov dynasty. After a tour of Western Europe in 1697–1698, Peter began sending Russians to Western Europe to receive military training. He also invited experts from Italy, England, Scotland, Germany, and the Netherlands to Russia to oversee the building of his ships, to teach navigation and engineering, and to help train his army. In November 1700 the greatly outnumbered but modern Swedish forces routed the Russian infantry—with its woefully inferior military technology—besieging the fortress of Narva on the Gulf of Finland. But before long Peter's military reforms paid off; by 1721 Sweden had acknowledged defeat in the Great Northern War and a new superpower had emerged on the European scene.

Conclusion

The seventeenth century in Europe was a time of tumult during which wars fought over religion gave way to wars fought primarily for dynastic glory and territorial expansion. Rulers sought to impose a more absolute form of government, partly as a way of gaining control over the resources of their country needed for war. They also believed that one head was better than many. But the death and destruction caused by wars, the high taxes they involved, and abuses of power, such as Louis XIV's decision to expel the Huguenots from France in 1685, provoked a strong reaction among European intellectuals. The religious radicalism that contributed to the overthrow of Charles I in England and flourished during the English Civil War provoked a strong reaction as well.

During the seventeenth century political philosophers such as Thomas Hobbes and John Locke advanced new theories about human nature and about the role and authority of the state. Natural philosophers speculated about the nature of the cosmos and the laws that governed the earth and the heavens, which they believed God had created. War and political maneuvering altered the political boundaries of the European states in the seventeenth century. Likewise, the scientific, philosophical, and cultural changes of that era altered humanity's understanding of itself, its conception of the divine, and its ideas about the world and the universe.

1. What factors led to the success of absolute monarchy in France?
2. What common themes emerge in the political development of Spain, Austria, Prussia, and Russia in the seventeenth century? Are there significant differences?
3. In what ways was the absolute monarchy of Kangxi in China similar to and different from the monarchy of Louis XIV in France?
4. What was the nature of the conflict between king and Parliament in seventeenth-century England? Did the Civil War resolve the conflict?
5. Why were war and political absolutism connected in seventeenth-century Europe?

Suggestions for Further Reading

Asch, Ronald G. 1997. *The Thirty Years War: The Holy Roman Empire and Europe, 1618–1648*. New York: St. Martin's Press.

Briggs, Robin. 1998. *Early Modern France, 1560–1715*. Oxford: Oxford University Press.

Coward, Barry. 2003. *The Stuart Age: England, 1603–1714*. 3rd ed. London: Longman.

Cracraft, James. 2003. *The Revolution of Peter the Great*. Cambridge, MA: Harvard University Press.

Monod, Paul Kléber. 1999. *The Power of Kings: Monarchy and Religion in Europe, 1589–1715*. New Haven, CT: Yale University Press.

Spence, Jonathan. 2002. *Treason by the Book*. New York: Penguin.

Suggested Websites

www.bbc.co.uk/history/war/englishcivilwar/index.shtml
This BBC multimedia website is a good source for basic information about the English Civil War and historical interpretations of different aspects of the war by prominent English historians, with links to related historical topics.

www.fordham.edu/halsall/mod/modsbook05.html

This website contains excerpts from a number of primary sources dealing with the topic of seventeenth-century absolutism, including passages from books by James I of England and Bishop Bossuet in France.

www.fordham.edu/halsall/mod/modsbook06.html

Like the previous link, this one is from Fordham University's modern European history website and is devoted to constitutionalism, with sources related to England and the Netherlands during the seventeenth century.

www.fordham.edu/halsall/mod/petergreat.html

This link contains excerpts from four primary sources dealing with the life and reign of Peter the Great of Russia.

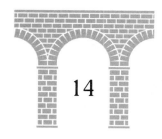

14 The Scientific Revolution and Changes in Thought and Society in the Seventeenth Century

The sixteenth and seventeenth centuries produced challenges to accepted truth in science, philosophy, art, and literature, in addition to the challenges to religious and political authority discussed in the previous chapters. The period witnessed many significant changes in virtually every realm of life and thought. If every age is to some degree an age of transition, the seventeenth century seemed to mark a more dramatic transition than most. In particular, the Scientific Revolution challenged the authority of ancient authors and contemporary religion with its discovery and advocacy of new ideas about the universe and the natural world—a challenge that reverberated throughout thought, art, literature, and everyday life in Europe and, perhaps surprisingly, in India as well.

The Shaping of the Past: Copernicus's *On the Revolution of the Heavenly Bodies* and the Scientific Revolution

A Polish astronomer provided the first important challenge to existing views about science in the first half of the sixteenth century. Nicolaus Copernicus (1473–1543) attended the University of Cracow in anticipation of a career in the Catholic Church. At Cracow, he was exposed to recent ideas about astronomy, including a book called *The New Theory of the Planets* by George Peuerbach (1423–1462). Peuerbach's book updated the work of the Greek astronomer Ptolemy and provided new astronomical tables that would allow more accurate prediction of the movements of the heavens. Copernicus's interest in astronomy deepened as he continued his education at the University of Bologna in Italy, where he also studied medicine, law, and philosophy. Astronomy was becoming an important issue for several reasons, not the least of which was an interest in calendar reform on the part of the church. Copernicus became aware of this interest at a conference in Rome in 1500.

Copernicus argued that Ptolemy's model of a geocentric universe, the ac-

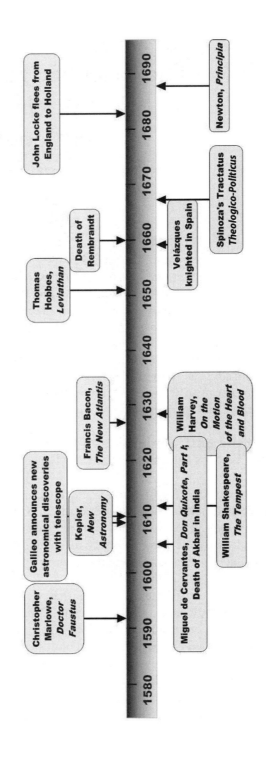

Andreas Cellarius, planisphere of the Copernican universe. This hand-colored, engraved chart illustrates the movement of the planets according to Copernicus's heliocentric theory of the universe. It appeared in *A Celestial Atlas, or the Harmony of the Universe* (1660–1661), published in Amsterdam by Joannes Janssonius.

cepted view until the sixteenth century, was wrong. Ptolemy posited Earth at the center of the universe, with all the other heavenly bodies, including a fixed crystalline sphere of stars, revolving around it. Ptolemy's system included the cumbersome device of epicycles, circles within circles, to account for the observed retrograde motion of the planets, which appeared to move backward in the heavens in their revolution around Earth. Copernicus eliminated the need for epicycles by postulating that not all heavenly bodies revolved around a single body. In fact, Copernicus said that only the moon revolved around Earth, while Earth, other heavenly bodies, and the crystalline sphere of stars revolved around the sun. The time required by each planet's revolution depended on each planet's distance from the sun. Furthermore, according to Copernicus, Earth rotates on its axis every twenty-four hours, causing the appearance of the movement of the heavens and the sun. Copernicus's heliocentric, or sun-centered, theory of the universe challenged accepted beliefs, apparently diminishing the importance of Earth because of its displacement from the center.

Copernicus, aware of the radical and potentially controversial nature of his astronomical ideas, waited until the year of his death (1543) to allow for the publication of his book, *On the Revolution of the Heavenly Bodies*. Protestants, who believed in the sole authority of the Bible and tended to take its words literally, initially voiced more opposition to the heliocentric theory than did Catholics because it seemed to contradict certain biblical passages, though their objections were not sustained over time. At first, the Catholic Church accepted his system, though as a theory rather than a fact—hypothetical speculation that served the purposes of calendar reform but did not necessarily reflect the physical nature of reality. But Copernicus did believe in the physical reality of the heliocentric universe.

The international influence of Copernicus's work is reflected in the further contributions of the Danish scholar Tycho Brahe (1546–1601), Brahe's German student, Johannes Kepler (1571–1630), and the Italian physicist and astronomer, Galileo Galilei (1565–1642). Brahe's observations led him to agree with Copernicus that the Ptolemaic system was obsolete and did not represent an accurate description of physical reality. But Brahe did not become a Copernican, instead devising his own system that did not include Earth's rotation and that kept Earth in the center of the universe. Brahe made a significant contribution to the understanding of astronomy, however, through his demonstration that the celestial realm was not static and unchanging, a point he emphasized in conjunction with his observations of a comet in 1577. Kepler, who shared the quality of theoretical brilliance with Copernicus, made use of the vast amount of observational data that had been accumulated from Brahe's impressive observatories at his castle at Uraniborg. Influenced by the medieval concept of the "music of the spheres," Kepler set out to demonstrate that perfect musical harmony existed in the movements of the heavenly bodies, thus proving the inevitable mathematical perfection of God's creation. To his surprise, he found that the heavens did not behave quite the way he thought they would. Expecting the planets to travel around the sun in perfect circles, a symbol of mathematical perfection, he found instead that they moved in ellipses, or ovals, that seemed to undermine his ideas about musical harmony. Kepler never completely abandoned his belief in the theory of celestial harmony, but to his credit he did not ignore the observational evidence that seemed to challenge that belief.

Galileo, building on the achievements of Copernicus, Brahe, and Kepler, helped to prepare the way for the accomplishments of Isaac Newton (1642–1727). Galileo was aided by the invention of the telescope, which he refined after it was invented by the Dutch. With this new instrument, which allowed him in 1610 to see heavenly bodies magnified by the power of thirty, he observed the irregular surface of the moon, the moons of Jupiter, the different phases of Venus, and the irregular shape of Saturn. These revealing discoveries altered the prevailing perceptions of the heavens by challenging the notion of the perfection of heavenly bodies. But Galileo went beyond these observational discoveries to become an ardent defender of the Copernican system, thus landing him in a great deal of difficulty with the Catholic Church. Galileo made it his business to see that the Copernican theory gained wider acceptance, even if that meant pointing out places where the Bible was inaccurate. Far from objecting to the Copernican theory, leading churchmen had in fact praised it because it allowed accurate calculations to ensure the appropriate celebration of the holy days on the Christian calendar. But now the church formally objected to the physical reality of the Copernican system in a 1616 ruling by the Congregation of the Holy Office that affirmed the veracity of the scriptures and the inaccuracy of Copernicanism.

As a physicist interested in the study of motion, Galileo made important discoveries related to the pendulum (an object suspended from a fixed point will move back and forth in equal times), gravity (objects naturally move downward unless the medium surrounding them exceeds them in gravity), mechanics (bodies will not move horizontally unless some external force compels them to do so), and kinematics (bodies of unequal weight fall at the same rate of speed). But Galileo's defense of the Copernican system was based on his observations rather than on mathematics or physics. Later in the seventeenth century, Isaac Newton explained exactly how the moons of Jupiter discovered by Galileo stayed in their orbits. Newton conceived of his theory of gravity not because of an apple falling on his head, as the legend goes, but through careful scientific reflection over a number of years. Newton eventually came to the conclusion that gravitational force between one body and another orbiting body is directly proportional to the masses of both bodies. Perhaps his most revolutionary idea was that the force of gravity connects all material particles in the universe.

In 1687 Newton published his main ideas on physics in his *Principia*, consolidating the mathematical approach to the study of nature, which ran counter to the previous English inductive tradition of observation and experiment and to the prevailing philosophy of the Royal Society of scientists in England. Newton worked in a tradition that believed in the existence of atoms, tiny particles of matter not visible to the naked eye that constantly interacted with each other. He believed that every motion had to have a cause and that force lies behind every motion. In the *Principia*, Newton defined the relationship between the moon's movement and Earth's gravity in terms of the universal role that gravity plays in the cosmos. But he believed that gravity operated according to the laws of physics and mathematics, not as some sort of mysterious, magical principle.

In 1543, the same year as the publication of Copernicus's famous work,

Andreas Vesalius (1514–1564), a Dutch physician, published *On the Structure of the Human Body*, with elaborate illustrations and thorough descriptions. From 1537 to 1544 Vesalius taught anatomy and surgery at the University of Padua, where he performed dissections in front of his students, greatly advancing knowledge of human anatomy. The tradition he began there was carried on by his student, Gabriele Fallopio (1523–1563), who discovered the fallopian tubes and taught at Padua, and the Englishman William Harvey (1578–1657), who furthered his education at Padua after beginning his studies at the University of Cambridge. Harvey was an adherent of Aristotelian philosophy, which emphasized the perfection of circular motion and stressed the search for "final causes." Both concepts contributed to Harvey's discovery of the circulation of the blood. In his *On the Motion of the Heart and Blood*, Harvey suggested that the heart actively contracts in a motion called the systole, and rests when it expands in a condition called the diastole. The contraction of the heart causes the dilation of the arteries, which carry blood away from the heart to other parts of the body—the pulmonary artery, for example, carrying blood to the lungs. Harvey discovered that veins carry blood back to the heart, hence the circulation of the blood.

Although Harvey was influenced by Aristotelian ideas, he, like Kepler, was prepared to reject his preconceived notions if experience taught him otherwise, one of the most important characteristics of the movement known as the Scientific Revolution. Harvey's contemporary Francis Bacon (1561–1627) was not so much a scientist himself as he was a major spokesman for the Scientific Revolution and a strong advocate of the ideals of experimentation and observation. Bacon did not stress knowledge for its own sake but believed that science had a practical role to play in ameliorating the life of human beings. He believed that only scientists and inventors working together could fulfill human potential by harnessing the forces of the universe on humanity's behalf. A prominent political figure in England who rose to the position of Lord Chancellor under James I, Bacon sought to encourage useful technological inventions as much as he promoted the importance of scientific discovery. His major works, *The New Organon* and *The Great Instauration*, both of which appeared in 1620, laid out his scientific philosophy and encouraged the implementation of the scientific method to create a new body of learning that would usher in a new age of peace, prosperity, and scientific, medical, and technological advances. Before he died, Bacon wrote a utopian work titled *The New Atlantis*, which was published posthumously in 1627. Bacon's ideal society was devoted to "the knowledge of causes, and secret motions of things; and the enlarging of the bounds of Human Empire, to the effecting of all things possible." To this end, Bacon speculated about the digging of deep caves in imitation of mines for producing artificial metals, the grafting and inoculating of fruit trees, and technological advances in furnaces, textile works, and engines, including machines that "imitate the flight of birds" and "boats to go under water."

The Frenchman, René Descartes (1596–1650), shared with Bacon a confidence in human reason and a desire for a new approach to learning that did not rely on the inherited knowledge from the past. Whereas Bacon stressed induction through observation and experiment, Descartes relied on deduction, using the rational powers of the human mind. Descartes started with the epistemological question: how could he know that any knowledge he had was correct? The problem with Bacon's inductive method was that it relied on the senses, but Descartes could think of many instances when our senses deceive us. But there was one thing, Descartes believed, of which he could be absolutely certain—that he existed. He came to this conclusion based on his inability to imagine that someone else was thinking his thoughts, leading him to his famous conclusion: "I think, therefore I am" (*Cogito ergo sum*). Furthermore, Descartes believed only God could have provided him with the notion that God existed—therefore, God must exist as well. And if God existed surely he would not deceive humans intentionally. On this basis, Descartes developed the confidence that, if he used reason properly, he could learn truths about the material and natural world. Descartes contributed to the Scientific Revolution in a different way than Bacon, but he did contribute through his promotion of the scientific method, his distinction between mind and extension, and his emphasis on the application of mathematics to scientific problems.

Most scientific thinkers in sixteenth- and seventeenth-century Europe were Christians, although their scientific achievements are often anachronistically taught or studied without reference to their religious beliefs. To do so distorts the context of their thought and the historical significance of the Scientific Revolution because their ideas about nature and human nature could not be separated from their ideas about God. Kepler, for example, was a philosopher as well as a scientist; he believed that his work in astronomy served a larger purpose in revealing the magnificence of the divine power that underlay the creation of the physical world and the celestial universe. Descartes remained a life-long Catholic, content to accept religious faith as a mystery not subject to rational analysis. Newton believed in a mechanical universe, but he was also a natural philosopher and a religious scholar who pursued alchemy and theology in addition to his study of physics and mathematics. The Swiss physician and medical scholar known as Paracelsus (1493–1541), an important forerunner of the work of Harvey, combined medicine with religion to such an extent that his real contributions to the Scientific Revolution have frequently been called into question. Paracelsus's main contribution was his criticism of existing medical knowledge, with which he was thoroughly familiar. He also

Francis Bacon, *The New Atlantis*

We have dispensatories, or shops of medicines. Wherein you may easily think, if we have such a variety of plants and living creatures more than you have in Europe (for we know what you have), the simples, drugs, and ingredients of medicines must likewise be in so much the greater variety. We have them likewise of diverse ages and long fermentations. And for their preparations, we have not only all manner of exquisite distillations and separations, and especially by gentle heats and percolations through divers strainers, yea and substances, but also exact forms of composition, whereby they incorporate almost as they were natural simples.

We have also diverse mechanical arts, which you have not, and stuffs made by them, as papers, linen, silks, tissues, dainty works of feathers of wonderful luster, excellent dyes, and many others; and shops likewise as well for such as are not brought into vulgar use amongst us as for those that are. For you must know that of the things before recited, many of them are grown into use throughout the kingdom, but yet if they did not flow from our invention, we have of them also for patterns and principals.

We have also furnaces of great diversities and that keep great diversity of heats; fierce and quick; strong and constant; soft and mild; blown, quiet; dry, moist; and the like. But above all, we have heats in imitation of the sun's and heavenly bodies' heats, that pass divers inequalities and (as it were) orbs, progresses, and returns, whereby we produce admirable effects. Besides, we have heats of dungs, and of bellies and maws of living creatures, and of their bloods and bodies, and of hays and herbs laid up moist, of lime unquenched, and such like. Instruments also which generate heat only by motion. And farther, places for strong insolations; and again, places under the earth, which by nature or art yield heat. These divers heats we use, as the nature of the operation which we intend require. . . .

We also have engine-houses, where are prepared engines and instruments for all sorts of motions. There we imitate and practice to make swifter motions than any you have, either out of your muskets or any engine that you have; and to make them and multiply them more easily and with small force by wheels and other means, and to make them stronger and more violent than yours are, exceeding your greatest cannons and basilisks. We represent also ordnance and instruments of war, and engines of all kinds, and likewise new mixtures and compositions of gunpowder, wildfires burning in water and unquenchable. Also fireworks of all variety both for pleasure and use. We imitate also flights of birds; we have some degrees of flying in the air; we have ships and boats for going under water . . . also swimming-girdles and supporters. We have divers curious clocks and other like motions or return and some perpetual motions. . . .

Source: Sidney Warhaft, ed., *Francis Bacon: A Selection of His Works* (New York: Odyssey Press, 1965), pp. 451–452, 454.

What do these passages reveal about Bacon's views on the potential benefits of science for humanity? Would these benefits create the kind of scientific utopia Bacon envisioned? Have we created a society that lives up to Bacon's vision? What do you think he would say about our current level of technology?

combined medicine and surgery, which had not been common in the Middle Ages. But as a sympathizer with the Protestant Reformation, he relied a great deal on the authority of the scriptures at the same time that he rejected the authority of Galen and Aristotle. Michael Servetus (1511–1553), who was burned at the stake as a heretic in Calvin's Geneva for his anti-Trinitarian ideas, also rankled religious authorities by his use of dissection, which led him to discover the circulation of the blood through the lungs.

The portrayal of religion and science as separate spheres during the Scientific Revolution usually derives from Galileo's conflict with the Catholic Church over the Copernican theory. Galileo challenged the church's position by arguing that the church was foolish to ignore physical evidence, even if it contradicted the Bible. However, Galileo did not challenge the truth of Christianity—he merely wanted the church to support the Copernican system because he believed that clerical opposition would prevent further advances in science. From the church's perspective, it could not admit that it was wrong about astronomy because, in the midst of the Counter-Reformation and with Europe embroiled in religious conflict, people might question its infallibility in other areas.

How can we ultimately account for the Scientific Revolution and the remarkable collection of individuals who contributed to it, only a select few of whom appear in this text? Science received strong support during the sixteenth and seventeenth centuries because of the practical needs of an age obsessed with navigation and warfare, though how much impact this encouragement had on the achievements of the Scientific Revolution is open to question. The printing press made scientific texts more widely available to scholars throughout Europe. But the printing press also worked as an instrument of conservatism; in medicine, for example, printers perpetuated the classical texts of Galen and ignored the visionary work of Paracelsus. Most of the main contributors to the Scientific Revolution had some university education. But most universities at that time were bastions of tradition, embracing the value of classical learning rather than promoting new knowledge and innovative discoveries. Despite their exclusion from universities, women played a role in the scientific revolution, mostly as patrons of learning and of salons that allowed thinkers to meet and exchange ideas and knowledge. But, despite their role and interest in science, women did not receive encouragement or support for their own scientific

Visit Rice University's Galileo Project website for information and images related to Copernicus, Galileo, and the Scientific Revolution at http://galileo.rice.edu/sci/theories/copernican_system.html.

activities. One explanation to account for the Scientific Revolution would be to consider the publication of Copernicus's *On the Revolution of the Heavenly Bodies* as a shaping moment that changed people's views of the world and their attitudes toward scientific authorities. Copernicus obviously did not accomplish this change alone, as the work of contemporaries like Paracelsus and Vesalius demonstrates. However, the Copernican view of the universe became the most important symbol of the need for a better understanding of the universe, the world, and the role of humanity within it. For the Copernican system challenged more than just Ptolemaic astronomy; it encouraged challenges to the Christian view of humanity at the center of God's creation.

Political Thought in the Seventeenth Century

Challenges to traditional authorities in religion and science inevitably gave way to challenges to other types of authority, including political authority. Therefore, it is no coincidence that in the seventeenth century monarchs and thinkers concerned with political stability found it necessary either to reaffirm the legitimacy of political authority or to find new foundations for that authority. In France, for example, Cardinal Richelieu believed in the divine right of kings, though he stressed the need for kings to rule in accordance with divine law and to respect God. Monarchs must set a high moral example for the rest of the kingdom and cannot expect more of their subjects than they demand of themselves. Richelieu believed that kings especially would have to answer to God for any abuse of power or unjust acts, a common characteristic of divine right theory. Other thinkers formulated political theories that would justify resistance to authority in certain instances. A French Protestant named Philippe Duplessis-Mornay (1549–1623), an adviser to the Protestant king Henry of Navarre, is widely regarded as the author of one of the first works of political theory that supported the notion of political resistance against a legitimately established government. In *A Defense of Liberty Against Tyrants* (1579), the author affirmed that God's law represents a higher law than that of the state and has higher claims to people's obedience. The author of this tract used examples from the Bible and history to justify the position that people need to follow God when divine precepts contradict those of the king. Other writers also sought to establish new foundations for political authority that would take the concerns of the people into greater account. Baruch Spinoza (1632–1677), a Sephardic Jew whose family had settled in Amsterdam, developed a highly rationalistic philosophy, organizing his philosophical principles in the same way that mathematicians would set about to construct their proofs. Spinoza inclined toward democracy as the form of government that best allowed human beings to freely employ their reason in order to live in a way most pleasing to them. Although Spinoza's radical philosophy did not include room for the Judeo-Christian notion of sin, since he regarded everything as a part of God, he did believe that the power of reason gave human beings the ability to understand that certain actions and behaviors were preferable to others.

Like Spinoza, the Englishman Thomas Hobbes (1588–1679) was a materialist philosopher who challenged religious justifications for political authority. He developed his political theories in the midst of the English Civil War, which affected him profoundly. Appalled at the violence and anarchy that beset England in the 1640s, he sought to establish a philosophical foundation that would prevent such a catastrophe in the future. Hobbes shared many views with divine right theorists, including the belief that subjects should give absolute obedience to their kings and to the civil law of their country. He believed that the subjects' duty was passive obedience and that religion should teach people to expect their reward in the next life, not in this one. But in his most famous work, *Leviathan* (1651), Hobbes went beyond divine right theory to develop a political philosophy based not on religious sanctions but on a realistic view of human nature.

Both Hobbes and his younger contemporary John Locke (1632–1704) based their political theories on speculation about the origins of civil society. Whereas Hobbes had a negative view of human nature, describing life in the state of nature as "solitary, nasty, brutish, and short," Locke had a more positive view. Locke believed that God had endowed humans with a natural understanding of human equality through their ability to perceive the similarities between others and themselves. Since those similarities suggested the inherent immorality of harming the "life, health, liberty, or possessions" of another, Locke believed that human beings were naturally social and peaceful. Civil society, for Locke, arises from the desire of individuals to band together for the purpose of enhancing their happiness and prosperity and from the desire of the community to preserve the law of nature and punish anyone who transgresses it. Hobbes, in contrast, saw civil society as replacing the law of nature, according to which anyone could legitimately harm another for one's own benefit. Hobbes postulated that civil society originated when people decided to give up some of their rights and freedom as individuals in order to enter a political association that would protect them from the predatory nature of others who sought power over them. Hobbes based his theory on an altogether negative view of human nature, describing the human quest as a never-ending search for power, which must inevitably come at the expense of other humans. According to Hobbes, an individual who agrees to live under the civil law cannot withdraw allegiance from the law, which has effectively replaced the law of nature that predated it. The creation of civil society for Locke, on the other hand, was the result of a social contract among participating individuals that could be dissolved if necessary by those who had voluntarily entered into it. This meant that laws and institutions derive their authority only from the agreement of the members of society, not from any divine right given to the ruler from above. Both Locke and Hobbes repudiated divine right theory, but for Hobbes the rulers or "Leviathans" had complete authority to fulfill their duty, even to use terror to force people to recognize the ruling power.

Hobbes expressed a strong preoccupation with order because of the political instability that he witnessed in his own lifetime. Locke, writing under the restored Stuart monarchy following the English Civil War, feared tyranny more than anarchy, as is reflected in his rather positive view of the state of nature. Hobbes was more concerned with establishing a strong foundation for state authority to preserve order than he was with justifying monarchy per se. Locke believed that, under certain circumstances, kings might be exempt from the laws of the country, but they did not possess unlimited authority nor were they ever justified in exercising tyranny against their own people. In their own ways, both Hobbes and Locke developed an important strain of political thought whose opposition to divine right monarchy contributed to the eighteenth-century movement known as the Enlightenment and to the American and French Revolutions.

Art and Literature in the Seventeenth Century

Literature and art always have the dual ability to reflect and shape an age at the same time. In the seventeenth century, literature and art reflected the challenges to established truths that came from changing ideas in religion, science, and political thought. But they also contributed to challenges to accepted truths, beliefs, and social practices. Either way, literature and art had stronger links with political authority during the seventeenth century than at almost any other time. Some of the most accomplished artists of the seventeenth century found employment in the service of powerful monarchs and popes and contributed to a defense or justification of absolute monarchy. Writers of this period either affirmed or challenged traditional values and established authorities, but they all responded to the concerns of their age.

Baroque art and architecture, characterized by elaborate decorative schemes and a grand scale, seemed uniquely suited to support the ambitions and pretensions of seventeenth-century rulers. Monarchs such as Philip IV of Spain and Louis XIV of France, as well as popes such as Urban VIII (r. 1623–1644), used art and architecture to express the grandeur of their position as rulers who held their authority directly from God. Baroque art is characterized primarily by the use of exquisite colors, a sense of movement among the shapes and figures, and an irregular arrangement of figures that frequently blend into one another. Baroque art is often associated with the Catholic Counter-Reformation because it expressed

Gian Lorenzo Bernini, bronze baldachino, St. Peter's Basilica. Pope Urban VIII commissioned this canopy combining sculpture and architecture built under the cathedral dome and over the site of St. Peter's tomb.

a spiritual vision meant to awe the viewer. Gian Lorenzo Bernini (1598–1680), the primary architect employed by Urban VIII, sought to enhance the glory of the papacy through such works as his magnificent tabernacle over the tomb of St. Peter (1633) and his sculpture *Ecstasy of Saint Teresa* (1645–1652), a sublime portrayal of religious mysticism in stone. But Bernini also did a marble bust of Louis XIV in 1655 that idealized Louis as an absolute monarch. The palace of Buen Retiro in Spain reinforced an image of the Habsburgs cultivated by the Duke of Olivares through numerous works of art, including twenty-four coats of arms representing the various kingdoms within the Spanish empire, five paintings by Velázquez of members of the royal family on horseback, and a number of paintings depicting important military victories of the Habsburgs.

Greater insight can be gained into the realities of Spanish power, however, from Miguel de Cervantes's famous novel, *Don Quixote* (Part 1, 1605; Part 2, 1615), which remains one of the masterpieces of world literature. Cervantes (1547–1616) turned the Spanish past and its ideals into a subject for ridicule rather than praise. Don Quixote seeks to imitate the chivalric knights of medieval romances by traversing the countryside performing feats of valor and rescuing damsels in distress; instead, his deeds frequently cause more harm than good, he is tricked into believing lies, and his lady in distress is neither sweet nor beautiful, in spite of the hero's protestations to the contrary. Cervantes observed that nobility does nothing to protect people from misfortune and that wealth cannot prevent the disasters that destiny frequently imposes, including those caused by human emotions.

In England, the poetry of the English cleric John Donne (ca. 1572–1631), while reflecting the continuing influence of religion upon literature, often suggests a kind of Christian pessimism that emerges at troubled times and holds that humanity can never be whole while alive on this earth:

> There is no health; physicians say that we,
> At best, enjoy but a neutrality.
> And can there be worse sickness than to know
> That we are never well, nor can be so?

Donne's verses also illustrate how recent currents of thought—such as Copernican theory—had contributed to a general feeling of despair and uncertainty:

> And new philosophy calls all in doubt,
> The element of fire is quite put out;
> The sun is lost, and the earth, and no man's wit
> Can well direct him where to look for it.

Donne's poetry thus suggests that the new scientific advances were slow to be accepted or assimilated into people's consciousness at that time. This strain in early modern English literature involving a fear of natural science can also be seen in Christopher Marlowe's play *Doctor Faustus* (ca. 1592), about a philosopher who trades his soul to the devil for knowledge. Marlowe understands the temptation to which Faustus succumbs as a product of his own age and the rapid expansion of knowledge, but also recognizes the danger that the quest for knowledge poses to traditional religion. William Shakespeare gives a more favorable portrayal of the magician-philosopher in quest of knowledge in his character Prospero in the play *The Tempest* (1611). But Shakespeare also includes witches in plays such as *Macbeth* (1606) to emphasize the dangers of forbidden knowledge.

Finally, the lives of three of the most renowned painters in European history suggest that the artists of this period cannot be divorced from the political values of their society. Diego de Velázquez (1599–1660) was not merely a hired artist, but a full participant in the life of the Spanish court, where he developed a close relationship with the king himself and sought for years to have his noble ancestry recognized, an honor bestowed only in the last year of his life. Peter Paul Rubens (1577–1640) was a Flemish baroque painter from the town of Antwerp who counted Maria de' Medici, the mother of Louis XIII, and Charles I of England among his patrons; he left France when he lost the confidence of Cardinal Richelieu, who suspected him of sympathies for the rival Habsburgs. Rubens later went to Spain as a diplomat for the Netherlands to negotiate for the reunification of the United Provinces with his native Spanish Netherlands. Even the famous Dutch painter Rembrandt van Rijn (1606–1669), largely known for the deep introspection of his numerous revealing self-portraits, bought a large house in the Jewish section of his native Amsterdam and bought expensive clothes that would have identified him with the wealthy merchants whose portraits he painted and who dominated Dutch politics as much as the kings of rival nations dominated theirs.

Everyday Life and Social Conditions in Seventeenth-Century Europe

In many respects social conditions did not change significantly from the sixteenth to the seventeenth century, at least not compared to the changes that have occurred since the seventeenth century. Europe remained an overwhelmingly agricultural society, but the age did witness an increase in commercial activity that further enhanced the role played by towns and cities. In Western Europe, capitalism and individualism continued to erode the feudal and corporate traditions on which medieval society had been based. Seventeenth-century wars and revolts caused considerable upheaval in society throughout Europe, bringing social change and instability in their wake. In an age that contained much uncertainty, people sought some measure of control over their lives by finding scapegoats for their problems in the form of witches and by using rituals and symbols to reinforce a sense of community identity and order in their lives. European society in the seventeenth century remained hierarchical, but some of these developments contributed to at least a degree of social mobility, particularly in England.

Opportunities for social mobility arose in England—and to a lesser degree elsewhere—from, for example, outstanding military service, university education, or royal favor. In addition, agriculture was becoming more commercial, allowing successful farmers to grow more prosperous and rise in social status. A dynamic and fluctuating economy—in short, an increasingly capitalistic society—created more opportunities for those who knew how to take advantage of them, but it could ruin or impoverish even wealthy families who did not manage their money properly or adjust to the times. Finally, wars and revolts not only reduced the population but also altered the relationships among those who survived.

In Europe there was not as great a distinction between life in the towns and cities and life in the countryside as one might imagine; agricultural laborers continued to reside even in large cities like Paris and Amsterdam, while increasing numbers of rural residents worked at industrial tasks for part of the year. Many people who lived in the city most of the year worked for part of the year in agricultural settings, especially during harvests; meanwhile, many people from the countryside traveled to the nearest town or city once or twice a week to bring their goods to market. Markets, which were held every day in large cities such as Paris, provided excellent sites for social interaction and exchange of ideas and information, as well as goods and produce. In towns with large markets, indoor halls for commerce were constructed to supplement the open-air markets. Because of unsanitary conditions and increased exposure to infectious diseases, the death rate exceeded the birth rate in cities, meaning that population growth in urban areas continued to come from migration from the countryside. The seventeenth century witnessed a growing trend toward large, shared residences, especially on the outskirts of Paris and London, to accommodate the numbers of those who migrated. The prosperous cities of the northern Netherlands welcomed immigration from the south because they needed skilled and unskilled workers to sustain their economic progress. But a growing class of poor immigrant workers combined with overcrowded, unsanitary conditions and a general lack of medical knowledge to contribute to crime, poverty, epidemics, including plague, and social inequality, all of which accompanied a greater degree of commercial prosperity in seventeenth-century towns and cities. The seventeenth century had not yet witnessed significant improvements in sanitation over conditions in the Middle Ages, leaving city streets so dirty or muddy that sometimes bridges were built to allow people to cross the street. Otherwise people wore high platform shoes or even stilts! In the Netherlands, however, an elite group of merchants possessed growing wealth and a willingness to pay for higher levels of welfare, better hospitals, improved housing, and a system of waste removal that was ahead of its time and improved the quality of water in the canals.

Throughout Europe, however, agriculture was still the backbone of the economy, and the labor of the peasant classes still supported whatever prosperity different regions experienced. In Eastern Europe, large landowners turned increasingly to serfdom to ensure the labor supply necessary to sustain their prosperity at a time when serfdom had almost totally disappeared in Western Europe. In Western Europe, markets in towns provided greater economic incentives and opportunities, allowing peasants to work for themselves and contribute to the commercial economy instead of merely supporting the wealth of powerful landowning nobles. There farming was becoming a more individualistic occupation, especially in England. An effect of the increased social and geographical mobility of the period was the trend toward the diminishing importance of kinship, leading people to cultivate a larger network that included friends and neighbors. This did not mean, however, that kinship ceased to be important. Relatives still frequently congregated and assisted each other, but kinship became just one of several forms of social connection that people might use to help them successfully navigate through life.

On their own, women had little opportunity to improve their social position, which derived entirely from their husbands or fathers. Conservative attitudes toward women were reinforced in this period by the patriarchal nature of the state, in which the king was often portrayed as the father of his subjects. In England, at least, widows proved an exception to the rule that every family should have a man at its head. English widows retained custody of their children and control over whatever property their husbands left them. On the Continent, there was more pressure on women to remarry, perhaps because patriarchal attitudes ran even deeper in societies more accustomed to political absolutism. Throughout Europe, unmarried women were particularly vulnerable and suspect for undermining what was thought to be the natural order of society—at the same time that the wars and plagues of the period contributed to a surplus of young women, while inflationary and economic pressures delayed the age of marriage for both women and men.

The result of these conditions—a growing number of unmarried women in a society increasingly suspicious of them—contributed to the European witch-craze, the accusation, trial, and execution of perhaps 60,000 people, mostly women, accused of witchcraft. The accusations resulted mainly from the role that witchcraft played in popular culture throughout Europe, but the witch-craze occurred because of the preoccupations of secular and religious authorities determined to eradicate social deviants. The social and economic changes and insecurity of the sixteenth and seventeenth centuries made people suspicious of others and created the kind of competitive tensions in local towns and villages that might provoke accusations of witchcraft. Women were particularly vulnerable because they lacked power; old, single women all the more so because they often lacked family support and could be seen as superfluous members of a society in which resources were scarce, especially during times of war and social upheaval. It was thought that those who lacked power or economic resources would possess greater motivation to engage in witchcraft, which would provide them a measure of power over their enemies. On the European continent, witch hunts flourished mainly in the decentralized territories of Switzerland and Germany and in those regions of France most remote from the power of the monarchy. Large-scale accusations tended to occur at times of social upheaval when local authorities could ignore the evolving codes of law and justice being implemented by centralized government. For example, the biggest witch-craze in seventeenth-century England occurred amid the turmoil of the English Civil War and was associated with the "witch-finder" Matthew Hopkins, who went from village to village preying on people's insecurities and promising to rid them of their witches.

The Reformation indirectly contributed to the witch-craze in Protestant areas because it removed many of the symbols and rituals that had provided a sense of protection and meaning in the lives of many people. Rosary beads, small devotional items known as *agnus dei* ("lamb of God"), crosses, and other images were generally not acceptable in Protestant areas, while holy water, the sign of the cross, and the mass itself were eliminated. Although Protestant churches varied greatly in their use of images, stained glass, and church ritual, many Protestants demanded the replacement of the ritual of the Catholic mass by services centered on preaching and the reading of the Bible. Protestants looked for signs of God's favor in the everyday occurrences of their normal lives. Catholic areas staged elaborate processions that included great pageantry, such as the Corpus Christi processions; when England became Protestant, the people did not do away with these processions altogether, but rather replaced them with those of a more civic nature. Community activities and rituals reinforced a sense of common identity and often involved the participation of both religious and secular authorities, even among English Puritans. The ways in which social rituals reflected the political ideas of a given society can also be seen in France under Louis XIV, where fathers enacted the role of the king in the family and received gestures of deference similar to those that the king received at court, such as being seated at the head of the table, with the rest of the family waiting to drink until after the father had his first sip of wine.

Early Modern India: Thought, Culture, and Social Change

Seventeenth-century India was a religiously and culturally diverse subcontinent, much of which fell under the authority of the Islamic Mughal dynasty (1526–1707). The cultural diversity of the region and the political domination of the Hindu majority by the Mughals created fertile ground for a blending of cultural influences and a flourishing civilization. Indian thought remained rooted in the philosophical traditions of the past, though important trends rendered it anything but stagnant. For example, despite a tradition in which it was difficult to separate views on science or nature from prevailing religious conceptions of the universe, by the sixteenth century a theistic tradition had emerged in south India that affirmed the dual realities of both God and the physical realm of the senses. Science received a potential boost in India with the rise to power of the Islamic Mughals, when India's most important achievements in mathematics combined with Islam's long intellectual tradition favorable to science and natural philosophy.

Astronomy was one science in which Muslims had made advances and in which the Mughals took a special interest. Indian astronomers used the astrolabe, which was advanced and refined by Indian craftsmen building on the work of Arabs and Persians, to make astronomical observations throughout the seventeenth and eighteenth centuries. Two Indian accounts exist of the 1577 comet that was observed by Tycho Brahe in Europe. The famous Mughal ruler Akbar (1542–1605) was inspired by the event to order that astronomers research the potential consequences of the comet's appearance. (The astronomers decided that the comet did not pose a threat to India.) In the eighteenth century, Indian astronomers made impressively accurate observations without the aid of a telescope. The Hindu astronomer Jaganāth, for example, imbibed Islamic and European approaches to science and utilized quadrants and dials to make a number of observations, and the Mahārāja Sawāi Jai Singh II (1686–1743) established observatories at five separate locations, including Delhi.

Interest in astronomy aside, India did not develop the kind of strong traditions in science and technology that emerged in seventeenth-century Europe. India had its own religious and philosophical traditions that permeated and greatly affected attitudes toward science in Indian culture. Indian thought generally recognized the beneficence of nature and suggested the goal of understanding and conforming to nature rather than trying to harness its powers or conquer nature for the benefit of humanity. No Indian Francis Bacon emerged to point

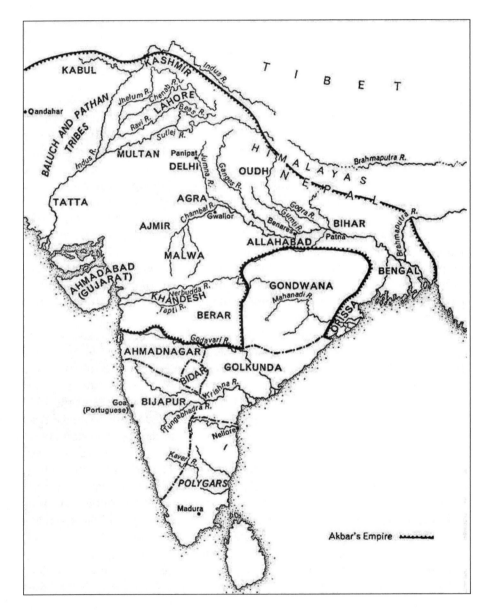

India under the Mughal Dynasty, 1605 (*Source: An Historical Atlas of the Indian Peninsula* [Oxford University Press, Bombay, 1961])

toward science and technology as the means of improving human society and the quality of human life in the future. In the seventeenth century Islamic scholars—in India and elsewhere—turned their attention away from science and back toward intensive study of the Quran. Even those Indian thinkers who attempted to understand nature sought a deeper, underlying spiritual reality. The Hindu belief in reincarnation and karma—that everything that happened in this life affected the next life—meant that Indians generally did not seek an understanding of the world outside of that spiritual context. While Europeans turned to observation and experience as the primary means of understanding the world and the cosmos, Indians believed in an ultimate unity that existed among all things, thus downplaying the significance of isolated experiences. By the end of the seventeenth century state-sponsored scientific institutions, such as the Royal Academy in England and the Paris Academy of Sciences in France, had emerged in Europe. In India, imperial interest in scientific endeavors peaked with Akbar and largely withered after the beginning of the seventeenth century.

In the early seventeenth century the Islamic and Hindu religious traditions were affected by continual close contact with each other. For example, the Sufi tradition of Islamic devotion flourished in India; Sufism emphasized the presence of the divine within each individual, the cultivation of a connection with that divine presence, and exercise of personal physical and moral discipline, frequently inspired by a charismatic holy man. In the similar Hindu tradition known as bhakti, spiritual leaders attracted followers who were devoted to a particular deity and who cultivated a unique spiritual regimen. Bhakti developed in India to a large degree in response to the Muslim conquest and the moral dilemmas that it posed. Over the course of Mughal rule, a wave of bhakti spiritual leaders emerged to call people back to faith as an answer to the perceived threat to the Hindu social order offered by Islamic rule. The bhakti leaders suggested that flaws in the social order of India had made it susceptible to conquest, singling out the caste system as the major problem.

Another shift in Hindu thought that occurred under Mughal rule included a greater attention to worldly affairs that encouraged in some an attitude of political resistance instead of passive acceptance. Ramdas (1601–1681) was a notable political theorist in India whose thought encouraged the revolt of the Marathas against Mughal rule. Just as religion was associated with ideas of political resistance in Europe, Ramdas emphasized religious freedom as a motive for Indians to rise up against the Mughal dynasty. Ramdas encouraged devotion to the Hindu god of strength, Hanumana, and inspired the architect of Maratha independence, Shivaji (1627–1680). Building on the Indian traditions that recognized the validity of world experience, Ramdas totally rejected the politically passive strain in Indian thought.

As far as Islamic thought was concerned, a new direction was explored at court under the reign of Akbar. Mirroring the questioning of orthodox Christianity in Europe during the Reformation, Akbar began to question orthodox Islam and became dissatisfied with certain aspects of the religion, such as its claims to exclusivity and its prohibition of human and natural images in art. Like an Indian Henry VIII, in 1579 Akbar proclaimed himself the head of the Islamic faith in India and appropriated the power to rule on matters of religious doctrine. However, after he was forced to put down a rebellion in 1580, Akbar rejected Islam entirely and initiated a new religious faith, the Din Illahi. Akbar temporarily replaced Muhammad in the role of divine prophet and expected people to prostrate themselves before him as they had previously done in mosques. This imperial cult did not extend far beyond the court, however, and did not affect the practice of Islam by the vast majority of the Muslim population.

Indian culture in the seventeenth century comprised a unique blend of Muslim and Hindu influences, mostly as a result of Hindu accommodation to Muslim rule. The arts in particular revealed a blending of Hindu and Muslim styles. Mughal emperors exerted a strong influence and control over art and culture, but this did not prevent Hindu influences. Indian dancers, for example, combined Hindu styles and themes with Persian dress. Islamic poetry flourished among the scholars who populated the Mughal court, while miniature Islamic paintings were produced for private consumption rather than for public view; yet these poems and paintings frequently reflected Hindu stories and traditions, which blended with Persian themes and forms. The modern languages of Hindi and Urdu represent a blend between Persian and the native language of northern India. In architecture, characteristic Islamic vaults and domes were found in combination with Hindu columns and balconies. In northern India both Hindu and Muslim culture influenced a form of folk opera called *nautanki*. Nautanki combined poetry and ballads based on popular romantic, courtly, royal, and religious legends, closer to the types of folk stories found in Shakespeare's plays than to later European opera. The most well-known

Explore more about the culture and art of India at the official website of the National Museum in New Delhi at www.nationalmuseumindia. gov.in/index-2.html.

Take a virtual tour of the painting collection at the famous Louvre Museum in Paris at www.louvre.fr/llv/musee/alaune.jsp?bmLocale=en.

European Love, Indian Love

Love, a constant in all cultures, was a common artistic theme in the sixteenth century. The first painting—by the Italian mannerist Giulio Romano (1499–1546)—portrays a couple relaxing in an interior setting under unusual circumstances. In the second image, attributed to Manohar (ca. 1597), the couple is relaxed and surrounded by nature.

What are the most striking similarities between these two pictures? Are there significant differences? What might account for the similarities? What might account for the differences? What is the significance of the third figure in Romano's painting? What do you think these two illustrations reveal about the nature of the two societies that they represent? Can we gain historical insights from comparing two paintings of a relatively simple subject?

Giulio Romano, *The Lovers,* **ca. 1525** (*Hermitage Museum, Saint Petersburg*)

418

Manohar, *The Lovers,* **ca. 1597** (*Freer Gallery of Art*)

▲▼ ▲▼ ▲▼ ▲▼ ▲▼ ▲▼ ▲▼ ▲▼ ▲▼ ▲▼ ▲▼ ▲▼ ▲▼

nautankis dealt with historical themes reflecting values generally associated with the European chivalric tradition, such as courage and loyalty.

Socially, India in the seventeenth century appears to have been developing a capitalist economy—prior to the influence of European colonialism that commenced in the eighteenth. During this period, transfers of property between members of different social castes and between residents of different villages became much more common. Agricultural society, therefore, underwent some significant changes, most importantly the breakdown of village unity, an increasingly important role played by merchants, and the relative decline of the previous landowning class. The changes in land ownership reflected a loss of power and prestige among certain families and a degree of social mobility for some members of inferior castes. As in Europe, places of prominence were reserved for certain individuals and families in ceremonies and parades in an attempt to emphasize and preserve the hierarchical structure of society. But as new landowners and merchants immigrated into towns and villages and attained prominence, such rituals would have been restructured to accommodate the new social realities.

Conclusion

Throughout the seventeenth century a tension existed between the desire to reinforce authority and the desire to challenge authority. In science, the conflict between Galileo and the Catholic Church best exemplifies this tension. Galileo could not ignore the physical evidence that supported the Copernican system while the Catholic Church believed that to concede error in one area of its teachings would throw others open to question. The idea of political resistance flourished alongside a new emphasis on the divine right of kings and the construction of absolute monarchies. Thomas Hobbes devised a theory to provide a more realistic basis for the power of the state, while John Locke developed the idea that the state could not trample on certain rights of the people. People struggled with social change, and even those who benefited economically still demonstrated a certain insecurity that led to accusations of witchcraft and reaffirmations of rituals designed to hold society together.

By the end of the seventeenth century, the cumulative impact of the Scientific Revolution had given educated people more confidence in the powers of human reason and human ability to understand the world and the universe. Not everyone shared this viewpoint, but philosophical skepticism became more common and some thinkers began to dispense with Christianity altogether as an explanatory scheme for their understanding of the world. This new found confidence in human reason produced in the eighteenth century the intellectual movement known as the Enlightenment. Religious intolerance had not disappeared, wars still raged, the churches remained a powerful influence in people's lives, and social injustices were still obvious. But people began to believe that—whether through social and political reform, a better understanding of human nature, the replacement of Christianity with a more rational view of God and the universe, or economic progress—humanity could solve its problems on its own. That was one of the main legacies of the challenges to accepted truths and the establishment of new authorities that occurred during the seventeenth century.

1. What were the main contributions of Copernicus, Brahe, Kepler, Galileo, and Newton to the Scientific Revolution and the understanding of the universe? Why did their work mark a shift in the general approach to science in the early modern period?
2. Did Hobbes and Locke support or challenge monarchical authority?
3. How did literature and art reflect the intellectual and social atmosphere of the seventeenth century? In what ways did literature and art contribute to or oppose the challenges to traditional authorities that characterized the period?
4. Describe social conditions in seventeenth-century Europe. What was the relationship between town and countryside? What factors contributed to the European witch-craze? Why were most accused witches women?
5. What impact did Mughal rule have on Indian thought, culture, and society?

Suggestions for Further Reading

Cowan, Alexander. 1998. *Urban Europe, 1500–1700*. London: Arnold.

Gingerich, Owen. 2004. *The Book Nobody Read: Chasing the Revolutions of Nicholas Copernicus*. New York: Walker.

Metcalf, Barbara D., and Thomas R Metcalf. 2001. *A Concise History of India*. Cambridge: Cambridge University Press.

Shorto, Russell. 2008. *Descartes' Bones: A Skeletal History of the Conflict between Faith and Reason*. New York: Doubleday.

Sobel, Dana. 2000. *Galileo's Daughter: A Historical Memoir of Science, Faith, and Love*. New York: Penguin.

Wrightson, Keith. 2000. *Earthly Necessities: Economic Lives in Early Modern Britain*. New Haven, CT: Yale University Press.

Suggested Websites

www.fordham.edu/halsall/mod/modsbook09.html
This website provides a good set of primary sources relating to the Scientific Revolution and associated topics.

www.historyteacher.net/APEuroCourse/WebLinks/WebLinks-Scientific Revolution.htm
This website provides links to primary sources on numerous topics related to the Scientific Revolution.

www.ibiblio.org/wm/paint/auth/velazquez
Famous works of the Spanish painter, Diego de Velázquez, can be found on this website.

www.rijksmuseum.nl/index.jsp?lang=en
This website from one of the great museums of Europe allows exploration of many great Dutch works of art from the seventeenth century, including those of Rembrandt.

www.sscnet.ucla.edu/southasia/Culture/Archit/Mugarch.html
The culture, art, and architecture of Mughal India is covered on this website.

Epilogue: The Shaping of the Past and the Challenge of the Future

In his epic *The Decline and Fall of the Roman Empire*, the eighteenth-century British historian Edward Gibbon stated that "history is little more than the register of crimes, follies, and misfortunes of mankind" and that "wars and the administration of public affairs are the principal subjects of history." The reader of this text will undoubtedly find much within its pages that might seem to confirm Gibbon's assessment. Furthermore, there are plenty more examples of historical "crimes, follies, and misfortunes" if one looks for them. However, I hope that this text has demonstrated that Gibbon was wrong in both the above quotes and that history is much more than he believed. In spite of the best attempts of some individuals to bring about death, destruction, and devastation, others in the past have worked equally hard to provide meaning to the human experience, improve the lives of others, create a better world, and preserve the environment of the planet that we inhabit. Sometimes human beings become confused and cause devastation in the process of trying to achieve the positive goals—and one of the most important roles that a historical text like this can play is to help readers distinguish between the two in the past in the hopes that a better world in the future might result. If I have had a particular agenda in writing this book, this has been it.

Even history textbooks are written by human beings with their own particular perspectives, backgrounds, and views of the past writing at a particular point in historical chronology. That is unavoidable. But what I have attempted to do here, within the confines of a relatively brief text, is to help readers understand some of the diverse forces that have shaped the past, as well as those that might be currently at work in shaping our collective future. As the great French historian Marc Bloch pointed out in his famous work *The Historian's Craft* (1944), written shortly before he was executed by the Nazis during World War II, sometimes the forces at work in the present date back much further than ephemeral fads and events that might have occurred only a few years ago. The roots of our current democracies can be traced back to a distant past, as can the religious divisions in Islam and Christianity that continue to affect our lives and considerations about the future, particularly in a region such as the Middle East. But since we do live in such a global society in the twenty-first century, and given the events of 9/11 and subsequent developments, who would doubt that events in the Middle East, that are shaped as much by distant historical developments as they are by current realities, do not have the potential to impact us all at some level? This is a large reason why the Arab Spring of 2011 is so potentially significant and has garnered so much attention in the Western press. It is, therefore, not merely out of any concern for political correctness that this text has adopted a global and comparative emphasis, but out of the conviction that any understanding of history or the way in which it might shape the future of the West cannot be confined to an understanding of Western history alone.

In addition, a comparative study of the past, even by examining differences among nations within the West, can provide a sense of the future possibilities for nations and peoples in the present. For example, for many different countries around the world, beginning in the late 1970s, democracy has been seen as preferable to dictatorship. This trend, effectively highlighted by Francis Fukuyama in his important and controversial book *The End of History and the Last Man* (1992), in regions such as Africa and Latin America has resulted from historical experience that diverse countries have had with both systems and the conclusion that democracy, whatever flaws it might possess, is better for most people. Of course, some dictatorships remain in these regions and elsewhere, most notably in China. Russia seemed to be headed back in that direction until a new wave of protests aimed at the power of Vladimir Putin in December 2011. The uncertain state of affairs in Russia is just one example of why it is premature to speak of the end of history. However, unlike the North American revolutionaries who founded the United States, today, in an age of tremendous global awareness and the ready and rapid availability of information and communication from around the world, people have numerous examples of both systems before them and can make judgments at least about what they want the political futures of their country to look like. There is no question that increased information about Western Europe contributed to the revolutions in Eastern Europe in 1989 or that the Internet and social media such as Facebook and Twitter had a role in inspiring the more recent revolutions in the Arab world.

Another challenge of the future involves the ability of national leaders—and individuals living in democracies who have the ability to influence their leaders—to discern what policies are most likely to be effective in preventing people and regimes in other countries from negatively impacting their countries or the world in general. Before she was assassinated in 2007, Benazir Bhutto, the prime minister of Pakistan and the first woman to head an Islamic state, made the case that democracy in the Islamic world was necessary in order to combat extremist forces and radical terrorism. But it is possible that the United States, by virtue of its being a democracy, has alienated many Muslims from democracy because of its heavy-handed dealings with states such as Iran, which it has sought to prevent from becoming a nuclear power, and its support of authoritarian regimes in countries such as Saudi Arabia. By contrast, it seems that American support for democratic student activists in Serbia helped to cause the downfall of the war-mongering dictator of Serbia, Slobodan Milošević, in the 1990s. If Russia moves closer to dictatorship, should the United States and the European Union take a stand at the risk of starting a new Cold War or should they use other means to ensure friendly relations with their former rival? In the 1990s the European Union decided to admit the former Communist states of Eastern Europe to membership despite concerns about the economic burdens and immigration problems that many feared. Now the European Union conducts controversial negotiations with Turkey about admitting an Islamic state in which the military is more influential than in most democracies. Would membership in the European Union further isolate Turkey, which provides a good example of a secular, democratic state within the Islamic world, from other Islamic states?

Turkey and Iran provide two examples of Islamic countries that increasingly feel the tension between the desire for democracy and the support for Islamist politicians who wish to impose the Islamic law known as the sharia. Meanwhile, increased religious repression has become one of the hallmarks of Russia's drift back toward dictatorship. There is a fine line between respecting the religious beliefs of others and challenging people of a different faith when their values lead them to commit terrorist acts such as the 9/11 attacks or impose a strict, repressive form of their faith by force, as was the case with the Taliban in Afghanistan. The Israeli-Palestinian conflict in the Middle East has resulted from the desire of some Muslims to destroy the state of Israel and their refusal to acknowledge Israel's right to exist as well as from Israel's sometimes haughty and repressive measures toward the Palestinians and its expansion into Palestinian territories against the will of local residents. Never was Benjamin Franklin's proverb that "a quarrel never would last long if on one side lay all the wrong" more true. It is certainly a challenge of the future to discern when it is necessary to take a stand and when, in the interests of peace, to use an understanding of the past as a means to get beyond present difficulties to create a better future for all parties involved.

Of course, Gibbon had a point in emphasizing the importance of the role that war has played in history. Wars are not just about changes in boundaries or the expansion of empires on a map; they change the lives of people and alter the future of generations. In the twentieth century the two world wars, the Vietnam War, and civil wars around the globe have had such a profound influence that—even if some of the developments of the period would have occurred without them—it is impossible to distinguish what would otherwise have happened. But one of the lessons of 1989 has been that monumental changes can occur in history without warfare and with relatively little bloodshed. Yet as long as there are thugs who use money and military strength to impose their will on their own subjects or neighboring populations, it would be naive to think that war will soon be eliminated as an option or a part of history—the challenge will be to know when it is the best or only option and when it might exacerbate the very problems it seeks to cure, which, given the unpredictability of history, is always a possibility.

Another place that the past has brought us to is a world in which people of many different backgrounds increasingly interact and live side by side. This has been the result of a process that has been going on for a very long time, of course, but it has never been truer or more widespread than at the beginning of the twenty-first century. In England, the archbishop of York was born in Uganda, while the bishop of Rochester is of Pakistani descent with Muslim ancestors. In 2006 more than 20 percent of London's population had been born in another country, and London ranked tenth among the world's cities in this category, behind, for example, Miami, Toronto, Hong Kong, Melbourne, and Amsterdam (Dubai ranked first, with more than 80 percent of its residents foreign-born). Relocation around the globe has become less a phenomenon of immigrants assimilating into the culture of their adopted homeland and more a recognition of the reality that one global culture is emerging in which virtually anyone can blend in virtually anywhere. The challenge of the future may very well involve less conflict between different groups and more refinement of the ability of individuals to get along with people from a wide variety of national or cultural backgrounds. The problems in the Balkans in the 1990s provide perhaps the best example of what can happen when people cease viewing others as individuals (as they ceased under communism) and revert to thinking of others as members of a different group. But we live in an age in which people increasingly have the ability to define themselves, and this becomes its own challenge when viewpoints can diverge so significantly over, say, secularism vs. religious fundamentalism, whether in the United States (with its red and blue states), Turkey, Iran, or Israel. The challenge is for such societies as a whole to continue to resolve their differences through a democratic process, to minimize hatred and demonization of the other, and to avoid violence.

Whatever challenges the future poses, and here I have mentioned only a few, they all will unavoidably be faced with reference to the past. I do not know that I totally agree with George Santayana's (1863–1952) famous dictum that "those who cannot remember the past are condemned to repeat it" because I do not believe that history ever truly repeats itself. But I do believe that to ignore the past—as if that were even possible—is a recipe for disaster. Forgiveness and reconciliation, whether between Germany and the Jews, the Japanese and the Chinese, Vietnam and the United States, may be necessary before peoples and nations can comfortably and successfully move forward, but they can come only with recognition of what happened in the past, not by ignoring it. The same will be true in the future for Israelis and Palestinians, Muslims and Christians, Bosnians and Serbs, among many other examples. Historians cannot predict what will happen in the future, but by pointing to the past and helping others to understand it, they can potentially influence the future in a positive direction—if not, what would be the point of writing history, unless as a mere intellectual exercise?

In his 1997 reflective work *On History*, Eric Hobsbawm (b. 1917), himself a renowned Marxist historian, argued that, although historians might have their own political identity, they have a responsibility to rise above that when considering the past. While we cannot completely escape our personal identity or the moment in history when we write, I have tried to follow Hobsbawm's advice in composing this text. No doubt some of my preferences, such as the preference for democracy over dictatorship or for religious tolerance over religious intolerance, have come through, but this too is unavoidable. The possibility of completely objective, morally neutral history is an illusion. But I have tried to do justice to each of the civilizations considered in the comparative sections, to thoughtfully select and present those facts and developments that might assist readers in understanding the past, and to show the many interconnections between periods that have resulted from a more distant past continually shaping a more recent past: hence the special emphasis on "the shaping of the past." We live in an interesting time, and I hope that this text has helped in the reader's understanding of it and the role that the past has played in shaping it and will continue to play in the shaping of the future, which will soon be yet another part of the past.

Index

About the Author

Kenneth L. Campbell is a professor of history at Monmouth University in West Long Branch, New Jersey. He received his PhD in British and European history from the University of Delaware and is the author of *The Intellectual Struggle of the English Papists in the Seventeenth Century* (1986). His recently completed manuscript—*Windows into Men's Souls: Religious Nonconformity in Tudor and Early Stuart England*—reflects his continued interest in the religious history of early modern England. He is currently working on a history of Ireland.